THE GERMAN NOVEL

THE
GERMAN NOVEL

STUDIES

by

ROY PASCAL

**PROFESSOR OF GERMAN IN THE
UNIVERSITY OF BIRMINGHAM**

MANCHESTER UNIVERSITY PRESS

Published by the University of Manchester at
THE UNIVERSITY PRESS
316–324, Oxford Road, Manchester, 13

1956

Printed in Great Britain by Butler & Tanner Ltd., Frome and London

Contents

Foreword

THIS book is not a history of the German novel, for I wished to discuss at some length the novels I hold to be of the highest worth, with the object of finding out, as far as I might, what it is that makes them good novels ; and a history would unavoidably include a host of works which have little claim to literary merit. Even so, many works of distinction have been passed over. I decided to limit myself to a fairly coherent historical period, and for this reason have not included the first great German novel, Grimmelshausen's *Der abenteuerliche Simplicissimus* (1668–9). Goethe's *Werther* and *The Elective Affinities* have been omitted, mainly because his *Wilhelm Meister's Apprenticeship* called for very full treatment and I did not wish to give so much more space to Goethe. Readers well acquainted with German literature will notice the omission of novels that are an essential part of German literary studies —for example Hölderlin's *Hyperion*, Novalis' *Heinrich von Ofterdingen*, the novels of Jean-Paul Richter, those of Immermann and 'Jungdeutschland', of Freytag and Spielhagen and the Naturalist school, of the Low-German writer Fritz Reuter, etc. All these have importance in the history of German culture ; but the poetic qualities that some of them possess do not belong primarily to the form of the novel.

No attempt has been made to survey the modern novel. There is a considerable number of modern German novelists who have a distinct artistic personality and deserve attention —Heinrich Mann, Jakob Wassermann, Alfred Döblin, Hans Fallada, Anna Seghers, Hermann Hesse, Robert Musil, Hans Carossa, Franz Werfel, Hermann Broch, Ernst Jünger, and no doubt others. I have simply limited myself to the work of the two writers who are widely accepted as the most significant of the moderns, Thomas Mann and Franz Kafka.

The book falls into two halves. In the latter part I have discussed in more or less chronological order the work of five novelists, and my method calls for no particular explanation. The first part, however, is devoted to a peculiar brand of novel, the so-called 'Bildungsroman', studied here in its four most eminent examples from Goethe to Thomas Mann. It is perhaps necessary to justify the separate examination of this category. Germany (under this term I include here all the German-speaking lands) has been notoriously less successful in the sphere of the novel than France, England or Russia; it is less well known that in Germany there developed a distinctive type of novel—the German species of the novel, it has been called—to which some of the greatest German novels belong. This seemed to call for special attention, and the rather lengthier discussion of Goethe's *Wilhelm Meister* is intended to serve as an introduction to the whole type.

Though my purpose was to write primarily of the aesthetic qualities of the works under discussion, it has been necessary from time to time to indicate the social environment of the authors and their general outlook. It is impossible to divorce the novel, or any other art-form, from its social and spiritual environment; and with all the writers I discuss, the novel was a medium for the expression of an outlook. I might take as my motto a statement from Goethe's *Maxims and Reflections*:

The novel is a subjective epic, in which the author takes leave to manipulate the world in his own manner. The only question is, whether he has a manner; the rest comes of itself.

This 'manner' is of course not a mere technical trick, but a mode of looking at the world, which is expressed in the author's theme and story, his composition, and his style.

I have limited my attention as far as possible to the novels themselves, and have concerned myself very little with literary influences, even less with the categories of literary historians. Two terms, however, have been frequently used, 'romantic' and 'realistic', and it is perhaps necessary to say a prefatory word about them. Romanticism is a complex phenomenon, but by 'romantic' I mean that aspect of Romanticism that was more marked in Germany than elsewhere—the yearning for metaphysical values as opposed to moral, the preference for dreams over practical social reality, what Grillparzer called 'that inconstant dreaming, that capacity for boding without clear image or idea '. By ' realism ' I do not mean any particular philosophical doctrine, any literary school or artistic technique, but a general attitude which takes various forms. It involves a recognition of the philosophical validity, ' reality ', of the world in which human activity takes place, ' a respect for the right and significance of every thing ', as Keller put it. With this goes an acceptance of the moral claims of the social world on every member of the community, a profound interest, as Liddell puts it (*A Treatise on the Novel*, 1947), ' in the enormous range of happiness that is specifically human '. And this philosophical and moral attitude is allied to an aesthetic delight in the observed world. I have had to make frequent use of these terms, ' romantic ' and ' realistic ', not because of any prejudice on my part, but because the German novel seems to take its shape as the result of a con- stantly renewed struggle, explicit as well as implicit, with the contrary trends that these terms denote.

Little is known in Britain about the German novel, but I have tried to discuss it in a way that is understandable to readers who know no German. In the text, quotations and some titles are given in English translation. In those cases where I have wished to draw attention to the style, I have given the original German in the Appendix.

I wish to thank Dr. S. S. Prawer and my wife for encourage- ment and helpful criticism.

Foreword

THIS book is not a history of the German novel, for I wished to discuss at some length the novels I hold to be of the highest worth, with the object of finding out, as far as I might, what it is that makes them good novels ; and a history would unavoidably include a host of works which have little claim to literary merit. Even so, many works of distinction have been passed over. I decided to limit myself to a fairly coherent historical period, and for this reason have not included the first great German novel, Grimmelshausen's *Der abenteuerliche Simplicissimus* (1668–9). Goethe's *Werther* and *The Elective Affinities* have been omitted, mainly because his *Wilhelm Meister's Apprenticeship* called for very full treatment and I did not wish to give so much more space to Goethe. Readers well acquainted with German literature will notice the omission of novels that are an essential part of German literary studies —for example Hölderlin's *Hyperion*, Novalis' *Heinrich von Ofterdingen*, the novels of Jean-Paul Richter, those of Immermann and 'Jungdeutschland', of Freytag and Spielhagen and the Naturalist school, of the Low-German writer Fritz Reuter, etc. All these have importance in the history of German culture ; but the poetic qualities that some of them possess do not belong primarily to the form of the novel.

No attempt has been made to survey the modern novel. There is a considerable number of modern German novelists who have a distinct artistic personality and deserve attention —Heinrich Mann, Jakob Wassermann, Alfred Döblin, Hans Fallada, Anna Seghers, Hermann Hesse, Robert Musil, Hans Carossa, Franz Werfel, Hermann Broch, Ernst Jünger, and no doubt others. I have simply limited myself to the work of the two writers who are widely accepted as the most significant of the moderns, Thomas Mann and Franz Kafka.

The book falls into two halves. In the latter part I have discussed in more or less chronological order the work of five novelists, and my method calls for no particular explanation. The first part, however, is devoted to a peculiar

PART I

THE BILDUNGSROMAN

CHAPTER I

Johann Wolfgang von Goethe

WILHELM MEISTER'S APPRENTICESHIP

No other German novel has enjoyed anything like the esteem and prestige of *Wilhelm Meisters Lehrjahre* ; its influence on the German novel-tradition has remained pervasive and profound. Yet it is a ' problematical composition ', as Goethe called it,[1] with faults that are often magnified in its progeny. If we compare it with the novels of Goethe's contemporary, Jane Austen, it is clear that it probes deeper into human fate and shapes situations and characters that were beyond the imagination of the English writer ; at the same time it is, in a peculiar sense, far less mature as a work of art than such works as *Emma*, not only in the indefiniteness of its general shape, but also in the imprecision of many characters and events. This immaturity belongs to its whole nature. For while Jane Austen, like all classical novelists, was concerned to show characters choosing between certain moral alternatives within an unquestioned socio-moral reality, the main task for Wilhelm Meister is to discover the validity of this reality and of moral decision altogether. The novel is the story of this discovery.

Intricate psychological processes are involved, and numerous variant attitudes are described. And its deliberate complexity is made more difficult because of the way in which it was written. Goethe did not start out from his conclusions, but came to them during a long period in which the work lay fallow. He wrote what are roughly the first five books in the early Weimar period, between 1777 and 1785, the version that is known as *Wilhelm Meister's Theatrical Mission*. He picked it up again in 1793 and finished it in 1795, rewriting the early books and adding three more. The theme was radically altered, and every reader can detect the change of style between the earlier and later sections. Because of this, it is helpful to discuss first the earlier version.

3

WILHELM MEISTER'S THEATRICAL MISSION

The theme of the *Mission*, the *Sendung*, can be rapidly summed up. Wilhelm Meister is the son of a prosperous merchant. As a child he is fascinated by his puppet-theatre, later by the real stage. He falls in love with an actress, Mariane, and in revolt against 'the clogging, dragging burgher life' he determines to run away with her and devote himself to the theatre. The shock of discovering her to be untrue to him throws him into a severe illness. Sent on a business-trip, to learn more about the world and trade, he falls in with the members of a disrupted troupe of actors, and rebuilds the troupe round himself, spending some weeks with them acting at a Count's mansion. Ultimately he goes to the town 'H' to join the troupe of a famous director, Serlo, and devotes himself with enthusiasm to the theatre as his profession, with the first object of producing *Hamlet*. The *Sendung* closes with his signing a contract with Serlo; it was to be concluded by the account of the production of *Hamlet*, and probably the establishment of a National Theatre. Wilhelm realises his mission (viii. 877); what was potentially within him comes at the end to fulfilment.

His object is more complex than it appears. Partly it is as an actor and producer that he finds fulfilment for his own inherent taste and talent for the theatre. But he is also something of a writer, a 'Dichter', and the theme of theatre often merges in that of poetry, about which he rhapsodises to Werner, his prosaic brother-in-law. The poet finds meaning in the world, 'he lives the dream of the world as a man awake' . . . 'hence the poet is at one and the same time the teacher, prophet and friend of Gods and men' (viii. 598–9),[2] and Wilhelm admits to his ambition, his feeling of being 'called' to be a poet. This theme fades out of the story, but of course it gives substance to Wilhelm's devotion to art, even as a mere executant.

Wilhelm's mission is, however, not only a matter of subjective impulse; it embraces the 'sublime purpose' of creating a National Theatre. Viëtor rightly stresses the great moral

importance of this apparently merely artistic intention.[3]
In a Germany split up by political, religious, and social
divisions, the theatre was one of the main agencies of cultural
and moral education, the only place where the intellectual
leaders could meet the German public. Wilhelm and his
actor friends are always discussing, we are told, ' the great
influence of the theatre on the cultural development of a
nation and the world '. In this sense, the *Sendung* is the story
of the ' education ' of Germany, rather than that of Wilhelm
Meister, who, since he discovers that his first intimations were
' right ', is not educated, but educates. Goethe is actually
referring to contemporary theatrical developments, for Serlo
is the great actor-producer Schröder, and ' H ' is Hamburg
where Schröder made his reputation.

The development of Wilhelm's own personality is less well
worked out than the creation of a National Theatre. Wilhelm
is not one with the actors, who are embroiled in their petty
jealousies, anxieties, interests ; nor is he a practical man like
Serlo. We are interested in him because of his idealism,
his poetic sensitiveness, his candour, his human kindliness
and goodness. He holds the actors together, helps them
and shelters them, and tries to give them a deeper appreciation
of their calling and their plays. But we do not see how he
himself profits and develops through his art, though this
theme is suggested from time to time. His discovery of
Shakespeare is a turning-point in his artistic life, and the
discussion and production of *Hamlet* is the culmination of the
novel ; but it is something more which is tantalisingly left
fragmentary. On reading Shakespeare, Wilhelm says, he
learns immeasurably about mankind, but also ' these few
glances I have taken at Shakespeare's world incite me more
than anything else to make swifter progress in the real world
and to mingle in the tide of fates ' (viii. 802–3). Jarno, the
nobleman to whom he is speaking, encourages him to quit the
trivial society he is in, and Wilhelm appreciates his advice,
though without acting upon it. We see too that a new idea
of life dawns on Wilhelm when he first comes into high society
at the Count's mansion (viii. 794). But these hints are left

in the air, and we cannot discover any intention in the unfinished *Sendung* of a further development ; they become all-important for the *Lehrjahre*.

The main theme of the unfinished novel is, then, Wilhelm's participation in the foundation of a national theatre, his contribution to the aesthetic education of Germany. Its charm lies in the incidents and characters Wilhelm meets in his progress. With great subtlety and humour Goethe shows how this idealistic, candid youth gets involved, by chance, with a variety of theatre-folk, and against his intention becomes a focal point for their livelihood, building up intricate personal ties in the process. The incidents have almost always an element of the accidental, the unforeseen, as in a typical eighteenth-century novel. There are delightful character-sketches. There is Werner, who becomes Wilhelm's brother-in-law and head of the business, a prosaic yet kindly Philistine, whose greatest enthusiasm is bookkeeping by double-entry ; Mariane, the actress, whose untidy room is a joyous revelation to the proper young burgher. Above all the troupe : Melina, who wants to make money out of the theatre, and cares for nothing else, Philine, the light of heart, generous and wayward, with no thought for the morrow, who always takes the easy course and yet is ready to abandon all scheming for a whim ; and all the rest who make up a company. It is brilliant realistic characterisation, and we can understand how Wilhelm gets fettered, ensnared by these people.

Associated with them are two mysterious creatures, who have captivated nearly all readers. Mignon, a girl of about twelve years of age, leaves a company of acrobats where she is maltreated and attaches herself with a fierce jealous devotion to Wilhelm, her protector. No-one knows where she comes from, she belongs nowhere ; she seems hardly to be of this world, insisting on dressing as a boy, and scarcely articulate except when she sings entrancing songs of mystery and longing—' Kennst du das Land '—' Nur wer die Sehnsucht kennt '. And there is an old harper who attaches himself to the company, also of mysterious origin, a homeless minstrel, burdened by a tragic guilt of which he sings in ' Wer nie sein

Brot mit Tränen ass ' ; a terrible song of guilt and punishment. These two stand apart from the realistic turmoil ; they remain unexplained in the *Sendung*. Wilhelm becomes, willy nilly, their patron. They seem to embody the pure beauty which lives outside the normal world, the beauty he seeks, more lovely and more terrifying than anything the real world offers.

WILHELM MEISTER'S APPRENTICESHIP

In 1819 Goethe wrote :

The beginnings of Wilhelm Meister had long lain untouched. They arose from an obscure surmise of the great truth that man would often attempt something for which nature has denied him the capacity . . . yet it is possible that all his false steps lead him to something inestimably good : a surmise that is more and more unfolded, clarified and confirmed in Wilhelm Meister, yes, and is even expressed in the clear words : ' You appear to me like Saul the son of Kish who went out to seek his father's asses, and found a kingdom '.[4]

It is questionable whether this statement is true of the *Sendung* ; but it does define the *Lehrjahre*. We now learn with surprise that Wilhelm's conception of his capacities and aim is erroneous, that he finds something quite different and much nobler than he sought. Schiller, in the admirable letters in which he commented on the novel, defines the new theme : ' Wilhelm Meister steps out of an empty and imprecise ideal into a definite active life, but without forfeiting his power of idealisation '.[5] It could not be meant that the ideal of a national theatre was ' empty ' or ' imprecise ' ; what we are to understand is that his ideal of himself, the idea of his personal calling, was both. Schiller's remark suggests therefore, and rightly, that all the stress is now, not on the external object of Wilhelm's life, but on his own personal self-fulfilment : that is on ' Bildung ', the formation of personality. Only now does the novel become a ' Bildungsroman ', *the* ' Bildungsroman '. Wilhelm is now no longer the artist who is to educate the public. The essential point is, as Grillparzer noted, that he is not an artist, not a true ' Kunsttalent ',[6] he is now a representative, not an exceptional, human being.

The *Lehrjahre* takes over much of the earlier material, altering its arrangement, making additions, and conducting the story to a new conclusion. I shall first outline the additions and the new theme, and then examine the meaning the older material acquires through the framework in which it is now placed.

A significant new note is struck through the interpolation of a long letter Wilhelm writes (Book 5, Chapter 3) to explain to Werner (and himself) why he signs the contract with Serlo. The emphasis is here on his need for personal development and purification : ' What does it help me to manufacture good iron, if my own inner self is full of flaws ? ' And he continues :

'To put it in a word, to develop myself, entirely as I am, that was obscurely my wish and intention from childhood.'

He contrasts the nobility and the bourgeoisie ; in Germany only the former may achieve ' personal development ', the middle class can only gain a living and at best develop the intellect.

' The burgher may not ask : '' what are you ? '' but only '' what have you got ? '' . . . If the nobleman gives everything through the display ['' Darstellung ''] of his person, the burgher gives nothing through his personality and should give nothing. . . . The former must act and affect the outside world ['' wirken ''], the latter must perform and accomplish. . . . But it is just for that harmonious development of my nature, which my birth has denied me, that I have an irresistible bent—'

and to become ' a public person ' he thinks the means for him, a burgher, is the theatre (vii. 311–14).

This letter is pivotal. Not because it gives the clue to the meaning of the book, as Korff suggests.[7] Wilhelm's aim ' to develop himself, entirely as he is ', is to be shown to be an illusion ; his idea that the stage is the proper method is wrong. But the passage is pivotal since it places the objective of personal development, the fulfilment of personality, in the centre of the picture, giving quite a new importance to Wilhelm's earlier remarks about the nobility and Shakespeare, and to Jarno's reproof.

The production of *Hamlet* is a great success and Wilhelm feels himself near to his goal. But after a while the public grows weary of *Hamlet*, and more popular trivial plays are put on. The troupe grows more and more intractable. Wilhelm leaves to visit a nobleman who has played fast and loose with an actress's feelings, in order to speak plainly to him about his heartless behaviour. Before his departure he comes into possession of a manuscript, ' The confessions of a beautiful soul ', which fills the whole of Book 6. It is the autobiography of a noblewoman who is carried irresistibly by her own inclinations to renounce the world and live in the contemplation of God ; he reads here of a woman who discovered her own personality and lived utterly for it. The noble circle he now meets is introduced by this autobiography, and in them he discovers a group of people of distinctive character, all active in their various ways, all unhesitatingly following their own peculiar bents. Attracted first by their personalities, he learns through them to admire practical activity. He has read what the Uncle of the ' beautiful soul' has said : ' Man's highest merit is after all to control circumstances as far as possible ' (vii. 436), and recognises with shame that he himself has both ignored and been at the mercy of circumstances hitherto. Now, conscious that he is guided by these people, the ' Society of the Tower ', who unknown to him have guided him in the past, Wilhelm recognises the need for activity within a community. He learns that activity demands self-limitation, but that personal one-sidedness is compensated and rounded off in the community, in which all one-sidednesses combine into a whole. At the same time he discovers a son, the child of Mariane, and marries ; the family roots him in society.

But it is necessary that we should examine more closely the goal which Wilhelm is approaching. If we leave it as ' activity ', even as ' a transfigured practical life ' (Korff), we are left with an unprincipled admiration of activity like Nietzsche's ; if we admit ' one-sidedness ' without examining what justifies, in Goethe's view, the choice of specialisation, we cannot see the difference between Werner and Wilhelm ; if we say ' community ' without asking ' what sort of community ', we open the door to all sorts of misrepresentation.[8]

Wilhelm enters into a society predominantly of nobles. These men and women incorporate the ideals he had defined in his letter to Werner.   They follow their own inward bent, they realise their personalities, freed by their social station from sordid cares and calculations, and by their characters from convention.   They are all reformers and educators. Lothario, the man they all look up to, has fought under Washington in America, and is engaged in bold schemes of agricultural improvement.   He would abandon the privileges of the nobility, considering that feudal burdens should be lifted from the peasantry, noble estates should be taxed, entail abolished, and class-distinctions removed.   This company of aristocrats seeks to establish a new society based on achievement, one that will make each man a full citizen and encourage the development of his potential powers (vii. 463, 545-6).   Goethe was aware that he was placing Utopian principles in the mouths of ' miserable landed gentry ', and in the *Wanderjahre* we see that the whole society is to emigrate to America, where the moral and social hindrances to their schemes do not exist. Also, the *Lehrjahre* ends with four ' Missheirate ', as Schiller called them, marriages between nobles and bourgeois : Lothario and Therese, Jarno and Lydie, Wilhelm and Natalie, not to forget Friedrich and Philine.   Thus Wilhelm is entering a new type of society in which the best of the nobility and the bourgeoisie unite, the spirit of which is contrasted explicitly, even harshly, with the withered laborious hypochondria of Werner, with the misanthropic pietism and foolish arrogance of the Count, and with the illusoriness of the world of the theatre.[9]

Because of the character of this society Wilhelm can see the justice of Jarno's opinions about the necessity of specialisation.   Jarno tells him, and the others illustrate the theme in practice, that each individual, to be anything, must be one-sided, and that the totality he seeks can only be achieved

socially, in the co-operation of one-sided individuals (vii. 592).
But one-sidedness does not profit the individual if it is something merely imposed, by birth or necessity. Wilhelm learns
from ' the beautiful soul ', and from the others, that ' man is
not happy until his boundless striving sets itself its own limits '
(vii. 593) ; the choice he is to make is to come from within,
to be determined by his personality.[10] Thus he chooses, in
the *Wanderjahre*, to become a surgeon, moved by his aesthetic
delight in the body as well as by social obligations. The
doctrine of one-sidedness cannot satisfy Wilhelm if it is associated with the society represented by Werner or the Count ;
it can do so only in relation to the new, projected society, in
which one-sidedness and personality are not opposed. Activity
in such a framework is also, he learns, the only way to come
to self-knowledge ; without it thought remains imprecise and
cloudy. ' Thinking and doing, doing and thinking, that is
the sum of all wisdom. . . . To test doing against thinking,
thinking against doing.' These are Jarno's words in the
Wanderjahre (viii. 285) ; more generally it is stated later on :

How can one get to know oneself ? Never by contemplation,
but certainly by activity. Try to do your duty, and you will
immediately know what is in you. But what is your duty ? The
demand of the day (viii. 307).

This then is the kingdom that Wilhelm finds, instead of the
national theatre, or poetry : specialised activity within a
worthy community, renunciation of much in the interests of
what is essential, the consequent building-up of personality
and true self-knowledge (in this sense the community of
emigrants of the *Wanderjahre* is called the ' Renunciants ').
Wilhelm emerges from his apprenticeship when he understands all this, when he prepares to enter a new life on these
conditions and with these aims. This is what is meant by
' Bildungsroman ', the story of the formation of a character
up to the moment when he ceases to be self-centred and becomes society-centred, thus beginning to shape his true self.
 In a sense, therefore, this novel is didactic. We notice,
however, a great difference from the normal didactic novel.

Running along with the general stress on activity, on social service, there goes an emphatic appreciation of the distinctiveness of each personality. There is no one ideal of man. What attracts and instructs Wilhelm in his new acquaintance is that each is himself, unique. ' The beautiful soul ', Lothario, Jarno, Therese, Natalie, all have sharply differentiated personalities ; yet each tolerates the others, realising they are complementary to one another. They do not seek to make Wilhelm like themselves, but to encourage him to find his own self. He brings, in fact, a very special element into their community. Early on, when Jarno expresses himself in his blunt way about the Harper and Mignon, Wilhelm wrongly calls him ' a heartless worldling ' ; but there is meaning in it when he says that his own sympathy for these unfortunates is worth more than all Jarno can offer him (vii. 207–8). Later, Wilhelm is shocked at the indifference with which Jarno and the others hear that he has discovered Felix to be his son. Therese is indifferent to imagination and art, both she and Natalie are insensitive to the beauty of nature. Lothario tramples on other people's feelings. All these nobles, even Natalie, show a certain impoverishment of the heart—Wilhelm himself had told the actors that the nobles lack that happiness which comes from inward warmth (vii. 227). He retains to the end his warmth of heart, his generous humaneness, which make him the confidant of people in distress. It is a true bourgeois feature in him that he will not lose.

It is one of the peculiar elements in the novel that, from the beginning of his adventures, this ' Society of the Tower ' has been interested in Wilhelm's education, guiding it in certain ways. The novel here links up with the conventional mystifications of eighteenth-century literature, omniscient guardians, unexplained interventions, etc. ; and it links up with the contemporary development of secret societies, the Free Masons in particular. But there is a profound and rational meaning behind this apparatus. In his letter to Werner, Wilhelm speaks of developing ' out of himself ' ; in actual fact he discovers that he has needed the guidance of others—' You do not remain alone, you form yourself in

society' (*Urworte. Orphisch*). He, like everyone, is educated
by influences from outside as well as by his own inner movement. The 'Society of the Tower' symbolises the world,
and like the world its members apply different educative
methods. The Abbé, the educator-in-chief, believes man is
educated by his own errors ; Jarno uses the corrective of
caustic and blunt sarcasm ; Natalie intervenes to help with
a loving hand. All are right in their way, together they make
up the total process of education (see vii. 558–9, 565–6, 590).
And again, Goethe subtly shows how precarious the results
are. Wilhelm, fully in accord with his friends, makes the
first really sound, clear decision of his new life. He becomes
betrothed to Therese, the woman who is all practical efficiency.
And immediately, through outward events and his own feeling, he discovers it was a wrong decision : ' Again and again
my eyes are opened to myself, always too late and always in
vain ' (vii. 650). In the fickleness of his little son he recognises
the image of himself and of man : ' You are a true man '
(vii. 610). We are never allowed to sit back with the comfortable feeling, now all is resolved, all is plain ; though much
progress is made, one problem is solved, as Goethe was fond
of saying, only to give rise to another. Thus the book, like
so many of Goethe's works, closes (as the *Wanderjahre* closes)
not with a final certainty, but with an infinite prospect, comparable with the indeterminateness of life. Goethe once called
Wilhelm ' a poor dog ', for as he said it was Wilhelm's indeterminateness, his infinite ' plasticity ' as Schiller called it,
that made it possible for Goethe to show clearly ' the interplay
of life and the thousand different tasks of life '.[12]

THE UNITY OF THE NOVEL

So far only the ' what ' of Goethe's novel has been discussed ; we must now turn to the ' how '. And first, the composition. How does the new intention fit on to and alter the
earlier version, the *Sendung* ? Here very subtle changes of
pattern can be noticed, as if a kaleidoscope had been ever so
gently shaken.

on which he is wrecked. That the actors speak of the dignity
of their profession in the *Sendung* is lightly humorous ; in the
Lehrjahre it is ironical and grating. The jealousies and follies
that rend the troupe at the Count's mansion, which Wilhelm
believes can still be overcome, have no longer the simple
gaiety of the picaresque novel ; ultimately these personal
defects, and the taste of the public which is their correlative,
defeat him. Wilhelm takes these difficulties to be accidental
and trivial hindrances in his way, and even when he turns
away from the theatre in discouragement, he fails at first to
see any deeper meaning in his disappointment. But Jarno
brings him up sharp. In recounting the life of the troupe,
Jarno tells him, Wilhelm is merely describing the world. So,
Wilhelm's delusions and failure with the actors are representative of his delusions and failure with the world, and at the same
time the means of his education.

The discussions on *Hamlet* take on quite a different meaning
too, although they are substantially the same as in the *Sendung*.
Much attention has always been paid to Wilhelm's interpretation of the play, and it is certainly original and interesting.
But the question is, what meaning have these long discussions
in relation to Wilhelm's pilgrimage. Why is *Hamlet* singled
out for discussion and production ? Why is Wilhelm such a
success in the title-role, while he fails in others ? Jarno, his
Mephistophelean friend, tells him outright :

' He who can only play himself is no actor. If you cannot trans-
pose yourself, in disposition and figure, into many characters, you
do not deserve this name. You for instance have played Hamlet
and a few other parts quite well, for they suited your character,
your figure, and the mood of the moment. That would be good
enough for an amateur theatre and for anyone who sees no other
way open to him. . . . One should guard against a talent that
one cannot hope to practise in perfection ' (vii. 591).

Jarno expressly associates Hamlet with Wilhelm himself.
The point is, Hamlet engrosses Wilhelm because he is an
objectivisation of Wilhelm's own inward uncertainties. Wilhelm sees him as a ' pure, noble, highly moral being destroyed
by a burden he can neither carry nor shake off ', a man torn

by doubt ; in analysing the conflicts in Hamlet's mind he
unwittingly reveals the conflict within himself, of which he is
not yet conscious, and the task of his life, which so far he has
misunderstood. The discussions on the play, particularly
those on Hamlet himself, subtly illuminate Wilhelm's own
character, his own inadequacies ; they circle round the issue
that Goethe later called the theme of his novel—' the great
truth that man would often undertake something for which
nature denied him the capacity '.   In the *Sendung* the deeper
bearing of the Hamlet discussions is not made clear to us,
and we cannot say how far the author was conscious of it.
The surmise can be detected, however, in the *Lehrjahre*, if we
see the discussions in the context of the whole novel.   The
comment on *Hamlet* in *Poetry and Truth* leaves us in no doubt
about Goethe's intention.   Here, discussing the influence of
English melancholia and misanthropy on the young Germans
of his generation, Goethe refers specifically to the meaning of
Hamlet for them : ' Hamlet and his monologues remained
ghosts that haunted all young minds '.[13]   It is precisely the
' ghostliness ' of his artistic aims and his life on the stage that
Wilhelm unconsciously reveals in his preoccupation with
Hamlet.   Thus the production of *Hamlet* is the climax of his
theatrical career, but at the same time its conclusion ; from
this point he sets out to seek his ' kingdom ' ; the search for
the ' asses ' is abandoned.

The visit to the Count's mansion likewise shows the clarification of an ' obscure surmise ', to such a degree that we can
almost speak of a change in function.   It is here that Wilhelm
gets an inkling, from his first contact with high society, that
the world is different from what he had thought (*Sendung*, viii.
794).   Here Jarno, whom he calls his friend, tells him he is
wasting his time with the troupe, and in directing him to
Shakespeare encourages him in his impulse to take an active
part in life.   But these hints do not lead, in the *Sendung*, to
anything specific, nor can we guess that any new direction in
Wilhelm's life was to arise out of them.   The primary purpose
of the visit is to show how harmful to the theatre and the actors
is the dilettante, tasteless, class-proud patronage of the nobility.

In the *Lehrjahre*, however, while all these elements are present, new additions attract our attention primarily to the problem of ' Bildung '. Wilhelm is persuaded, against his better feelings, to dress up as the Count in order to play a trick on the Countess ; when the Count, unexpectedly returning, sees in a mirror what he takes for his own image, he believes it to be a presage of impending death ; he falls victim to an obsession, abandons all his worldly responsibilities, and joins the sect of the pietists. Wilhelm and the Countess, yielding to impulsive emotion, embrace, and in the embrace a medallion the Countess wears presses painfully on her breast. Her feeling of sin turns into an obsession that she has a cancer there, and she joins her husband in his pietism.

These two incidents flow into the main stream of the novel. Wilhelm can never overcome his remorse, for he recognises that his irresponsible and impulsive behaviour has caused irreparable harm to the two, and it is a tangible symbol of the falsity of his theatrical life and aims. And the Count and Countess, reappearing as the relatives and friends of the ' Society of the Tower ', illustrate the perversities which attend a *fainéant* nobility, forming a useful foil to the rather idealised nobility that Wilhelm admires. They, like the Harper, fail to live worthily, because of 'an *idée fixe* that has no influence on active life ' (vii. 373) ; the harsh mockery with which their friends speak of them startles and shocks Wilhelm, yet it tells him indirectly that he needs, equally severely, to repudiate his own earlier *idée fixe*.

Of particular interest is the later treatment of Mignon and the Harper, since Goethe's development of their characters and story has provoked the sharpest criticism. He does not leave them in the mysterious twilight in which they appear in the *Sendung*. We discover their past. The Harper is an Italian monk, and Mignon is the child of his union with his sister, whom he loved without knowing her identity. They are outcasts in every sense, morally and psychologically. The 'Society of the Tower' puts the Harper, who suffers from attacks of homicidal insanity, under the tuition of a wise clergyman, who succeeds in restoring the old man to health, though he

can remain balanced only if he carries round with him a
bottle of poison, the assurance that he can at any moment
dispose of his life.   Felix is discovered, as they think, to have
drunk the poison, and the old man cuts his throat ; saved
in the nick of time, he tears the bandage from his throat and
dies.   The efforts of the Society, so successful with Wilhelm,
fail with this psychosis ; there are dark regions where even
their wisdom is unavailing.

A more subtle process takes place in Mignon : she can be
said to pass like Wilhelm through phases of development, a
metamorphosis ; [14] but with her it is a purely natural, almost
physical development rather than a moral one, arising from her
adoring love for Wilhelm, and indicating her growth from ' a
hermaphrodite ' to the threshold of womanhood.   After the
night that Philine spends with Wilhelm, Mignon changes.
Suffering a terrible shock out of childish jealousy, she sullenly
submits to Wilhelm's reasonable advice to become a pupil of
Natalie's, but is subject to repeated hysterical attacks.   She
accepts guidance, and dresses as a girl ; but she is ill, and no
one can restore her.   She dresses in the white costume of an
angel, which symbolises her withdrawal from ordinary life,
her longing for death.   When she sees Wilhelm in the arms
of his betrothed, Therese, her heart breaks and she dies. [15]

Schiller made rather curious observations on these two
figures, Mignon and the Harper, linked both by birth and
nature.   He noted, with acumen, that all the other characters
are ordered in a ' planetary system ' at the end of the book,
but these two are outside, ' linking it with something distant,
something greater ' ; but at the same time he considered their
' monstrous fate ', their psychoses, were due to the ' unnatural-
ness' of a superstitious religion. [16]   The statements are contradictory, and there is no evidence that Goethe intended here
any criticism of Roman Catholicism.   In both these persons
we are made aware of obscure forces, an unmastered fate, a
mysterious beauty, which do not fit into the normal world and
cannot be controlled by it.   There are hints in Wilhelm and
Felix of forces which cannot be brought under full control by
reason ; here in the Harper and Mignon these forces dominate.

But, while in the *Sendung* these characters represent the highest beauty, a sort of elusive, incomprehensible ideal, in the *Lehrjahre*, while they may be loved, they are not idealised, but shown as ineffectual, dangerous. It is surprising, even repellent, to find that Mignon's death passes almost without comment. Wilhelm, conscious that all his efforts to help Mignon have resulted in her destruction, dismisses the problem from his mind ; a pompous funeral-ceremony is a substitute for personal feeling. Mignon is embalmed as if for ever to be removed from the natural, healthy process of life. Yet Goethe's development of the characters and the meaning of the Harper and Mignon is consistent ; and we can see that it is a misreading to make Mignon the centre of the story, to call her, as did Friedrich Schlegel, in his review of *Wilhelm Meister*, ' the mainspring ' of the work. Here is the core of the Romantic criticism of the book, as we find it in Novalis, who attacked the book because he observed, more accurately than Schlegel, that Goethe in a sense condemns the ' natural poesy ' of Mignon's character. The idealisation of Mignon is the commonest source of a misunderstanding of Goethe's novel ; few people can both appreciate the ' poetry ' of her existence, and recognise that it is the beauty of immaturity, even of disease.

In reference to *Wilhelm Meister*, Grillparzer, himself much of a Romantic, made a most apt comment on the Romantic conception of beauty :

That the Germans attribute so high a value to this unsteady dreaming, this capacity for boding without clear image or idea, is the very misfortune of this nation. . . . They think it is something peculiar to their nation, but other peoples know this state of mind too, only with them boys in the end grow into men. I do not speak as one to whom this dreamy daze is strange, for it is my state. But at least I recognise that one must work one's way up out of it if anything is to be achieved. Monks and hermits may intone ' Hymns to the Night ' [Novalis], but active men need the light.[17]

Goethe would have approved the whole of this statement as summing up the theme of his novel.

Beside all these particular problems of composition, there

still remains the central question, how does the main theme of
the *Sendung*, the idea of a theatrical mission, contribute to the
realisation of the ultimate purpose of the *Lehrjahre*. If it is
merely an ' error ', it lasts an unconscionable time, and is
artistically scarcely justifiable.   The problem is raised directly.
When Wilhelm deplores the void of his life with the troupe,
the wise Abbé, his moral guardian, answers : ' Everything
we encounter leaves traces behind. Everything contributes
imperceptibly to our education.'   He admits that it is often
difficult to recognise what contribution a particular experience
may make, so gives the wise advice that the safest thing is
not to think over it too much, but just do the immediate task
(vii. 454)—in this spirit the ' Renunciants ' in the *Wanderjahre*
are pledged never to talk about the past or the distant future
(viii. 44).   The permanent influences of Wilhelm's theatrical
experiences are indeed difficult to perceive, and never made
explicit ; he drops his old acquaintances and interests completely.   Only a most attentive reading will discover relationships here.

The formal link between Wilhelm's old and new life is his
reading of the ' Confessions '.   How is this book a spiritual
bridge ?   We note the title, ' the beautiful soul ' : so, it is
still a question of beauty.   But the beauty is now a moral
beauty, a beauty of life and temperament, not a beauty which
belongs to a realm distinct from the moral and social world.
It is the beauty of Iphigenie, issuing from the identity of
feeling and moral purpose, from the union of duty and inclination, as Schiller defined beauty.   In the case of ' the beautiful
soul ' herself, this beauty is still restricted, not exemplary,
because the outer world, activity, is neglected, because she
develops without struggle, almost without being conscious of
her aim (vii. 407).   The views of the Uncle which she reports,
provide a correction of herself.   He asserts that a larger harmony, a larger beauty, must be sought, that man must through
activity bring his environment into harmony with himself
(vii. 436).   Hence he admires above all ' resolution and
pertinacity '.   The activity he pursues and recommends, like
that illustrated in many characters in the *Wanderjahre*, is good

because it is useful ; but usefulness is the way to the true and
the beautiful (viii. 73), for the beautiful is exactly this harmony
within the character, and between the character and the outer
world.   Natalie is more truly a ' beautiful soul ' than her
aunt, because her inner self is entirely and serenely fulfilled
in service to others ; she is both a ' realist ' and ' a purely
aesthetic nature ', as Schiller remarks.[18] No man can be
happy and harmonious, says the Uncle, unless he is systemati-
cally active : ' It is always a man's misfortune if he is made to
strive after something with which he cannot unite himself
through regular self-activity (' Selbsttätigkeit ') (vii. 438)—by
' Selbsttätigkeit ' he means an activity which springs from his
own character and will.   For the Uncle art is a necessary condition too to moral training, for it is a means of training our
' sensuous nature ', of refining it so that we do not fall a victim
to an ' unregulated fancy ', to false sentiment (vii. 439–40).
It is not without significance that the art that most enchants
this ideal group is that of choral song, where each part becomes
lovely only in combination with others.

These ' Confessions ' have the deepest educative influence on
Wilhelm.   He learns through them a new ideal of character,
beauty of character based on complete inner harmony and
self-certainty ; and he learns of the task that faces him, of being
active in such a way that a harmony is established within
himself, and between himself and a community, so that
practical social existence itself may be beautiful.

It is only too easy to misunderstand this theme, to ignore
it, to reject it.   For the Romantics it seemed the negation
of beauty, which resides for them in the world of presentiment
and fancy.   Sentimental Philistines reject it too, for they
want the beauty which is an alleviation, a leisure-time entertainment, a comforting delusion.   Carlyle, on the other hand,
with his puritan asceticism, could approve heartily the doctrine
of activity and work, but completely failed to see the aesthetic
aspect of Goethe's intention.[19] Schiller understood it best
and Korff has well brought it out in his chapter on *Wilhelm
Meister*.[20] The beauty of the harmonious, purposeful character and of his work is exemplified in a somewhat idealised

form in the *Lehrjahre* through the description of the few noble
characters with whom Wilhelm consorts or through that of
his own appearance in contrast to the withered Werner. It
emerges in the *Wanderjahre* in relation to certain characters,
with their true beauty like Frau Susanna, or their false faces
like ' The Fifty-year-old Man '. It comes out also in the
beauty of the well-managed estate of the Uncle, in the beauty
of the operations of spinning, which Goethe describes with
such loving attention. Goethe's praise of systematic and
skilful work has always an element of utilitarianism in it ;
but he values it in the conviction that usefulness implies a
harmonious relationship with society, a combination of personal and social interests, and that it alone can make a man
harmonious in himself, can fuse opposing qualities in him,
can give him beauty. In this sense Wilhelm's early search
for beauty, his mistaken feeling of a ' mission ' for the theatre,
his desire to find fulfilment for his talent and to be a cultural
educator, all these trends find fulfilment in his later life. His
life with the troupe was not merely an error ; it fostered
and developed his inherent tendencies. It not only taught
him the falseness of an ideal of art which is not associated
with personal and moral ' Bildung ', but it firmly established
in him an aesthetic purpose—the purpose of making the
totality of existence harmonious, beautiful. In this complex
sense *Wilhelm Meisters Lehrjahre* is the fundamental document
of Weimar classicism.

FORMAL AND STYLISTIC CHARACTERISTICS

In a famous passage in Book 5, Chapter 7 (vii. 330–1),
Goethe presents the conclusions of a discussion on the relative
merits of the drama and the novel which certainly represent
his own views at the time he was writing *Wilhelm Meister* :

> In the novel, as in the drama, we see human nature and action.
> The difference between these genres does not lie simply in their
> outward form. . . . In the novel, opinions [21] and occurrences are
> above all to be presented ; in the drama, characters and actions.
> The novel must move slowly, and the views of the main character
> must, in one way or another, obstruct the unravelling of the whole.

The drama must speed, and the character of the hero must drive on towards the issue, and only meet obstructions. The hero of the novel must be passive, or at least not highly effectual ; we demand of the dramatic hero impact and deeds. Grandison, Clarissa, Pamela, the Vicar of Wakefield, even Tom Jones are, if not passive, yet retarding characters, and all occurrences are in a sense moulded upon their dispositions. In the drama, the hero moulds nothing upon himself, everything resists him, and he clears and shifts hindrances out of his way, or else succumbs to them.

They agreed too that chance might properly be allowed free play in the novel, but that it must always be steered and guided by the dispositions of the characters. On the other hand, fate, that urges men without their co-operation through incoherent external circumstances to an unforeseen catastrophe, belongs only to the drama. Chance may produce pathetic situations, no doubt, but never tragic ; fate on the other hand must always be terrible, and becomes in the highest sense tragic, when it brings disconnected deeds, innocent and guilty, into disastrous association.

We cannot at the moment consider how far this definition applies to the novel in general.[22] That the distinctions drawn between novel and drama are not completely satisfactory is immediately discovered by the company, for they agree that Hamlet himself has the ' disposition ' of the hero of a novel— another gentle hint at the relevance of Hamlet to Wilhelm Meister. Goethe's definitions, based largely on the English novel of the eighteenth century, lead to the conception of the ' Bildungsroman '. The hero is not a man of action or will, he does not influence the march of events, even retarding them rather than propelling them. He is interesting above all for his disposition, his moral views and sentiments, his moral personality. In the midst of apparently fortuitous occurrences, he gives the latter a unity within his disposition, he ' moulds ' them though he does not cause or control them. The occurrences are of little importance in themselves, but acquire a meaning when reflected in his character. Thus Goethe lays all the stress on the disposition of the hero, on his ' Bildsamkeit ' as Schiller and Friedrich Schlegel called it, his educability. There is no fatal clash between circumstances and character ; the outcome is inherently there in the character from the beginning.

C

Hence, and here Goethe's definition leads on from the English novel to the ' Bildungsroman ' proper, a moral meaning is given to the outer world, however haphazard its scenes and occurrences may appear. There is a moral logic that connects events, that leads the Harper and Mignon to their pathetic end as it leads Wilhelm to his ' happy ending '. The novel has therefore an exemplary purpose—to show ' how man, in spite of all follies and errors, led by a higher hand, yet comes to a happy ending'.[23]

There is something ' garden-like ', as G. Müller well puts it, about the composition of the *Lehrjahre*. An almost bewildering variety of characters and incidents is disposed in a plan which belongs not to nature but to a gardener, who ensures to each plant the soil and position which enable it to flourish. Wilhelm, specific as he is, demonstrates a typical process ; his ' Bildung ' has ' the objectivity and teleological direction of an organic process '.[24]

Goethe's concept of ' metamorphosis ' postulates two active factors : a set of influences from outside which are shaped by the formative dynamism within the organism. We see these two principles in the growth of Wilhelm. He meets a vast number of incidents, and his character gives them a meaningful shape. It is a peculiarity of Goethe's conception, and of the whole book, that events are never decisive ; there are no points at which the hero is suddenly brought to change course. He develops in time, but time is not broken up into clear, distinct turning-points. Almost unconsciously he absorbs what an occurrence offers, and its result takes shape slowly or quickly, according to the tempo of his inward growth ; the novel is ruled not by clock-time or historical time (its chronology is in fact rather shaky), but by organic time, the speed of which is determined by the inherent laws of the organism. Thus a confused series of accidents and incidental attachments leads Wilhelm to throw in his lot with Melina, Philine and the rest ; there is no precise challenge, no moment of decision, and his decision in fact comes from an irresistible urge in him which becomes dominant at that moment of his development. Again, the experiences at the Count's mansion

seem disparate and bewildering until Wilhelm, slowly maturing, gives them a meaning in the letter in which he announces
to Werner that he is signing the contract with Serlo. The
final decision, to enter into the circle of the 'Society of the
Tower', is poorly motivated if we observe only external causes ;
it is explicable only if we understand an inward movement
in Wilhelm which proceeds at a speed of its own. He seeks
to elucidate and understand the change, in order to be assured
that it is sound and permanent ; but the actual process
escapes analysis and is never the result of definable causes.
There is the same sort of movement in Mignon. Outer
events induce change, but it takes place in a way and at a
speed which is determined by her own nature, primarily as the
outcome of her leap from childhood to girlhood. Up to very
recent times few writers have been able so subtly to represent
the movement of this inward, organic time.[25]

It is evident that with this central pre-occupation, the events
of the novel have a function not met with in other novels of
Goethe's time. In fact Goethe uses many of the tricks of the
eighteenth-century adventure-novel, partly in order to satisfy
the taste of the reading public : chance meetings in inns,
abductions, robbery, fire, lost children, incest, secret societies,
mysterious figures with uncanny knowledge, etc. ; the reader's
curiosity is tickled by wilful suspension of the narrative or
arbitrary withholding of information. Straightforward narrative is often replaced by reminiscences of various characters,
letters, poems, lengthy conversations and reported speech.
Much of this ' dates ', and the variety irritates rather than
pleases. But we are the less disturbed by this paraphernalia
because of the primary interest in character and in growth
round which it is organised.

Wilhelm gathers in, so to speak, the spirit, the meaning, the
substance of all that goes on round him, transforms every obscure
feeling into an idea and a thought, expresses each individual thing
in a more general formula, brings home to us the meaning of all,
and thereby fulfilling his own character, most perfectly fulfils the
purpose of the whole.[26]

Throughout the book, the author intrudes in the ways usual

in the contemporary novel, through direct address to the
reader, short recapitulations at the head of some chapters,
references to ' our hero ', comments that the hero ' did not
know ' certain things, etc.[27] The presence of the story-
teller is equally, though more subtly, betrayed by the composition, by the often ironical juxtaposition of events and
opinions, by the prevailing clear, equable, somewhat detached
style. It is noticeable for instance that Goethe gives many
conversations in indirect speech, thus introducing the author's
personality even here, where the characters might be expected
to appear most immediately ; and in any case there is extremely little differentiation in the direct speech of the characters—they are distinguished more by the content, the
underlying bearing of what they say, than by the mode of
expression. In this respect the novel is characteristic of
Weimar classicism ; the variety of life is as it were filtered
through the medium of a clear, harmonious, serene personality.
This personality is indeed not felt as an ' intrusive author ',
something separate from the story related. It is not the
particular historical Goethe, but an imagined, idealised (somewhat avuncular) character, a bearer of the whole meaning
of the book, and ultimately, perhaps, its most important
character.

In general composition and conception the novel is a
unity. Just as Wilhelm's ' Bildung ' is the central interest of
the novel, so he himself provides the formal centre of its
composition—' the most necessary, not the most important
character '.[28] The author tells us more than Wilhelm is
conscious of, but he always takes his stand-point alongside
Wilhelm, so that only those events and that experience that
is available to Wilhelm is presented. Thus, from a purely
formal point of view, Wilhelm takes the centre of the picture
and forms the focus for the reader's imagination.

Thus there is a complex and subtle unity of composition in
Wilhelm Meisters Lehrjahre ; complex and subtle because the
novel does not present completed characters within a static
set of values, like for instance *Tom Jones* or *Vanity Fair*, but
shows a ' Bildung ' in the main character, a metamorphosis

of values as well as of environment. Yet no reader will feel this unity immediately, and most fail to grasp it altogether. And this is not only due to Goethe's ironical reserve, his delight in veiling himself, in testing the reader by subtle hints and connections. Nor is it due to faults in the actual composition, some of which Schiller pointed out.[29] The main cause lies in the style ; in this respect the book lacks unity.

The parts of the *Lehrjahre* which were taken over from the *Sendung* are outstanding for their fresh liveliness, the realistic descriptions, the clear delineation of a number of characters who have the startling uniqueness, almost the irresponsibility of life. Goethe writes with an amused, friendly irony of characters who refuse to obey rational principles. With this go the deeper notes of Mignon's and the Harper's songs, expressing a longing and a despair which interpret a sub- terranean stream within Wilhelm's own naïve and candid character and give to his apparent harmlessness a strength and substance that on the surface it lacks. Totally different is the style in the later books. In a note to guide the com- pletion of the book, Goethe summed up in abstract terms what he intended to do with his characters. ' Wilhelm, aestheti- cally moral dream. Lothario, heroically active dream. . . . Mignon, madness of discordant relationships.'[30] Useful as this note is for the interpretation of the novel, it is even more revealing from the point of view of the style. The char- acters are to acquire an abstract meaning, they stand for general psychological types, they become allegorical. The ' Confessions ' still has the liveliness of actual experience, based as it is on documents of Goethe's friend, Fräulein von Klettenberg. But otherwise the later books are pale and abstract, the lessons and experiences are theoretical, and they do not strike home to our imagination. Natalie, for instance, is a completely ideal character, who educates and loses Mignon, who hears of Wilhelm's adventure with Philine, furthers his match with Therese, and ultimately marries him herself, with unaltered serene equanimity. Wilhelm's early life is full of the substantiality of experience ; his later education is theo- retical. Hence we cannot help feeling that in his adventures with the troupe he was a real person among real persons, while in the later part, and in the *Wanderjahre*, he is an unreal ghost walking among other ghosts.

And this directly reverses the theme of the book ! Compared with Natalie, Philine, the whimsical light-of-love, is rooted and real ; there is more harmony, confidence, wholeness in her ' If I love you, what's it to do with you ? ' than in any action or thought of the later characters. The haphazardness of person and incident in the first part seems solid ; the subtle linking of persons and incidents in the later part seems ' romantic ' and more than far-fetched. Mignon and the Harper seem sufficient in the mystery of their early appearance ; when their characters are explained, they seem to lose all substance. The climax of the first version is a real event, the creation of a theatre and the production of plays ; the climax of the other is a set of aphorisms (Wilhelm's articles of apprenticeship) and a marriage which is unattended by passion or even by union. This is the great weakness of the book, and it cannot be overlooked. The lack of sensuous reality in the later books is not merely a regrettable weakening of artistic quality ; it almost fatally injures the whole meaning of the novel, and is the chief cause of the misunderstanding of the work.

The novel ends with the winning of an outlook, a set of values, and a set of relationships ; with this Wilhelm's apprenticeship is concluded. He is now on the springboard of the social world, ready ' to mingle in the tide of fates '. How will he fare, what struggles will come ? Goethe felt a conclusion was necessary. He composed the *Wanderjahre*, yet this again tells us only of preparation, moral preparation above all, for active life, represented as the New World to which all the society of ' renunciants ' will emigrate. Goethe thought once of a *Meisterjahre*, but without result. In the light of the subsequent history of the German novel, we must consider this fact as being of great significance. We find again and again, in Stifter, in Keller, in Thomas Mann (*Der Zauberberg*), that the ' Bildungsroman ' leads up to the decision to take part in social life, but halts at the threshold, or deals summarily and feebly with the later fortunes of the hero. Viëtor is no doubt right in calling the ' Bildungsroman ' ' *the* German species of the novel ';[31] and it is characteristic that while no other national literature can show novels comparable with the German in illuminating the moral and spiritual development of man from subjective pre-occupations to the affirmation of objective activity, German literature is extraordinarily poor in novels which present the main theme of the nineteenth-century European novel, the problems of actual social life.

It seems that the urgency of the message of *Wilhelm Meister*, so well understood by Grillparzer, remained ; it provided the stimulus for Germany's greatest novelists, and limited the range of the German novel. Goethe understood something of this when comparing his work with Walter Scott's novels. The rich variety of great events in British history was lacking in German, he believed, so that he himself was forced to choose the ' most wretched material ' for *Wilhelm Meister*— ' itinerant theatre-rabble and miserable landed gentry '.[32] In order to provide the Society with a worthy field of activity, he had to idealise them and send them to a Utopia. Since Goethe's time German novelists seem to have been dogged by the conviction that German circumstances were not adequate to the needs of the full personality.

CHAPTER II

Gottfried Keller

GREEN HEINRICH

THE publication of *Wilhelm Meister's Apprenticeship* occurred
at the moment when Romanticism was asserting its hold
over the whole younger generation in Germany, and its theme
was decidedly anti-romantic.   Yet few of the Romantics could
resist it—Friedrich Schlegel wrote an enthusiastic review, and
Novalis' early comments were extremely favourable.   Its form
was imitated in many Romantic novels, with results that
show how little it was understood.   Tieck, in his early novels,
made sensitive artists his heroes, and sought to depict their
artistic education ; but they remain vague characters incapable of maturing, irresolutely submitting to exaltation and
agitation.

By far the most important of Romantic novels in the *Wilhelm
Meister* tradition is Novalis' *Heinrich von Ofterdingen*.   After his
first enthusiasm for Goethe's novel, Novalis had rapidly come
to see that it was fundamentally anti-romantic, ' a Candide
directed against poetry ', as he called it.   He composed his
own unfinished novel as a refutation of *Wilhelm Meister*.   It
is the story not of the education of a young man, but of the
unfolding of his poetic spirit, his ' Gemüt '.   Its opening
subtly, fascinatingly, announces its theme :

His parents were already in bed and asleep, the clock on the
wall ticked away monotonously, the wind roared past the clattering
windows ; at intervals the room grew bright in the gleam of the
moon.   The young man lay restlessly on his bed and thought of
the stranger and his tales.   It is not the treasures, he said to himself, that have awakened in me so ineffable a longing ; avarice is
far from my thoughts ; it is the blue flower that I long to see.   It
lies constantly in my mind and I can imagine and think of nothing
else.   I have never experienced anything like this ; it is as if I had
hitherto been dreaming, or as if in my sleep I had passed over into
another world ; for in the world in which I have been living, who

30

would have bothered himself over flowers, and certainly I have never heard of so strange a passion for a flower. Where can the stranger really have come from ? None of us has ever seen a man like him ; yet I do not know why I was the only one to be so captivated by his speech ; after all, the others heard the same and nothing like it happened to them. And I cannot even speak of my queer state of mind ! I am so rapturously happy, and only when the flower is not fully present in my mind am I at the mercy of a deep inward urging : no-one can or will understand this.

Without rhetoric or stress, with the insistence of the simplest expressions and an insinuating melody of phrase, the book takes its direction and announces the basic motifs—the stranger, the blue flower, the dream-world, the mysterious and restless urge away from the prosaic world. The novel is to unfold this seed ; Heinrich von Ofterdingen is to become a poet, and in so doing to transcend the real world : ' The world becomes a dream, the dream becomes the world '. A mighty theme ; here Romanticism challenges Goethe. But the challenge is not sustained on the artistic level. It belongs to the theme that earthly realities are dissolved into unearthly. All clear contours are lost, the characters thin out into allegorical abstractions, and the novel widens and widens until no end can be imagined. Important as this novel is, it demonstrates more conclusively than weaker works how unsuited the novel is to the Romantic purpose.

There is more substantiality in Jean-Paul Richter, particularly in the eccentric individuals and the domestic interiors he creates. But his sentimentality, his rococo-Romantic extravagances, his lack of discipline are not only immensely irritating ; they cause the central characters to blur and vaporise.

Even the novels of the following generation, with its avowed anti-Romantic, satirical purpose, suffer from the Romantic tradition. Sentimental idealisation, highfalutin and whimsicality in the Jean-Paul manner, mix queerly with social and political satire of a rather abstract kind. The most significant German novelist of the 1830s was Immermann, a recalcitrant Romantic, who in his two important novels, *Die Epigonen* and

Münchhausen, seeks a way through old Romantic values and
pretence to the realities and moral responsibilities of the
contemporary world. But the hero of *Die Epigonen* remains
elusive and indeterminate, and Romantic mystifications still
disfigure the work. The story of the sturdy farmer of the
' Oberhof ' in *Münchhausen* has a plasticity and coherence
which have made it justly famous, and its function is to stand
as the counterpart to the vacuity of the aristocratic *fainéants*.
But it is not organically linked with the rest of the novel, and
once again the central hero does not develop, but wavers
irresolutely between the two worlds of solid substance and
glittering form. It is a curious and interesting phenomenon
that in the short story, the ' Novelle ', to which genre one
can almost reckon the ' Oberhof ' episode, German writers,
including Romantics, could achieve masterpieces ; in the
novel there is failure after failure.[1]

It was only in a new generation, in the years after 1848,
that the theme and form of *Wilhelm Meister* were truly assimilated. It is remarkable that the two direct heirs of Goethe
were a Swiss and an Austrian.

The one great novel of the Swiss author, Gottfried Keller,
is curiously like *Wilhelm Meister's Apprenticeship*. It is the
story of the growth of a child to manhood, of a would-be
artist who discovers that his true calling is service to society,
the Canton of Zürich.[2] His error is not unprofitable. Heinrich's devotion to art, to his imagination, detaches him from
the conventional round of life, from the vulgar concepts of
success and failure, from the thoughtless egoism of the
Philistine. He learns both to renounce, and to pursue the
ideal purposes of social living ; in his final capacity as a
modest administrator he becomes a man of trust, a mediator,
a representative of communal life. But, much as Keller
avowedly learned from Goethe, and in particular from *Wilhelm
Meister*, his novel is no glib imitation. It is, as Keller repeatedly
said, ' the fruit of personal experience '; its problems were
those of Keller himself, and its material is often autobiographical. He toiled at it for many years, and the labour of
composition bears witness to Keller's own severe struggle with

his experience. The first published version of *Der grüne Heinrich* appeared in 1854-5, the product of seven years of work. He refashioned it in the 1870s, and the novel in its final form appeared in 1879-80.

Poverty, and the devotion of an ignorant mother, isolate the child, Heinrich Lee, from normal active society, for which his imagination provides a rich substitute in the loneliness of his attic or among the strange objects and stranger conversations in a neighbour's junk-shop. His set-backs at school, which are due to a combination in him of imaginative intelligence and clumsiness, promote ' an excessive pre-occupation with himself '.[3] He invents scenes in which he is the central and important figure, often to his own harm and that of others. When taken to task for using ' bad words ', he tells his masters that bigger boys have tortured him and forced him to use these words, thus getting them into serious trouble, and producing in himself only a profound satisfaction at being believed. In order to manifest his own importance, he steals and spends the savings his mother had painfully put by for him. Expelled from school for a childish outburst of exuberance, his consequent isolation further intensifies his search for a compensation, and his choice of the artist's profession grows obscurely but naturally out of this isolation. When his mother places him with a commercial artist, the soulless mechanical labour further provokes him, so that he seeks for an outlet in the most romantic compositions. Leaving this employment, at which he has learned nothing, and thrown on to his own resources, he is not only without the prospect of an income, but also more and more cut off from his fellows. His occasional visits to cousins in his parents' native village introduce him to a natural, cheerful, healthy community ; his uncle the parson laughs at his pictures and sets him to copying real trees. But though the boy is happy here, and some of his diffidence is overcome, it is not his community ; and when he returns home he sinks ever deeper into ' the fantastic pursuits of his isolation '.[4]

He learns from an artist who temporarily resides in his town something of the discipline of art, and decides he must

study in Munich.   Here he lives for some years, supported in
the main by his mother.   But his isolation from the community becomes more and more complete, and his paintings,
romantic at first, lose more and more in content till he spends
his working hours filling a huge canvas with an infinite cobweb
of lines.   He makes a little money painting flag-poles for a
popular celebration, and almost succumbs to the attraction of
settling down in modest artisan contentment.   But a feeling
of idealistic responsibility prevails, and he resolves to return
home, abandon his false career, and devote himself to the
service of his homeland.   On the way he is entertained at
the mansion of a Count who is a disciple of the materialistic
philosopher Feuerbach.   Here Heinrich abandons his old
beliefs in a personal God and immortality, which had dis-
tracted him from recognising his responsibilities in this world,
and had encouraged him to maunder along in the vague hope
that ' the Lord will provide '.[5]   Thus secured in spirit, he
returns home ready to devote himself to the service of man,
in a democratic community whose principles he approves.
His mother, worn out by sacrifice and disappointment, dies
as he arrives, and chastened by the realisation of his guilt,
he works in a humble capacity to develop the social and moral
consciousness of his fellow-citizens, making few claims on
personal happiness.

In the first version Heinrich is so shattered by his feeling
of guilt towards his mother that he himself breaks down and
dies.   To his friend Hettner, the literary critic, who had
criticised this ending as being inorganic and inconsequent,
Keller defended it with the argument that, in ignoring his
duty to the family, Heinrich had disregarded the very basis
of society ;   time and the tolerance of the public would have
forgiven him, but his own conscience was too tender to accept
any excuse.   It was only as a result of a long experience that
Keller came to see that in this personal story he was describing
a fate ' for which no-one is guilty, or everyone ';   that there
is a ' psychological-social ' solution to a guilt like Heinrich's,
through nature and work, even though his feeling of guilt,
his consciousness of error, remains with him as the principle

of his personal renunciation.[6] The culmination of the first
version forces everything into the perspective of the fate of an
individual ; that of the final version asserts the vitality of
social life and makes the individual, even in his eccentric
course, a representative man.

SYMBOLICAL REALISM

Attention has been drawn to the symbolism which underlies
the incidents of *Wilhelm Meister*. The novel is not a simple
tale but the account of an inward development and education,
and every occurrence has a function in this education. It is
the same with *Green Heinrich*. On one level we have a story
rich in reality (not only ' thirsty for reality ', as Keller called
Wilhelm Meister) ; on another level, a series of experiences,
including anecdotal digressions, which as they accumulate
build up a human life in terms of its basic factors. Though
the novel was ' the fruit of personal experience ', Keller had
much more than an autobiographical purpose ; if his own
childhood was its basis, he wrote to Hettner, it was not
' because ' it was his, but ' although ' it was his.[7] His ' experience ' included his thought, and his novel was the fruit of his
whole wisdom. The principle of its composition is in fact
Keller's search for the fundamental structure of a human life.

We can discover this symbolical structure of the novel most
easily in the incidents which were added in the final version,
when Keller was more sure about his intentions. For instance,
he adds to Heinrich's financial resources a small paternal
legacy, which enables him to take up his studies at Munich.[8]
This legacy is held by the peasant community in his native
village, and he goes there in order to ask the trustees that he
may have it in order to complete his training. He is in a
state of inward revolt against the community, and half-
defiantly, half-timidly, he tells the peasants that with this
money he will quickly equip himself for a successful career.
The canny peasants are suspicious of the very idea of an
artistic profession, and can scarcely believe that success can
be gained so easily. Only through the advocacy of Heinrich's

rather easy-going uncle are they brought to relinquish their trust and give the security to Heinrich. The scene is described with great mastery, its focus being the anxiety and boastfulness of the young man who feels himself superior to these shrewd, limited peasants who are reluctant to relinquish their responsibility for him. At this moment of his life, he tears himself finally from the ancient bed of his family, from the ancient community, and he does so with a glad heart. But the proceedings also impress him with involuntary respect, he feels embarrassed and troubled as he sees the title-deed taken out of the box where it has been safely kept along with the property of widows and orphans, and is reminded that it is three hundred years old.

A feeling of the importance of the transaction sank into me in the end and oppressed my mind. I saw myself, the object of serious injunctions and legal procedure, both passive and responsible, without having, in my view, committed any crime or being about to do so, and with redoubled zeal I sought to escape from this unfree situation. 'They know damn all about freedom', the student sings about the Philistines, not noticing that he himself has only just started to learn something about it.

So, at the moment in which Heinrich rejoices to free himself from the community, the seed of social responsibility has dropped into him.

Other extensions of the text serve the same purpose. In the final version, Keller filled out the incident of painting flag-poles with a meeting between Heinrich and a little sempstress, Hulda. A cheerful simple girl, she offers him apparently a chance of a happy home; and only by accident does he find that her affection is given to all and sundry. The sketch of Hulda's character is delightful, and the incident reveals most deftly the dilemma facing Heinrich at that time. We can fully agree with Keller himself that ' it was not a bad motif to give an apparent justification for Heinrich's descent into the lower spheres of obscure unpretentious labour '.[9]

Early in the book there occurs, in both versions, the little tale of ' das Meretlein '. Heinrich sees a girl's portrait in the village, and tells the story of little Emerentia as he culls it from local gossip and the diary of a parson. It is a masterpiece that has always been admired, but is frankly a digression, and what we must ask ourselves is, what function it has in Heinrich's story.

A hundred years before, Emerentia, the child of an unhappy first marriage, had obstinately refused to pray or go to church. Her father and stepmother had placed her with the parson of the village whose efforts to correct her utterly failed. She was kept from other children, as her influence was considered to be harmful, and she wasted away in misery. Certified as dead, she was being carried to her grave when she stirred, and, taken from her coffin, she ran away, being ultimately discovered well and truly dead. She lives on in popular gossip as a bewitched child, yet there is more pity in the legend than horror.[10]

The tale is occasioned by Heinrich's refusal to say grace at the request of his mother. She tells him he will have no dinner if he does not say grace ; but when he obstinately persists, she gives way, and with sobs and tears he sets himself down to enjoy his food. Instead of reflecting on the causes of Heinrich's irrational obstinacy, Keller then tells the tale of Meretlein, who is destroyed by the failure of the adult world to make allowances for the complex processes in the child's mind. The tale tells us, subtly and indirectly, of the problem besetting both Heinrich and his mother.

The artistic propriety of the longer tale of Zwiehan, introduced in the final version, is more questionable. Heinrich sees a skull lying in a churchyard, and carries it with him to Munich. Often embarrassed by this lugubrious and cumbrous companion, he at last throws it away on his return home after using it to frighten a brutal forest-guard. The symbolical meaning of Heinrich's attachment to it is made explicit by the story of the man whose skull it is, a shiftless fellow who assumed the identity of his brother and lost thereby personality and well-being. The story may well be felt to be a digression. Keller himself wrote that he had a bad conscience about it since Zwiehan might appear ' somewhat too evident an allegory and prototype of someone who loses his own nature and person '.[11]

But if this symbolical structure is most clearly to be detected in the insertions and additions to the novel, it is also no less present in the apparently most simple parts of the narrative, and governs the composition of the whole. It is there in the contrast between the loneliness of mother and child in the city, and the social bustle of the village. All the incidents of childhood, the child's fancies about the weathercock, the reveries in Frau Margarete's curiosity shop, the lies at school, his spell-bound participation in the production of Goethe's *Faust*, all centre in one theme : ' what is dream and what is reality ? ' The theme is, however, never abstract, and the incidents have nothing of the appearance of allegory ; nor is the problem specific to Heinrich, for it is the problem of his friends and neighbours too. His and their fancies arise out of the nature of their lives, out of their psyche and situation. The novel is psychologically as profound and revealing as the great autobiographies of Rousseau or K. P. Moritz. Yet Keller is not concerned simply to uncover the causes of the perilous luxuriation of fancies. He shows how fancies arise as a compensation for a narrow and socially frustrated life, particularly in the poorest sections of the population ; he shows the moral errors these fancies may induce. But he also shows how necessary the imagination is, what a spur it may be in the development of personality and the improvement of social behaviour. He is as critical of the matter-of-fact ' realists ', the men of practical success, as he is of those who fail to come to terms with reality.

Often enough Keller makes his point explicitly, as an author's comment. He tells of the lad with whom Heinrich vies in self-importance, so that each begins to lie and steal in order to impress the other. This lad, we are told, later in life becomes a common thief and his sisters, whose minds are perverted by an indulgence in sentimental novelettes, become lights-of-love. They are likened to sectarians who indulge in indiscriminate religious exaltation and lose consciousness of practical reality. But, adds a sympathetic comment, these excesses of the poor indicate ' the needs of the heart and the search for a better reality '.[12] Such incidents and anecdotes are therefore all closely interwoven with Heinrich's own obscure search and aberrations. As rich an account of childhood as *David Copperfield, Great Expectations,* or *Jane Eyre,* it surpasses them in two ways : the child is more contaminated, and his moral growth, more endangered, is more substantial, while at the same time his experience acquires a social representativeness.

For instance, Heinrich very early in life feels hostility to the external forms and simple beliefs of the church. He is sent to confirmation-classes, for confirmation is also a civil initiation-rite, and invents very heretical answers to the dogmatic questions which are discussed. Half-shy, half-precocious, he dreads the public ceremony, and he defiantly wears his customary green suit at the confirmation service, instead of the almost obligatory frock-coat, feeling pleasure at challenging the convention of the ' better ' citizens and associating himself with the poor whose poverty puts formal dress and full citizenship out of their reach. His views and behaviour are explicable in the light of his reserved and sensitive nature, which rebels against vulgar opinion and public show ; his irregular education since his dismissal from school also fosters unorthodox opinions. But at the same time he is representative. He notes how readily, in the confirmation-class, the better-class boys respond to their religious instruction ; how the sons of artisans and factory-workers, grouped at the back of the room, are slow, inattentive and turbulent. Different from the latter in his intelligence and sensitiveness, Heinrich yet formulates the resistance of a whole social group to the state-church, the church of the upper-classes. In fact he tries to interpret the idea of the Divine in terms of republican freedom and personal self-determination.[13]

As Heinrich grows into adolescence, the struggle within him between reality and imagination, nature and the ideal, community and isolation, is embodied in his love for Judith and Anna, a double love which is as profound psychologically as symbolically. Anna lives with her book-loving father in

D

an isolated house some distance from the village ; a friend of
Heinrich's cousins, she is different with her gentle, reserved
disposition and fragile, slight body.   Her education in French
Switzerland, her accomplishments, make her still more remote
from the lusty village girls.   Heinrich loves her as an ideal
being, silently and shyly.   The kiss they exchange in the
excitement of the village Carnival celebrations provokes con-
vulsive tremors in her frail body, and Heinrich feels he has
committed ' a breach of trust '; henceforth their love is
expressed only in indirect attentions.   She is struck down by
consumption and after a long illness she dies ; her death
marks the end of Heinrich's youth, for immediately afterwards
he does his military service and then leaves for Munich.

If Heinrich's love for Anna indicates that the idealistic
quality in him, though good, is too ethereal to subsist in this
world, his love for Judith shows his more corporeal, earth-
bound needs.   He hardly recognises it as love, it is intimacy,
happiness, security, love-play.   She is a young widow, a
villager, healthy, sure of herself, who educates him in simple
healthy feelings.   He grows accustomed to relieve the strain
of his ideal love and the sick-room by calling on Judith, to
chat and play, to discuss himself, his ideas and plans.   Her
half-motherly affection for him is without sentimental idealisation.   He tells her of a heartless trick he has played on his
Zürich art-master, and begs her to assure him that, as he is
repentant, he can dismiss his oppressive feeling of guilt.   She
roundly answers :

' No fear !   The reproaches of your conscience are very healthy
crusts for you, and you can chew away at them your whole life
long, I shall not butter them with my forgiveness.   I could not
do it anyway ;   for what cannot be changed cannot be forgotten,
I know enough about it, I think !   In any case, I unfortunately
do not feel that you have grown disagreeable to me ;   what are we
here for if we do not love people as they are ? ' [14]

Heinrich does not call his affection for Judith love.   Anna
is his love ;   and he is often tormented by his faithlessness to
his ideal, for even when Anna is ill he continues visiting
Judith.   Judith is a natural necessity, which at this stage he

half despises. After Anna's funeral, when he notes with some
discomfiture that he is less mournful at her death than exalted
by the feeling of being a chief mourner, he swears an oath
that he will never see Judith again, so much is he convinced
that his relations with her have been wrong and insignificant.

The whole relationship to the two girls grows subtly out of
his own youthful indeterminacy ; its ambivalence and con-
tradictoriness interpret his dilemma. His feeling for neither
can satisfy him, for the one is too ethereal, too much a product
of his juvenile idealism, the other too natural and instinctive.
But in the last part of the book he meets Judith again. He is
now different, and has accepted his task as a servant of the
republic ; but she too is different. After some years as an
emigrant in America, where she has proved her quality, she
returns a mature woman to find a sphere in which her humane
feeling can develop a beneficent activity. His meeting with
her is again symbolic, the climax of his reconciliation with the
people, with nature ; she is a symbol of what may grow out
of the raw material of life. In friendly association with her
he is relieved of his remorse for his mother's death. ' Heinrich
gets over this death years later, and only from the moment
when Judith returns and, the very personification of nature,
pronounces him free of guilt.'[15] Judith represents the logic
of time and nature, which frees Heinrich as it does Goethe's
Faust—with the difference that Heinrich does not forget his
responsibility and remains chastened in spirit to the end.

A striking feature of the composition of the novel is the
parallelism between the elaborate descriptions of two Carnival
celebrations. That at the village forms the framework for the
development of Heinrich's love for Anna and Judith ; that
at Munich is a turning point in his artistic career. Both
symbolise, in themselves, the contraries which tug at Heinrich.[16]

His native village and the neighbouring places decide to
enact Schiller's *Wilhelm Tell* ; the scenes are distributed over
the valley, and all the members of the community enter with
zest into the day-long celebration, choosing characters like their
own and embroidering the action with their own invention.
The seriousness and solemnity of the myth of their national

liberation is permeated by the jollity of a true popular festival ; it is a true communal rite, in its theme and its form, and imagination here is not opposed to reality, but rises out of it, purifies and strengthens it.   An early incident of the day strikes the key-note.   There is a procession of villagers with their cattle round the valley, and a surly toll-keeper holds it up, insisting that, according to law, all cattle passing his barrier must be taxed.   Wilhelm Tell, in real life a substantial inn-keeper, comes by chance on to the scene, and without a word he quietly lifts the bar and tells the people to pass.   Heinrich is in fact dismayed to observe that the villagers remain them-selves even in their costumes.   He sees one of the principal ' national heroes ' busily bargaining over the sale of an ox just before the show begins ; he is indignant when he hears Tell, in the dinner interval, vigorously persuading the local sheriff to take a new road past his inn, so that he may gain the custom of the traffic.   But the sheriff explains to Heinrich that a vigorous community cannot exist on altruism and renunciation, and needs the energetic self-interest of its members.   The whole celebrations do not obliterate the villagers' consciousness of their real existence, but enhance it. The fruitful function of the Carnival is seen on the following day, for floods are pouring into the valley, and all the people come out to build dykes in the threatened places.

Heinrich has been enlisted in the celebration as his artistic skill and historical lore are useful ; and the whole experience is a valuable lesson for him in communal life.   He must of course remain an outsider, for this is only a narrow, rural community, and he has to find his way to the larger com-munity of the state.   He discovers rather painfully that he does not truly belong, for in the flood-labour he is too unskilled to help.   But he has learnt much, and it is after this experience that, returning home, he begins to love Goethe's works and to appreciate, in place of the romantic extravagance of Jean-Paul, Goethe's ' love for all that has grown and become established, his respect for the right and importance of every thing, and his feeling for the coherence and depth of the world '.   Heinrich has learnt that poetry and beauty can be discovered in reality ; that ' poetry is something living and reasonable '.

The Carnival at Munich serves an opposite function. When arguing over his legacy, Heinrich had scornfully told the village trustees that art was now divorced from the handicrafts and freed from the need of long apprenticeship. The Munich Carnival is an ironic comment on this theme. The artistic community re-enacts scenes from the heyday of German art, the Germany of Dürer, when the culture of the different classes of society was remarkably homogeneous, and when the artist-craftsman was a typical figure. The rich, elaborate costumes and festival, the temporary social unity in this make-believe, only underline its falseness ; for this Munich world of artists has no roots in reality, in the common people or the community, no more than its patriotic fervour has any practical meaning. One of Heinrich's rich artist friends, Lys, who is amusing himself with a simple burgher girl, neglects her shamefully in the course of the festival to run after a wealthy and sophisticated woman. The girl finds comfort with a tradesman ; but Heinrich is so incensed that he challenges Lys to a stupid duel, which ends harmlessly.[17] The idle purposelessness of the Carnival is emphasised by the outcome for Heinrich and his friends. His two closest acquaintances give up art and devote themselves to politics and business. He himself falls into complete isolation, and it is now that he occupies himself with a large canvas that he patiently covers with an immensely intricate spider's web of gray lines (Heinrich is the first of the abstract painters). Art that is divorced from real life, life that is divorced from community, become empty and desolate.

Thus there is a consistent interweaving in *Green Heinrich* of incident and general theme, a consistent symbolism of structure. In the early parts of the book fusion of symbol and reality is perfect. But after Heinrich's arrival at Munich this fusion is less satisfactory. Something of the emptiness of Heinrich's life as an artist enters into the work itself. The Carnival at Munich seems unnecessarily long, and the detailed descriptions of characters, the prolonged carousal, are tedious.

The incidents of his years in Munich have nothing of the spatial and atmospheric precision of his earlier life (with the exception, characteristically enough, of the episode of the flag-poles and Hulda, for this evocation of the *plebeian* world is fresh and charming). The long dream at the end, which introduces Heinrich's decision to go back home, is an inappropriate form to indicate his change of mind ; the stay at the Count's mansion, the introduction to Feuerbach's philosophy, is poorly motivated and somewhat forced. And the return home, the acceptance of social duty, is told in summary, general terms ; Judith herself is now an abstraction, not a living woman, and Heinrich is whittled down to a shadow. The novel has, from a formal point of view, much the same weakness as *Wilhelm Meister*. As we come closer to Heinrich's decision to leave the world of imagination for the world of reality, the writing itself loses in plasticity, the theme emerges in an abstract didactic form and loses its poetic quality. Keller perhaps deliberately avoids describing this Swiss society as it actually was, with its factories, banks and social conflicts ; he shows the process of Heinrich's development, but not the life into which he enters.[18]

FORM AND STYLE

If a comparison between *Wilhelm Meister* and *Green Heinrich* throws an illuminating light on the specific quality of the theme of the latter, it is also remarkably instructive as regards its form. We have seen that the first version of *Wilhelm Meister* was composed as the straightforward consecutive story of the hero, and that, in the final version, Goethe made the story of Meister's childhood retrospective and told by the hero himself. Keller reversed the process. The childhood was originally inserted, as Heinrich's autobiography, after an opening section describing his arrival at Munich, and the whole of Heinrich's later artistic career was recounted in the third person. In the final version, the novel begins with the story of Heinrich's childhood, and the whole novel is written in the first person as Heinrich's own account.

Goethe's procedure is closely associated with the ironical

flavour that his novel persistently revels. The account of Meister's childish delight in theatre and drama, since we hear of it only from his own mouth, leaves the genuineness of his artistic calling in doubt. The ironical, if sympathetic, description of his life with the troupe follows organically upon this ; and again, his turn to social activity is so sudden, so dependent on external guidance, so insecure, that ironical tones prevail to the end of the *Lehrjahre*. Nothing however is further from the tone of both versions of *Green Heinrich* than irony and, in the first version, the abrupt contrast of the story of his childhood with his situation in Munich is not only clumsy (for the insertion is very long) but also entirely without aesthetic function.

Keller decided to put the whole novel into the first person before he contemplated changing the conclusion. As early as 1871 he thought of starting with a brief account of Heinrich's death, and then giving his life-story as the dead man's autobiography, and he kept to this plan till 1878. On Theodor Storm's suggestion, and after deciding that Heinrich should live on ' quietly and obscurely in unpretentious but regular employment ', Keller then gave the novel its present form of a life told by the hero from the view-point of maturity.[19]

In transforming it thus, Keller had done more than remove the inappropriate ' elegiac ending ' from a book whose character was, as he said, ' otherwise full of the will to life (" lebenswillig ") '.[20] Although Heinrich misconceives his calling, there is no such contradiction between his early life and his final decision as there is in *Wilhelm Meister*. The childhood tells of a continual conflict within him between reality and imagination, between the public and private self, a conflict which gives the undertone to his life as an artist, and which issues organically into his decision to return home. The experiences of his youth enter into the substance of his being, and in returning to his native land he rounds off the cycle of his experience, while Wilhelm Meister passes on into a totally new environment. Further, the world Heinrich returns to serve is this real world of his early life, while Wilhelm Meister serves a society which is still to be created. Heinrich's past could not be treated in a detached ironical manner, nor could his present be conceived except as deriving out of the past, of which we are continually reminded throughout the course of his stay at Munich.[21]   The unity of the form of the narrative is as appropriate to *Green Heinrich* as its variety is to *Wilhelm Meister*.

It is imaginable that the whole novel might have been written in the third person ; it is certain that it would have lost thereby.   By retaining and extending the use of the first person, Keller was able to find a simple and unifying principle for the selection of episodes, and was freed from any concern for insignificant biographical detail.   The imagined author remembers only what is significant for him, those incidents where something important was at issue ; he is seeking to clarify his purpose and his problem, and the moments of crisis (using the word in its widest significance) naturally remain prominent in his consciousness.   But Keller was concerned not only to portray, but also to comment, to make the meaning of events explicit.   This current commentary, which extends to general questions such as religion and politics, was not only less mature in the first version ; in the parts written in the first person it was often inappropriate to the youth of the pseudo-author and, in the parts written in the third person the intrusions of the author were oppressively frequent.   In the final version, purified by a wiser head and a riper taste, the commentary is that of the hero himself, and as such is an organic part of the tale.   We know who it is that is making the comments—in this sense the conclusion of the book, the mature wisdom of Heinrich, is present from the beginning, and the actual story only confirms what is subtly and some-times vigorously evident in each incident.   The dualism of author and incident that sometimes vexes in the earlier version has disappeared, and in the final form, the political, philo-sophical, aesthetic or moral comments form an organic part of the hero's reality.

Keller therefore never seeks to reproduce the world simply as a child, a ' greenhorn ', might see it.   His style reflects, without disguise, the mature man who recaptures, through

memory and imagination, the world of the child, illuminated
by the understanding.   It is a peculiarly dense style, inclining
even to clumsiness at times.   It is thronging with things, with
material, psychological and social actuality ; yet impregnated
with reflexion, which gives a shape to the experiences recounted
and builds up, with them, the process of the book, the
' Bildung ' of Heinrich.   In the account of Heinrich's excuse
for using swear-words we can find a characteristic example of
the fusion of imagination and mature reflection, and can
observe how his material, descriptive and reflective, is ordered
by his underlying purpose.[22]

A few days later, to my surprise, our teacher kept me behind,
together with the four boys whom I had accused [of teaching me
to swear], who seemed half-men to me, they were so much ahead
of me in age and size. A clerical gentleman appeared, who
usually gave us religious instruction and was chairman of the
School Board ; he sat down at a table with the teacher and told
me to sit beside him.   The boys, on the other hand, had to line up
in front of the table, and waited for what might come.   They
were now asked, in a solemn voice, whether they had uttered
certain words in my presence ; they could answer nothing and
were completely astounded.   Thereupon the clergyman said to
me : ' Where did you hear the things from these boys ? '   I was
straight off the mark and answered unhesitatingly with dry precision : ' In Brüderlein wood ! '   This is a thicket about an hour's
journey from the town, which I had often heard mentioned though
I had never been there in all my life.   ' What happened then, how
did you come to go there ? ' they went on with their questions.
I told them how one day the boys had persuaded me to go for a
walk and had taken me out to the wood, and I described in detail
the way bigger boys take smaller ones along with them on a lark.
The accused were beside themselves and gave tearful assurances
that they had either never been there or only long before, and least
of all with me, glancing at me with startled loathing as at a vicious
snake.   They started to overwhelm me with reproaches and questions, but were told to keep quiet, and I was summoned to describe
the road we had taken.   It straightway lay clear before my eyes,
and I named the roads and paths that lead to the place, fired by
the fact that they were contradicting and denying a fairy tale in
which by now I myself believed, since I could not otherwise account
for the present scene.   I knew the way only from the merest

hearsay, but though I had scarcely paid any attention every word slipped into its proper place. I went on to tell how we had gathered nuts on the way, had made a fire and roasted some stolen potatoes, and had thrashed a peasant boy who had tried to stop us. When we came to the wood, my companions climbed up tall firtrees and began to yell, calling the clergyman and the teacher by nicknames. I had hatched out these nicknames long before in my heart, thinking over the appearance of the two men, but had never mentioned them out aloud : this was an opportunity to strike home, and the anger of the two gentlemen was as great as the astonishment of the boys I was using as a pretext. After they climbed down from the trees, they cut some long switches and ordered me to climb a little tree and shout out the nicknames. When I refused, they tied me to a tree and beat me with their switches till I said all they wanted, including the indecent words. While I was shouting they crept away behind my back, a peasant came up at that moment, heard my bad language and caught hold of me by the ears. ' You bad boys,' he shouted. ' You wait. I've got this one ! ' and he gave me a few slaps. Then he too went away and left me standing there, and it was growing dark. I managed to wrench myself free and tried to find my way home through the dark wood. But I lost my way and fell into a deep brook, in which I waded and swam until I got out of the wood, and so, after surmounting many dangers, found the right way. And then I was attacked by a big billy goat, and fought him off with a stake I quickly tore out of a fence.

At school they had never seen me display any such eloquence as in this tale. Nobody thought of asking my mother if I had ever arrived home at night and wet through. Instead they connected my adventure with the fact that it could be proved that one or other of the boys had played truant just about the time of which I was speaking. They believed me because I was so young, as well as because of my tale ; the latter fell quite unexpectedly and ingenuously out of the blue of my normal silence. The accused were innocently condemned as unruly wicked young people, since their obstinate and unanimous denial and their just indignation and desperation only made the matter worse. They were given the severest punishments, were put into the school pillory, and over and above this were thrashed and locked in their rooms by their parents.

So far as I remember, I was not merely unconcerned over the disaster I had caused, but felt a sort of satisfaction that the poetic justice of my invention had been so smoothly and visibly rounded off, that something striking had occurred, that action and suffering had taken place, and all in consequence of my creative word. I could not understand how it was that the maltreated boys could make such a fuss and be furious with me, since the story had taken such an excellent and natural course and I could intervene as little as the ancient Gods could alter fate.

[In a concluding paragraph Keller tells of the attitude of the boys to him in later life, and of the mingled shame and anger with which he remembers the whole incident.]

This little anecdote illustrates, of course, the manner in which the boy's imagination drowns the truth. It is a brilliant example of Keller's ability to describe, in all its plastic truth, the physical and visible actuality which interprets the attitude of the characters. But it in no way rests at the actual reality as the hero saw it at the time of which he writes. Not only does the mature story-teller give an explicit summing-up of the motives and feelings of the young boy, and his later relations with his abused schoolmates. The whole description is pervaded by a wider knowledge and understanding than the boy could have had. Thus the author explains to the reader what the ' Brüderlein wood ' was, or suggests why the authorities did not test the truth of his story. He explains how the very expostulations of the other boys fired his imagination. Subtly, too, the boy's tale moves from the past subjunctive, a form appropriate to an invention : ' I went on to tell how we *had* gathered nuts . . . *had* made a fire, etc.' (the German uses the past subjunctive), to the simple narrative past, so that this invented tale as it proceeds gains imperceptibly in confidence and persuasiveness. Thus at every moment the events are presented in digested form ; past and present, the actual experience and the matured wisdom, impregnate one another.

Keller delicately suggests the psychological grounds of Heinrich's prevarications. The invention arises in the first place from the boy's desire to throw the responsibility for his use of swear-words on to bigger boys. But something deeper is at stake than the question of moral honesty. He picks on bigger boys whom he admires, not on boys he wants to have punished ; he embellishes the account with all manner of realistic detail. The real trouble is his exhibitionism, and in the course of exalting himself he loses consciousness of reality and thinks his tale is more satisfactory than reality. He does not only deceive his foolish masters and the other boys' parents ; he deceives himself. The result is injustice, rankling anger, and above all a disharmony between the boy and society, between the boy and reality. The incident embodies the whole theme of the book : the narrowness of elders who are unreasonably concerned over the words the child innocently uses ; the imaginative compensation the boy discovers and the power of the imagination over himself and others ; the resultant disharmony and dislocation, which make the imaginative world even more attractive and the way back to reality even more difficult.

In relating the hero's imaginative world with the actuality for which it is his compensation, Keller provides a running criticism of this actuality. The theme of the book, the discovery of ' the poetry of what is living and reasonable ', is not only Heinrich's spiritual development, but also the development of the social reality to which he learns to devote himself. Keller does not idealise the Canton of Zürich as an idyllic corner of the world. His German friends sometimes found his Swiss patriotism quaint and strange, but he was by no means a sentimental patriot. He vigorously opposed attempts to foster a specific local-Swiss art and literature, considering that they simply furthered a reactionary philistinism.[23] His affirmation of the Zürich democracy was not the result of a practical commonsense acceptance of an inescapable reality ; it arose from his conviction that, imperfect as it was, it still provided a satisfactory framework for human relationships and humane aspirations. His attitude to it was the reverse of sentimental. Most of his shorter stories are notable for the caustic humour with which he satirises the shortcomings of his fellow-countrymen, shortcomings that distort their characters, limit their powers of enjoyment of life, and harm their neighbours and the community. The same acerbity is present in *Green Heinrich* even when Keller shows the most sympathetic insight. Keller's humour, which fuses his sympathy and his criticism, is never passive and sentimental ; its basis is his belief that the aberrations he describes can be corrected, and that the society in which his characters are placed offers the possibility of improvement. This democratically organised community is not good as it is, much needs to be done, as we are explicitly told in the last part of the novel, if it is to be made a fitter place for humane values ; but it is healthy and educable, like Heinrich himself. This positive critical realism is not only the social message of the book ; it is the secret of its poetic quality. The book belongs to Switzerland, to Keller's generation ; no German or Austrian author of the time could be so fully at home in his world, and could come to so harmonious a reconciliation of beauty and reality.

CHAPTER III

Adalbert Stifter

INDIAN SUMMER

> I have probably written this work because of the rotten-
> ness prevailing, with some exceptions, in world-political
> relationships, in moral life, and in literature. I have tried to
> confront our wretched degenerate condition with a great,
> simple, moral force.

THUS Stifter writes of his novel, *Der Nachsommer*, ' Indian
Summer ', to his friend and publisher, Heckenast.[1] This
' Bildungsroman ' has therefore, like all Stifter's mature works,
an avowed didactic purpose which links it with *Wilhelm Meister*
and *Green Heinrich*. But his statement also indicates a marked
divergence from Goethe and Keller. While they describe the
development of a young man towards integration into society,
Stifter here contrasts society and the ' moral force '. While
Goethe sketches a set of social principles and relationships
which may be made worthy of human endeavour, and Keller
recognises in his native democracy a worthy framework for
the humanism of his hero, Stifter builds for his hero a private
existence which is an asylum from the stresses of wider social
and political life.

We are here faced not simply by a different temperament
and outlook, but also a different social environment. *Indian
Summer* (1857) was written in that decade when Schopenhauer first became widely read, a decade, for the Austrian
and German middle class, of disillusionment and pessimism.
The first version of *Green Heinrich*, which was written in this
same decade and while Keller was living in Berlin, bears
witness to this pessimism, even though the author was a Swiss
who welcomed the democratic reform of the Swiss constitution
which had been successfully carried through in the 1840s.
The course of events in Austria, Stifter's homeland, had been
entirely different. The revolution of 1848 had taken a radical

turn which alarmed Stifter and his friends, it had kindled
national risings that threatened the doom of the Austrian
Empire. A mild and timid liberal, Stifter had lost heart, and
acquiesced, though without enthusiasm, in the return of the
old order. From 1848, perhaps from earlier still, he considered that political excesses were due to a lack of moral
education ; the ' hollowness of our morals and literature '
was the cause of the misguided violence and the failure of
the revolutionary effort to establish constitutional government.
He became an inspector of schools in the hope of contributing
to the moral education of his countrymen ; and his books
he hoped would be valued from this point of view.[2]

Indian Summer is on the surface not a work of pessimism or
regret ; if it were, it could scarcely be a ' Bildungsroman '.
Yet Stifter deliberately placed its action thirty years back,
before the crises and discouragement of 1848. And though
the theme of the novel is entirely positive, affirming the beauty
and worth of the mode of life its chief characters construct,
there are such high fences erected between their world and
the normal world, between their characters and the normal
run of men, even between their stylised language and normal
speech, that it has something of the beauty of the cactus which,
after years of devoted tending in the conservatory, blooms so
radiantly at the end of the book. Around the world of the
novel are glass walls which suggest the fears and despondency
that often assailed the author.

THE STORY

The original core of *Indian Summer* is the tale of ' the happiness of two old people ', Risach and Mathilde, the background
of which is related only towards the end of the novel. We
get to know the Freiherr von Risach very early in the book,
and his influence is decisive in the education of the young hero,
Heinrich Drendorf. He devotes his declining years to his
country estate, more particularly to horticulture and the
beautification of his home, which contains ancient and modern
works of art and specimens of all the marbles and woods of

his native land. Beauty, science, and practical purpose are here harmoniously combined. The place is a sanctuary for birds, whom he feeds and protects because they keep down the number of harmful insects. In the first place he was called 'the old bird-friend' or 'the old bird-catcher', and when he describes the habits of the birds to Heinrich he finds a touching symbol for his own old age. After the young are fledged, the parent-birds, he says, enjoy a period of leisure before migrating :

'Towards autumn there comes again a freer time. They have as it were an Indian summer and play for a while, before they leave.' [3]

Von Risach exchanges regular visits with an old and intimate friend, Mathilde, who seeks his advice on all important matters. Her son lives with Risach as his pupil, her daughter Natalie treats him as a father. In Book 3 he tells Heinrich their story. As a young man he had become the tutor of her brother at their country mansion, and had fallen in love with Mathilde. For some time they hid their love. When he insisted on revealing it to her parents, they were deeply disturbed by the secrecy of the two, and asked that the lovers should wait for a few years before binding themselves, particularly as Risach had still to make a career. Risach fully accepted their reproaches and proposals, but Mathilde, though she was ready to consider herself to be bound by filial piety, rebelled passionately against his acquiescence. When after some years he had sought to approach her again, she refused to see him. Both married, and met again only after many years, when they were widowed. Mathilde now remorsefully had recognised the error of her passionate resentment, but Risach had guided her to understand that, while the past cannot be made good, the present offers the chance of a new relationship of a different beauty ; and they live on in intimate trust, in the happiness of an 'Indian summer'. Heinrich overhears a snatch of conversation which interprets their misfortune and their happiness. Mathilde's childhood-home had been famous for its roses ; and Risach's constancy to her is expressed in the mass of beautiful roses he cultivates before his house—Heinrich always calls the house ' the Rose House '. As the two old people are standing by the fading roses in the late summer, Mathilde says :

' As these roses have withered, so has our happiness withered.'

And Risach answers :

' It has not withered, it only has a different form.' [4]

The Risach-Mathilde story, although told only in retrospect, is of vital importance in the construction of the whole novel, for it alone contains the elements of error and suffering, and only in relation to this error and suffering can the quality of their happiness, and that of the young pair, Heinrich and Natalie, be evalued. Mathilde's youthful outburst is the only expression of spontaneous, overflowing feeling in the book ; her error, touching in its natural violence, is deliberately intended to indicate the unreliability of the impulsive heart, which destroys its own happiness. It is she who makes Risach suffer throughout his life for his original lack of candour towards her parents. But another ' error ' is imposed on him, for he has to make a career in a sphere for which he feels no real calling. As an official, an administrator and diplomat, he rises high in the civil service and gains signal distinctions, being raised to the nobility. But public service brings him no happiness, and at the height of his career he retires into private life. Enriched by his savings, a legacy, and his wife's dowry, he devotes himself to his country seat, to agricultural improvements, the restoration of works of art, setting an example to the neighbouring gentry and finding, in this secluded life of his own choice, happiness and moral purpose. His life has had no ' summer ', but he has found a serene and fruitful ' Indian summer '.[5]

The story of Risach and Mathilde is essential to the novel, for the theme of the latter is, in the main, the transmission of their wisdom to the young pair, Heinrich and Natalie, who ' are fortified for their future earthly happiness through the simple peaceful happiness of the older folk ' [6]—a transmission of wisdom not by direct injunction so much as by

E

example and imperceptible influence.   Sheltered and guided
by wisdom and love, the young man and woman respond without error to the promptings of their elders; their very educability
is, as Mathilde says, the sign of their moral distinction.[7]

Heinrich Drendorf is the son of a Viennese merchant in
affluent circumstances.   He has been surrounded by love and
understanding from childhood, and all his tastes and desires
are moulded by piety to the family.   With an independent
income, which he manages most prudently, he devotes himself
to the study of the natural history, particularly the geology,
of his native land.   On one of his expeditions he takes shelter
from a threatening storm in a country house, Risach's home,
and the old man invites him to stay, showing him his garden,
his marbles and fine furniture, his workshop for the restoration
of antiques, and his house.   Heinrich returns there several
times, meeting Mathilde and her daughter Natalie and visiting
their mansion.   He grows deeply attached to them and their
way of life, and through them acquires a steadfast idea of his
purpose in life.   He marries Natalie and settles down as
Risach's presumptive heir.

The complete lack of incident and accident, tension, struggle,
plot, is deliberate.   As Stifter said in the preface to his collection of tales, *Bunte Steine*, greatness was to be found, in his
view, not in earthquake and tempest, but ' in the stirring of
the air, the rippling of the stream, the swell of the sea, the
greening of the earth, the radiance of the sky, the glistening
of the stars '.   ' Greatness is always simple and gentle, like
the universe itself.'[8]   What he is concerned to show in *Der
Nachsommer* is a profound moral achievement which is reached
by the almost imperceptible unfolding of character and the
gentle acquisition of values which are placed within easy reach
of the young pair.

The groundwork of Heinrich's character is piety—piety to
the family and piety to things—which is expressed, in its most
exalted form, as a somewhat undefined veneration of the God
who has ordained things as they are.   This piety has to be
developed to become a principle of activity, determining wider
human relationships and the choice of a profession.   Heinrich

is from childhood ' a great friend of the reality of things ',[9] and from this characteristic stems his devotion to science, to the study of the earth's crust. He observes ' with awe ' the boulders brought down by mountain torrents, and as he penetrates into the secrets of the origin of geographical features he is filled with a religious feeling of self-enrichment.[10] But it is only from Risach that he learns to integrate this scientific interest and religious feeling into the rest of life.

He learns from Risach how science and morals may be wedded through the agency of beauty. Things are not only to be respected ; they are to be improved through loving care. The roses, above all, are improved by every possible means, sheltered from frost and sun, carefully selected, transplanted and pruned, given appropriate earth and position. Fruit-trees are pruned, grafted, scrubbed, the garden is carefully fenced against intruders of any sort. Native marbles and woods are polished and shaped into beautiful objects, into precious panelled floors, over which Risach and his guests walk only in felt shoes. The choicest works of art, above all a Greek muse, are placed in the best light, to be observed and studied with leisurely reverence. As Heinrich learns to appreciate this operation of man upon nature, from the level of usefulness to that of sensuous beauty, from the level of need to that of adornment, from the practical to the ideal, he undergoes a moral development. In the Risach household he imbibes the charm of an ordered, self-controlled life, whose beauty flowers from the intimate, loving, serene fusion of nature and morality.

Heinrich's attitude to his science changes. At the instigation of Risach his interest becomes more purposeful, and he sets himself the task of completing a geological survey of a restricted field. But he grows interested too in the people of the region, the sturdy peasants who assist him and become his friends, their artistic products. He learns to see the landscape with new eyes, as an artist, in relation to ' colour, air, light, mist, clouds, distance, sky '—factors that as a geologist he had always tried to ignore. He collects specimens of marbles and trains a rural stone-mason to shape them into beautiful objects

for his family and friends. He studies ancient buildings and
their decoration, old altars, and the methods of artists ; by
watching modern craftsmen and restorers, by drawing valuable
pieces of old and modern furniture, he trains himself to understand the artist's craft ; he helps his father to beautify their
own home. Beneath it all he feels at times a melancholy
unease, as if all this widened interest and activity needs something else to crown it, to give it purpose : there is something
disturbing at the bottom of his heart. The question arises,
' whether art, poetry, science circumscribe and complete life,
or whether there is still something further that embraces life
and fills it with far greater happiness '.[11] This ' something
further ' is there in the family life at home, which comforts
him, it is there in Risach's and Mathilde's households ;
Heinrich discovers it in the end in his love for Natalie, which is
at the same time an eternal bond for the establishment of the
family, and as such the basis upon which he can securely
build his future career.

Both feel, immediately, that their love can come to fruition
only if it has the approval of their parents and Risach ; their
first step is to ask their consent, which is gladly given. The
experience of their elders, embodied in their upbringing,
enables them to escape the error of Mathilde and Risach.
Equally, Heinrich is enabled, through the example of his
parents and Risach, through their guidance and forbearance,
not least through their material affluence, to avoid choosing
a profession which might be incompatible with his character
and talents. He has slowly been able to fit himself for the
science he prefers, and their wealth enables him to settle as
a private gentleman.

Though the decisive settings for Heinrich's development are
his parents' household, the mountains, and the country seats
of Risach and Mathilde, Stifter does not utterly ignore the
wider social relations. Risach's character and standing have
been shaped in distinguished service to the state ; Heinrich's
father is a hard-working merchant whose business ability alone
has made it possible for him to give a sheltered and graceful
environment to his children. Both withdraw to the country,

to the life of country gentlemen, as the ripe result of their experience. Heinrich from the beginning is a reserved, naïve boy, shy in society, who only too readily seeks the privacy of the family and his scientific pursuits. But Risach recognises that he must have a wider experience, if his character is to become firm and his inclination for the Rose-House type of life is to be more than a choice of the easiest road. So he tells him he should go more among people, when he is at home in Vienna. Heinrich does so, he mixes with different circles, talks with middle-class people, diplomats and soldiers, noblemen. But he finds little to attract him in the business of the city, except the salon of a princess where noblemen and men of letters meet, and the friendship of a jeweller, with whom he studies precious stones. Engaged throughout the winter on his private studies, he passes through social life as a detached observer. In conversation Risach tells Heinrich that city and country are necessary to one another ; but Heinrich swiftly reaches the older man's somewhat contradictory conclusion that town and country are ' mutually incompatible ', and that only on the land can one find permanence and beauty.[12] The description of city life is in fact perfunctory ; even more perfunctory (one paragraph only) is the narrative of the two-year tour through Europe that Heinrich undertakes in order to gain experience of the great world, and it is not meant in any way to alter his disposition or ideas.[13]

One thing more is necessary for Heinrich. Free of inner problems, never at odds with his family and Risach, he has to show that he is not merely docile, but has acquired firmness and maturity. After his betrothal, a series of incidents indicate this. He travels with his father to the latter's birthplace, and on this journey for the first time enters into a mature relationship with his father, appreciating him as a man, not merely respecting him as a father. Heinrich then takes his sister on an excursion into the mountains, and shows himself an expert in guiding an inexperienced and weaker person. Lastly he himself climbs in midwinter up to a glacier, an exploit considered impossible by the mountain peasantry. These undertakings, which in their modesty are true to the whole character

of the book, mark his ripeness for marriage, for establishing
and guiding a family. So Risach, during the somewhat protracted solemnities of the wedding and the legal settlements,
can sum up Heinrich's goal :

' It is the family that is needed by our times, it is more needed
than art and science, than trade and commerce, prosperity, progress, or whatever may be called desirable. Art, science, human
progress, the state, all rest on the family. . . . Once you stand
on the ground of the family—many can achieve much without
contracting marriage—but once you stand on the ground of marriage, you are only a man if you stand upon it wholly and purely.
Work then for art or science as well and if you achieve something
unusual and excellent you will rightly be praised ; serve your
neighbours as well in communal affairs and follow the call of the
state, if need be. Then you will have lived for yourself and for
all times.' [14]

THE LIMITATIONS OF SCOPE

It is characteristic of the ' Bildungsroman ' that the hero
is a naïve, innocent young man, well-meaning even in his
errors ; the persons among whom he moves are never evil,
and most of them give good guidance, directly or indirectly.
In Stifter's novel these characteristics are taken to an extreme.
All the characters are harmonious and tranquil, all circumstances conduce to the happiness of Heinrich Drendorf, and
there is a complete absence of internal stress and external
seduction or conflict, of religious or philosophical struggle.   It
conjures up, like Shakespeare's *The Tempest*, a world where the
powers for good are beyond effective challenge or infection.
But, more idyllic than *The Tempest*, there is scarcely an echo
in *Indian Summer* of former strife and present danger, of
human imperfections.   Contemporary critics often commented
unfavourably on the idyllicism in Stifter's works, and he often
promised himself that he would write something with action,
conflict, tragedy in it.[15]   He did not succeed in this, though
he tried to do so in his historical novel, *Witiko*, and the bearing
of *Der Nachsommer* is limited by its very tranquillity, its
unproblematicalness.

Heinrich's development contains no element of conflict or error. Brought up in an exemplary family, where each member has for the others affection, respect, consideration, he has merely to follow the gentle slope of his inclinations. In the Risach household he meets a repetition of the same relationships, so much so that when the two families meet each finds in the other identical tastes, habits, and views ; the complex harmony of Wilhelm Meister's world, made up of very different voices, is here replaced by something approaching the simplicity and monotony of unison. Even the servants chime in, in subdued tones, perhaps an octave below, respectful, contented, affectionate. The elder Drendorf's life-story is the smoothest account of the winning of material prosperity and family bliss. Were it not for the Risach story, we should have no inkling that there are stresses and strains in human nature. But if the tranquillity of an ' Indian summer ' may be accepted as the deserved goal of the elders, how dangerous and strange to make this the goal of the young people who have not yet reached their summer ! In the world of *Der Nachsommer* there is a lack of moral strenuousness.

But not only on the psychological and philosophical plane ; on the social, too. It is characteristic that most of the many discussions in the book, particularly the opinions of Risach, which represent the summit of Stifter's wisdom, circle round art. Very few deal with social problems, and the only major discussion on equality and freedom is trivial and facilely optimistic.[16] We have no glimpse of the urgent social and political problems of Stifter's times—he placed the action of the story in the 1820s, just before the conflicts that issued in the Revolution of 1848 were declared, and before railways and factories had brought their complications into Austria.[18] On Risach's suggestion, Heinrich sets out to get a wider experience of men and things, but all he does is to pass through certain social circles in Vienna ; social and political activities remain far from his ken. Compared with the amusements and interests of his Vienna acquaintance, the life of Risach and the country gentry seems substantial and fruitful ; and Heinrich chooses the latter with the comfortable feeling that his primary duty is to order satisfactorily his own private life. As Heinrich's father says : ' If each man lives in the best way for himself, he serves human society best.' [18] There is no hint that national and social problems may profoundly affect the nature of personal values and the shape of personal life : one of the themes of Goethe and Keller.

Characteristic is the manner in which reference is made to the growing specialisation of science, which raises a faint echo of the great problem of ' one-sidedness ' that Wilhelm Meister and his friends have to face. In Stifter's novel, all that Risach tells Heinrich is that the growing specialisation of the sciences will ensure great advances in knowledge. The psychological and social implications are not touched on.[19]

In *Wilhelm Meister*, landed gentry and bourgeoisie become allies in the effort to found a new society, essentially bourgeois in its economic activities and social relations. In *Indian Summer*, the bourgeoisie (Stifter insisted that Heinrich's family belongs to the wealthy bourgeoisie [20]) turns into landed gentry. There is no derogation of bourgeois activities, it is true. Heinrich is never ashamed of his father's business, and Risach, himself of middle-class origin, praises trade and gladly, as he says, returns through the marriage of Heinrich and Natalie to the class from which he had risen. Mathilde herself, though the mistress of a great estate, is not an aristocrat. But even Heinrich's father, as well as Heinrich, settle as landed gentry, for them the ideal life, the only life where men can achieve fulfilment and moral satisfaction.

In this, Stifter is paying tribute not to the nobility as a privileged class, but to their form of life. Risach, the bourgeois by origin, brings movement into this mode of life. By example and advice he inspires his neighbours to improve their land and stock. Like Lothario in *Wilhelm Meister*, Mathilde has commuted the feudal dues of her tenants, the tithes and payments in kind, into cash rents, the relationships of bourgeois society. Material progress, usefulness, is a principle of this group of enlightened landowners ; change is envisaged without alarm, as a natural principle of life. In the same way as Risach grows old without regret, simply using every opportunity to the best advantage, so he is continually altering and improving his estate and garden. When his heirs, Heinrich and Natalie, wish to promise him that they will for ever preserve the Rose House as he has arranged it, he reproves them for this mistaken idea of piety, and tells them they must go on improving and changing things after his death.[21] Change is necessary, is often desirable ; but the guarantee of its rightness and value is that it is controlled and ordered, that it takes place gradually and with a minimum of disturbance.[22] Thus the most thorough examination, thought, and consultation precedes all changes in Risach's and Mathilde's households. The same principle holds good for changes in social status. Birth is not decisive, but talent must make its way, if it is not to err, without rebellion and violence. The servant-craftsman Eustach and his brother rise slowly, encouraged and furthered by Risach, to the positions of artists and companions, as their talents and moral qualities are proved. Risach himself is the ideal of the master, selflessly concerned to make the most of his subordinates, just as he is the ideal tutor to his foster-son and the ideal guide to Heinrich.

This idyllic relationship between the social classes, between master and household servants, is of course deliberately exemplary, and it illustrates Stifter's view that the conflicts of his times were due to excess and passion, to the lack of ' moral freedom ' in his contemporaries.[23] But it leads him to avoid, in the novel, the real social conflicts that were there, or were emerging. Even on the land we get only a glimpse of the farmers and farm-servants, and always they are in the role of faithful, contented retainers. The rather numerous and obtrusive household servants carry out with alacrity the often pettifogging tasks put on them, and like the farmers show in a respectful but cordial fashion their delight in the happiness of their betters.

The social basis of the moral principles of the novel is indeed extremely narrow. It is not by accident that we are precisely informed about Heinrich's handling of the income his father gives him. The wedding is accompanied by a detailed and exact account of money-settlements which put the

seal on the happiness of the marriage, ensuring its complete
propriety. Whether this money has been acquired solely by
inheritance and marriage (Mathilde), or through services to
the state (Risach), or through trade (the elder Drendorf), it
finds its proper purpose, it is 'moralised', in the form of
landownership and investment ; the ideal form of life is that
of the *rentier*. The importance of the family is stressed in this
respect too ; for inheritance and marriage play a large part
in the accumulation of wealth in each family, and above all
with Heinrich and Natalie. One is reminded of Stifter's
innocent wishful dreams, in the midst of his isolation and
money-troubles in Linz, for a lottery-prize which would allow
him to build a country-house and devote himself to his
writing.[24] There is no hint in the novel of the questionability
of the *rentier* ideal or of the social conflicts it engenders.

This class, the landowner with his ample means, is in
fact the hypostasis of the 'Biedermeier', the independent
bourgeois relieved of the pressures of unsatisfactory employment and vexatious superiors and free to pursue his own
interests and hobbies. Here the family and home can be
tended without distraction. The family itself is narrowed to
the simplest proportions, cumbersome relatives are lopped off
with the gardener's skilful pruning-knife, property remains
concentrated since the families have but one son and one
daughter. Round the family runs a fence like that round
the Rose House, keeping out all intruders ; individuals are
fenced too by strict conventions of respect, and Heinrich, when
visiting at Risach's or Mathilde's, always carefully locks the
door of his room. The word 'hegen' gives the key-note of
this existence, for it indicates both 'cherishing', the tender
nurturing of the garden, the home, private life, and 'hedging
round', protection from the outer world.

Because of these drastic limitations to the scope of the world
represented in the novel, its moral bearing is also narrowed ;
and in particular morality sometimes tends to appear in the
form of propriety and convention. Astonishing, by contrast,
is the freedom and unconventionality of manners and morals
in *Wilhelm Meister* and *Green Heinrich* ; scarcely ever, in these

novels, does mere propriety usurp the place of moral relationships. Heinrich Drendorf's distrust of impulse and his desire not to violate the sanctity of other people's privacy, on the other hand, impose on him an exaggerated restraint. For instance, when he twice meets Natalie by chance, he urgently seeks to withdraw in order not to offend her ; and we feel the offence is more to propriety than to her or to morality. The piety which leads him to refrain from inquisitive questions in his relations with Risach and Mathilde borders at times on the purely conventional notion of propriety ; after a first impulse he scrupulously avoids inquiring what the name of his host is, until Risach tells him himself, and only after his betrothal does he learn, again from Risach, the surname of his wife-to-be. Stifter describes with approving solicitude the propriety of the behaviour, mode of address, or clothes of the two families. Orderliness and cleanliness are for Stifter fundamental constituents of the moral life, and the novel betrays almost an obsession with them ; books must always be placed back on the shelves, curtains be frequently washed, clothes of course kept always neat and clean ; gardens, parks, paths are kept in meticulous order.[25]

The world of *Indian Summer* is therefore but a fragment of the real world, both psychologically and socially. Without conflict, ruggedness, spontaneity, all its phenomena are prepared for and controlled. The book is in conception closer to the ' Novelle ', the short story, than to the normal novel, for the ' Novelle ' properly abstracts a particular moment and situation from its total environment—and Stifter is one of the masters of the ' Novelle '. But the work has its validity as a novel, and reflects with extraordinary homogeneity a general situation and moral process. Within its high fences, we see the interaction of man and nature, the marriage of the individual self and the outer community, of the moral force and nature : the mutual education of man and nature. All the book is inspired with a deep love and veneration for the world ; ' what is, is holy ',[26] both man and nature, both are capable of being made moral, useful, beautiful. Both are fundamentally good and ' innocent ',[27] and the development of

Heinrich, the clarification of his personality and purpose, shows how this innocence may be preserved and enriched in loving co-operation with other human beings and with nature. Stifter's attitude has been called pantheistic, but it is wrong to put any philosophical label on it ; it fits on to any religious or non-religious belief that affirms the goodness of the world, above all any belief that affirms the power of man to mould his circumstances and himself for good. So unchallenged is this belief, as it shines through the tranquil serenity of the course of the novel, that modern critics have detected a ' hidden melancholy and mourning ' in it, the consciousness that it represents a world that can never be.[28] There is considerable truth in this interpretation. Yet it is never explicit, never even hinted at, in the book, and its strength is that this narrow world is tangible and concrete, and in its concreteness and objectivity appears true ; and that by its very existence, as Stifter intended, it makes a moral existence more possible. We can apply to *Indian Summer* the words Stifter used to define the character of an earlier work : [29]

If I could make the thing as I would, it would be simple, clear, transparent, and as soothing as the air. The reader would move in the book through well-known beloved things and be gently entranced and encircled, as one passes in the warm air of spring in the sunshine among the sprouting seeds, and grows happy, without being able to say why.

THEME AND FORM

In few novels is the form and style so integral a part of the theme as in *Indian Summer* ; it is above all its form that reconciles us to the limitations of its scope, or even makes us oblivious of them. It is written in the first person, for it is the tale of his own life told by Heinrich Drendorf. But Stifter has not set himself the task, as did Keller, of relating the past from the standpoint of the present, of illuminating the past constantly through a style which expresses the wisdom of maturity. His aim is, to capture at every moment the particular stage of mental development the hero has reached,

to show only what the hero can see and understand.   If some
incidents and things are dwelt on, others passed over rapidly
or ignored, the cause is found in the bent of mind, the spiritual
capacity of Heinrich Drendorf.   Thus the original crisis which
not only explains the relations of Risach and Mathilde but
also is the centre of gravity of the whole moral structure of
the novel, is related very late in the book by Risach himself,
at a time when Heinrich has at last become capable of understanding it in its full meaning.   At all stages narrator and
hero are identified.[30]

Stifter's method was ably interpreted in one of the very
few appreciative reviews of the novel on its first appearance,
in relation to Heinrich's visit to a performance of *King Lear*.
Heinrich tells how he walks to the theatre in the rain, and
puts his coat in the cloakroom, having tucked his cap into
a pocket.   There follows a rather lame account of the plot
of the play.   The performance deeply moves him, and at the
end his eyes are attracted to a young woman who he sees is
also deeply moved : it is one of the few ' incidents ' in the
story, for the girl is Natalie, who is to become his wife.   He
then tells how he goes to the cloakroom, gets his coat, takes
his cap out of the pocket, and walks home, where his mother
is waiting up for him.   Why is this first strong aesthetic
experience and the first meeting with Natalie encased in so
lame an account of the play, above all in such trivial detail ?
Partly, no doubt, because Stifter continually insists that small
everyday things are of importance.   But there is another
reason that the critic, Julian Schmidt, suggests : ' Stifter did
not want to describe the play or the walk to the theatre, but
the impression on the soul of his hero.' [31]   That is, he wanted
to describe the play, the walk, the theatre in terms of the open
but immature mind of this young man, on whom important
and unimportant experiences as yet make an equal impact.

This patient, unimpassioned attention to detail characterises
the style of the whole novel.   Heinrich describes with meticulous care, sometimes directly, sometimes through the mouth
of Risach, the plan of the Rose-House garden, the culture
of the roses or cacti, the inlaid floors, the decoration and

furniture of rooms, the restoration of antiques, the pictures, engravings, the marble figures. Misled by normal expectation, the reader at times may expect that there is some dramatic function attached to this method—for instance, he might think that Heinrich's visits to the cloakroom at the theatre are to lead to some significant incident. But no ; the object or action is described for its own sake, it does not advance or retard the external action of the story. Or rather, not for its own sake, but for the sake of building, through these myriad concrete details, a picture of the life and the spiritual constitution of the characters.[32]

There is not only no passion in the book ; there is no psychological probing. The characters appear only through the medium of their appearance, their observations on matters of common interest, their behaviour. The concreteness and detail of the descriptions and of the conversations illuminate the serenity that has been won, the tenderness with which the activities of this sheltered life are pursued : through the orderliness, the care for detail, we imbibe the whole ' moral ' of Stifter's book. For, with all their concreteness, these descriptions are not descriptions of an objective, impersonal reality. They show the operation of man upon nature, the ordering and beautifying of nature through which man manages to order and beautify his own character. As, for instance, Risach tells Heinrich of the habits of the birds in the sanctuary of the garden, he unfolds to him in a bird-lover's terms the whole course of life as he would have it, up to that Indian summer he himself has reached. Though he prepares nesting-boxes for the coming year, he is not concerned for the individual birds after they migrate ; it is the cycle of one year, of one life, with which he is concerned, not with matters beyond the needs of his knowledge and the bounds of his control.

We do not therefore have to turn to the moments when emotion is declared to discover feeling in the novel ; the characters' relationship to things is impregnated with feeling, for the things in themselves and for family and friends. But it is the thesis of the book that this feeling is legitimised, moralised, only if it takes the concrete form of worthy behaviour. Hence it is not only Heinrich's inexperience that causes him to refrain from statements about his or other people's feelings, but also his whole moral training and character which holds feeling back until it is sifted by reflexion and moulded into behaviour. The attraction of Risach's character and household is expressed above all in Heinrich's desire to return there, in his readiness to follow Risach's advice and his patient study of what the older man commends. As a guide Risach shows a similar piety. He does not tell Heinrich that the Greek statue in his house is of high artistic quality, but leaves the young man to find this out for himself; and when Heinrich asks him why he had not told him it was beautiful, he answers that it was much better that he should discover it without help, which might misguide him.[33]

Particularly characteristic is the method by which we are told of Heinrich's growing love for Natalie. We become aware of it only in the most indirect manner, and, being experienced readers of novels, we even know more about it than the story-teller himself. When he leaves the Rose House after his second visit, on which he had met Mathilde and Natalie, he is pursued by a feeling of unexplained sadness, of unease, which he overcomes only by scientific work in the intimacy of his home. This unease appears from time to time, but is never allowed to be the object of probing or description. He notices too that Natalie, on a later visit, has become somewhat restless and frequently takes long walks alone. When they meet, as she is resting on one of these walks, she tells him about her walks in simple, concrete terms. Only after the declaration of their love can we interpret his unease, and her restlessness, for now she quietly tells him: 'I felt much pain for your sake, when I walked over the fields.' [34] Throughout the book there is a chaste reserve with regard to feelings, but they are nevertheless powerful. It is wrong, in my view, to use the phrase 'disembodied chasteness' to denote the character of the scene where Heinrich and Natalie declare their love.[35] The feeling of the two is ardent and simple, not disembodied; but it is avowed only when it springs from, and chimes in with, the whole moral personality. For this reason, the climax of the scene is their decision immediately to ask for the consent of their parents.

As in other relationships, there is a danger that even in love morality lapses into propriety, and that Heinrich's behaviour towards Natalie becomes stilted. Thus, when they meet on the day after their declaration of love, Heinrich refrains from asking Natalie what has been the outcome of her talk with her mother until, at the end of a long conversation, she tells him with a blush that her mother approves their union. Neither of them says anything more on the subject. We are to understand this restraint, in Stifter's sense, as the evidence of Heinrich's pious trust in Mathilde, in whose judgement he is ready absolutely to concur, and of his trust in Natalie. If parental consent is withheld, they will love one another ' for ever ', but will part for ever. But we must doubt the strength of a feeling which, conscious of its innocence and goodness, is so restrained, and we can scarcely attribute this restraint to anything but propriety. Stifter was not, however, concerned to give us a ' genre ' study of ' Victorian ' propriety, but to show us examples of fully moralised characters. It might be suggested that when propriety usurps the place of morality in the novel (as also when we feel too strongly the idyllic character of the whole) we get a glimpse of the unspoken conflict between reality and the world of this novel ; we then remember that Stifter himself, like his contemporaries in his view, much fell short of the ideal of harmony he presents, and needed to be bolstered up by purely conventional forms of behaviour and intercourse. We see in this tendency, too, evidence of that distrust of nature, of that gnawing uncertainty, which always lowers on the horizon of this apparently soothing book.

So anxious is Stifter to present in Heinrich a character of complete innocence and harmony, that we are conscious at times not only of a deep-seated distrust of impulse, but also a distrust of intelligence. Heinrich refrains from drawing certain conclusions not only out of pious respect, but also out of an unwillingness to put two and two together. For instance, he only slowly comes to the conclusion that the estate named

' Der Sternenhof ' is Mathilde's home, when it has been very clear for some time that this is the case.[36] Or he laboriously tells that a coach goes slowly because no doubt the travellers had made caution their law ; or explains that the temperature rises as he descends from a mountain expedition because the air in the valleys, in the late autumn, is warmer than that on the high mountains.[37] There is a polemical disingenuousness in all this, or ' coquetry ', as Julian Schmidt called it.

Despite these small blemishes, Heinrich's intelligence, feeling, morality, his whole personality unfold according to a steady law that is revealed in the changes of things as of persons. Time becomes a tangible process. Quietly and regularly the seasons change, each with its use and beauty. A great master of nature-description, Stifter never makes his descriptions an end in themselves. Just as the roses are constantly improved, so their blooming is never a mere repetition, and each summer the characters, Heinrich particularly, but Mathilde too, learn more from them ; at the end of the novel a cherished cactus, which flowers extremely rarely, blooms as a symbol of their happiness, the crowning of long labour, and it seems we have been waiting for it through the seasons, with the patient and active expectation of the gardener. So also the mountains change from summer to summer, as Heinrich learns to penetrate their secrets and see them more fully, until that final excursion when he mounts to the glacier in midwinter and sees the snow-caps above and the clouds beneath him. Time steadily advances. In the regular round of the year change takes place ; it is change that Heinrich studies over the immense distances of geological time ; and like nature, the human beings also change, but steadily, in a regular procession, with the acquiescence that is in nature.

As Heinrich tells his story, this quiet movement issues from the very form of his sentences. At all moments he, or the speakers he reports, seem to acquire a resting-point which is at the same time an outcome and a starting-point. All that Risach tells him has mature finality about it, the product of ripe experience and thought ; and at the same time it sets Heinrich thinking or urges him to further study and work.

F

There is constant communication, and constant stimulus, yet
the stimulus is always in consonance with the past. We have
seen examples in the words of Risach and Mathilde in front
of the fading roses. ' As these roses have withered, so has
our happiness withered,' she says ; and Risach answers : ' It
has not withered, it only has a different form.'   Or in Risach's
words about the birds : ' Towards autumn there comes again
a freer time. They have as it were an Indian summer and
play for a while, before they leave.'   All the sentences have
a ring of completedness about them ; and yet, at the same
time, in their context, and in their unassuming simplicity,
their lack of emphasis and rhetoric, they lead onwards, pro-
moting meditation—not so much active thought as a patient
rumination through which they will slowly be assimilated.
In Risach's mouth such phrases have the precision that denotes
mastery ; but they have also a gentle falling cadence which
subtly insinuates their truth and implications into the ear of
the listener.

The many and long conversations in which Risach instructs
and encourages Heinrich all have this tranquil movement,
through which Heinrich's modest questions and suggestions
are corrected and developed. On his first visit, Heinrich
ventures to sum up his impressions : ' You have here a charming estate,' he observes ; and Risach answers : [38]

' Not only the estate, the whole country is charming, and it is
good to dwell here when one comes from among men where they
are a little too close to one another, and when one brings back
activity to further the powers of one's being. At times, too, one
must take a glance inside oneself.   Yet one should not be constantly
alone even in the loveliest country : one must at times return
again to one's social circles, even if it were only to refresh oneself
in the company of some splendid ruin of a man, a relic of our
youth, or to gaze up at some strong tower who has preserved himself. After times like these, country-life re-enters, like a soothing
balsam, into the opened spirit.   But one must be far from the town
and untouched by it. The changes wrought by the arts and
crafts come to appearance in the town ; on the land, those which
have been engendered by manifest need or the influence of natural
objects on one another. The two are mutually incompatible, and

once you have the first behind you, the second appears almost as something permanent, and then the beauty of constancy lies quiet before the mind, and the beauty of the past is revealed to meditation, drawing us in human transformations and the transformations of natural things back into an infinity.'

The gentle rectification of Heinrich's statement is characteristic, for it is as much a development of an incomplete thought as it is a correction. Risach's statements are not dogmatic and oppressive, he cautiously yet clearly seeks his way through qualifying words and phrases, until he can reach the smooth cadence of the phrase ' country-life re-enters, like a soothing balsam, into the opened spirit '. He does not rest here, however, with this comforting, motionless image, but continues his meditation until we are engaged with him in reflections which lead ' into an infinity '. As often, this part of the conversation closes with the remark of the narrator : ' I answered nothing to this speech, and we were silent for a while.'

It is not only Risach's mode of life and outlook that Heinrich assumes in the course of the novel, but also, in a sense, his mode of expression, which ' falls like a soothing balsam into his opened spirit '. He describes events and people at first in an almost gauche manner, confining himself to the simplest statements of what he saw or did. Signs of a deeper consciousness or feeling are only indirect, as when, too shy to look at Natalie when she leaves a room, he sees her and her brother in the mirror : ' But I saw almost nothing more than four identical dark eyes turning away in the mirror.' [39] In the same detached way Natalie describes her walks round the Rose House :

' I like to go walking where I do not feel confined. I walk between the fields and the waving corn, I climb up the gentle slopes, I walk past the leafy trees and go on till a strange landscape gazes at me, where the sky over it is as it were a different one and holds different clouds. As I go, I muse and think. The sky, the clouds in it, the corn, the trees, the bushes, the grass, the flowers do not distract me. When I am tired out, and can rest on a bench, as here, or on a seat in our garden or even on a chair in our room, I think I shall not go so far another time.'

And Heinrich describes his walks and explains to her the lie of the land in similar terms.[40]   But though Heinrich's narrative never loses this naïve concreteness, it acquires something more as the novel progresses ; the development is most pronounced in the two long conversations with Natalie.   The first leads from simple exchanges about their walks to the first avowal by Heinrich of an awareness that there is a ' radiance ' in the world, of a quest, beyond his science, for ' something unknown and great '.   And the second conversation, which culminates in the confessions of love, circles round the theme of the beauty of the fountain at which they meet, the water, the air.   Their thoughts here, the cadence of their speech, enter the Risach sphere.   Heinrich tells how he had risen early, to enjoy the morning air : [41]

' It is a unique, soothing restorative, to breathe the pure air of a serene summer,' she answered.
' It is the most exalting nourishment that Heaven has given us,' I answered.   ' This I know, when I stand on a high mountain and the air lies wide around me, like an immeasurable sea.   But not only the air of summer is refreshing, that of winter is so too, all air is so, that is pure and in which there are no particles that repel our nature.'

On the following day, as he points out to her the distant mountains, they come to compare the works of nature with the works of man : [42]

' Works of art lead the eye to them, and rightly so, they fill us with admiration and love.   Natural things are the work of a different hand, and if they are observed in the right way, they too arouse the highest wonder.'
' I must always have felt the same,' she said.
' For many years I have observed the works of creation,' I answered, ' and then, too, as far as was possible, I have got to know works of art, and both delighted my soul.'

Thus the style of life, the personal development, that Stifter has made the theme of his novel, comes into evidence not only through the content of his story, through the ideas the characters express and the decisions they take, through the form their daily life acquires, but also in the very tone and fall of voice, which reveals the deepest recesses of their natures. This recurrent voice lacks variety, for it sounds in all the characters ; it is a carefully, almost consciously modulated voice, lacking stress and passion, betraying at hardly any point whether it is the outcome of stress that has been mastered, or whether it is habit and simple nature. The stylised monotony of its beauty invites the same criticism as the whole scope of the novel, yet its enchantment makes us forget the difficulties, the precariousness, of personal and social life. Is this the monotony of a life shorn, in the interests of harmony, of its exuberant powers ? or is it the monotony of which Risach speaks, ' which is so sublime that it seizes the whole soul as abundance, and as simplicity embraces the All ' ? [43] Its power, as its weakness, is that of the whole book, and it interprets to perfection the charm of a form of life of whose inaccessibility Stifter was painfully aware.

CHAPTER IV

Thomas Mann

THE MAGIC MOUNTAIN

THE last important 'Bildungsroman' is Thomas Mann's *The Magic Mountain* (1924) a deliberate revival of a type of novel which in the Wilhelmine era was felt to be obsolete. In the later nineteenth century, 'Bildung' came to mean 'culture' as the term is used in such phrases as 'a cultured gentleman'; its more substantial moral meaning was ignored. The novel began to concern itself primarily with social and political questions. The most representative novel was Freytag's *Soll und Haben*, a crude success story; the most challenging works were Spielhagen's garish studies of social tensions; the most solid achievements were the novels of Raabe and Fontane, which modestly explore the possibilities of compromise between humane values and a bleak social reality. The Nietzschean or Wagnerian protest against this positivism found at first no counterpart in the novel. But in the early years of the new century, while the realistic novel became sharper and more precise in its social criticism—as with Heinrich Mann—new trends, nourished on irrationalistic philosophy, imposed a new character on the novel, to be exemplified above all in Thomas Mann's *Buddenbrooks* and the works of Kafka. In this new generation, from whatever standpoint the author sets out, individual and social values seem to drive in opposite directions. Only after the First World War do these issues, so closely related in the traditional 'Bildungsroman', come together again.

Thomas Mann calls *The Magic Mountain* 'a story that, in a queer, ironical, almost parodistical way, attempts to renew the old German "Bildungsroman" of the Wilhelm-Meister type, this product of our great bourgeois epoch '.[1] It was a deliberate attempt to renew a literary form which Mann felt belongs to an epoch which is past, and this incongruity gives it a peculiarity, a 'queerness', to which we must be attentive. But the self-irony of Mann's statement is not meant to suggest that his novel is an experiment in antiquarianism. It was written at a time of significant change, both in Mann himself and in Germany, and its theme is that of the spiritual trans-formation of a whole people. Like all Mann's larger works, it is the story of an epoch, and as in them all, in this novel the alternatives facing his characters represent the dilemma of a whole nation.

The novel was written in the aftermath of the First World War, when Germany was painfully seeking the way from an autocratic empire to a democratic republic. In this period Mann, formerly a spokesman of the anti-democratic tradition, proclaimed his belief in the republic, particularly in his pamphlet *On the German Republic* of 1923. This is the theme of *The Magic Mountain*, but only in a concealed, non-political form. Mann's early literary works were emphatically non-political. Convinced with many of his artistic contemporaries of the collapse of 'bourgeois' positivism and rationalism, he was preoccupied with the conflict between normal bourgeois routine, psychologically healthy and practically efficient, but spiritually hollow, and the richness of the inward life of the artist which was in his view socially disruptive and morbidly menaced. 'The soul of the poet', he wrote in 1913, 'is yearning, and the last, the deepest yearning is that for release in death.'[2] Three great artist-philosophers of political reaction dominated his mind : Schopenhauer with his contemplative pessimism, Wagner with his indulgence in grandiose feelings of destruction and death, Nietzsche with his irrational vitalism.

But it was only during the war that Thomas Mann drew the political consequences of his attitude. In the *Reflections of a Non-Political Man* (1918) he associated his scathing attack on Western rationalism and humanism in favour of German irrationalism with an attack on democracy in favour of German autocracy. German middle-class culture, he believed, flour-ished only because of the protection of the authoritarian, aristocratic power-structure of the state, of Prussianism in short—he defined this bourgeois culture as ' power-protected

inwardness '. While in his post-war political pamphlets he
abjured this political Prussianism, in *The Magic Mountain* his
hero wrestles with the seductions of inwardness, the bourgeois
response to and nourishment of Prussianism.   It is a deeply
personal story, for the hero, like those of Goethe and Keller,
grows through experiences which were the stuff of Mann's own
spiritual life ; but Mann claimed for it a representative validity
—he called it ' an ideal leave-taking from much that had been
loved, from many a perilous sympathy, enchantment, and
temptation, to which the European soul inclined '.[3]

The spiritual and social maladjustment of man is in this
book infinitely more threatening, more catastrophic, than in
the earlier ' Bildungsroman '. The world in which Hans
Castorp moves is sick, in love with its sickness, and all Hans
Castorp's experiences are enclosed in the tuberculosis sanatorium, the Berghof, at Davos, among the diseased.   The
sanatorium serves a double function.   Partly, in contrast to
the real world, it is a place of unchallengeable routine and
irresponsible freedom, where time is forgotten, from the
seductions of which Castorp is to be weaned.   Partly it is a
mirror of the world itself, in which he experiences in a distilled
form the conflicting issues of the modern world.   Sickness is
here, as in the Romantic tradition and in Mann's first novel,
Buddenbrooks, a means and sign of spiritual distinction ; but it
is also, in the Goethe tradition, something to be overcome.
Hans Castorp is sharply differentiated from his cousin Joachim,
the cadet-officer, who looks on the sanatorium only as a place
to cure him.   Joachim says to Hans : ' We are here to get
healthier, not wiser ; to get healthy, cured, so that they will
set us free and dismiss us with a clean sheet to the plains.'[4]
He wants simply to get back to the military service that suffices
for his needs.   But for Hans Castorp it is a place of education,
and he has to become wiser in order to be cured.

Hans Castorp is a ' simple ' young man, brought up in the
comfort of a solid Hamburg merchant family, an orphan and
an only child.   Having qualified to become an engineer, he
comes at the beginning of the book to the Berghof to visit his
cousin.   In the course of his visit suspicious symptoms come

to the surface, and the doctor diagnoses a tubercular infection of the lung. He stays on for seven years until, at the end of the novel, he returns to the plains to enlist—it is 1914. Medically, his case is never absolutely clear ; he never loses a slight fever, but does not get worse, and we are left in doubt whether it was ever necessary for him to stay. But he wants to stay, and remains there for years after the doctor has dismissed his case. The sanatorium offers him experiences which he has been deprived of in the plains, in his profession and familiar surroundings : the enterprise of his sea-faring forefathers, Mann tells us, has turned in him into ' an adventurousness in the spiritual and intellectual realms '.⁵ It is the explorer's fever for ideas and personalities that is his real sickness, as it is the means of his spiritual growth. Hans Castorp is not critical of the world he has left, except in the sense that he is utterly indifferent to it, its opportunities and values. But he is acutely stimulated, fascinated, by this sanatorium world overshadowed by death, by death itself.

The great majority of his companions, sick and dying, are frivolously or desperately determined not to face up to death. Some, like Joachim, only think of return to normal life. Others exploit their situation to escape from the moral restraints of normal life, and their feverish desire for life is only an escape from reality. The dying are carefully kept out of sight and mind. At first Hans Castorp inclines to the illusion that there is something venerable about sickness, and is puzzled that so many of the patients are as stupid as healthy people. But he retains the conviction that constant contact with death can make a man see normal life with different eyes and become more sensitive to its ' crudity ' and ' cynicism '.⁶ Hans Castorp is therefore a patient by inclination more than by necessity ; he has a ' sympathy with death ', as Mann called it, which is at the same time a curiosity about life, a craving for experience, and which leads him to break the normal taboos of the sanatorium. He curiously observes death in its many forms, fascinated by the delusions and fears of the dying. He has pity for them, paying them visits and taking them flowers. His efforts are not much appreciated, but in his almost morbid curiosity lie the seeds of love for his fellows, an unconscious solicitude for life, which gradually becomes a deliberate commitment to life.

The many macabre scenes through which he passes seem at first, however, only to prove the triumph of death over life. The skeleton of his own hand, which he sees on the X-ray screen, makes him look with fascination ' into his own grave '. His doctor, Hofrat Behrens, who drowns the unpleasant facts of disease under an exuberant flow of jocularity, analyses in a conversation with Castorp the organism into its chemical elements. The loveliness of the female figure is due, he informs his greedy listener, to fat ; the body is water and albumen ; life is oxidation, and death is the same : ' Tja ', he exclaims, ' living consists in dying—*une destruction organique*, as some Frenchman said. It smells of it too.' But the doctor, the humanist by profession, recognises the specific quality of life : ' Life means that in the changes of matter the form is preserved.' In Hans Castorp's mind, however, the lesson is different. ' Why preserve the form ? ' he asks ; and on the rather shocked answer : ' I say, that isn't the least bit humanistic, what you are just saying,' Hans rather cynically closes the conversation with his ' Form is folderol '.[7] His subsequent studies in physiology, anatomy, embryology make him think of life as a ' fever of matter ', as a mere moment of pause in the process of continual dissolution, as ' the rainbow over the waterfall or the flame '; each organic entity reveals itself, on closer examination, as a manifold of elements responding automatically to stimuli. Form and individuality are simply matter grown sensitive and corruptible. Through these reflections we see how deeply Hans Castorp has become immersed in the deathly, timeless, purposeless ' existence ' in the sanatorium, which is the negation of activity, will, of life itself.

His predilection is furthered by the assistant doctor, Krokowski, a devotee of the new depth-psychology of Freud. In his lectures Krokowski breaks up the familiar concepts of love, morality and health, into unconscious urges. Illness, he tells his audience, is psychologically determined and is the result of profound instinctive yearnings. Castorp is repelled by the man, and scarcely shares the feverish fascination with which the other patients listen to ideas that shatter the normal moral inhibitions ; but the doctrine fortifies him, too, in his moral relaxation. As the years pass, Krokowski progresses from depth-psychology to occultism, and Castorp's attitude to this ' psychical research ' is a characteristic mixture of curiosity and disgust. He takes part in a séance, and at his request the medium causes his dead cousin to appear, dressed in the field-grey uniform and steel helmet of the war that is to come. But Castorp is overcome by shame, and abruptly breaks off the séance. It is not the truth or untruth of psychic phenomena that is here in question, but the right or wrong of meddling with them. Castorp leaves the room with a ' threatening nod ' to Krokowski ; he has chosen for life, light, responsibility.[8]

Hans Castorp's ' sympathy with death ' finds its emotive climax in his love for one of the patients, Madame Chauchat, a Dostoyevskian type of Russian that Mann's generation turned into a symbol. Castorp first becomes aware of her because she always bangs the door on entering the dining-room ; the negligent grace of her bearing and appearance subtly challenges the normal proprieties. She condenses all the unease he has felt from childhood about the bourgeois virtues of work, orderliness and social service. For many months he studies her from a distance, dwells silently upon her, talks discreetly about her, till his passion is common knowledge among the inquisitive sensation-loving inmates. As the culmination of his physiological studies, and in the fever of carnival, he summons up the courage to tell her his desire for her. But the next day she leaves the sanatorium, and though he waits years for her return, the liaison is never resumed.

This episode is entitled ' Walpurgis Night ', and Castorp's friend Settembrini illuminates some of its incidents with quotations from the witches' rout in Goethe's *Faust*. But the ' evil ' is more problematical than in Goethe. In their conversation, Clavdia Chauchat teases Hans because of the German preference for order instead of freedom, she mocks at

the humanistic notion of morality, so harsh and inhuman from
her point of view.   She tells him (her words recall some of
Mann's own proclamations in *Reflections of a Non-Political Man*) :

> ' It seems to us Russians that one ought to look for morality not
> in virtue, that is, not in reason, discipline, good behaviour, decency
> —but rather in the contrary, I mean in sin, in abandoning oneself
> to danger, to what is harmful and consumes us.   It seems to us that
> it is more moral to lose oneself and even to let oneself perish than to
> preserve oneself.   The great moralists were not virtuous men, but
> adventurers in evil, men marked by vice, great sinners who teach us
> to bow like Christians before misery.'

She believes that this doctrine is not for him, the young German
brought up in a good bourgeois family.   But he tells her that
he is more than this, there is his illness, his fever, and this
fever is ' nothing but his love for her '; it makes all else
valueless.   And he bursts into a passionate declaration of love
which is exalted by his consciousness of the death that resides
in the body : ' body, love, death, these three are one '.   All
the knowledge of the mystery and beauty of the living body
that he has accumulated in these months in the sanatorium,
a knowledge always directed to disease and corruption, is
fused in this rhapsodic declaration of love for the beauty of
the ' human image made of water and albumen, destined for
the anatomy of the tomb '.[9]   As a keepsake she leaves with
him, at his request, her X-ray photograph, a ghostly body,
faceless, marked by the shadow of disease.

It is a diseased and feverish love.   After its brief consum-
mation Castorp stays on hoping to renew it, but when Clavdia
returns, the companion of another man, there is no question
of renewal.   This passion, absorbing as it is, is not a personal
fulfilment ; there is something theoretical about it, it serves
something else—it is not accidental that Castorp declares his
love in a foreign tongue, French.   In a later conversation
when he tells Clavdia that he is not a passionate man, she
replies lightly, but with a sure touch :

> ' It is extraordinarily reassuring to hear you are not a passionate
> man. Anyhow, how could you be ? That would be odd in a
> German, Passion—that is, to live for the sake of life. But every-

one knows that you Germans live for the sake of experience. Passion—that is, self-forgetfulness. But you are concerned with self-enrichment. *C'est ça.* You have no notion that that is revolting egoism, and that some day it will make you the enemies of the human race.'[10]

So we too are not concerned primarily with the story of Castorp's love for Clavdia, with this relationship that comes to so undramatic a close. We are to see it as one element in his experience : ' eating the pomegranate ', it is called. It is an important step in his development, it asserts his new wisdom against the disapproval of his cousin and his mentor Settembrini ; but it itself is a phase in his general moral development, and its significance can only be understood against the background of his philosophical discussions with Settembrini, Naphta, and Peeperkorn, the three outstanding characters from whom he learns.

Of these, Settembrini is the educator by instinct and principle, irrepressible in his self-appointed role of mentor but also moved by a genuine affection for Castorp. Ill enough to be a permanent patient, he tries from the beginning to persuade Castorp to break away from the sanatorium and return to work in normal life : not like Joachim to traditional duties, but to share in the work for human progress. For this Italian in a humanist of the old school, an optimist who believes in mankind's power to perfect itself, a democrat who believes that social institutions can be steadily improved, a rationalist who believes that man can be educated by reason and science, an idealist who believes that truth, justice, freedom may be reached. Even on this remote mountain he is collaborating in grandiose literary schemes for the enlightenment of man. In many conversations he struggles to wean Castorp from the fascination of disease and death, from his greed for experience and his love for Clavdia Chauchat. Experience is necessary to man, he tells him, but there are dangerous experiences which threaten to submerge the will, and these must be avoided. Disease is something to be overcome, and death has meaning only as a means of new life. He is the type of ' Zivilisationsliterat ' that Mann had bitterly derided in the

Reflections of a Non-Political Man, but Castorp affectionately listens to him, and respects him in spite of his threadbare suit and his slightly ridiculous rhetorical phrases and gestures. He learns quite a lot from him, but bit by bit the pupil becomes the equal and critic of the master. He allows himself a sly irony, sometimes parodying Settembrini's words. This grandiloquent humanism, he feels, is inhuman in its abstract moralism and idealism. He sees that Settembrini, for all his bold belief in man, tries to ignore certain aspects of reality and even fears certain experiences ; that he is frightened of risking his health when invited to return to the plains to take part in a great scheme for the welfare of mankind. Castorp throws off his tutelage when he takes the plunge with Clavdia ; on the same night he addresses them both with the familiar ' du ', Settembrini in challenge, Clavdia in bold solicitation.

The weakness of Settembrini's philosophical position is fully shown up in the perpetual arguments between him and Naphta, at which Castorp is often present. Settembrini moves to lodgings in the village and introduces the young man to this house-mate of his, a Jew turned Jesuit, whose illness has prevented him from being ordained a priest and who teaches at the local grammar school. Yet as the Italian gets worsted in the arguments, Castorp turns more and more towards him, and against his subtle and sinister opponent.

Naphta is the receptable of all the anti-liberal irrationalism to which Mann himself had confessed his allegiance in the *Reflections of a Non-Political Man*. He convincingly shows the absurdity of the concept of absolute truth : ' truth ', he says in Nietzsche's words, ' is what profits us '. He shows the confusions and contradictions in the bourgeois concept of freedom. He ridicules the illusions of bourgeois individualism, attacks the disintegrating power of capitalism, sneers at nationalism. The real needs of man are in his view his irrational desires for community, for obedience, for the conviction of a supernatural destiny ; and Naphta is ready to welcome totalitarianism and terror, even communism, as the means to a renewal of spiritual life. He tears Settembrini's beliefs to pieces ; all the latter's scientific philosophy is revealed as a patchwork of material interests and expediency, irrelevant to men's deepest needs ; his ' rational ' principles turn on closer examination into mutually incompatible demagogic slogans, like peace and nationalism, liberty and capitalism, spiritual enrichment and scientific progress.

Castorp often finds these arguments persuasive, for Naphta's paradoxical intelligence gives shape to his own modest doubts about Settembrini's views. But he also begins to see with alarm the implications of his revolt against Settembrini, the gloomy and inhuman terror of an existence where man abandons reason and individuality, where social life is stripped of value, and the dark instinctive forces are worshipped. As Naphta himself is devoid of love and kindliness, so his system is ferocious and inhuman. And though Settembrini is often reduced to a mere indignant protest, a rhetorical flourish, yet his protest against Naphta's inhumanity becomes more significant for Castorp than the logic of the other :

' I like you all the same. You may be a windbag and organ-grinder, but you mean well, you've got better intentions and I like you better than that sharp little Jesuit and terrorist, that henchman of the Spanish torture-chamber with his beaming spectacles, though he's nearly always in the right when you quarrel . . . when you two pedagogues scrap over my poor soul like God and the Devil in the Middle Ages.'

These quarrels culminate in an absurd duel, in which Settembrini fires in the air and Naphta shoots himself, his last nihilistic act. But Castorp acts as Settembrini's second, and when he leaves the sanatorium for good, it is Settembrini who sees him off, for Castorp is at last leaving for the real world. But he is leaving to fight for Germany, against the nations who incorporate Settembrini's principles, and Settembrini's final leave-taking indicates only too clearly the insufficiency of his philosophy :

' Addio, Giovanni mio ! I wished you to take a different sort of journey, but so be it, the Gods have willed it thus and not otherwise. I hoped to discharge you to take up your work, but now you will fight among your people. . . . Fight bravely, where blood binds you ! No man can do more than that now. But

forgive me if I devote the remainder of my strength to incite my
country on the side to which the spirit and sacred self-interest
point the way.   Addio ! '

His doctrine is full of contradiction, and it is not a guide to
the young German in the modern world ; but a deep affection
and mutual respect binds them.   Hans will fight, he answers
the call of the nation, and this is more in accordance with
Naphta than with Settembrini ; but something must result
beyond the scope of either, and it will owe most to Settembrini.

But before this decision Castorp has become acquainted
with a man who presents him with still another attitude from
which he profits.   When Clavdia Chauchat returns to the
sanatorium, she is the ' travelling companion ' of a wealthy
planter from the Dutch colonies, Peeperkorn.   A man of
enormous vitality, Peeperkorn undermines his health with his
excessive eating and drinking.   Even in the sanatorium he
continually breaks all the rules.   He is a child compared with
Settembrini or Naphta ; he can speak about practical matters,
though otherwise he can rarely finish a sentence, vaguely
indicating what he thinks by a gesture.   As a personality,
however, he towers above the rest.   Castorp cannot explain
this mystery, but he submits to his influence ; not for a moment
does he think of competing with him for Clavdia.   But this
giant also has his weakness.   He is secretly terrified of the
decline of his vitality ; Castorp notices in his eyes, now and
again, a ' panic horror '.   Life which he worships in the
simplest form of enjoyment brings with it old age and impotence.   And Peeperkorn commits suicide, abdicates, frightened
with the symptoms of age in himself, terrified, as Castorp
sadly comments, over the ' collapse of feeling in face of life '
which for a Peeperkorn is a ' cosmic catastrophe '.[11]

From all these people Hans Castorp learns much.   Unformed
like the traditional hero of the ' Bildungsroman ', he listens
and observes modestly and affectionately, and if he disagrees
or criticises he does so hesitantly, even surreptitiously.   Yet,
imposing and self-confident as they are, each of his teachers
consciously and unconsciously cancels out much of the others,
and Castorp has to find his own way between them.   He

seeks to govern and manage himself—' sich regieren ' he calls it—and this purpose itself is a mark of his growth. Intellectually he cannot master all the complexities of the problems they set him, and his development is largely an unconscious moral process, springing from the sources of personality, rather than a conscious mastery of intellectual problems. It is evident in his affection for Settembrini and Peeperkorn, but only a startling incident makes him conscious of a change and a decision in himself.

This experience occurs in the midst of the confusions of the arguments between Settembrini and Naphta over freedom and service, reason and instinct, man and nature, and it crystallises Castorp's response. He has learnt to ski and makes a lonely excursion in the high mountains. Something of his ' sympathy with death ' inspires his delight in this adventure, a deliberate courting of danger, comparable he thinks with the moral perils of the intellectual arguments he has been listening to. But also there is a new courage in him, a feeling of human dignity as he challenges these indifferent silent peaks, ' an ironical mockery of their mighty meaninglessness '.[12] He is overtaken by a snow-storm and in a distressed state rests in the meagre shelter outside a hut. A painful effort to find the way home lands him back at the hut, utterly exhausted, and he realises his situation is serious. His head gets fuddled with a drink of port wine that he happens to have on him, and he has a dream which makes clear to him the decision which has been ripening within him for many months. He sees an idyllic scene beside a southern sea, a happy and courteous company of men and maidens, mother and child ; and in the background, within a temple, a horrible scene of human sacrifice. As his horror awakens him, his thoughts continue his dream. The grace and courtesy of the human scene, he thinks, is the essential human response to the horrors which also are human ; the dream of life encompasses both. Death and sickness belong to life, they must be faced ; not as an end in themselves, but as a spur to make life beautiful and worthy. And he will hold to those who, bearing in mind the horror of life, seek to make the human

G

community fair and friendly, ' for all the interest in death and disease is nothing but a sort of expression for that in life '. Death cannot be overcome by reason, but by love : ' For the sake of kindness and love man must not let death dominate his thoughts.' As Castorp comes to the end of his reflections, he suddenly sees the weather has cleared, and in a few minutes he is safely back in the village.[13]

It is a new attitude ; but only an attitude. Hans Castorp does not make any practical conclusions, and stays on for years at the Berghof, observing and talking. Peeperkorn comes, Joachim dies, Castorp participates in the new fashion of psychic research. If it were left to him, perhaps he would never shake out of this existence. But the growing tensions in the real world of the plains disturb this eyrie too. Tensions grow, personal irritations, there is a horrible fight between an Anti-Semitic patient and a Jew : in this period of disintegration there occurs the duel between Settembrini and Naphta. Then comes the news of war, and the inmates start dispersing homewards. And now, at last, Hans Castorp, who has lost all personal connections with his native land, has lost all consciousness of time, leaves the magic mountain :

He saw himself freed from the spell, redeemed, liberated—not by his own strength, he had shamefully to confess, but turned out by elemental external powers, for whom his liberation was very much a minor matter.

One last glimpse is given of him on the battle-field as the author takes an affectionate farewell of his creation :

Farewell, whether you live or die. It is a poor outlook for you. The desperate dance which whirls you away will last many a long year, and we would not bet heavily on your chance of survival. If we are to be honest, we are not much concerned about it. Adventures in the flesh and the spirit, which heightened your simplicity, have let you survive in the spirit what you are hardly likely to survive in the flesh. Moments came, when out of death and the riot of the flesh there dawned on you a dream of love, which you took as guidance. Will it be that out of this universal festival of death, this malign fever, which sets the rainy evening sky afire, love one day shall arise ?

SIGNIFICANT AND SYMBOLICAL REALISM

On the surface this novel seems to belong to the realistic tradition. In the description of interiors, above all in the delineation of character—through dress, gesture, phrase—Mann displays a precision of observation that approaches virtuosity. We are prepared for this artistry if we know his earlier works, yet there is a considerable maturing in comparison with *Buddenbrooks*. There is complete ease in the author's relationship to his readers. He does not hide his identity, and frequently offers incidental comments, often of an ironical character, or allows himself general reflections. This confident intimacy with his readers does not mean, however, that the narrative focus is disturbed, as it is at times in *Wilhelm Meister*. Castorp is not only the main character, the hero, of the theme, but also it is he who determines the range and character of the experiences and thoughts that are presented.

In *Buddenbrooks*, for instance, there is a somewhat clumsy alternation between the setting of fixed scenes and the subsequent action ; in *The Magic Mountain* description and action are fused. It begins with Castorp's arrival at the Berghof, and the sanatorium and its inmates are described as he meets them. The time-chart of the novel has nothing of the arbitrariness of the time-lapse of *Buddenbrooks*, and it illustrates again Castorp's function as the artistic as well as moral centre of the novel. In his first days at the sanatorium the new scenes and people are described extensively, and time seems to stretch out endlessly. Soon, however, the day, filled in and shortened by the sanatorium routine, disappears as a time-unit, and the narrative advances in larger strides, marked by the seasonal changes or periodic examinations that are important for Castorp. Soon even these melt into one another, and the progress of time is like (and likened to) the ebb and flow of the tide, a perpetual motion in an unchanging element. Just as Castorp loses all sense of time, so the time-lapse of the novel loses all precision ; time is recovered only when the outer world rudely invades the illusory isolation of the sanatorium.

In the same way, the descriptions in the early part of the book are rich in precise detail, almost in the naturalistic style, corresponding to the greedy curiosity of the newcomer. Later, discussions, reflections, dreams come to predominate, and descriptions of external appearance occur more rarely, and only when, for some reason, Castorp's curiosity is aroused. In fact, when Peeperkorn arrives, it is Castorp himself who, in a conversation with Behrens, describes his appearance. When the author playfully adds : ' we could not have done better ourselves ', he is only emphasising the dominant role his hero plays in the artistic composition of the work.[14] It may seem strange that we are never told what happens on the night of Castorp's declaration of love. From one or two hints we get to know that Hans and Clavdia spend the night together, but we are expressly excluded from his confidence, even though he tells a friend the whole story. It may be that Mann, like an oldfashioned story-teller, enjoys puzzling us ; but above all, this reserve itself tells us how jealously Castorp guards the treasure of this experience.

Only in one instance is this unity of standpoint broken. After some acquaintance with Naphta we are told in twelve pages the story of his life hitherto, and this section is an alien body in the organism of the novel.[15] It is not only that the synoptic cogency of this narrative of Naphta's life contradicts Castorp's natural mode of perception ; but the account has a sharp sarcastic ring about it that does not correspond at all with Castorp's character or experience. He can be severe with simpler characters, but Naphta, at least at this stage, is far too complex to be summed up thus by him. At the end of the synopsis, Mann lamely tries to justify it by saying : ' Hans Castorp learnt of these things in conversations with Naphta ', but the excuse seems only to add a fresh difficulty —for how could the wily Naphta lay himself open to so sarcastic an interpretation of himself? By contrast the progressive self-revelation of Settembrini utterly accords both with his character and Castorp's ; and how right and satisfactory is the half-dark of Peeperkorn's past.

There is an extraordinary richness in the realism of this

novel, then, since what is noted reveals both the outward world and the developing mind of Castorp. In earlier works Mann had been fond of the leitmotif, a fixed mannerism or turn of phrase which labels a character. It is used much more sparingly in *The Magic Mountain*, for the characters themselves resist the over-simplification that the leitmotif suggests. Settembrini's flamboyant check trousers do reappear in Castorp's consciousness from time to time, growing more threadbare as time passes. But the slamming of the dining-room door, which always signals Clavdia Chauchat's entry, ceases when, on her return, Peeperkorn opens the door for her. The characters have their distinctness, their mannerisms, but Mann does not try to make the label and the man identical ; behind the typical phraseology or gestures of a Behrens or Peeperkorn we occasionally glimpse an unspoken anxiety that the mannerism vainly seeks to hide. Castorp has his fixed habits, but what is most important, he develops. Mann shows, often with delicious humour, how Hans and even Joachim learn from the conversations of the others, how they apply the phrases and attitudes they have observed to clarify their own disputes, how in fact Hans in particular grows wiser. Thus he reproves his cousin for his ' dualism ', a word he has just learnt from Settembrini ; or a phrase Clavdia had once applied to himself comes in handy when he makes his reckoning with Naphta.[16] There is an extremely subtle pattern of such influences which show Castorp's gradual absorption of experience.

It is clear that realism is not an absolute aesthetic principle for Thomas Mann, for only that is described which has significance for the hero at a particular moment. After Castorp has spent some time at the sanatorium, we are as oblivious as he to much of the routine of life, and it is only an exceptional event that awakens a consciousness of the environment, as for instance Castorp's first visit to the lodgings of Settembrini and Naphta, his first meeting with Peeperkorn, and so forth. The amount of the outward world which appears, even the shape in which it appears, is determined by and indicates Castorp's state of mind ; the technique

might be called ' significant realism '. Sometimes this outward reality seems indeed to intrude on Castorp, to be observed
despite himself, in the way things have.   When he has the
long-awaited conversation with Clavdia after her return, we
are told that he is sitting in ' a plush-covered chair in renais-
sance style '—but the author playfully adds ' if you really
want to see it ': i.e. Castorp cannot avoid noticing the chair,
he knows it is quite unimportant what sort of chair it is, and
yet he will always associate this interview with this chair.[17]
As Weigand points out, chairs have quite a ' symbolic ' importance in this book ; there are, too, the reclining chair of the
patients, which once starts an important metaphysical argument, the ' chair of triumph ' in which Clavdia listens to
Castorp's declaration of love, the bare cane chairs of Settembrini's revolutionary grandfather.[18]

All the incidents of the novel, and the manner in which
they are presented, are then both scrupulously realistic and
also indicative of Hans Castorp's development.   But they are
significant not only in the simple sense that they represent the
elements of his inner wrestlings ; they also link his personal
theme with a more general one, and in this respect become
symbolical.   Many direct indications lead us unavoidably to
look further than Hans Castorp for the meaning of *The Magic
Mountain*, in the same way as Castorp himself is led to look
for the meaning of his love for music, for Schubert's *Linden
Tree*, in which he recognises with surprise and dismay the
fascination of death against which he is now on his guard.
It is at this point that in a generalisation Mann gives an
indication of the symbolic character of the novel as a whole :

We will put it thus : an object which is of the spirit, that is, a
significant object, is significant precisely because it directs us
beyond itself, because it is the expression and exponent of a more
general spiritual entity, of a whole world of feeling and attitude
which has found in it a more or less perfect symbol,—which determines the degree of its significance.   Further, the love for such an
object is likewise significant.   It tells us something about the
person who loves it, it characterises his relation to that general
entity, to that world that the object represents and that is consciously
or unconsciously loved at the same time.[19]

This ' general entity ' is indicated plainly in the last words of the novel, where Mann explicitly relates the emergence of love out of Castorp's ' sympathy with death ' to the emergence of love out of the ' festival of death ' of the world war. It is hinted at in the penultimate paragraph where he writes, in the role of an affectionate author, that he has told the story for its own sake, not for Castorp's—words which recall an earlier statement that while Castorp is an ' average ' sort of fellow, ' we are inclined to give his fate a supra-personal significance '.[20]

So, parallel with the personal story of Castorp, there runs a more general theme. This sanatorium is the world itself, assailed by a disease which may be fatal or not, which may have spiritual or material causes. How is man, and how in particular is the German, to face this insidious foe?—or, one must say, how is the German middle class to face it, for all the emphasis is on Castorp's bourgeois character, subject to the contrary pulls of Settembrini and Clavdia, ' West ' and ' East ', finding his own way yet owing much to each. Settembrini's playful reference to Joachim as ' the hope of the Prussian army ' is not an idle comment ; and when Clavdia tells Hans that Joachim is worse than he knows, she is defining the hollowness of the Prussian ideal of service. In this sanatorium-world Mann takes care to introduce us not only to various moral types but also to national representatives, for the disease is international. Settembrini is not only a democratic nationalist but also an Italian ; his flamboyance and seediness reflect the past glories of Italy as well as of positivism. Clavdia Chauchat is the Russian, as Mann understood it from Dostoyevski. In Naphta there merge the mysticism and authoritarianism of the Eastern Jew and the European Jesuit. The incurable illness of Settembrini, the cure of Castorp, the suicides of Peeperkorn and Naphta are all directly symbolical of the doctrines for which they stand. The incidents of the novel and the order of their occurrence all have a symbolical meaning. Carnival is the time appropriate for Castorp's declaration of love both because its excitement gives him a reckless courage and because it is, symbolically, the time when the dark forces oust order and reason. The growing tensions in the outside world, as we approach 1914, take symbolical shape in the personal quarrels of the inmates of the sanatorium, the duel of Naphta and Settembrini, the degrading scuffle between the German Anti-Semite and the Jew, both already in the last stages of disease.

The Magic Mountain differs from the earlier ' Bildungsroman ' in the explicitness of its cultural analysis ; this term may properly be used, for its theme is the character and problems of German civilisation at a particular historical moment. In this, it is a typical work—' Everything Mann has produced is part of the criticism of culture.'[21]   He has proposed different solutions, but the terms in which he has defined this problem do not greatly vary in *Buddenbrooks*, 1901, *Reflections of a Non-Political Man*, 1918, *The Magic Mountain*, and *Doctor Faustus*, 1947.

This underlying theme adds greatly to the significance of *The Magic Mountain*, but it creates pitfalls too, which Mann has not always successfully avoided. The generalisations with which he operates are sometimes specious, shallow, irritating —for instance the concepts of ' East ' and ' West ', the concept of the Italian, the German, the Russian. Sometimes the symbolical meaning a character bears is too heavy and drowns his artistic reality—this is so particularly in the case of Naphta, who is a receptacle for a host of tendencies which remain on the plane of mere argument and paradox, and whose suicide is psychologically badly motivated and, if one considers him as a representative, unconvincing.

With some acquaintance with Mann's political and cultural essays, the reader is bound to recognise some of these generalisations as Mann's own, and to accept them or reject them according to his own political philosophy. In fact, however, perhaps by an almost unconscious artistic instinct, Mann has largely avoided making the novel the equivalent of a political or cultural essay. The general, allegorical references of the novel are nearly all made by the characters themselves, not by the author. It is Settembrini and Castorp who make generalisations about East and West, about Germany as ' the land of the meeting-place ', it is Clavdia Chauchat who describes the character of the German, Castorp who calls the Germans ' the delicate children ' of the world. Such phrases, when used by Mann in the *Reflections* and elsewhere, provoke dissent or agreement, but in the novel they have a full aesthetic validity, since they both illuminate a problem and characterise the person speaking. The love of Castorp for Clavdia is overloaded with symbolical meaning, to such an extent as hardly to fit into the category of genuine feeling ; yet here again this perversity is the very expression of a diseased mind and body, and its over-intellectual content interprets the doom which is set on their relationship.

Thus, while we are continually reminded of the symbolical reference of an incident or character, of the general issues of a historical period, Mann avoids too explicit and rigid an allegorical system. It is part of his times, part of our times, that the individual is conscious of belonging to wider entities of nationality, class, outlook, and can know himself only by understanding his inheritance and allegiance. The social doctrine of tolerant humanism, love, service, to which Castorp slowly attains, is at the same time the recognition of the fact that he must see himself in some sense as a representative, as a responsible member of a group. But Castorp is a representative figure—not an abstract, ideal summation of the dominant characteristics of a group, for instance of the Germans or the German middle class, but an average man of the middle class, who experiences the dilemma of his times in a peculiar, individual way, and whose achievement is limited, imprecise, provisional. Scenes and characters scarcely ever lose this individuality, and in figures like Settembrini or Behrens Mann has created personalities who have the fluid exuberance of reality as well as the significance of a type or representative.

In a speech given at Lübeck in 1926 Mann spoke of some of the ideas he associated with *The Magic Mountain*. He spoke of the middle class as being essentially German and embodying the ' idea of the meeting-place '; he asserted that it was doomed as a class, crushed between international capitalism and communism, but proclaimed his faith in the permanent

value of its cultural achievements, its ' humaneness, humanity '.
But how much of all this is actually there, in *The Magic
Mountain* ? There is no international capitalism, no working
class, not even the German bourgeoisie. There is no question
of doom or revolution. The novel is infinitely more cautious
and delicate than the essay. And though it urges us continually to reflect on the grave underlying social issues of the
times, it leaves the imagination free to absorb this story as an
individual occurrence.

MANN AND THE ' BILDUNGSROMAN '

We ask ourselves, at the end of a fascinating book, has the
spiritual transformation of Castorp really acquired substance,
will his life ' in the plains ' take on a correspondingly new
shape ? The change in Mann himself, and in many of his
contemporaries, came as the result of profound shocks, war,
defeat, revolution, impoverishment, effort. Hans Castorp's
development, however, is the result of almost purely intellectual experiences, and it remains somewhat indefinable and
intangible ; his new, positive attitude to life has no precise
social content, far less indeed than Wilhelm Meister's, Green
Heinrich's or even Heinrich Drendorf's. He goes to take his
place in the fighting ranks of his countrymen without asking
what they are fighting for or what the outcome will be. It
seems he exchanges one illusory world, the sanatorium, for
another, the power-state ; one ' festival of death ' for another.
And Thomas Mann disclaims concern for Castorp's fate in
this ' fleshly ' world ; though one might have thought that just
at this point the whole theme of the novel must prove itself,
only here, in the real world, can Castorp show what he has
become. No doubt Mann was wise in refusing to commit
Castorp. At the end of the novel he has become a representative German, and Mann was well aware in 1924 that the way
out of the ' festival of death ' had still to be found and secured.
But this uncertainty places a troubling question-mark against
the whole of Castorp's moral education, his ' Bildung '.

In this respect, Mann is true to the tradition of the ' Bildungsroman ', in spite of the fact that in the others there is no such abrupt breach between personal education and the social world. All the ' Bildungsroman ' were written in the aftermath of revolution and social turmoil, and all make a reckoning with the principles of social life. It is their distinction that the intricate processes of personal development are guided by principles of social conduct. In Goethe these principles, influenced by the French Revolution, have a Utopian character, and lead his ' renunciants ' out of Germany. In Keller the reformed constitution of his Swiss republic gives his hero the solid ground he needs for an active social life. Stifter, repelled by the revolutionary liberalism of his day, made the family the basis from which social improvement might come. Mann's hero finds a far less secure anchorage. Among the bewildering experiences of the sanatorium Castorp gains, not real allies and companions, not a job or a home, but only an attitude of mind. He enters a world infinitely more bewildering than that awaiting the other heroes of the ' Bildungsroman ', more acutely threatened, much less amenable to rational decision ; and his author is much less sure about the outcome. Perhaps this is what Mann meant when he called his novel something of a parody of the older ' Bildungsroman '. In spite of differences, however, essentially the same pattern is evident ; what has changed is society itself, which now propounds infinitely more puzzling and difficult problems.

Other peculiar features of *The Magic Mountain* do not conceal the fundamental unity of character and purpose that links it with the earlier novels. Bruno Walter, Mann's lifelong friend, said retrospectively of the early Thomas Mann : ' There was the danger that his urge to contemplate life and to mirror it poetically would cause him to become lost to life itself ' ; [22] a statement strikingly near to the whole theme of the ' Bildungsroman '. Castorp has, typically, to choose between the fascination of the inwardly directed life and the demands of social being ; he has to ' renounce ' in order to mature. The sanatorium serves as a misleading but enriching experience, like the theatre with Wilhelm Meister or painting with Green Heinrich ; it, also, mirrors the world and is the medium through which valuable experience is gained. Castorp's final decision, like that of his prototypes, is primarily the result of an inward debate, of partly conscious, partly unconscious rumination over his experiences and the views put to him by the persons he meets. There are differences. The aberrations of the others are not so catastrophic. The choice for Castorp is not simply between dream and reality, between unhappiness and happiness, isolation and community, but between death and life. The sanatorium has nothing of the innocence of the troupe of actors or the painters' fraternity, it is a house of the dead, utterly cut off from the living, and even its humours are macabre. Castorp himself lacks the capacity for simple restorative experience. His friendship is reserved, distrustful, ironical, and even his love for Clavdia is a ' phlegmatic passion ', curiously perverted and unfruitful. Stifter's hero, like Meister and Green Heinrich, is candid and trustful ; Castorp is naïve only in his curiosity, otherwise he is always on his guard. But all these differences belong to the general situation Mann was faced with : an imperilled world, gripped by catastrophic obsessions, rushing towards war and revolutions. Mann's novel is a recapitulation of the great theme of the older ' Bildungsroman ' from a standpoint where the full bearing of this theme was revealed. His work gives a new significance to the older novels, for it shows that the ' Bildungsroman ' was not merely a particular variety of the novel, but had been, and still was, the novel-form in which the deepest spiritual issues of modern German society could take tangible shape.

PART II
NOVELISTS

CHAPTER V

Jeremias Gotthelf
1797–1854

THE PARSON'S AESTHETIC

IF Gotthelf is to be labelled, he must be called a realistic novelist, the first in German literature. A contemporary of Balzac and Dickens, this Swiss writer strikes off from the track of the Romantics, Tieck, Novalis, Arnim, Hoffmann, in whose work the world of fantasy takes precedence over the world of social experience and reality. He also stands in opposition, formally as well as in social attitude, to the ' Young German ' novelists of the 1830s, with their concern for social theories. Of all contemporary German writers, Immermann comes nearest to the realistic novel in his description of peasant life and industrial conditions, but his realistic bent is fatally twisted by Romantic elements. Gotthelf's work makes a great break in the German tradition, and for this reason it is of advantage to sketch his personal situation and general philosophical outlook, which for all their peculiarity give useful pointers to the genesis and significance of realism in the novel.

Albert Bitzius, who wrote under the pseudonym of ' Gotthelf ', was born and bred in the Canton of Berne. The son of a clergyman of the Established Reformed Church, he studied theology at Berne and (for a year) at the University of Göttingen—his only period of residence outside Switzerland. After two or three rural curacies and a short incumbency in Berne, he was vicar in the lowland parish of Lützelflüh from 1831 till his death in 1854.

His adult life coincides with a period of great social transformation in his Canton and in Switzerland as a whole. In 1830 the old Bernese oligarchical system was replaced by a liberal-conservative régime, which itself was overthrown in the 1840s by a radical movement which laid the basis of the modern

democracy and of a new Swiss federal constitution.   All social
institutions became the subject of violent political argument,
including the particular concerns of parish priests, the schools,
poor-law, and the Church.   Gotthelf, like nearly all his contemporaries, was deeply embroiled in the public controversies.
A stout supporter of the earlier liberal reforms, he became
dismayed at the success of the radical revolution and the
decline of piety towards secular and ecclesiastical authority.
From the middle of the 1840s he threw himself heart and soul
into the struggle against radicalism, and became notorious
for the ferocity of his criticism of popular trends and personalities, opposing to the bitter end the compromise which
established a stable liberal democracy.

Confined throughout this period to his parochial work, he
sought through his novels to urge his views on a wider public.
They were written, frankly and emphatically, to serve moral
and practical needs as he understood them ; and he was
so outspoken and provocative that he was sharply criticised
even by those, like Gottfried Keller, who recognised in him
' a great epic genius ', while the half-century after his death
found him unpalatable.   A French study of 1913 first showed
a full appreciation of his literary quality, and particularly
since the publication of Walter Muschg's *Gotthelf*, numerous
investigations, particularly by Swiss, have risen above the
limitations of political or religious partisanship.   Above all,
the magnificent edition of his complete works and his corre-
spondence has made his work accessible in its true form, and
has provided the critical apparatus peculiarly necessary in
Gotthelf's case.[1]

All Gotthelf's novels were written with a direct moral purpose, and nearly all are focused on the peasants of the two
Emmental parishes he knew intimately—the weakest of them,
Jacob the Journeyman's Travels through Switzerland, the story of
an artisan who roams further afield, shows the limitations of
his knowledge and sympathy.   Round a specific theme, the
treatment of village paupers or schoolmasters, the blind trust
in quack-doctors, the establishment of a co-operative cheese
factory, there collect others, which may be reduced in the

end to the essential theme of the maintenance of the peasant farm and family. He denied any purely literary ambition.[2] In the preface to his late novel, *Zeitgeist und Bernergeist*, he wrote that ' he had entered the lists for God and the Fatherland, for the Christian home and the future of minors, knowing that his books would never be products of art '. He had scarcely been conscious of becoming a writer, he told a correspondent, ' but the poor, the schools were at stake '.[3] ' The world pressed on me so long until it pressed books out of my head, in order to throw them at its head.' [4] His Swiss friends begged him to moderate his attacks on institutions and persons, his German publisher advised him to cut out politics from his novels ; but the polemical intention was the very *raison d'être* of his writing, and he would not have written had the novels not been a medium for his propaganda.

He carried on a perpetual guerrilla warfare against the ' cultured ' classes, their aesthetic tastes and their literature. His aim was to become a ' writer for the common people ', a ' Volksschriftsteller '. But he saw the great weakness of the usual sort of didactic literature, made up of a dose of religion, a dose of morals, suppressing unpleasant aspects of reality, frowning on the lustier pleasures of life, and often idealising other classes, particularly the educated, as a model for the simple people. He wished to ' enliven ' as well as instruct, to put the truth of life as fully as possible before his readers, to embrace all aspects of peasant life and other classes or institutions with which they were in contact.[5] Half a farmer himself in his upbringing, often at loggerheads with the ' lords of Berne ', he was so deeply persuaded of the dignity and worth of the peasant-class that he neither sought to make its manners conform to some other standard, nor feared to criticise it.[6] As a parson he was engaged in a constant and sharp struggle with the peasantry ; as a countryman he was sufficiently of the peasantry to identify himself with the values of its way of life, and to describe it ' in its own especial peculiarity '.[7]

To these conscious motives was added a purely subjective impulse, which he noticed from time to time in retrospect.

H

His cousin Carl Bitzius, who greatly admired his work, remonstrated with him for the bitterness with which he attacked people and types of which he disapproved, telling him that these faults lessened his influence. Gotthelf answered in a most important confession. He spoke of the frustrations that he suffered in the rigid, bureaucratic, traditionalist society of Berne :

> From all sides I was lamed, held down, I could nowhere find an outlet for free activity. If I could have worked it off by riding, if I could have gone riding every second day, I would never have taken to writing. I now understand that a wild life was surging in me, of which no-one had an inkling. . . . This life was bound either to consume me or to break out in some way. It broke out in writing.

And he adds that only now does he notice that the heroes of his first two novels, *The Mirror of Peasants* and *The Schoolmaster*, are, like himself, ' thwarted characters '.[8]

To this recognition that his works were not the calculated outcome of a merely moral impulse, but issued out of his own inner turmoil, was added in course of time a further discovery about himself. It is best illustrated by his comment on *Anne Bäbi Jowäger*. This novel was begun at the request of the Berne Medical Commission, which asked Gotthelf to write a book attacking the common belief in quack doctors, and it sets out to show what damage arises from this habit of mind. But, even from the start of the book, other themes enter in : the harm of false types of religion, the dangers of narrow-minded obsessions, even the value of certain types of superstition ; and all these separate themes are swallowed up in the exposition of the characters of the peasant family. When the book was finished, a two-volume work, it was too expensive to be distributed as a popular pamphlet, and in any case did not at all meet the requirements of the Medical Commission (just as so many of his other works found disfavour among Gotthelf's religious colleagues). Reflecting on this problem, Gotthelf wrote :

> As soon as I set about a piece of work, a spirit comes into it, and this spirit is mightier than I, and life comes into every person, and

this life claims its rights, wants to grow to full stature and assert its rights in all directions. So it happened in this story : the characters asserted their rights and swamped the actual moral intention, pushed it into the background.[9]

Gotthelf's imagination was repeatedly seized by his own creatures. In some of his works, where he was not so captivated, the moral theme dominates to the disadvantage of the work, and the characters fail to take on life, being viewed from without, over-simplified, often harshly and unsympathetically treated : this is the cardinal weakness of *Jacob the Journeyman*, *Der Herr Esau*, of much of *Zeitgeist und Bernergeist*, and several of the shorter tales. But where Gotthelf's imagination was seized, the moral theme deepens into the reality and problematic of a character and a whole life ; the reader does not deduce a simple moral lesson, with the pat answers of moral superiority, but is made aware of the tangle of qualities that make up a character and a life.

This process of artistic creation produced another contradiction in Gotthelf's work which he failed to face. He wrote expressly for the people he wished to improve, peasants, labourers, villagers in general. But his novels (as distinct from his contributions to almanacks) were little read by such. His own parishioners seem only to have been obscurely and resentfully aware that their parson was using them somewhat ruthlessly as his ' material ', while he was read above all by the educated classes.[10] This was so even with the earlier works published in Switzerland ; his later were published in Berlin by a liberal, Springer, primarily with German and educated readers in mind, though Gotthelf himself never ceased from his vicious digs at Germans, at the educated, at liberals.[11] There was then a confusion in his purpose which he never disentangled—and a most salutary one, which saved him on the one hand from an excessive utilitarian parochialism, and on the other from thraldom to the moral and aesthetic conventions of the cultured classes.

The main conscious principle of all Gotthelf's work was that it should ' strike home ' with the people ; for this reason he was contemptuous of all aestheticism and jeered at the

accepted formal proprieties. His lack of artistic restraint is
only too evident, and injures all his books, even the best, and
not only in superficial ways. His most obvious fault is his
continual moralising. He interrupts his tales with frequent
moral generalisations which often develop into long digressions, even sermons. Hardly has he begun a story than the
digressions come, thick and fast, often ponderous and violent.
The narrative of his greatest novel, *Anne Bäbi*, is distressingly
interrupted, in the second volume, by a series of long digressions ; for instance, the account of the birth of a child is held
up by thirteen pages on the whole duties of a midwife, while
a little later there is a thirty-page digression on the relative
functions of doctor and parson. Sometimes racily written,
sometimes rhetorically unctuous, these digressions are the
greatest hindrance to a wider appreciation of his quality.
More serious, because more injurious to his imaginative conceptions, is the violent prejudice which leads Gotthelf to
caricature certain types. Townsmen, particularly officials, are
always presented in the blackest light, radicals too, even if
they are peasants, schoolmasters and innkeepers often, whom
he felt to be the enemies of the parson ; with a true peasant's
prejudice Gotthelf is often extremely harsh to farmhands,
maids and artisans. His social, moral and religious pre-
conceptions often prevent him from penetrating into these
characters, and they seem to be possessed of some perverse
devil. Most of the novels written in the later years of his
life, when radicalism was rampant in Berne, are seriously
damaged by these prejudices—the radical agitator, Eglihannes,
a poor peasant, and his schoolmaster confederate in *The Cheese
Factory*, the radicals and officials and schoolmasters in *Zeitgeist
und Bernergeist*, are sheer caricatures ; the last-mentioned novel
has a viciousness in it which is destructive of art—though,
like *The Cheese Factory* and *The Peasant in Debt*, it is rich in
scenes and characters of the best Gotthelf quality, when his
sympathy comes into play.

Gotthelf himself was confused in his conception of art. He
never emancipated himself completely from the views evident
in his diary of 1821, in which he identified beauty, in the

popular romantic way, with the picturesque, the idyllic, the exotic. It was only duty, he said at one time, that drove him to contemporary themes ; his own taste was for something more remote in time.[12] The artistic quality of his realistic novels entered in as it were by chance, without premeditation. ' I just flopped into writing novels. . . . If there is anything artistic about them, it is by instinct.' [13] His constant polemic against art is due to his identification of art with the faded romanticism of his day. Yet he recognised, too, that his more conventional historical and legendary short stories were his ' weak side ' ; [14] even of his best legendary tale, *The Black Spider*, which is framed within a delightful contemporary setting, he wrote that this was not ' the right path ' for him.[15]

He was indeed confronted with a formidable aesthetic problem, the question of the artistic properties of the realistic novel. Most of his remarks on the beauty that he sought to represent in them show a decidedly moral interpretation of beauty. Every man, he writes, can give aesthetic delight if he expresses, in his being and actions, the spirit that ' moves invisibly within him '. A fence skilfully made can have ' more spirit ' than many so-called cultural products.[16] Uli's skill as a worker shows that he is ' a man with a soul '.[17] A fruitful landscape, a well-tended farm, a clean and orderly house, are beautiful. Feeding pigs and painting pictures are equally noble tasks : which is the better ' is a matter of the loyal spirit ' in which the task is done.[18] In this passage Gotthelf jocularly calls the pigs ' natural art-products ', and obstreperously takes sides for practical work against ' art ' ; but underlying his thought is the belief, which he can hardly find words to justify, that pig-feeding, fence-making, hay-making, can be beautiful : that beauty arises in some manner from the satisfactory accomplishment of human duties.[19] His love of the vital powers of man leads him, in conscious derision of ideals of elegance and propriety, to delight in a coarse, earthy exuberance and grotesque humour that links him with Rabelais and Fischart. He may also be associated with Dickens and Balzac in respect to the immense material richness of their imaginative worlds and their defiance of conventional artistic canons. The words of Georg Büchner might be applied to Gotthelf : ' I demand in all things—life, vitality, and that's enough ; we do not need to ask whether it is lovely or ugly.' [20]

At the beginning of *Les Paysans* Balzac writes : ' I am going to make you dream with real things ', instead of ' delicious fancies '. This is what Gotthelf sets out to do ; but he would add, ' in order to tell you how you should behave '. He gives us a world which is in many respects a faithful mirror of actual persons and circumstances, admired as such by his contemporaries who knew the actuality. At the same time he gives us characters such as have never existed, which yet have all the substantiality of truth.[21]   With an unrivalled knowledge of peasant psychology and the ' technique and tactics ' [22] of peasant life, he has created stories of entrancing ideality, which, for all their faults, have an artistic form in the whole and in the parts which arises out of the very particularity of their conception and intention. We have to seek to define the secrets of his composition and form. But first we have to enquire into the philosophical principles which drove this clergyman to construct his dreams out of the elements of actual social life, and to make an improved participation in real social activity the purpose of the aesthetic experience.

GOTTHELF'S RELIGIOUS OUTLOOK

The themes of Gotthelf's novels are always social. They grow out of the moral, psychological, religious problems and development of his characters, a development which not only takes place in a precise social and practical environment, but is shaped and proven by this environment. Moral qualities are exactly mirrored in the farm, the family and the village community ; goodness or badness is expressed in the most tangible forms of well-being or disorder, prosperity or bankruptcy, harmony or discord. Thus social activities enter as a decisive element into Gotthelf's system of values ; he gives them a spiritual meaning, he ' sanctifies ' the practical world, as one critic states.[23]   Just as we can find the source of Keller's realism in his materialism, so we can discover the source of Gotthelf's in his religious outlook.

As a student and a clergyman Gotthelf's chief interest was the practical work of a parish priest, primarily in a rural community. He took no part in theological controversies, except to insist that the first responsibility of the Church was to the great mass of the common people. What his actual personal beliefs were cannot be defined with precision. He knew the main trends in modern theology, particularly the ' scientific ' school of Germany, and had studied the modernist D. F. Strauss. In a letter he darkly hints at unorthodoxy in his private opinions :

There was a time when I was a materialistic rationalist, and many would still call me so, if I were to dispute with them over Balaam's ass, and the prophet Jonah, over the corporeal begetting of Christ, the descent into Hell . . . Yet I am no rationalist, for such a man only recognises as true what lies within the frontiers of human knowledge. For where would faith come in, surmise ? Yet I am also not among the supernaturalists, and would never defend a single so-called miracle with such and in their way . . . I take miracles as they are given, and use my reason neither to defend them nor to attack them.[24]

But from the rare remarks about his private beliefs we can construct very little ; and in any case to little point. What was important for Gotthelf, and is important in his work, is the religion he preached and advocated for public use. His violent opposition to village sectarians, to advocates of a more inward religion, to the modern philosophical school of theologians, was not based essentially on theological disagreement but on his conviction that these trends were harmful to the moral and practical needs and the spiritual constitution of the common people.

Gotthelf expressed his point of view several times, and with emphasis. In the letter of 1840, already quoted, he goes on to justify the established church as the outward form of a ' firm faith ', because this form ' represents the standpoint of the masses ' and is the avenue to the hearts of the people. It would be sin on the part of the preacher to throw his inmost

thoughts among the people ; he has to ' hold to and master '
what is established ' through the people ', and ' bring life into
it '. The people believe in Heaven and Hell ; the preacher
must not confuse them with more complicated thoughts.[25]
Thus too he insisted on the necessity of ' precise ecclesiastical
forms '.[26]

As he grew older, he identified himself more and more with
the beliefs and practices of his flock—his partisanship for the
traditionalist peasant grew in every way as he grew more
alienated from the political movement of reform. In the
earlier books, however, the dichotomy between his private and
public tenets is consciously grasped and justified, most fully in
the behaviour and arguments of the wise parson in *The Schoolmaster*. As opposed to the parson at Schnabelweide, who
ignores both the practical and intellectual interests of his flock,
and the rash parson at Gytiwyl, who is always alienating the
peasants by his reforming zeal, the wise parson seeks to improve
his flock by shrewd tactics, playing on their weaknesses, hiding
his own beliefs in order bit by bit to raise the peasants out of
their stupid practices and superstitious religion. Thus he tells
the schoolmaster, one must not start telling the peasants about
natural science, but for the time being must encourage them
in their belief that the lightning is sent by God, for if they
begin to doubt this sort of thing, they will start to doubt
everything, and the whole structure of their morality will
collapse.[27]

To some extent, therefore, Gotthelf's religious principles,
particularly as advocated in his homiletic works, in which his
novels are to be included, were tactics. Yet here we discover
a profound philosophical principle, which has the most
direct relevance to his artistic realism. It is the most general
form of his recognition of the truth and validity of the outer
world. In *Anne Bäbi* he asserts that there are two holy books
given by God to man, the Bible and life, and that true religion
arises from the study of both.[28] The body is created by God
as well as the soul, each penetrates the other, and both need
equally careful tending.[29] Thus he sharply attacked all excessive preoccupation with the state of the soul, because it injures

practical life and with that the soul itself. He shows how an ascetic vicar, with his insistence on sin and contrition, so confuses a simple woman, Anne Bäbi, that she attempts the worst crime, suicide. His continual attacks on sectaries were based on the same principle (continual attendance at prayer-meetings means that dinner is not ready to time, and family-harmony destroyed), and brought his closest friends to expostulate over his injustice to their characters and intentions.[30]

As a result there is a forthright materialistic, secular flavour to Gotthelf's religion. Moral goodness and badness are rewarded and punished in a direct and tangible fashion in terms of material welfare ; rewards come, if not as the direct outcome of hard work and piety, at any rate as ' poetic justice ', as a gift from Heaven, through the unexpected rescuer like Hagelhans in *Uli the Tenant Farmer*, the salary-increase at the end of *The Schoolmaster*, the inheritance in *The Mirror of Peasants*, the nobleman in *The Peasant in Debt* ; or as a divine punishment like the sudden death of the wicked Hans in *Zeitgeist und Bernergeist*. The destruction of Uli's crops by the hailstorm is taken by all the characters as a judgement of God. No wonder Keller described Gotthelf's deity as ' the ancient weather-God ',[31] though if we examine more closely this and similar incidents we actually see that Gotthelf is careful to show that he is defining the peasant's view, not his own, in such cases. The interweaving of the material and spiritual called forth protests of a more subtle character from Gotthelf's religious colleagues. A correspondent said no one would think the author of the novels was an evangelical clergyman ; they smack of pantheism, Hegelianism ![32] Religious reviewers wrote that Uli the farmhand was led by circumstances, not by principles. To the latter Gotthelf answered that this is true, but therein lies ' the higher connection ', i.e. Uli is none the less led by God.[33] Gotthelf not only enjoyed, in a most robust fashion, the achievements and simple pleasures of peasant life, but he also, provocatively, relates them to the highest spiritual values. Thus, in *Uli the Farmer*, he says the call to the harvest-feast, after the hard days in the fields, is a foretaste of the call to Heaven.[34] Anne Mareili, after dropping in on a confirmation class, identifies her lover's home with Heaven ' in an almost blasphemous manner ', writes a modern commentator.[35]

It is not my concern to examine here the validity of Gotthelf's religious principles. Keller already noticed how suited his religious conceptions were to the isolated peasantry of whom he wrote. Their greatest shortcoming is that they allow for no change in the peasantry ; just as Gotthelf fought bitterly to preserve the peasantry in its old-fashioned mode of life, so he fought bitterly against the new religious ideas which accompanied the modernisation of Swiss society. In his early works, indeed, he is concerned for a gradual and cautious ' enlightenment ' of his peasants ; but with the growth of radicalism, which he more and more interpreted as an anti-religious movement, he fought in the last ditch on the religious as well as the political front. It is, however, the meaning of his religious attitude in relation to his art that concerns us here. His subordination of all other considerations to the practical and social welfare of his flock, his veneration of practical life in its peasant-form, his ' sanctification ' of practical life, is the philosophical key to his art. No other German writer describes with such love, and such truth, the whole circle of earthly tasks. He is a puritan of the true line, for whom service in this world is service to God :

> Who sweeps a room as for Thy sake
> Makes that and the action fine.

His realism, in all the complex meaning of the word, springs from this deep respect, this reverence, for earthly life ; for all his savage intolerance and his narrowness, which prevented him from writing about other social classes with any truth or understanding, Gotthelf is inspired, with regard to the peasantry of his time and parish, with the humanism which is at the root of all the great German novelists, from Goethe to Thomas Mann. The artistic weakness of his last novels, *Zeitgeist und Bernergeist* and *The Peasant in Debt*, must in the last resort be be ascribed to the weakening of his faith in man, or more exactly, of his faith in man's capacity to create social forms in which the best human powers can flourish.

THE PRINCIPLE OF COMPOSITION

Gotthelf is justly admired for the brilliance of his ' scenes from village life '. With an intimate knowledge of rural life, he describes peasant characters, not greatly diverse, in the ever-recurring round of their lives, with an incomparable freshness and humorous tolerance. Yet his purpose was not at all to depict or explain this class to remote townsfolk ; he did not, like Auerbach, deliberately exploit a new literary field. Nor did he seek out, like the Romantics, those aspects of rural life which suited certain aesthetic or metaphysical require-ments. He stands firmly within peasant life, and his object is to show how this life may be made spiritually and prac-tically a success, a moral problem of dire urgency to him as to his characters. His main novels turn on decisions of vital material and moral importance which face the main characters, through which the personality fully establishes itself. The principle of composition is the development of personality at these points of decision.

Some of his novels are weak precisely because the characters fail to develop. His first novel, *The Mirror of Peasants*, is unsatisfactory since the hero is too much of an ' innocent ' to experience any great expansion or deepening of his being (like Oliver Twist or David Copperfield). In *Zeitgeist und Bernergeist*, the good and the bad peasant and their wives and children all lack inward development and therefore seem rigid and stereotyped. The hero of *The Peasant in Debt* and his wife, who earn our respect and sympathy by their hard work, owe their material failure largely to their spiritual narrowness,[36] and for this very reason the book fails aesthetically. *Käthi the Grandmother*, lacking spiritual struggle and development, inclines towards the idyll. These stories are in many ways as ' true to life ' as the great novels ; but they are more the story of circumstances than of people, they do not uncover the potential resources of the peasant character. As a rule, Gotthelf seems wisely to have reserved the short-story form, the Novelle, for tales in which the characters are set from the beginning, e.g. excellent sketches like *Hans Joggeli der Erbvetter* or *Michels Brautschau*.[37]

The development of which Gotthelf's peasant characters are capable is strictly limited within the potentialities of their mode of life. They move, as it were, within two concentric rings, the centre of which is formed by the practical necessities of the farm and family. In the narrower ring they accomplish what is necessary to keep the farm together, to lead a life that is secured and decent. But they can break through to the wider ring, where spiritual needs greater than those of immediate material interest are tended, where the farm is seen as a trust received from the past to be delivered to the children, where marriage is not merely a practical partnership but also a spiritual companionship, where the family becomes a spiritual entity. In both cases, the characters move in a world of clear objective values, and goodness lies in conforming with material and moral necessities. Thus, in the last resort, the theme is the moral energy which this form of life engenders. In some of his characters this moral energy is perilously intense, as with Anne Bäbi, whose almost dæmonic devotion to her family turns her obstinate protective instinct into a fearful threat for her child and grandchildren ; Eisi, in *The Bankruptcy*, has something of the same dæmonism which enables her to come unbroken through the miseries of bankruptcy. As a rule, however, Gotthelf is not capable of depicting, like Balzac, the energy of evil ; evil appears usually with him as the outcome of the calculating and petty egoism of radicals, or the foolishness of a Hunghafen Hans, or the weakness of character of the malignant Joggeli and his innkeeper son. He is above all concerned with the resources of good.

In itself, skilful work and management shows this inward power, which Gotthelf unhesitatingly labels as the ' divine ' element in man. It is Uli's skill as a farmhand, we are told, that marks him as ' a man with a soul ' instead of a ' clod '.[38] In the first chapter of *Uli the Farmer*, Gotthelf defines three decisive stages in a man's life, where his inner quality comes to light : first, in the choice of a mate, ' in the struggle for which the man's divine shape first shines forth'; then, in the struggle for material prosperity, the founding of a secure family existence ; then, in the resistance against crude materialism, the recognition that man exists not so much to acquire wealth as to content his soul. Thus most of his stories are love-stories : not in the sense that they lead to a conventional happy end, but in the sense that in his choice of and struggle for a wife a man shows what his quality is ; thus too his stories often continue into married life where the struggle is renewed in a different form. Keller pointed out how materialistic are the calculations that lead Gotthelf's peasants to the choice of a wife.[39] A cash-dowry may not be essential, but the girl must be healthy, hard-working, sweet-tempered, if Gotthelf is to approve the match ; and he is extremely harsh to matches which are promoted by sentiment alone. Keller added that such calculations are necessary in the peasant-class, where the woman must preside over an extremely important group of tasks. But he is wrong in suggesting that ' love ' does not enter into these matches.[40] On the contrary, the marriages of Peter Käser, Uli, Jakobli Jowäger, Resli, Felix are true love-matches. But the love of the men is deter-mined not by feeling which is dissociated from or at variance with their practical lives, but by a feeling whose genuineness is due to the fact that their whole disposition is shaped by the obligations and honours of peasant life. That their feeling chooses a suitable girl shows how solid and monolithic is their character.[41] Their calculations are sometimes less true than their feelings, but we are not misled by their failure sometimes to think as clearly as they feel.

The two *Uli* novels unfold the potentialities and the prob-lematic of peasant existence more fully than the others, for Uli, a destitute farmhand, has to win his way to independent ownership, while most of the other young heroes are well-established by birth. His own good nature leads him to respond with trust to the moral counsel and practical help of his first master, Johannes. Under his guidance he becomes an excellent worker and learns to abjure the normal pleasures of the farmhand—the inn, sports and merry-making, girls.

He becomes foreman at a rich but neglected farm, and there establishes order and prosperity. With his savings he may now think of marriage, and he naturally thinks of a peasant heiress, his master Joggeli's daughter, who flirts with him, and then marries a tradesman. In a parallel situation to his, Vreneli, an illegitimate poor relation of the farmer, manages the women's side of the farm, always humiliated by the farmer and his daughter. But though they are close allies and friends, Uli does not think of marrying a poor girl like her. Both, at the end of their patience with their perverse master, decide to leave the farm. The farmer's wife, afraid for the future if they go, conceives the plan of marrying them and handing the farm over to them on lease. She takes them on a two-day excursion to Uli's old master, which itself suggests a wedding-trip. On the way she unfolds her plan, and Uli begins to see how advantageous and agreeable it is ; Vreneli, more sensitive than Uli, puts up a stout resistance, for she fears that Uli's readiness is based more on calculation than on love and respect. Only on the morning after their return, when they meet at the water-trough to wash, does their feeling suddenly overcome them both. Even on the wedding-trip, Vreneli has to chide Uli for his concern with money, and though he responds to her spirit, we can detect a source of future struggle.

Uli has made his way to a ' happy ending ' through hard work and thrift. But the second volume, written some years later, rudely shatters any sentimental illusions the reader might have nursed. After a first prosperous year, Uli shows himself over-anxious at the harvest-feast about the cost of the obligatory hospitality. He becomes obsessed by saving, and begins to cut down expenses, dismissing good workers and engaging poorer ones at lower wages. He quarrels with his wife over her freer hand, for she tries to live up modestly to the charitable obligations of a farmer's wife. He tricks a peasant over the sale of a defective beast and gets involved in a lawsuit, in spite of the plain reproofs of his wife. Vreneli at first, in her customary spirited way, keeps up her end, and they are in a fair way to becoming a ' typical ' couple, a close-fisted, narrow-minded husband and a nagging wife. But she learns, with the help of the old farmer's wife, to be patient and gentle, and to try to influence him indirectly. He is reformed at the end, but, and this is typical in Gotthelf, only with the help of massive material allies. The peasant he has swindled curses him ; and as he hastens home from the law-court, troubled in his conscience, he sees a terrible hailstorm destroy his crops and end his hope of independence. He takes it as a judgement of God, and has a nervous collapse, which is succeeded by a dangerous illness. In his slow convalescence, nursed by his wife and helped by old friends, Uli comes to see that he had almost lost the truly valuable things in his obsession with money, and he resigns himself to a new start as a humble farmhand. Then again, in true Gotthelf fashion, a *deus ex machina* appears. Vreneli's father, a wealthy peasant, turns up, and sets them finally on their feet ; thus virtue is rewarded in the same way as Joggeli's moral failings and those of his son and daughter bring them ultimately to material distress.

It can be seen that Gotthelf in no sense attributes extravagant moral powers to Uli or Vreneli. The first effort Uli makes, to subordinate everything to his goal of becoming a peasant, almost exhausts his moral resources. These exclusive qualities of thrift and labour, so essential to the labourer, threaten the farmer, who needs something more. Uli's success as a farm-hand almost fixes his character for ever, and he is rescued for a human existence only by the terrible shock of material disaster and the moral support of Vreneli and his first master. Within this framework the routine of farm life has from year to year a changing character, and appears ever fresh : his various visits to market, buying and selling beasts ; the first harvest-feast as a farmhand at Joggeli's, and the first as a farmer ; the excursion with Vreneli when they become betrothed, the later wedding-trip, and the trip that Vreneli makes to an old friend, when Uli goes out to meet her on her first absence from their home ; the storm at hay-harvest in the first book, and the hailstorm at the end. These are not consciously contrived parallels. The life is so regular and limited in range that its incidents are necessarily repeated, but always in fresh variations because of the change in moral situation and problem.

In the earlier book, *Sorrows and Joys of a Schoolmaster*, Gotthelf is less successful in showing development in his main character —perhaps because the parson-schoolmaster relationship was in actual life one of extreme difficulty. Peter Käser learns to behave as is fitting in a member of his profession, but he remains to the end perky and conceited, needing sorely the help of his wife, Mädeli, and the counsel of his friends the parson and the somewhat misanthropic Wehrdi. It is Mädeli, the daughter of a ne'er-do-well cobbler, who grows spiritually. She has a high ideal of her husband's calling, and fortifies him in his best impulses. When he asks her to marry him, in desperate need of someone to wash and mend and cook for him, she shyly asks how it is that he has not wooed her in the normal way, that is, by coming to her room at night ('Kiltgang'). He tells her that he has a higher ideal of courtship. But when her father ridicules his fancy-notions and tells him to spend the night with his daughter, Käser is ready to obey ; and now it is Mädeli who insists that he goes home, and from this time it is she who takes the lead, caring for her father and malicious mother-in-law, bringing up the children, reading the Bible and asking her husband what it means, so that he has to reflect over things he has hitherto taught mechanically. Unfortunately the form of this novel is seriously damaged in two ways. The story is told by Käser in the first person, and, as Gotthelf's friends noted, this ignorant little schoolmaster makes comments which are quite out of character. And in the second volume we are taken into extensive details about school reforms in the Canton that have merely an historical interest.

In composition *Anne Bäbi Jowäger* is the most complex of all Gotthelf's works, and the most dramatic. Here all the characters develop, all actively contribute to a first dire crisis which is solved by the marriage of Jakobli, and beyond it to fresh crises which severely test them all. Anne Bäbi is the devoted wife and mother who rules the household with her sharp and dreaded tongue. She spoils her little son with her suffocating care, and almost kills him through her obstinate belief that his small-pox can be cured by quack remedies ; he becomes a suppressed, melancholy simpleton. When a wise woman tells them that marriage will cure him, she sets about contriving a marriage that threatens disaster to them all. Terrified of the strapping would-be bride and her rapacious family, Jakobli manages to thwart his mother's plans by falling ill. With the monosyllabic support of the farmhand Sämeli, and the vociferous help of the old maid, Mädi, who thinks he really wants to marry her, he frees himself and marries a simple affectionate orphan. The father, accustomed to bear his wife's nagging in silence, rouses himself to protect the girl and his son, and Anne Bäbi becomes reconciled to this meek and cheerful daughter-in-law, whom she can favour and bully. When a child is born, she takes charge absolutely, and actually kills the child with her ignorant solicitude. Almost deranged by a young vicar's talk about sin, she attempts to commit suicide. This character develops a baleful power that almost extinguishes the life of the family ; and yet she is in essence the very principle of the family. Mädi the maid is a variant of her mistress, for she too only enjoys grumbling and furious outbursts of temper, and yet she too is utterly attached to the family.

The timid, suppressed, pock-marked Jakobli takes the first step to independence almost unconsciously, escaping an unwelcome marriage by falling ill : with the same passive resistance, when the girl's relatives come to try to hold them to the contract, he and his father outwit them by the simple ruse of hiding in the farm-buildings. He can woo Meyeli only because his mother, in high dudgeon, washes her hands of any further plans, and the way in which he wooes and marries his bride gives her the worst forebodings about the treatment she will receive at the hands of his mother. Jakobli can in fact never protect her from his mother. But a process of moral development has actually been set up in him. When the first child is born, Jakobli suddenly starts to think of the future, to buy fresh stock, to build bigger middens, to acquire more

I

fields. For the first time, to the astonishment of his father,
he shows initiative. And it is characteristic of Gotthelf's truthfulness that these new interests threaten to drive everything
else out of his narrow head, and he begins to neglect his wife,
not noticing that she is ailing.

Meyeli is a willing, devoted girl, accustomed to serve and
demanding little in return. Less robust than most of Gotthelf's
' heroines ', and necessarily playing a minor part in Anne
Bäbi's household, she develops in a way which has no parallel
in Gotthelf's other novels. She gropes after something deeper
than the practical relationships of the farm, and strikes up a
timid friendship with the country doctor and the parson's
family. This friendship cannot take her outside the peasant
world ; but her grief at the doctor's death reveals spiritual
capacities which cannot be satisfied within the practical scope
of peasant life. Gotthelf seems not to have been able to find
an outward shape for these inner stirrings in Meyeli, for in
the later stages of the book the novel takes us into a new
sphere, that of the doctor and the parson's family, which
stands somewhat apart from the main theme of the novel.
The book closes abruptly as Meyeli enters the parsonage to
share her grief with the parson's daughter. The ending of
other books is abrupt, but in a different way. Readers often
wanted to know more about the future fate of his characters,
but Gotthelf felt that, having set them on a clear course, he
had said enough. In Meyeli's case, however, there is a real
indeterminacy ; we cannot guess what will come out of these
stirrings within her.[42]

It will have been noticed that the more profound spiritual
struggles take place in Gotthelf's women, and in this respect
he is true to the social class he is describing. The peasant
woman must have many of the characteristics of the man—
she is in charge of house and maids, the provider of food,
responsible for the vegetable garden, for hemp-patch and flax-
patch, for the butter and eggs and pigs ; in the smaller households she works in the fields, too, and sells on the market.
But she is also responsible for the children, and for the poor :
her spirit decides the moral quality of the home. She may

become a tyrant and gossip, the variety of her tasks invites her to be a slut, her seclusion makes her ignorant. She must reckon with menfolk who are absorbed in practical tasks and have nothing gentle or subtle in their make-up ; and in hardship, for instance on the loss of a child, she may easily become melancholy, or seek comfort in sectarian religion, neglecting her duties. The peculiar task Gotthelf sets his ' heroines ' is to learn patience and forebearance, to turn from a lion to a lamb like Vreneli, without losing grip on practical duties. It is usually a hard task, needing the sustenance of sanctions and examples bearing a religious, supernatural authority. The peculiar capacity and obligation of the peasant woman provide the dynamic of the first part of *Money and Spirit*, which deals more expressly than any other of Gotthelf's novels with the religious element in peasant life.

The setting is a harmonious family, a wealthy and honoured peasant, slow and conservative, a wife who is active and bountiful in the traditional way, with their three grown-up children. The husband, Christen, through ignorance and an ' aristocratic ' self-confidence, loses £250 for which he has been trustee, and he takes the damage to his property and his honour very much to heart. He urges his wife to be less open-handed with the poor, and when she persists, an alienation begins which affects the whole household. The married couple no longer repeat together the Lord's Prayer before going to sleep—communal grace and prayer are always in Gotthelf a sign and means of family unity and well-being. Both feel resentful and injured. On the Sunday before Whitsun, Christen asks for a cake with his coffee, and finds that Aenneli has given the last away to her clientèle. There is a sharp flare-up, the children take sides, and Resli, the heir, asks bitterly what people will say if they hear that they have been quarrelling again, and on a Sunday.

The word strikes home in Aenneli's heart, for in the narrow peasant community public esteem is the touchstone of personal self-esteem. What, she thinks, will people say if no one from their house goes to Church, the public meeting-place, on this Sunday before Whitsun ? She goes, alone and miserable,

and straightway finds comfort in being among the congregation.   The parson preaches on the Last Supper, and exhorts
them all to consider each meal as if it were their last.   Aenneli
goes home pondering what memory she would leave behind
if she were suddenly to die.

Her daughter has got dinner ready, Resli is anxiously looking
out for her.   Christen has spent the morning dully and hopelessly turning things over in his mind.   They eat in silence,
each thinking the others are resentful and angry, and quickly
separate.   Aenneli stays in the deserted house and weeps.
Roused by a chance visit, she walks round the buildings, sees
how the pigs, the flax, the fruit are flourishing, gazes over the
goodly fields, and reflects how all this rich beauty comes from
the harmonious mingling of sky and earth ; and quickly trans-
poses the thought into that of the harmony between Heaven
and man, the spiritual harmony that brings blessing to human
relationships.   She knows she is ' the hinge on which the fate
of the house turns ', and therefore feels that she bears the
essential responsibility for the quarrel ; with ' heroic humility '
she decides to take the first step to reconciliation by reciting
that night the Lord's Prayer.   When the others come home in
the evening, she pours out the coffee herself, serving Christen
first, and giving him the skim of the milk, which he particularly
likes.   The atmosphere lightens, and Christen becomes so talka-
tive that the children think he has spent the afternoon drinking.
When the others have gone to bed, Aenneli goes round the
house, tidies everything, locks the door, sees that the fire is
out, and with a beating heart goes up to bed.   After a hard
struggle, likened to that in the Garden of Gethsemane, she
begins to say ' Our Father ' ; Christen jerks bolt upright in
bed ' as if the fire-bell had rung ', and joins in.   Weeping,
they beg each other's forgiveness ; peace is restored.

The children discover it indirectly, for the next day Christen
is always popping into the kitchen to light his pipe, while
Aenneli is always running out to the stables to ask him a
question.   Christen tells Resli he must go to Berne market to
buy some fresh stock, a tremendous privilege for the youngster,
while Aenneli starts planning some new dresses for her daughter.

On the Saturday evening they tell their children of the wrong they had done, and propose that they all go to Church the following morning. The parson takes as his theme the need to detach oneself from worldly goods and to prepare oneself in spirit for the next world, and they all feel the message is for them, confirming their new harmony.

What has happened? The parson (and Gotthelf) talks in religious terms; but this religious message is embodied and fulfilled in purely secular, practical terms. Aenneli, and her family, are enabled to rise above the immediate, brutish response to the situation; they are lifted out of an unreflecting routine to a high vantage-point with a far perspective. They recognise that they are members of a community; they see the farm as a whole, the year as a whole, the family as a whole. Special circumstances and rites are necessary to enable them to achieve this new and truer view: the special quality of Sunday, the solemnity of Church, the congregation, the deathly, Sunday stillness round the house, the mysterious elevation of sermon and prayer.

And what is the outcome? Immediately, the question of Resli's marriage is raised, to which the rest of the novel is devoted. Readers have often criticised the book for falling, in fact, into two unrelated halves; yet between these two halves there is the closest tie. The religious experience has not turned these peasants away from life, but to it, and in a new sense. The parents recognise that they are growing old, that they must provide for the future, that they must give way to their children. They face the reality of the whole process of life, but gladly, objectively. Aenneli indeed has a presentiment that she will soon die, and is serenely set on seeing that a new mistress shall be there to take over when she goes; the novel closes, not with the marriage of Resli, but with the death of Aenneli, at which the lovers come together: the lesson of their experience is that death and marriage are not an end or a beginning, but productive functions in the life-process of the family. This wonderfully delicate book is the fullest exposition in Gotthelf's work of the function of religion in the peasant family; it is the peasant's philosophy, through which he can rise to understand and control the totality of his life.

The title of the novel, *Money and Spirit, Geld und Geist*, (' Geist ' here is a very difficult word to translate), seems at first sight less applicable to the story of Resli's courtship. Resli loves the daughter of a wealthy farmer, and their marriage is entirely suitable from a material, monetary point of view. Anne Mareili's father is a coarse, tyrannical, miserly man, who plans to marry his daughter to an old man so that his family will inherit the latter's property ; the two lovers stand in opposition not to any interests of their own, but solely to an avaricious father.   But, as Grob has shown, what distinguishes their love-story and gives it its peculiar delicacy is the manner in which they vary from the typical, while remaining within peasant-bounds.   On their first meeting at a dance, they do not reveal the ' famous ' names of the families to which they belong, since they wish to be taken at their own worth.   Both are so deeply aware of the significance of marriage that they are slow to admit their love, and Anne Mareili confesses hers by mutely placing her hand in Resli's and bursting into tears. Her father is willing to allow her to marry him, providing a contract is signed by which Resli disinherits his brother and sister, and this Resli refuses to do, even though Anne Mareili bitterly resents his abandoning her.   And only after dropping in on a confirmation class does Anne Mareili forgive him, and walk to his home to place herself unreservedly and humbly in his hands.   Their marriage is the victory of youth and love, but it has a deep spirituality because it springs from the candour and moral seriousness of their characters.   While it conforms with all the essential conditions of peasant life, it shows at all points a victory over the merely practical and conventional.

The later novels are coarser in fibre.   Felix, of *The Cheese Factory in Vehfreude*, the arrogant son of the wealthiest peasant of a village, loves a poor orphan, and bit by bit his love makes him gentler and more respectful to her ; but in his social behaviour he remains a tough, class-proud ' aristocrat ' to the end.   In *Zeitgeist und Bernergeist* all the characters are fixed from the beginning, moral superiority consists in conformity with Gotthelf's political views, and material prosperity is the crass test of morality.   In *The Peasant in Debt* a *deus ex machina* (a wealthy, crusty, conservative old landowner) ensures that hard work and thrift lead to a happy end.

Individual scenes and characters are as brilliant in these novels as in Gotthelf's best.   But he is so involved in denigrating radicals and politicians that he tends to be content simply with static descriptions of the ' worthy ' peasants, as if their mode of life and character were good in itself.   Our sympathy is claimed on principle, and there is only the slightest indication in Felix or Anne Marei of that deepening of character, that development of moral personality, which forms the theme and the principle of composition of the greatest novels.

THE TECHNIQUE OF GOTTHELF'S REALISM

A duality in Gotthelf's artistic quality was recognised from the first by his closest friends, for they admired both the truth of his representation of peasant circumstances and characters, and the ideality of his moral purpose and of certain of his characters.[43]   He defined his aim as ' to place conditions clearly and vividly before the eyes of the people ', ' to reproduce the face of the people ';[44] yet he commonly omitted from his novels certain aspects of peasant life, and gave a subjective colouring to many others.[45]   He was concerned to create exemplary characters and exemplary decisions, even though he did not cross the frontier of the possible ;   he was always, and emphatically, a clergyman, writing with didactic and religious intention.

But the ambiguity of his ' realism ' arises essentially from a vulgar interpretation of this term.   If realism is defined as ' the reproduction of reality ', Gotthelf is no realist : in any case such a phrase is meaningless.   Introducing a work which professed to be truthful reportage, *The Floods in the Emmental*, Gotthelf recognised the limitations of the realistic writer :

The author has described as faithfully as possible what he saw and heard.   Those who have experienced such events know how

men see with different eyes, how differently they apply colours to
what they have seen. Later it is impossible to decide who has
seen correctly and told correctly, and all one can do is to eliminate
what bears obvious marks of delusion or deceit.[46]

The problem of realism arises, however, from something
else than the inevitable partiality of a particular point of view.
In this very work of reportage, by far the most illuminating
incident is the purely imaginary scene suggesting the drought,
where a peasant, disturbed in his sleep by the disconsolate
lowing of his beasts, gets up in the dark to count his savings,
and sets out with a heavy heart to buy hay. It is this power
of abstracting from reality, of condensing it, reducing it to a
new shape, that makes Muschg say that Gotthelf ' creates out
of nothing ' [47]—a phrase which is patently untrue, and yet
usefully calls attention to a creative activity that is common
to all the great realists. It is right to call him a ' realistic
novelist ' because of his fundamental and successful effort to
present to us, with a deep, often humorous tolerance, the
essential characteristics, material and moral, of a social group ;
because he reaches after no other values than are realisable in
social practice, convinced that this social world of the peasantry
has a dignity worthy of all human effort. The term involves,
too, his whole attitude to his art, which was not for him a
means of self-purification, irrelevant indeed to any inward,
personal problems he might have had, but directed with great
simplicity of intention to the improvement of man within the
bounds set by actuality. His artistic technique must be
appraised therefore, not in the light of any aesthetic dogma,
but in relation to the whole intention of his work.

It is scarcely necessary to observe that Gotthelf treats the
passage of time not naturalistically, but according to the needs
of his conception of the story. He can pass over a long period
rapidly, and expatiate on those moments when a significant
event, a significant conversation reveal a moral situation or a
crisis. Nor has time for him a value in itself, he does not
conceive development as a slow imperceptible growth, as it
appears for instance in *Wilhelm Meister*. His characters are
not, like those of the ' Bildungsroman ' proper, young people

who are slowly, obscurely taking shape as they grow up. They are 'led by circumstances', they develop through precise outer stimuli. Time is for him a process of connected events, and his theme is events, the concrete substantial events in the process of the year, in the process of a lifetime, through which the characters establish themselves in their rock-like individuality.

Though all the elements in Gotthelf's characters are observed from experience, his characters are never ordinary. These elements are concentrated, and the story is contrived so that they appear, even in their complexity, in pure and essential form. The characters possess an intensity of life which rarely if ever is met with in experience, like the characters of Balzac. Gotthelf said that there are Anne Bäbis everywhere, tyrannous, pig-headed scolds ; but his Anne Bäbi is unique, she develops all the potentialities of the type, she is dæmonic. Precisely because the inner logic of her type is developed on such a scale, we come to true knowledge of all the modifications in which it ordinarily appears—just as we can best understand an experimental subject by submitting it to extreme tests. Gotthelf's method corresponds to that normal mode of judgement which leads us to recognise a unique specimen as a type : we say, ' So-and-so is a typical grandmother ', and we mean that she combines in an extraordinary degree, exceptionally, the various qualities which are usually present only partially in the grandmothers we know. Only the exception is the type.

Similarly, the incidents of Gotthelf's tales have an intensified simplicity that is life-like yet more than life-size. Gotthelf does not attempt to describe the whole year or all the occupations of peasants, but to distil out of them what Muschg has called ' the forces engendering and consuming life '.[48] The decisive events of peasant life are few, recurrent, and of great simplicity ; but, in presenting them in their peculiar significance as moments of moral testing, Gotthelf gives them an ' unnatural ' vividness. They absorb and develop the moral energy of his characters ; through them the lineaments of personality receive their stamp : nothing in the modern novel is nearer to the spirit of the ancient epic than these incidents.

When Meyeli enters the Jowäger household, the customary formulas of greeting, the attitude at the meal, are tense with meaning and decide future relationships. In betrothal scenes, the girl's shy reserve, and then her rush of speech as she speaks of practical matters, so often repeated in minor variations, sum up that combination of self-esteem and trust that ensures that the marriage is well founded. Uli's love of his wife, in a time when it is threatened by his obsession with money, emerges without conscious expression in that scene when, missing her sorely on her first absence from their home, he goes to meet her and brings her, footsore, back home in the trap. Such scenes are too numerous to mention. They have a poetic intensity which derives from the single-minded concentration of the characters on the event which, maybe trivial in itself, demands all their attention and reveals their innermost powers. Market-days always have this importance for the peasant ; in the novels they are thrilling incidents. When the inexperienced peasants of Vehfreude go to the great cheese-market at Langnau to seek a buyer for the first products of the communal cheese factory, the bustle and confusion reaches bewildering, almost terrifying proportions. So too, the subsequent delivery of the cheeses to the merchant is an event of capital importance. All the village is involved in the preparation of the horse-teams and carts, and the young peasants drive through the countryside like young heroes ; the drive home develops into a chariot-race. From time to time Gotthelf jocularly compares his peasants with the Homeric heroes, and the comparison bears examination.

Gotthelf's technique in these scenes is not realistic in the vulgar sense. He simplifies or magnifies an incident in order to reveal its meaning to an individual or a community, even though the persons concerned are unconscious of its full bearing. Often, for serious or comic purposes, he allows himself exaggeration. In *The Cheese Factory*, Felix's protracted bargaining over the sale of a pair of horses, through which he comes into daily contact with the family of his beloved, takes on a monumental character. When Uli and Vreneli, as farmers, give their first harvest-feast, beggars and dependents come ' snowing ' along, begging for alms and crowding round the kitchen door, and the farmhands themselves eat and drink without end. If a wealthy peasant lad is seeking a wife, the farmhouses buzz with gossip, pedlars chase here and there with messages, mothers and girls go visiting, the whole country-side is agog. Gotthelf's humour often takes a grotesque turn, like that of Rabelais or Fischart ; but it is a means to reveal, with a kindly tolerance, the characteristic preoccupations and values of the class he describes.

Because these incidents are conceived dynamically, in rela-tion to a particular moral situation, they have great variety and individuality ; yet the underlying purpose of Gotthelf's art is to reveal the typical. His tales are designed as typical events, typical problems, and these again are ordered according to the actual standing of the persons : the wealthy peasant, the small farmer, the labourer, the innkeeper. Often indeed he is unduly sweeping in his summation of individuals under classes, and at times he gives maids and servants, innkeepers, religious sectaries, lawyers and townsfolk only the general abstract characteristics of a disliked type. He has a trick of style, sometimes effective, sometimes irritating, which illustrates this search for the typical. Often he gives in outline, as an ' author's comment ', a typical occurrence ; and then shows his characters conforming to the rule. He describes a peasant home on a Sunday afternoon, the wife disturbed by a visitor, her walk round the farm ; and then we see how it actually happens thus.[49] The course and outcome of Gritli's spa-visit is exactly foretold.[50] In *The Peasant in Debt* the innkeeper describes at the beginning how ignorant peasants are cheated by sharpers, and the novel itself simply fills in this framework. Sometimes he will describe a typical reaction, and continue : ' But it was not so with these people ',[51] indicating two or more typical modes of behaviour.

Behind the vividness and individuality of Gotthelf's scenes and characters, we always discover the typical, and an examina-tion of his style shows how consistently it serves this purpose.

Take for instance the opening of *Anne Bäbi Jowäger*, one of the
rare examples of set description in Gotthelf's novels :

> Hansli Jowäger was a good sort of man, and Anne Bäbi, his wife,
> meant well, but in her own fashion.   Hansli Jowäger still wore
> side-of-bacon coats, waistcoats with flaps over the pockets, and even
> though he did not wear knee-breeches, his trousers were slit up
> to the knee, and the long slit was rarely buttoned up.   His hat
> had no high crown ; but the brim was all the broader, and when
> he stumped it to market, he liked to rest his chin on his stick while
> he was bargaining for a cow.   His wife Anne Bäbi did not plague
> him on the score of vanity.   On high Sundays she wore her grand-
> mother's wedding-dress, and she saved her own wedding-dress for
> her offspring.   She still wore shoes with solid soles, but cut broad,
> so that she could hardly hang on with her toes, and she had as yet
> never spent a penny on fine Aargau aprons.   She would be
> shamed, she said, to slip such a rag on, in which you could not even
> blow your nose heartily without it poking out on the other side.
> Hemp and cotton mixture, that was the foundation of a household,
> she used to say.   Hansli Jowäger had married his Anne Bäbi
> only after the death of his mother, when both were well beyond
> thirty.   He did not want to annoy his mother with a daughter-in-
> law, he said ; everybody knows how it goes, when two stand at
> the same hearth.   The fruit of this marriage was a son, whom they
> called Jakobli and held dear as their only late scion, and who was
> to become a paragon of virtue and piety before God and man.

The opening sentence introduces the whole character of
these two peasants, not their appearance at a particular
moment.   Gotthelf tells us what Hansli *usually* wore, and adds
the negative ' he did not wear knee-breeches ' in order to
associate him indirectly with an even older fashion.   Straight
away he describes a typical activity, bargaining for a cow at
market, and a typical gesture.   Hansli is a typical small
peasant, shrewd in his narrow way, with rigid principles ; his
misguided piety to his mother foreshadows his forbearance
with regard to Anne Bäbi herself, avoiding difficulties rather
than meeting them.   The treatment is even more selective in
the description of Anne Bäbi.   She sees the world as fixed for
ever, is economical, shrewd in her narrow way, coarse, and
her whole wisdom is summed up in a small group of practical,
ever-repeated axioms.

Gotthelf uses many local and dialect terms in the passage, and reports the usual phrases of the two, which embody their wisdom. The repetition of their names gives a taste of their obstinate self-assertion. At the same time Gotthelf does not hide his identity as the story-teller ; the opening phrase, with the dialect ' uf sy Gattig ' ('in her own fashion '), indicates his critical detachment. He approaches his tale with a characteristic sympathetic humour, and he will not be chary with direct comment, guiding our response with value-judgements even in the very adjectives he uses. The last sentence is openly satirical, with the highfalutin ' scion ' and ' paragon ', like the word ' offspring ' earlier on. For all its precision, this opening paragraph does not give a mere static description. It sums up characters already shaped and established, a routine of life and work with which we are already on terms. So, we do not wait for something to happen in order to start the story off ; it has already started, and the next paragraph continues, quite naturally : ' Once, when Jakobli was two years old . . .'

Description and action are never separate in Gotthelf's work, as Keller pointed out.[52] He sees all situations under the aspect of the human energies which respond to them, make them, change them. A co-operative cheese factory may not seem promising material for a novel, and in *The Cheese Factory* Gotthelf does not shirk factual description of its working. But his account of the co-operative contract, the choice of a site, the making of the cheeses, the daily delivery of the milk, the tensions between the cheese-maker and the peasants, the passionate discussions in each home, the buying and selling of cows, the inquisitiveness over other people's deliveries, the watering of the milk, the highlights of the sale of the cheeses and the share-out at the end of the season, all these make a drama of fascinating intensity and often uproarious humour—not to speak of the struggle between wife and husband, for with the establishment of the factory a domestic revolution took place, in that the milk was transferred from the province of the woman to that of the man.

Even the landscape is rarely described, for nature is essentially the material of the peasant's labour, not an object of

contemplation. Gotthelf rudely polemised against the romantic
delight in picturesque scenes of nature, considering it a typical
falsification by the cultured townsfolk. A peasant, he writes,
observes on a journey only the practical things—not the
landscape or the tints, but the corn, beans, flax, and hemp.[53]
Gotthelf himself, the story-teller, scarcely ever pauses to observe
a scene ; such short nature descriptions as he gives are very
rare, and merge immediately into action ; usually nature and
man are mingled.

It was a cold morning, the mouth's breath seemed like heavy
smoke, the snow crunched under the feet, glittered and sparkled
like a field of diamonds, made the nose tight and cold, and there
was scarcely any difference any longer between a delicate maidenly
nose and an old brandy-nose.[54]

The gathering of the hailstorm in *Uli the Tenant Farmer* receives
exceptionally full treatment, but it does so because Uli sees
it coming as he hastens homewards, anxiously measuring his
pace against its speed ; there is a similar artistic principle
in the description of the storm when they are bringing in the
hay in *Uli the Farmhand*, for the desperate effort to outstrip the
storm brings Uli's anger with the slack farmhands to a head.[55]
Nature is described as an integral part of the peasant's
active experience. Gotthelf's peasants are not boors, blind to
the beauty of the landscape, but they can appreciate its beauty
only on very special occasions, when a particular event or
situation makes them peculiarly receptive. In the peace of
Sunday the peasant likes to lie on a hill, observing the fields
and the mountains beyond. The quarrel with her husband
makes Aenneli aware not only of the fruitfulness of the earth,
but also of its beauty. In a state of acute distress, more or
less ostracised by the community, Ankenbenz finds comfort in
the sight of the Alps under the moon, as he returns to his home ;
like Aenneli he sees sky and earth as symbols and lessons of
the greatness of God, but it is the beauty which drives the
lesson home.[56] Occasionally there are moments of interrup-
tion in the routine of the days, visits to distant friends or
wedding-trips, when the peasant lifts his eyes and sees the blue
Jura on one horizon, the snow-peaks on the other, and notices

the green of the grass, the cry of the migrant birds. When
Uli goes with Vreneli and the farmer's wife on the decisive
trip which is to end in a betrothal, the whole house is stirring
early, excited, in an unusual frame of mind, and as they set
out they see the Autumn landscape :[57]

> In a splendour of colour the withered leaves hung on the trees,
> in the lustre of their own evening glow ; beneath them stretched
> the young corn, green and cheerful, playing gaily with the sparkling
> dewdrops which were hanging on its spikes ; the sky extended
> mysterious and hazy over all, the mysterious womb of the wonders
> of God. Black crows flew over the ploughlands, green woodpeckers
> hung on the trees, swift squirrels ran across the road and inquisi-
> tively peeped at the passers-by from a quickly gained branch, and
> high in the air the snow-geese sailed in their well-marshalled
> triangle towards a warmer land, and strangely did their strange
> migratory song resound from the far height.

Enlivened by the scene, the travellers begin to speak—about
the farmhouses and the crops they pass ! The loveliness of
the scene enters their souls without comment ; its power is
indicated at most by the slightly elevated vocabulary and
rhythms Gotthelf uses.

The descriptions of human scenes and attitudes are likewise
embedded in the action. Gotthelf's resources in this respect
seem to be limitless, and every novel abounds in such scenes.
He can economically choose a single central symbol for a
whole situation, or can be richly expansive. The disaster of
the drought in *The Floods in the Emmental* or *The Cheese Factory*
is brought out by the constant lowing of the distressed cows ;
the tension between Uli and Vreneli appears subtly, on their
wedding-trip, when they argue in friendly fashion over Joggeli's
wedding-present. The conversation of Anne Bäbi flows in
torrential fashion, overwhelming everything. The discussion
of the peasant pair in *The Peasant in Debt* over the probable
price of a meal is miraculously plastic, an example of innumer-
able conversations in Gotthelf's novels. *The Bankruptcy* has a
whole series of customary scenes, from the funeral of the innkeeper to the selling-up of the inn—for instance, when it comes
to selling the wine in the cellar, the village women crowd

round the entrance, half-afraid to enter this arcanum, telling one another gruesome stories of the fabulous practices of inn-keepers with their wine ; they go down and forget their fears in sampling the wine. Carl Bitzius, Gotthelf's cousin and colleague, even had fears because of the brilliance of such scenes in this novel and *Käthi the Grandmother*. He told Gotthelf that this detail description (we might call it genre painting) should only be there for the sake of the action ; too much ' art ' of this kind would injure Gotthelf's moral purpose, it would appeal to the educated but not to the people for whom the books were written.[58] Carl Bitzius was over-simplifying the nature of Gotthelf's readers, and had far too narrow a view of his moral purpose, but this comment is valid in the general sense, and corresponds to Gotthelf's practice. These scenes never become, in the novels, an end in themselves, but are the signs and stages of a moral progress. Some of the short stories, on the other hand, seem to be almost sheer genre painting—what distinguishes *Michels Brautschau*, *Erbvetter Joggeli*, and *Wie Christen eine Frau gewinnt* from the novels is precisely the lack in them of spiritual development.

Gotthelf's technique of description is never impressionistic or naturalistic. He frequently uses general, typifying phrases like ' a lovely house ', ' in Sunday splendour ', etc. He allows himself the utmost freedom, selecting according to the degree of significance, terse here and expansive there, describing an action here, a gesture there, reproducing actual spoken words, reporting real or even hypothetical conversations ; determined only to show the total impact of a situation on characters who themselves are creating it. His method is well illustrated by the following passage from *The Schoolmaster*. The schoolmaster has been appointed to a new village. On his first visit, when he briefly notices the rich meadows, the mighty houses and muck-heaps (the signs of opulence), he has asked them to send him two carts to fetch his belongings. They ignore his request and he comes, a six-hour journey, to beg for the carts. He describes his arrival :[59]

I walked up to Gytiwyl and in the early morning, by one of the first houses, saw the church-warden watering a horse at the trough.

In haste, and without meaning it badly, I asked if they had not received my letter, and why no-one had come. He answered, they wouldn't allow themselves to be ordered by letter ; that would be a fine affair, if everyone only needed to order. If I wanted anything of them, I would have to go gently to win them over, and come myself, that's the proper way. A schoolmaster must not think he would be master in the village, they were at home there too. With that he led his horse into the stable, after it had been drying its wet nose for some time on his sleeve, and left me standing outside.

With great deliberation he filled his bucket from the bin, moistened the fodder, and emptied it, well mixed, into the manger, tidied the muck, and came out. There I addressed him again, very humbly : that was what I had come for, to ask for a cart, and he should not be angry because of the letter, I had just not had time, and thought a letter would lose no time, while I should have lost one or nearly two days. He hitched up his trousers and said, he would give a horse, and I should go to such and such, whose homes he pointed out ; if they also would go, he would be agreeable. With that he went into his house, without telling me to go with him. It was the same at the second house. As I knocked on the door, someone looked through the peep-hole, but quickly withdrew his head. Probably the head knew me, and inside they began discussing what it could be I wanted, and whether they should tell me to come in or not. The wife will have said : ‘ You go out to him, Hans, the sitting-room is not dusted yet, and we've only got warmed-up cabbage and sour milk, and we don't know what sort of a one he is, and so I don't want him to have his nose in everything.’ And the husband will have said : ‘ He will wait I expect, I'll just finish my dinner.’ And the wife opened the peep-hole again, first to see me and then to tell me : ‘ Someone's just coming.’ And while Hans slowly ate his cabbage with a fork and his curds with a spoon, and finally a piece of bread as dessert, he had to inform his inquisitive wife what could be the reason for my visit.

At last he came outside, gave me the same answer as the former, and sent me on to a third. There, a tall, stalwart woman was just carrying two pig-pails back from the stables, where she had been having her morning's pleasure over the spritely piglets and the colossal porkers, which, as the white pails demonstrated, were fed with as much cream as milk, in any case better milk than the people themselves had on their table. I am ready to bet, the wealthy gentry of Basel do not have such good cream in their coffee

K

as about four thousand Bernese pigs have in their troughs from
Martinmas to Shrovetide.

The woman was in good spirits ; she had probably just tied her
garters together and measured her darlings, and found that in the
last month they had again gained by almost a quarter.   She asked,
forthrightly, ' What would it be you're wanting ? '

The schoolmaster, knowing he is at the mercy of these hard
peasants, is in no mood for pictorial description.   He gives
the substance of the reproofs of the village magnate, indicating
his slowness by the nuzzling of the horse.   He watches anxiously
the deliberate routine of feeding, until the churchwarden,
jerking up his trousers, delivers his decision.   At the next
house he reports a conversation at which he only guesses, a
typical conversation, not an actual one, with the typical food
and unchanging ritual of eating, acutely conscious of being an
outsider and dependant.   At the third, it is the pig-milk which
sums up the prosperity and dignity of the peasant, and again
he tells us of a probable, a typical action, culminating in the
abrupt question, more like a command, which issues in a long
interrogation and a hospitable meal.   The first conversation
is given in indirect speech, with just a touch of dialect ; he
falls into dialect for the conversation of the second pair, using
dialect even for his own words here ; and Gotthelf allows
himself what is really an ' author's comment ' about the ' rich
gentry of Basel '.   The whole description is active, presenting
to us in different ways the helplessness of the poor little schoolmaster in face of his future masters, so self-confident and
inconsiderate, yet not without hospitableness in the last resort.
It tells us of an important occurrence, which not only shows
the peasants in their normal behaviour and activity, but also
sets the tone of his future relations with them.

The passages quoted give some idea of the quality of
Gotthelf's language.   It moves on several levels, not all of the
same artistic quality.   In his moralising digressions he is
sometimes rhetorical, heavy, parsonic, using the stereotyped
unctuous vocabulary and rhythms of the preacher.   The same
fulsomeness appears in some of his nature descriptions, where
he is only too likely to speak of dew like diamonds, stars going

chastely to their beds, the sun ' drawing the curtain ' like a
good mother, caressing the earth, with a plentiful addition of
metaphors which turn a natural scene into the text for a sermon
on God's goodness.[60] He uses many of the tricks of second-
rate romanticism—the inversions, rhythm, alliteration of idyll-
writers like Voss, the weak sentimentality of almanack-writers,
of the poorest literary quality. In his metaphors he had a
weakness for crude exotic terms like volcanoes, earthquakes,
rattlesnakes, etc. Where he seeks a beautiful or pathetic
effect he often betrays the fact that his conscious ideal of
literary beauty belongs to the feeble romanticism prevalent in
his youth.[61] In addition he is often obstreperously crude
and clumsy.

But often, too, even the digressions are written in a racy,
imaged fashion which is delightful, salted with anecdotes or
expressions which present situations and attitudes in their
living movement. A short digression on the ' sulks ' in women
vividly and grotesquely evokes a whole variety of attitudes.[62]
The relations between a doctor and peasant patients is put in
terms of typical behaviour.[63] The discussion of the general
relationship of a mother-in-law and a daughter-in-law is in
fact a group of typical situations, and has all the vividness of
a narrative.[64] Where his imagination clothes his ideas in
human shape, where they take on the substantiality of actual
existence, the digressions come to life and become an organic
part of the story itself, enriching it with numerous parallels and
variations.

His style is at its best in narrative, the narrative of the
behaviour, thoughts and feelings of his characters. It is dense
with material substance, like the stories, and like them full of
vitality and movement : there is no clear line of construction,
no purity and elegance of diction, just as there is nothing
comparable with these qualities in his peasants. His sentences
are usually long and tortuous, often clumsy in construction,
even containing obvious faults of grammar. But at every
turn, with every fresh onset of the sentence, something new in
tone is added ; the object is not merely more fully described,
but with every addition it appears in a new light, it gains

the complexity of a real, living thing and seems to have
unlimited potentialities.   Over and over again we seem to see
a whole host of stories which might arise from a particular
scene or person.   This style is not only suited to the bustle
of a market or a betrothal expedition.   It can be reticent
where need be, and a simple gesture can convey the most
intimate and profound feeling.   When Anne Mareili places
her hand in Resli's and bursts into tears, all her trust and
fear, her love and her maidenly reluctance are expressed.   The
wise master, Gotthelf tells us, knows that he can guide a
farmhand best by an odd word of reproof or advice, dropped
as they are working together, so that others hardly notice it,
and Gotthelf himself often uses this method.

The novels are full of direct conversation, for words are
consciousness, and however limited the peasants are, they are
not creatures of instinct, but rational people seeking to control
life.   Thus they only fully establish themselves when they
speak.   Scolds like Anne Bäbi are inexhaustible, of course, but
at critical moments all reveal more by speech than could be
described, the sly ones as well as the taciturn.   Nothing is
more profoundly revealing than the sudden loquacity of girls
when the man they have chosen offers them marriage.   Shy
till then, Mädeli or Meyeli suddenly can tell, not of feelings
or love, but of their lives, their experiences, with an artless
eloquence that tells of their utter trust in the man, of their
gladness at being wooed.   They speak of material things, like
Gretchen in Goethe's *Faust*, for it is in material things that their
spirit takes shape ; if Gotthelf tries to describe their feeling,
he fails badly as a rule.

Many of these conversations are in dialect.   Gotthelf's use
of dialect is extremely free.   Sometimes all the conversations
are in dialect, sometimes part ; sometimes dialect is used in
reported speech, and it overflows too into the narrative, in
odd phrases or connected sentences.   He is capable of giving
standard German words a Bernese twist, and he may slightly
alter a dialect phrase or word to conform in some degree with
standard German.   Even though he made a great effort,
especially in his later work, to make his books easily accessible

to German readers, he could not eliminate dialect. ' I intend
never to write in dialect, and little of it may be noticed on the
first twenty pages ; afterwards I am forced to use it, whether
I want to or no '; and he gives the reason, too : ' I must lay
Bernese German aside, I understand ; but if I do, I cannot
really indicate what I want to.'[65]

One has only to compare conversations rendered in standard
German, like many in *Uli the Farmhand*, and those in dialect,
to see the justice of Gotthelf's preference for dialect. He
himself produced standard-German versions of *Uli* and *The
Schoolmaster* which are feeble counterfeits of the originals ; his
occasional ' translations ' of dialect words are clumsy and
weak. He does not use dialect for folkloristic reasons, for
though he transcribes the dialect accurately he often wilfully
distorts it, and, as he said, would have liked to standardise it
all. But as soon as the peasants speak differently, they
become different people, their mode of consciousness becomes
distorted. One can see this even in the townsfolk of *Der Herr
Esau*, whom he wishes to deride. In their contacts with
the peasants their speech is given in a stilted standard German
in order to contrast their whole attitude with that of the
peasants ; but when their speech is given in dialect, their
character appears in fact, against Gotthelf's intention, to be
much nearer that of the peasants. The dialect forms, syntax,
idioms, as well as the vocabulary, closer to medieval German
than any other High German dialect, represent a mode of
consciousness essentially related to the way of life and moral
values of a peasant people. Gotthelf did not write out of
a ' cultured ' interest in dialect, he had no such aim as to
' preserve ' it ; he used it because it was the living speech of
the peasants of whom he wrote.

In the totality of his language, Gotthelf tried to do what
few other Germans have even attempted : to marry the spoken
language with the standard, and to provide a literary language
which has the resonance, the plasticity, the multiple suggestive-
ness of actual speech. If he failed to create an integrated
literary language out of the different elements at his disposal,
it is because of reasons out of his control : the different rate

and type of cultural and in particular literary development in different parts of Germany, the marked difference between the literary cultured language and the actual speech of the peasants, the separation of Berne and Switzerland from the Reich.

GOTTHELF AND THE EUROPEAN NOVEL

Just as the milieu of Gotthelf's novels is off the beaten track, so it is difficult to place him in any German literary tradition.   The most obvious influences to be observed in his work are those of the Romantic school, particularly the lesser Swiss romantic writers.   Clearly, too, he owes something to the didactic writers for the common people, particularly to Pestalozzi ; and his temperament and style link him with the older sixteenth-century writers, with their enjoyment of anecdote, their robust coarseness and taste for hyperbole. Yet these relationships are more misleading than significant, for he evidently belongs most closely to the great nineteenth-century tradition of the realistic novel.   The strange thing is that he seems to have been completely oblivious of his great contemporaries in this genre.   He knew something of minor writers like Eugène Sue, whose themes and sensationalism he abhorred ; but it is questionable whether he knew Dickens or Balzac, and there is no trace of their influence in his works. Yet he is, with all his faults, the greatest realistic novelist in German, the only one whom one inevitably compares with the great English, French, and Russians.

Such a judgement may seem to claim too much, and one must hurry to make qualifications.   He is scarcely read outside Germany, and widely appreciated only within Switzerland ; even here, apart from *Uli the Farmhand*, his works appeal only to readers of a somewhat cultivated taste.   His faults are glaring and put off the more naïve reader.   His moralising is direct, emphatic, ubiquitous and old-fashioned in its rigidity ; and he takes it so seriously that it cannot be ignored.   A great deal of imaginative tolerance is needed to remain sweet-tempered in face of his violent injustice to townsfolk, professors, lawyers, politicians, radicals and aristocrats, artisans, and his recurrent vicious jabs at Frenchmen, Germans, Englishmen and Jews. If one is over-sensitive to these negative aspects of his work, he seems a pig-headed, self-willed, rampageous backwoodsman, a typical product of an out-of-the-way corner, justifying himself by denigrating everybody else. None of the other great writers was so intolerant and narrow-minded.

He is supreme in his representation of the peasantry ; no other novels, of any time, can equal his in the richness, depth, inexhaustibleness of the material life and spiritual resources of the peasantry. Yet it is questionable whether even this supreme gift can put him among the greatest writers. The greatness of a writer does not depend simply on artistic accomplishment, but also on the scope of his material ; and Gotthelf's sphere is narrow. It does not matter that the area of which he wrote was provincial, and a matter of a few square miles. What is more significant is that the range of idea, problem and passion among these peasants is narrow. Some of the great passions and spiritual problems, of which the great European novelists made their contemporaries conscious, are ignored by him, denigrated even, for he derides any questioning of the values of peasant life and established religion. Political ambition, love, patriotic feeling never have in his works the impassioned, often fatal intensity they may have in those of Stendhal, Balzac, Tolstoy ; the tensions with established morality do not with him throb and vibrate as they do in *Madame Bovary* or *Anna Karenina* ; to a large extent he ignores the sensitive and imaginative capacities of man. Variations from the norm are treated by him, as a rule, as the result of pettifogging calculation and aberration, not as constituent forces of life in its modern form. The struggle of poor with rich, workers with masters, as he represents it, has no urgency, no moral substance, no fatefulness in it, none of the potency already understood by Mrs. Gaskell or Kingsley or Balzac.

That these qualities are absent, whether by deliberate intention on Gotthelf's part or because of his own temperamental failings, means that his achievement is slighter than that of his great contemporaries. But it means too that he did not, like so many of their German imitators, foist alien themes and characteristics upon his peasants, that he kept to the truth of his chosen milieu, and that within this milieu he could discover, uncover, all the vital resources that belong to it, that sustain and threaten it. Loving life, and concerned to show the dignity and worth of life, to point out how it may be worthily lived, endowed with a superb mimic gift, he has created an imaginative world which interprets the real world out of which it was built. It is a world of narrow range, characterised by simple problems and moving within the confines of a few simple recurrent events ; and precisely because it is so, his figures and scenes have a simplicity, clarity, and monumentality that recall the ancient epic.

CHAPTER VI

Wilhelm Raabe
1831–1910

RAABE'S SOCIAL ATTITUDE

THERE are many novelists of the middle nineteenth century who are superficially more interesting than Raabe. Some, like Gutzkow and the Naturalists, experiment more curiously with the novel-form, many are concerned with flashier themes —with psychological aberrations or acute social and political conflict. Many, like Freytag or Spielhagen, were more up to date and popular than Raabe. But Raabe's work, subdued in tone and modest in intellectual scope, has a solidity and integrity that, as time goes by, raise it more and more above that of his contemporaries.

His life was uneventful. Nearly all of it was spent in slow-moving provincial towns—Wolfenbüttel, Stuttgart (1852–70), Brunswick (1870 till his death). His contacts with the leading spirits of his time were of the slightest, and he remained untouched by the dominant literary and intellectual fashions ; nor did he associate himself with the regional novelists' ' childish ' revolt against modern times.[1] His response to the great political and social events of his times followed a conventional middle-class pattern. Before 1860 his longing to see Germany united and powerful was expressed with an elegiac pessimism. Later he joined the National Liberals and greeted the emergence of Prussia as the leader of Germany. After 1870 he remained loyal to Bismarck and the Reich, but he was deeply troubled by the character of German political life and by the social and cultural transformation of the country. He took no part in public affairs, and his letters give the impression of a reticent, somewhat drab personality. Only his first novel was a popular success, and the lack of recognition by distinguished contemporaries drove him back, somewhat in discouragement, on the circle of his provincial friends.

There is no great variety of theme in Raabe's novels. Most of them centre in the conflict between the humane personality and the circumstances that cramp or crush it. His best historical novels, *Das Odfeld* and *Hastenbeck*, dwell on ' insignificant ' characters whose quiet lives are temporarily dislocated by great but fundamentally irrelevant historical events. Most of his novels deal with the contemporary scene, and here the contrast between the private individual and the hostile world appears over and over again in the form of a contrast between childhood and age, between an old and a modern Germany, the small town and the metropolis, the world of artisans and that of modern industry, the world of comfortable easy-going local officials and that of the modern ambitious bureaucratic hierarchy. Yet, with some exceptions, Raabe does not sentimentalise this conflict and preserves himself from romantic idealisation of the past. For while he often indicts the modern age as soulless, he always represents it as necessary and real : ' Raabe does not merely see the actual world as present and established, but seeks to grasp it as necessary and morally binding.' [2] His personal sympathies go rather to those who cannot maintain themselves in the pressures of modern times, and his acceptance of change is not so much the outcome of a positive belief as the expression of a sincere and humane, sometimes despondent, resignation.

This ambivalence is the very heart of his imaginative world ; and it is the key to the humour which pervades his works. In the historical novels, his awareness of his reversal of normal values is interpreted by the sympathetic humour with which he treats the small characters who seek, like field-mice after the plough has destroyed their nest, to patch up their lives in the midst of cataclysms, and the irony with which the ' great ' are presented. In the novels of contemporary life, humour and irony cast a kindly veil over the fragile who are unable to adapt themselves to modern conditions as over the tougher ones who make a success of things. Raabe's frequent adoption of a ' reminiscence-technique ' in telling his tales is part and parcel of the whole bearing of his art, for the characters who tell their tales themselves not only bring home to us the two time-scales, of past and present, but also strike that humorously ironic and often self-deprecatory note that is so characteristic of Raabe.

ARTISTIC GROPINGS

Raabe's earliest novels are characterised by a wistful recalling of childhood or of simple provincial life, enlivened by a whimsical humour that betrays the influence of Dickens. His first novel, *The Chronicle of Sperling Street* (1855), has remained the most popular of his writings, but like *The Children of Finkenrode* (1858) it is evidently immature. When serious personal or social issues loom up, they are immediately shut out by a mist of sentimentality or humour. *Der Hungerpastor* (1864) has many of the faults of these earlier works, but it can be considered the opening of a new period, for Raabe tried to embody in this book the moral character of his times. It is, however, a much weaker book than his other two novels of the 1860s with which Raabe himself linked it, *Abu Telfan* and *Der Schüdderump*.[3] The hero, another Oliver Twist, does not develop at all, but passes through one experience after another ' as if it had never happened ', successful only in preserving his innocence. The description of his simple home is convincingly alive, but when he gets as a tutor into upper-class regions Raabe's imaginative powers fail. The author's valediction to the hero as a fighter for humanity, ' Keep your arms bright for future generations, Hans Unwirrsch ', is not more than an appeal for an innocent, dumb, quietistic avoidance of the great world.

Something of the same philosophy runs through *Abu Telfan*, but it is presented with an ironical ambiguity that corresponds to the novel's deeper, more sober realism. Leonhard Hagebucher, after some years spent in slavery in darkest Africa, returns to his native Nippenburg, a typical sleepy small town, where all his relatives are petty officials. He will not settle into a normal career, and makes friends with other misfits, a lady who has retired, after her husband's public disgrace, to an out-of-the-way, decrepit mill, and a young noblewoman who is also at odds with the demands of good society. He goes to the ' Residenz ', studying Coptic with an old professor, and plans to give public lectures on ' Life in Africa ' ; but after the first lecture the police stop him, for the authorities are shocked at the freedom with which he compares the native institutions with European. He is not content to devote himself to scholarship, like the professor, and his plan of escape through marriage also goes awry ; nor can he find solace in dreams like his friend, the tailor. Through the death of his father he finds his material existence secured, and he continues to live at home, finding spiritual refreshment in occasional visits to the mill.

Nikola von Einstein's story runs parallel with his. She gives way to the pressure of society and marries a man of the court, believing that she can preserve her inner independence by playing possum, ' sich tot stellen '; but as time passes her ideals are ' buried so deep ' that they are almost lost. She is rescued only by the fact that her husband is involved in a scandal, and broken in spirit she too finds refuge in the mill, in a life which is a ' dream ', which is death in life.

The theme of the novel is, then, how to preserve personality between the two crushing forces, the petty bourgeoisie and the court. As far as the latter goes, Raabe's description is shallow. There is sharp satire of the typical small court of the times, its petty preoccupations, its narrowness, conventionality—some of the sharpest pages in the whole of Raabe's work [4]—but this satire does not acquire a plastic, imaginative form. The ' vice ' and ' crime ' of the upper circles are vaguely described and luridly tinged, and betray a petty-bourgeois prejudice and narrowness in Raabe ; the two ladies at the mill seem themselves, in their grief and shame, to pay homage to the moral standards of their class. It is in his portrayal of the middle class that Raabe shows a great advance on his earlier work.

Several forms of resistance to the morals of the Spiessbürger are presented. There is Leonhard's uncle, an inspector of

ways and roads, a rolling-stone in some respects, a bachelor.
He has a stretch of prison behind him, for patriotic demonstrations in his youth ; his job keeps him on the move, and he
is excessively fond of a drink. But he encourages Leonhard
to challenge the family, he supports him when he is destitute,
he introduces him to the lady of the mill. And yet he is a
faithful member of the Spiessbürger club in the town, and
forms a link between Leonhard and the rest ; he is himself a
Spiessbürger whom the times have driven into misbehaviour.
Temperamentally akin to him is the rough old lord of the
manor, a country hobbledehoy, who is introducing modern
scientific methods into his farming and whose son is on the
way to marrying Leonhard's sister. And, as Leonhard settles
into his father's house, and starts to feel the need for ' a more
comfortable tranquil future ', we see that he is making his
peace with the Nippenburger. His uncle prophesies that he
will become town-clerk and join the club, and Leonhard
agrees. At the end of the book Raabe writes glowingly that
the world of the Philister is the necessary complement to that
of the mill, and that it is a profound source of German strength,
of German culture.

The theme is not worked out to our full satisfaction. The
change from hostility to reconciliation is too abrupt, and in
any case only suggested in general terms ; or, it might be
said, it is caused directly by Hagebucher's acquisition of his
father's property. But the inevitability of a reconciliation is
subtly suggested by the style in which the characters face their
problems. There is a rueful, comic note in Hagebucher's
description of his resistance and his ideals, which always
reminds us of the massiveness of the reality against which he
is pitting himself and of the uncertainty he feels. He dreams
of the dressing-gown, carpet-slippers and pipe of the philistine ;
he talks humorously of his love for the professor's daughter, as
if doubting its inner truth ; and when with the professor he
discusses the police-ban on his lectures, he closes ironically
with a request for another cup of coffee, while the professor
asks his daughter to fill his pipe ' with the tragic words, " it's
the first today " '. Where humour is absent, for instance in

the description of the mill and the court, sentimentality, melodrama, mawkishness make their appearance.

It has been observed that, in *Abu Telfan*, there are two themes akin to those of two philosophies—Feuerbach's optimistic naturalism and Schopenhauer's pessimistic contemplativism. In *Der Schüdderump* (1869) they appear again, and still to a large degree unreconciled, as alternatives : the more sensitive, fine-fibred characters are shattered by the crude world and find an insecure refuge only in moral repudiation of it ; the healthier, tougher characters build a worthy existence in spite of the ' horror of the world '.

Raabe opens this story with the description of a plague-cart, ' der Schüdderump ', that he once saw in a German town, and during the course of the story he refers several times to the rumble of the cart, the ever-presence of death. Yet the symbol only partly interprets his story. It begins with the return of Marie Häussler and her illegitimate daughter Antonie to her native village, where she is lodged in the Poor House and protected from the spite of the peasants by the gentry at the manor. Years before, her father, the barber, had taken her with him to win a fortune, and had abandoned her in her misery. She dies, and her daughter becomes the playmate of the little Junker up at the manor. When he goes away to school, she becomes a favourite with the aristocratic folk and lives with them. When she is eighteen her grandfather turns up, now a gentleman who has won wealth and honours through financial speculations in Austria and Italy, and he carries her back with him to Vienna, intending to marry her to a business-associate. Here she falls into a decline. Her old friends come to see her, discover too late how things stand, and stay till she dies.

Such a synopsis, however, does the work serious injustice. The theme is partly, it is true, the destruction of rural innocence and simplicity by the sophisticated materialism of the metropolis. But the conflict of innocence and the ' world ' exists in the village too. Tonie Häussler is linked with other outcasts who are treated with harsh hostility by the village folk, old and young, and by the parson and his family, who all

pay court to the once-despised Häussler when he returns as a
' gentleman '. But it is essentially deepened and complicated
by a conflict within the manor itself, which is the main scene
of the story.

The head of the noble family is Adelheid von Lauen, an
extremely capable, practical, cheerful woman, busy from morning to night in the house and farm. Under her wing live
two aristocratic dependents. The ' Ritter ' is a destitute
nobleman, wounded severely in the wars against France, a
chivalrous man of the old school, who smoothes over the
differences that arise in the family. It is he who rescues
Marie Häussler from the villagers' fury. He gives the Junker
his early education (on the principles of Comenius !), advises
that the lad must go away to school, and goes to Vienna to
make Tonie's last days happy. His counterpart is Mlle de
Saint Trouin, a proud and self-opinionated French emigrée
who lives on the idealised memory of the French court. She
needs someone to favour and to rule, and she too educates the
Junker, reading with him *Télémaque* till he revolts. She and
the Ritter make a pair, often at loggerheads, often exasperating
the practical Adelheid, both representing a world that is gone
and in many ways ridiculous, and yet both standing for an
ideal culture that makes Adelheid feel they are necessary to
her and the Junker. Thus there is a deep poignancy in the
struggle against the modern world, for from the beginning
we recognise that the idealistic characters belong to the past
and are unable to maintain themselves, in the simplest meaning
of the word, in the actual world. It is through the words of
the Ritter that the power of money is condemned, as he admits
his own powerlessness in his poverty, it is he who speaks of the
' horror of the world ', it is he and Tonie who recognise,
despite all, ' that life, vitality, is always in the right '.[5] Tonie
dies, the Ritter loses his wits, the Mademoiselle withers ; they
do not represent a social force. And Adelheid, who is always
uneasy about the adoption of Tonie and relieved when she
goes to Vienna, knows too that they have taken the child
partly because they want a ' plaything ' once the Junker has
gone away.

Her son, Junker Hennig, is also a positive, unsentimental character. He is a decent, lusty lad, without refinement of feeling ; 'he possessed in a high degree that animal feeling for the comforts of life that is also called " Gemütlichkeit " '. Tonie is devoted to him, and if he had said a word, she would not have accompanied her grandfather to Vienna ; but he has no inkling of her feelings. He goes to Vienna and discovers that she is ill and miserable. He is honourable enough to propose that she should come back with him and marry him, a proposal she refuses because she sees he makes it out of pity ; and he is greatly relieved at her refusal. He thinks he will satisfy his honour by fighting a duel with her fiancé, but succumbs easily to the charm of the latter, and finds Viennese society very much to his taste. After Tonie's death he comes home grieving, but he can hardly restrain a cheer as they drive into the farm, and his mind is already busy with the pleasant tasks of a gentleman-farmer. In Hennig and his mother Raabe presents a picture of people who are healthy and good, and even if they are not sensitive and refined, yet are appreciative of finer natures.

The moral of *Der Schüdderump* is often interpreted either as ' the victory of the canaille in the world ', or the victory of the pure in spirit, who refuse to accept the world.[6]   In fact, the theme is ambiguous.   In relation to Tonie, whose character is the least developed, the shadowiest, in the book, it may be so defined.   But we have seen that the other idealistic characters are presented with realistic irony, and that in between the idealistic characters and the ' canaille ' there exist the healthy practical people like Adelheid and Hennig.   Raabe is not so much providing a solution, as in *Der Hungerpastor*, not simplifying reality, but presenting it in its contradictory complexity.   It is a weakness of *Der Schüdderump* that the various attitudes are embodied in different persons, none of whom experiences an inner struggle of values ; in the best of his later work he was to show the contradictory forces of his times at work within one and the same individual.

FULL MATURITY

The year 1870–1 brought the fulfilment of Raabe's political hopes. A victorious war had been crowned by the creation of the Reich under a Prussian monarch ; the friction with his Swabian friends had been smoothed over (during and after the Austro-Prussian war he had been boycotted by his predominantly anti-Prussian friends in Stuttgart) ; his own party, the National-Liberals, was large and confident of exerting influence on Bismarck. Yet in these circumstances, and in the following decades, Raabe proved the integrity and delicacy of his feeling. His immediate response to 1870 was, characteristically enough, a sympathetic but ironical account of the patriotic idealism which had inspired the Schiller-centenary celebrations of 1859 (*Der Dräumling*, 1871), and from time to time he was to write with nostalgic and humorous regret of the early aims and hopes of the patriotic movement. *Gutmann's Travels* (1891) describes the love affair of a North-German patriot with a Bavarian girl within the framework of the first conference of the ' Nationalverein ' of 1860 ; its tone is illustrated by the remark of the hero to his mother : ' No sons of a nation could be more innocent and harmless than we in our concern for our fatherland.' [7] *Kloster Lugau* (1893) shows how personal difficulties dissolve as the protagonists enter jubilantly into the war of 1870. But, apart from these and two or three historical novels, the main body of Raabe's later work deals with the contemporary scene, with the moral problems which the new Germany created, with the changing values arising from new forms of social life.

Raabe was deeply disturbed by the materialistic greed that swept over Germany after the war. In the preface to the second edition (1890) of *Christoph Pechlin* (1872) he writes :

The wounds of our heroes were not yet closed, the tears of children, mothers, wives, fiancées and sisters not yet dry, the graves of the fallen not yet green : but already, so soon after the fearful war and the costly victories, things were very queer in Germany. As when in a great fire a cask of treacle has burst in the street and the mob and the guttersnipes set about licking it up ; in Germany the money-bag had burst open, and the coins were rolling over the streets, and only too many hands were stretching out after them. It almost seemed as if this was to be the greatest gain that the united Fatherland was to win from its great historical achievement.[8]

In earlier works he had tilted at financial speculators and the destructiveness of modern industry—in *The Forest Folk* he describes the mood of a society gathering in the jargon of the Stock Exchange,[9] and the mill of *Der Schüdderump* has lost its water and its usefulness through factories higher up the valley. But now he realised that a profound change was occurring in German society, a transformation ' from a peasant-people to an industrial state ',[10] a change from small towns of artisans and easy-going local officials to great cities of factories and a bureaucratic hierarchy, from humane and personal human relations to impersonal and mechanical, from the leisurely performance of traditional tasks to the agitated pursuit of material and social success. What makes Raabe's work profound is his criticism of both the present and the past, his realistic recognition of the necessity of change and of the moral loss involved. He escapes the melodrama of Spielhagen, the idyllicism of Storm, the hysteria of Nietzsche, and presents deftly and modestly the dilemma and truth of his times. His view was restricted socially and emotively, as we shall see, but within his modest scope he shows a purer integrity than any contemporary novelist except Fontane.

An exceptionally prolific author, some of his novels, and particularly his shorter tales, tend to propose a facile escape from, or solution of, the moral dilemma of which he was aware. *Christoph Pechlin*, for instance, is, as he avows in the (later) preface, an escape into farce, ' into dry jesting, into completely unemotional fun '.—' It is a privilege of decent people, when the times give rise to anxiety, rather to play the fool on their own than to be rogues among all the other rogues.' In *Villa Schönow* (1883) the Berlin entrepreneur Schönow, the embodiment of the new age that is shattering the past, is himself the defender of the cultural heritage and the more humane ideals of the past ; a comparable figure is the industrialist Asche of *Pfister's Mill*. And though Raabe indicates, in the rather extravagant self-irony of these men, their own consciousness of an unresolved conflict in their characters, there is an element of sentimental wishful-thinking in his conception of both. In *Restless Guests* (1884) the attraction of the ' social ' world and the prejudices of the vulgar are successfully resisted by the selfless piety of a young woman who devotes herself to the poor and sick in a remote mountain village, and who educates the more sensitive people who meet her ; but Raabe, with characteristic sincerity, recognises that this remains a personal solution for the few. The humane little group in *Old Iron*, who take pity on two helpless orphans and are content with a humble security, also form a little oasis in society, like the Ritter and Tonie in *Der Schüdderump*, ' alone in the desert of life '. In these novels, though the problematic of modern society is apparent, its sharpness is blurred through the focus Raabe chooses. His greatest works do not so much allow us to dwell on the ideal or desirable, as bring us face to face with the ambiguity, the ambivalence of life.

This effect is achieved even in his most popular humorous tale, *Horacker* (1876). The chief figures are two old-fashioned grammar-school masters, Eckerbusch and Windwebel, with their wives, and their friends, a village parson and his wife. A young villager, Horacker, the child of paupers, has escaped from a reformatory. The schoolmasters go for a walk through the woods, meet him on the way, find that he is desperate because he has heard that his Lottchen is in trouble, win him over by their sympathy, and persuade him to give himself up to the authorities in the village. As opposed to the authorities, who take the purely official view of Horacker's insubordination, and the common people, who spread rumours that Horacker is committing all sorts of dreadful crimes, the schoolmasters and the parson take a humane attitude to the lad and thus can help him.

Beneath this simple and uneventful story there lies a deeper theme. The elder schoolmaster, Eckerbusch, is ' the last Konrektor ', the last of a type of schoolmaster which had just been abolished. Deeply immersed in the classics, which he is fond of quoting on all occasions, he is also deeply embedded in the life of his little town, fond of his pupils, his drinking-club and skittles, a staunch friend of the unworldly old parson, whose favourite reading is Gellert. He resolutely refuses to accept the prevailing view of Horacker, but at the same time he knows how to speak to the peasants, how to manage them. His sympathy for the boy never loses the tone of the pedagogue. Finding a true companion in the rather despised art-teacher, he has a hearty distaste for a new master, the representative of the new Prussian spirit of abstract learning and discipline, a man who prefers composing Latin verses to a walk in the country. Eckerbusch's wife is a true comrade and helpmeet. She is always grumbling at her husband for cheapening himself, for his lack of dignity, but she knows his worth. Rumours spread through the town that the two excursionists have been killed by Horacker, and to comfort the anxious wife of the art-teacher she decides to take a carriage to the village. Incensed by the heartlessness of the Prussian master, she insists on his accompanying them, and on the journey magnificently gives him a piece of her mind.

The conflict between the schoolmasters is paralleled by that in the village. The peasants have discovered an old contract which demands that the parson should personally beg for his emoluments from his parishioners, and he is incapable of arguing against the re-introduction of the obsolete custom. But his sharp-tongued wife turns the tables on the peasants, and makes them so sheepish that they are even ready to damp down their arrogance to the poor outcasts, Horacker and Lottchen, as well.

Underneath the rollicking humour of this story, with its happy ending, there lies, then, a serious theme. But it is highly characteristic of Raabe that satire is directed not only against the peasants and the modern schoolmaster. Eckerbusch and his wife, the parson and his wife, are also treated with an expansive humour, their peculiarities and weaknesses are in no way hidden. They belong to an age that is dying out and the new generation will not be like them ; their humane spirit must be preserved, but we are not told in what form.

In *Old Nests* (1879) Raabe fully develops the implicit problem of *Horacker*. There is a significant reference in this book to Immermann's *Münchhausen*, a novel published in 1838, which Raabe complains is now taken to be ' light entertainment ' instead of ' a bitter-serious warning '. Immermann had made the notorious liar Münchhausen the symbol of the decadence of aristocratic culture, and had put in apposition to it a thriving peasant homestead, the Oberhof, and its sturdy independent farmer. But he had not intended the Oberhof to represent a changeless ideal. He had shown how the ethos of the traditionalist peasantry comes into collision with the ethos of the modern state, and how, admirable as it was, it has to change. Raabe recognised in Immermann a spirit akin to his own, keenly appreciative of the moral values within ancient forms of life, yet aware of the limitations and the doom of these ancient forms.

The story of *Old Nests* opens as a memory by the story-teller, Fritz Langreuter, a middle-aged scholar in Berlin, of the idyll of his childhood. There is the great country mansion of Graf Everstein, in which his mother is housekeeper, and the Graf's high-spirited daughter, Irene, the forester's cottage, and the forester's two children, Ewald and Eva. Near by is the neglected farm of Irene's plebeian cousin, Vetter Just, a great favourite whom they all make fun of because of his uncouth devotion to book-learning. It is an idyllic world, but economically insecure, and a scoundrel completes the ruin of nobleman and peasant. Farm and mansion are sold up, and the children scatter, with the exception of Eva, who stays on with her father. Ewald and Just, the one an engineer in Ireland, the other an emigrant in America, work with the sole object of returning. Vetter Just in the end returns to buy the farm, marries Eva, and uses his learning to introduce modern methods of farming. Ewald buys the mansion and hopes to establish himself there with Irene, now a widow who has many sorrows behind her. But he comes to realise that his idea of return was an illusion. They cannot recapture their childhood. The dilapidated mansion can be rebuilt, but it will not be the old one ; they cannot live there and be

themselves ; it is ' dead '. ' Man reminds himself by no means
often enough that he is alive, is life, and has to deal with
living things.' [11] Ewald and Irene leave for England, where
Ewald will continue in modern circumstances his career as
an engineer. He gives the mansion to Vetter Just, who sells
the stone to be used in the erection of a new bridge. And
the story-teller, himself firmly attached to his own life in
Berlin, reconciles himself to the destruction of a place so sacred
to them all with the words : ' All is right with the world.
It is true, the great comforting truth, that behind every thing
as such stands the world as such, appears clearly only on an
occasion like this.' [12]

The moral is not simple. Vetter Just can return, partly
because he is a naïve, generous man of simple wisdom ; Eva
can stay at home, because she always has a duty there. He
returns, however, not to enjoy the past, but to work, to improve
his farm, to play an active part in the rural community.
Ewald and Irene, the enterprising, gifted children, cannot
find due scope in the countryside, and above all cannot revive
the obsolete manorial life, however lovely it may have been
in the past ; the attempt would crush and destroy them.
Fritz Langreuter, whose life seems to have withered his feelings,
finds a compensation for the aridity of his metropolitan life
in his imagination : not ' my home is my castle ' but ' my
castle in Spain is my home '. The problem is the same for
all of them, but the solutions are various.

The clash of past and present is presented more concretely
in *Pfister's Mill* (1884). The story is told as a reminiscence
of a young Berlin schoolmaster, who is spending his honeymoon
in his father's mill, now just about to be broken up to make
room for a factory. He tells of the happy days of his childhood,
when the thriving mill was a favourite resort of the folk from
the neighbouring town. But the water of the millstream is
polluted by the effluvia of a beet-sugar factory, the guests
can no longer bear the stench, and even the mill-hands give
in their notices. His father wins a law-suit against the
factory, but he has read the signs of the times and knows that
the good old days and good old world are doomed. He is

broken in spirit, but before his death he is grateful that his
son has left the traditional calling of the family, and advises
him to sell the mill and invest the proceeds in industry.

Past and present are contrasted here, as always in Raabe,
not as opposed intellectual principles, but as two ways of life,
each with a different ethos, the character of which can be
experienced, not defined. The conflict cannot be reduced to
abstractions, but is present in behaviour and action. Thus
the value of the old miller's world appears in the latter's
jovial, expansive, generous and hospitable character, while
that of his son's world sifts through his comments, his humble
contentedness in his present occupation, his happiness with
his wife, his subdued regret for the tragedy of his father—
through his suppressed character, good but ineffectual, his
modest ideal of happy domestic life in the great, anonymous
city. The conflict emerges in the character of Dr. Asche,
the scientist who gives the miller the expert information which
enables him to win his suit against the factory. Asche was
in love with the old mill, with nature, and as a young man
resisted the impersonal discipline of the modern world. But
he has realised that, if he is to achieve anything, he must fit
into the new world, and he has become an industrial scientist,
has founded a successful dye-business that will pollute bigger
rivers than the millstream and shatter more existences than
the miller's. Asche is acutely aware of the conflict between
past and present in himself, and speaks with a rather tortured
and sardonic irony both of ' progress ' and of the mill of which
he is so fond. With characteristic savage irony he says to
Ebert Pfister, when he comes to help the latter's father :

And you, my lad, don't you imagine that I have come out to
Pfister's mill in order to distil end-of-the-world feelings from this
stunk-out idyll of your father's pub. Idylls are all very well ; but
in spite of a melancholy tear for Christmas, Easter and Whitsun,
I now intend to go quietly down among the philistines and there,
on that given, bitterly real soil, I intend to guzzle and swig with
the rest, to prosper, and if possible to propagate too.[13]

But it is he, the modernist, who shows a truer sympathy with
the humane values of the past than any of the miller's

small-town friends.   After business hours he studies Greek and
reads Homer.   He helps the old-fashioned idealistic poet of
the small town, who is a laughing-stock to the neighbours, a
drunkard who, in his way, shows the breakdown of the old
society.   It is Asche's attitude that finally convinces old Pfister
of the inevitability of change.

In all the more important novels, Raabe shows not only
the attractiveness of the old, small-town world, but also its
drawbacks, its moral and practical narrowness, its 'philistinism'.   Most of his heroes are engaged in a struggle with
the philistinism of the past as well as with the utilitarianism
of the present, and this theme is unobtrusively present in
Pfister's Mill too.   *Stopfkuchen* (1890) most clearly strikes at the
tendency to idealise the past ; in the character of the chief
character, Heinrich Schaumann, Raabe's imagination has
created the most adequate symbol of his resistance to, and
acceptance of, the real world.   It is, as Raabe said, his ' really
subjective book '.[14]

This tale is told by a middle-aged man, Eduard, a prosperous
settler in Africa, who visits his native German town, and
writes his account as he is on his way back home.   His visit
disappoints him until he looks up his old friend Schaumann,
and the main part of the novel is taken up by Schaumann's
own tale of his life, told in the course of a long summer's day.
The latter had been a fat, awkward boy, poor at school-work
and clumsy at games, perpetually hungry (hence his nickname,
Stopfkuchen), despised by his schoolmates.   He tells how he
had made friends with a girl living at a farm called the ' Red
Redoubt ', whose father was suspected of being a murderer
and therefore treated as an outcast by peasants and townsfolk
alike.   The ' Red Redoubt ' had become for Stopfkuchen a
refuge from vulgar values and prejudices, a symbol of challenge
to the philistines, and he tells how he came to live there,
married the girl, and himself became the farmer up at the
' Red Redoubt '.   Bit by bit he has found out who the real
murderer was, an old postman who plays a big part in
Eduard's idyllic memories of childhood.

As far as Eduard is concerned, the past lives as a romantic

memory, abruptly separated from the modern colonial world in which he lives. But he is prevented from dwelling on the past as he sees it or from telling the story of his own adventures : that is, we are not allowed to remain at the standpoint of another Ebert Pfister or Fritz Langreuter. Stopfkuchen insists that it is *his* story that is important, that it is he who has faced up to reality and found a solution. Stopfkuchen knows how cruel and shallow was the school life that Eduard wants to idealise, he remembers with justified bitterness how all the adults had pushed him, the grammar-school boy, towards a profession for which he had not the slightest talent or liking, how they had all tried to change his fundamental character. He had had a bitter struggle to ' be himself ', to find an outlet, as he ironically remarks, for his ' shamefully suppressed apti- tudes for comfort and human dignity '. Only by challenging all normal conventions had he linked his life with the outcasts in the ' Red Redoubt '. The farm was so named because it was built on the site of a redoubt thrown up in the Thirty Years' War, from which the town below had been bombarded and reduced to submission, and for Stopfkuchen it is still a place from which he can ' bombard the philistines down there '. Here he can survey the town without being engulfed in its pettiness, from here it and its concerns can even acquire a picturesque appearance—as they look down, in the sunlight, even the gaol, he remarks sarcastically, looks lovely, ' sheer fairy-tale magic '. With unobtrusive skill Raabe leads all the lines of the story, all the comments of Eduard, back to this Red Redoubt which is, as Barker Fairley has admirably shown, the focus of the story and the theme.

But Stopfkuchen is not an idealistic reformer, nor does he claim to be one. He is ostentatiously self-satisfied, lazy, sly and gluttonous. He has let his fields to a sugar-beet concern, of which he is a founder and shareholder, and thus has freed himself from the need of working. He makes no claim to have discovered a general solution, even though the problem he faced was a general one—perhaps for this reason Raabe makes him childless. Through almost incidental reminders that the story is told in a world of ocean-liners, railways and great industrial concerns, we grow conscious that the world is undergoing vast changes and driving to an unknown future, a theme which is reinforced by Stopfkuchen's interest in the bones of pre-historic animals found on his land. All Stopf-kuchen has done is to establish a form of life suited to himself and his own circumstances. The form of his victory is not exemplary and final, but personal and temporary.

It is no accident that the most positive of Raabe's characters, those who drive deep roots into the changing world, are them-selves in many ways ' philistines ', able to resist the harmful distortions of philistinism only because they themselves are so attached to a narrow round and are, or become, limited in their aims, like Stopfkuchen or Hagebucher. When Raabe broaches the problem of those who perforce leave the small town, the ' philisterium ', his heroes are characteristically vacillating, torn between two ideals, like Ebert Pfister and Dr. Asche. One of his last novels presents this dilemma in a peculiarly penetrating fashion. *The Vogelsang Documents* (1895) describes the life-story of a group of three children in the framework of the break-up of an old-fashioned suburb, the ' Vogelsang ', in a small town which has developed into a modern city. It was a real neighbourhood, where poor and rich, artisans and officials, rubbed shoulders and helped one another, just on the fringe of the town. But the old houses are sold and pulled down, factories, working-class tenements, music-halls take their place, and the old inhabitants leave for anonymous apartment-houses suited to their class and careers.

Of the children, the girl, Helene, is taken by her millionaire father to America, where she marries money. Velten Andres, the gifted, sensitive boy, who despises social success and money, follows her as a sort of symbol of his happy childhood and the old innocence. The third, Karl Krumhardt, accepts the guidance of his ambitious father, fits into all the conventions of the new life, marries into a ' good ' family, and has become a successful official.

The ostensible main theme of the book is the story of Velten, the man who despises all conventional values. He refuses to take advantage of the opportunities offered him, throws his career away, and in the end renounces his property, dying in poverty in a furnished room in Berlin. He is romantically attached to his old house and the old form of life of his childhood, but, fully aware of its passing, he burns all the precious relics of his father and mother, thus challenging the sentimentality as well as the practical sense of the townsfolk. But the central interest of the book is the attitude of Karl Krumhardt, who is the story-teller. Krumhardt writes from the secure standpoint of success and happiness, and we are continually reminded of his present position. But he is attached to his childhood, and is unaccountably burdened by his respect and admiration for Velten, whom he knows to be superior to himself, whose challenge he envies. Running throughout his tale, therefore, is a dual attitude : his consciousness that men like his practical father and himself are necessary for they keep things going, and at the same time his recognition that they are not happy with all their property and success, that the world they maintain is of dubious worth, and that it is those who follow their dreams who really ' conquer ' the world. He writes Velten's story down, he tells us, because it is such a burden to him : ' I have pulled him out into the world because I could no longer live under the same roof with him.' [15]

With easy but subtle artistry Raabe unfolds the moral dilemma of Krumhardt. As Krumhardt describes his childhood, the tension is slight, for his attachment to the ' Vogelsang ' and Velten can appear as the normal safe nostalgia of middle age. But when he describes Velten's return home, the events impinge directly on his own married life. His wife, a ' Honoratiorentochter ', is at first rather thrilled to meet a character so different from the conventional people she has grown up with, but bit by bit she gets horrified at Velten's misanthropy, and when he burns his family keepsakes she not only is resolved to keep him away from her home, but is horrified at her husband's continuing attachment to his friend. Krumhardt now feels fully the incompatibility of the two modes of life, and as in his childhood, accepts without hesitation the way of

propriety.   With the rueful, ironical stiltedness of a prudent
man of the world, he admits that he is grateful that his father
had kept him to the narrow path, and that he wants his own
children to conform to conventional standards.   Irony once
again is the mood in which the chief character can reconcile
himself to a reality which he knows is impoverished.   Raabe
makes Krumhardt the epitome of his time, estimable, useful,
and contented, yet uneasily conscious of the shallowness and
precariousness of his life and values.

THE STORY-TELLER

Raabe is one of the most subjective of novelists ; his personality obtrudes directly into his works.   Some of his novels
begin with general comments on the ' moral ' of the story he
is to tell, others begin with a short explanation of how he
came across the story.   His personal character—his delight in
oddities, his somewhat pedantic facetiousness, his attitude to life
—is expressed in all the elements of his style, which emphatically reminds us of the moral and cultural standpoint from
which the stories are told.   It is the reverse of a ' classical '
style, for Raabe seems always to be seeking some direct point
of contact with his readers.   In his mature work, however,
these subjective elements become fused with the whole theme
and themselves interpret its essential bearing.

In the early works, Raabe shows sharp observation of the
scenes and characters of small-town life, but his composition
is faulty.   The varied existences in *The Chronicle of Sperling
Street* are linked only in the memory of an old man ; in *Der
Hungerpastor* the hero passes through several milieux, each of
which propounds new problems without any corresponding
growth on his part.   But the characters and incidents of *Abu
Telfan* are more tightly disposed round a single moral situation,
and more firmly subordinated to the author's purpose.   *Der
Schüdderump* again is closely knit, and the only milieux which
are fully described are the Manor House and the Poor House,
the two poles of the theme.   In the mature works there is
a still greater simplicity and sobriety of construction, a more

austere selection of character and detail. Many of the novels are built round a slight and undramatic incident, and even where a life-story is related, as in *Old Nests*, *Stopfkuchen* or *The Vogelsang Documents*, events are only lightly touched on and closely related to the moral situation.

Because of this simplification of structure, certain central features of his later tales acquire so intense a meaning that they become symbols. Raabe rarely forces symbols into his works : it might be held that his imagination was not vigorous enough to condense experiences into simple plastic images. He begins *Der Schüdderump* with a description of the old plague-cart that gives a symbolic title to the novel, but this symbol is not adequate to the complex theme and seems rather forced. The macabre battle of the crows over the future battle-field of *Das Odfeld* is a rare example of a striking and poetic symbol of this kind. But at his best, a natural realistic feature of the tale emerges bit by bit with the force of a symbol. The ' Red Redoubt ' of *Stopfkuchen* sums up his isolation and security ; the death of the old postman expresses the end of Eduard's nostalgic idealisation of the past. The manor house of *Old Nests* sums up the loveliness and the deadness of childhood ; the Vogelsang suburb likewise. These symbols are not fixed, they change with time, and their transformation symbolises the conflict of values in the characters, and the nature of their decisions : the stone of the derelict manor house is used in the building of a bridge. The most harrowing and profound of all Raabe's symbols is the idiot in *Altershausen*, the old man with the mentality of a child, the embalmed past.

Even in his historical novels Raabe never shows much narrative skill. The variety of the early novels is provided by profusion of character rather than of incident, and later there is a marked lack of action. Yet there is tension in his works, for the small action there is involves a decision that brings a whole character into play. This decision may or may not be actually taken. Stopfkuchen, Ewald and some others take it, while many do not, like Krumhardt, Hagebucher or Ebert Pfister ; but the purpose of the novels is to lay bare the structure of the moral dilemma in which the characters are placed.

We see the characteristic clarification of Raabe's purpose and technique if we compare the historical novels *Unsers Herrgotts Kanzlei* (1862) and *Das Odfeld* (1887). The former, a story of burgher resistance to princely power in the age of the Reformation, describes numerous military engagements with the enemy and civil unrest within the city of Magdeburg. But events and figures are thin, sharply differentiated into good and bad, and there is no moral tension or development. The setting of *Das Odfeld* is also a battle. But it is one of the many indecisive engagements of the Seven Years' War, and the military events are of absolutely no significance. Though the sympathy of the main characters goes entirely to the Prussian allies, we see both armies engaged in purposeless fighting and senseless destruction and pillage. The real story is that of a small group of civilians, thrown out of a plundered homestead, who wander for two days over the battlefield, hiding from both armies. An old schoolmaster, the laughing-stock of the community, comforts them in their anxiety and distress, and guides them back to the devastated farm to take up their labours once again, richer in suffering and sorrow but also in wisdom and inner serenity. What is important is not, who will win, what great deeds will be done, but how the common people can grow wise through experience.

It is characteristic of Raabe that usually, in order to show this inner change, he makes extensive use of conversation. Description often seems a bare preparation for the actual speech of his characters, who suddenly acquire a sharp precision as they begin to speak. Dr. Wimmer, of *The Chronicle*, is a vague person until he begins to talk ; in *Der Hungerpastor*, the hero's uncle and aunt really live only when we hear them speaking. The most vivid moments of *Abu Telfan* are those when direct speech is reported : the verdict of the family-council on Hagebucher or the garrulous and rampageous exuberance of Uncle Wassertreter. Nikola von Einstein, who in Raabe's description remains a somewhat nebulous, intangible creature, suddenly springs to life in the reckless gaiety and

timid insecurity of her letter of submission.[16]   The substance
of *Horacker* depends on the actual quality of speech of the old
schoolmaster and his wife.   The stories of *Villa Schönow* and
Stopfkuchen are woven round the monological discourse of
Schönow and Schaumann.   But also in *Pfister's Mill* or *Old
Nests* the actual scraps of reported conversation interpret the
' problem ' of the story more incisively than the statements of
the rather naïve, timid tellers of the tale.   It is noticeable
that Raabe devotes extremely little attention to the lawsuit
and exterior facts in *Pfister's Mill* ;   the story is poised on,
and culminates in, the *words* of Asche and the old miller.

Many of Raabe's works are written in a form which makes
them ostensibly the tale of a particular teller, a form which
thus carries the use of direct speech to its ultimate conclusion.
In *The Chronicle of Sperling Street* and other early works, this
device is used as Storm frequently used it, in order to throw
the veil of distance over events, to soften their sharpness
through a mellow melancholy, and it allows Raabe to sentimentalise and idealise the past.   Later it is used in order to
intensify and deepen the problematic of events.

There is a certain sameness in the character of these pseudo-
narrators.   In *Pfister's Mill*, *Old Nests*, and *The Vogelsang
Documents*, they are all men with an academic education,
successful in their modest way, contented with what they have
achieved and their manner of life.   They have all, to some
extent, participated in the events they describe, but always
without energy and impact, themselves following normal
careers and accepting normal standards.   But they are all
men who are able to understand and sympathise with their
energetic or idealistic friends who have protested against the
conventions, and they suffer from a deep feeling of insecurity,
which often finds naïve, almost unconscious expression.   This
conflict is expressed in Ebert Pfister through the wry contrast
between the sadness of his tale and his present happiness,
through his wife's reluctance to let him dwell on his tale,
through his own subdued comments.   It is expressed in Fritz
Langreuter's awareness of the inhibitions within his own
crippled character ;   in Eduard's submission to Stopfkuchen's

garrulousness ; in Krumhardt's irony about his own career. Thus the story-teller provides us not only with a standpoint from which events are focused, but himself is the embodiment of the conflict of values which is the centre of his tale. The apparently incidental delineation of his present position and his character is as important as the tale he has to tell ; the story proceeds on two or three planes, which ultimately intersect in the story-teller's own person. Raabe himself seems to be most at ease when he adopts this device of the fictitious story-teller, and it gives his novels a depth that they sometimes lack.[17] It has a further advantage. Raabe's own style is somewhat laboured, clumsy, amorphous ; in these reminiscence-novels it appears, however, as the appropriate form of expression of the pseudo-narrators.

Raabe's handling of this technique is always deft ; in *Stopfkuchen* it is bold. Eduard writes down the story of his visit as he sits in the liner, on the way home to South Africa ; and the whole of the tale breathes his contented anticipation of his return to his farm and family in the new world. From the beginning we feel therefore that the old world of the small town and Spiessbürger has receded, has been overcome by new opportunities ; his visit has actually brought him little profit—except the meeting with Stopfkuchen. Then, as Stopfkuchen takes up his own tale, we are in the midst of a real and successful struggle at close quarters with the old world, and Eduard's temporary effacement illustrates the greater severity and worth of Stopfkuchen's struggle. The latter's own words, interrupted only by short pauses when Eduard describes their walk round the ' Redoubt ', the meal, the wife, make us feel the uniqueness of Stopfkuchen's life ; and as Stopfkuchen, after accompanying Eduard down to the town, takes his leave and returns to his fastness, we feel how lonely has been his struggle. Eduard now turns from his old friends of the ' Stammtisch ' with a deeper consciousness of the narrowness of their lives ; the funeral of the old postman acquires the symbolic character of the death of an illusion.

In an excellent article on Raabe's artistry, Barker Fairley has pointed out how deeply rooted in Raabe's artistic person-

ality are these various aspects of his technique—his groping
towards his readers, his lack of dramatic narrative, his use of
conversation.[18]   Fairley sums up his work as ' the most richly
conceived body of fiction in the German language '.   He calls
Raabe's composition, as opposed to the ' linear ' type of narrative, a representation of ' life in depth ', and compares it
with Rembrandt's.   Events and scenes are somewhat blurred,
or emerge only slowly from a dark background, because they
exist not for themselves, but in relation to the characters ; each
character itself emerges only in its meaning and reality for
others.   This is a rich conception of the novel indeed, and
as Fairley points out, a very modern conception too.   It was
not consciously evolved by Raabe, but arose ' out of his general
awareness, from the start, of what is involved mentally in
the process of narration '.   The unity of Raabe's important
novels, that is, of the later novels, lies in the mysterious and
elusive point of intersection of description and narrative in
the minds of the characters.   *Stopfkuchen* itself, as Heinrich
Meyer has said,[19] is a *non plus ultra* of composition, for the
story of Heinrich Schaumann is the point of intersection of
the colonial world, the small town, and the ' Red Redoubt ';
of the present, childhood, and the remote past unobtrusively
recalled by Stopfkuchen's collection of pre-historic remains,
which places the whole story in a perspective of infinite time
and gives it a depth recalling that of Hardy's great novels.

RAABE'S HUMOUR

Raabe is known most popularly as a humorous writer, and
it is easy to see his affinity with Sterne and Jean Paul (whom
he often quotes), and with Dickens and Thackeray.   Like the
former, he continually contrasts, to humorous effect, the
colourfulness of fantasy with the drabness of reality ; like
the latter, he delights in the oddities of life, in eccentric
characters and incongruous situations.   These elements are
evident in an undigested form in his early novels ; in his later
they merge into the general body of his work, in which his
humour gains a specific character and philosophic function.

M

All through his life Raabe kept one form of humour—farce, gay make-believe—as a refuge from an oppressive world. We have already seen how he wrote *Christoph Pechlin* as a piece of fooling at a time when he was bitterly disappointed over the materialistic greed of the years following the foundation of the Reich. Such works are based on accurate observation of characters, but with a conscious exaggeration of oddities, a frankly far-fetched plot, and much stylistic freakishness. They are at best a relaxation ; when such a character as Mutter Cruse, the old-iron collector in *Old Iron*, is placed in a serious framework, one is a little disconcerted by the determination of the author to avoid serious issues when they threaten to arise. In such situations Raabe's humour may easily become crude and tasteless ; it is certainly much overdone in *Villa Schönow*, where the misfortunes of a young boy and girl are heavily overlaid with an ostentatious and inescapable humour ; there is something of the same crudity in the historical novel, *Hastenbeck*.

In the first place Raabe's humour interprets a distrust of self, characteristic of the dejection of the patriotic and liberal middle class during the 1850s. In the early works it betrays a wistful consciousness of the contrast between the ideals within men, and the pettiness of their actual circumstances, and the contrast is humorous because it is accompanied by irony and distrust of self. *The Children of Finkenrode* displays this sort of humour in a variety of ways. The hero Bösenberg (who is the story-teller) is a smart, modern journalist, who can write of his job, his office, and his colleagues only with irony. His keenly anticipated visit to the scenes of his childhood is damped by the desolate inhospitability of the village where he changes from train to coach. The horses are ready for the knacker, the coach itself breaks down, and our hero enters his native town on foot, in a heavy downpour, unnoticed by anyone (Raabe often gets fun out of the contrast between exalted spirits and bad weather). Bösenberg spends his time in screwing up his courage to avow his love for a childhood friend, but discovers at the end that she is promised to another ; but this theme is always humorously treated, for at no time is he a character who takes himself seriously or who asks us to take him seriously. The triviality of Bösenberg's character is emphasised by the ironical bombast and preciosity of his descriptions. A child scratching its head is ' a native disturbing the harmless settlements of little backwoodsmen in the primeval forest of his head '. An umbrella is ' a silken storm-roof '. A chamber-maid is a ' nymph ', a pot an ' amphora '. Through this pervasive and irritating facetiousness Bösenberg escapes the responsibility of grappling with the real unsatisfactoriness of his life and profession.

In the later works this forced whimsicality develops into a philosophic humour. Its prevailing theme is the conflict between the humaneness of inner conviction and the cramping effect of actual concerns, but this conflict can be presented humorously because the tensions, though recognised, are left unresolved. Thus, the humour of Hagebucher's encounters with the police in the various states, as he goes from Africa to his home-town, introduces us deftly to the central theme of personal freedom. His father, and the other Spiesser, are both soberly and humorously described, for their mode of life has a value as well as being a challenge. The eccentricity of the former patriotic student, Wassertreter, his liking for a drop, his noisy exuberance, form a commentary on the times, which frustrate and injure the most generous. Similarly the comic treatment of the little professor, with his pipe and domestic comfort, his absent-mindedness, reveals the limitations of his protest against the pressure of society. The irony of Hagebucher is his manner of coming to terms with a reality too strong for him—Nikola tells him that ' he tries to hold his shattered life together through savage irony, and thinks he can rescue himself through the laughter with which he hurls himself into contradictions'. Hagebucher accommodates himself to the burgher world, and it is thus that his struggle appears in humorous form ; his humour anticipates his ultimate surrender, and is his revenge for it. The court of the small state is treated without humour, for Raabe does not accept a compromise with it.

This is the mature form of Raabe's humour, and it has

many gradations. A man like Krumhardt (*The Vogelsang Documents*) is the reverse of a humorist in the usual sense, for he is a prudent and pedantic lawyer, weighed down by the consciousness of his responsibilities, burdened and puzzled by the story he has to tell.   Only an occasional ironical comment, as when he remarks incidentally that he has married into one of the best families, allows us to see that he is conscious of the equivocalness of his career.   In *Gutmann's Travels*, the proceedings of the first conference of the ' Nationalverein ' are accurately reproduced, while the humour is apparently reserved for the love-affair of the shy young couple.   But the intertwining of the two themes, the fretting of young Gutmann through the long speeches, constitutes an essential commentary on the proceedings, which are thus made to appear far less important than the union of the couple ; it is a sort of tender farewell to illusions.   Raabe himself was later to call it a ' Bismarckiad ' ! So also the tender humour with which the old-fashioned, impractical old schoolmaster is described in *Das Odfeld* brings out most subtly both the fragility of the humanity he represents, and its deep roots.

More obviously humorous are those characters like Hagebucher who acutely feel a conflict of values within themselves, and express this through a fantastic and often fierce irony. Velten Andres is no social reformer, though he sets himself against the world, and his revolt expresses itself in savage irony of the ideal of success.   But he writes with the same bitter irony of himself, of his love for Helene and of his plan to become a tailor in order to be able to follow her to America. His mother calls his plan ' a tragic farce ', and Krumhardt asks himself at times if Velten's life is serious or farcical. Asche (*Pfister's Mill*), Schönow, Herberger (*Kloster Lugau*), all try to smother their unease with humour ; the more they devote themselves to practical business, the more their fancy luxuriates.   Schönow and Asche are not just self-opinionated, garrulous, powerful personalities ; their expansive humour expresses the tension in capable and enterprising men between their resolute realism and their humane idealism.   In less resolute characters, like Ebert Pfister, the humour is expressed more indirectly, through the unconscious apposition of values and circumstances in the shaping of the story. Ebert is not the man to face up to all the reality of his times, and so Raabe subtly shows him at times dwelling on his present happiness and hopes, at other times recalling with wistful idealisation the life of the old mill.

When this basic conflict of values is presented without humour, Raabe often falls into sentimentality, and particularly so when childhood or youth appears as the symbol of humaneness. In his early works childhood is a period of unsullied happiness, and scarcely any of his children suffer. His depiction of childhood has nothing of the power and insight of Dickens', for instance. Even the poorest of his children are sheltered by devoted parents or adopted parents, and his adults remember their childhood as an idyll in the country or rural town. He scarcely touches on the psychological stresses of adolescence. Characters like Hans Unwirrsch and Tonie Häussler grow up without conflict and are innocence personified ; even in a later work like *Old Nests*, where past and present are humorously and significantly contrasted, childhood is recalled as an idyll. But also when young people are treated ironically, as in *Gutmann's Travels* or *Horacker* or *Hastenbeck*, Raabe tends to sentimentalise them by exaggerating their helpless innocence in the midst of the big affairs of the world. In the best of his works we can glimpse, as in *The Vogelsang Documents*, the conflicts of age already present in childhood, and their presence in childhood is all the more poignant since the pseudo-narrator, Krumhardt, himself unconsciously tries to see his childhood as idyllic. *Stopfkuchen* is one of the rare works where (in contrast to Eduard's illusions) childhood itself is represented as full of conflict, embodying the limitations of the society in which the child grew.

The most curious and ambiguous of all the novels, in this respect, is Raabe's last, unfinished work, *Altershausen*. On the face of it, the theme is simple and characteristic. A distinguished medical man, at the end of a career full of honours, visits incognito the small town in which he was born, to recapture himself, the real self that the years have overlaid. Little

is changed, and bit by bit he rediscovers this ' better ' self of
his, which he had left behind at the age of eleven or twelve.
He meets again two old school fellows and feels that they have
done as well with their small humble lives as he with his.
What is startling, however, is that one of these, a lad he and
everyone else had much admired, is an idiot, whose mental
development had been arrested through an accident at the age
of twelve.   Here then is the picture of his childhood as it
was, preserved in its original form, yet macabre and distress-
ing, and even ludicrous.   It is a bleak statement that childhood is good but must be outlived.   Yet the distinguished
doctor still finds more comfort and substance in the company
of this idiot and his companion than in his own career, and
if there is grotesque humour in the behaviour of the idiot,
the finer irony is kept for the doctor himself.

Raabe's humour is seen at its deepest in *Stopfkuchen* ; the
humorousness with which Schaumann tells his story defines
exactly the measure of his achievement.   The very character
of his language—he uses the complex literary style of the
educated middle class, often with a parodistic relish which
reveals that this culture itself has become philistine—reminds
us at all moments of what normal people think about his
achievement.   He puts matters in such a way that momentarily
we are led to believe that all he has done is to win the right
to be lazy and comfortable ;   and this is indeed part of the
truth.   But his humorous concessions to normal views, his
refusal to idealise or dramatise his struggle, his almost ostentatious self-depreciation, only strengthen the impression of his
moral power.   As he imposes his tale and his views on Eduard,
we feel he is asserting his personality as against the philistines,
and Eduard's half-comic resignation to the role of a listener
is his vindication :

' Where does a man's fate spring from, at bottom, Eduard ? '
he first asked, and before I could answer (what could I have
answered ?) he gave his opinion : ' Usually, if not always, from
one point.   From my pram-days—you know, Eduard, I've always
been a little feeble on my feet—I can very well remember that
Sunday afternoon walk on which my Dæmon first directed me up

here, when my father said : " Praise be, wife, we shall soon find some shade behind the Red Redoubt. And it's high time this rascal walked on his own feet, what do you think ? "—" He's so feeble on his feet ", sighed my dear mother, and I'll never forget her for these words. Yes, Eduard, I've always been a bit feeble, not only in my head, but also on my feet, and that's the point in question. It's absolutely true that I have not managed to get farther in the world than the shade of the Red Redoubt. I really can't help it. That was my weak point, or if you insist, my strong point. This is where fate got hold of me. I struggled, but I had to submit, and I submitted with a sigh. [Your friend] the postman and [the book of] Le Vaillant carried you, Eduard, to burning Africa, and my feeble intellectual powers and still feebler feet held me fast in the cool shade of this farm. Eduard, you see, fate mostly utilises our weak points to make us attentive to what may be serviceable to us.'

This man was so impudently ungrateful that at this moment, I tell you, he fetched a sigh from the depths of his paunch. Naturally, only to make his contentment seem even more enviable. But I did not fall into the trap. I did not do him the pleasure of sighing too, still deeper and with more justification.[20]

Stopfkuchen's humour, embracing himself as well as the world, puts him in an unassailable position, so that contradiction and agreement both simply confirm his values. His wife, a simple woman, protests that he underrates himself ; but his apparent self-irony only shows how secure he is. ' In *Stopfkuchen* ', wrote Raabe, ' I felt myself most free and secure above the world.' [21]

THE LIMITATIONS OF RAABE'S RANGE

Raabe deserves a place among the important novelists of his time, for the sureness with which he grasped the moral dilemma of his world, and the truth with which he portrays it. But his limitations are such that he can only be accounted a minor writer. His works lack intellectual insight and the energy of passion ; and their social range is very narrow.

In several of the novels Raabe shows a character destroyed by the times, but the conflict is never passionate or bitter. Tonie Häussler, Velten Andres, even the miller Pfister, succumb

without a real effort, inwardly convinced of the unavailing-
ness of struggle. The most conscious of them are ironically
aware that they have no right to move the clock back, however
much they refuse to seek a place within this new world. Those
men who, though torn by misgivings, conform to the new
society—Schönow or Asche—overcome their unease by irony.
Raabe's contemplative tolerance prevented him from envis-
aging the process of his time as a dire conflict of energies, and
he lacks the exaltation of great effort and feeling ; his work
as a whole suffers from drabness. The sobriety and truth
of his work is much to be esteemed, especially when we compare it with the melodrama and hysteria of many of his
German contemporaries. But it not only betrays an emotive
narrowness in his temperament, but also a failure fully to
grasp the implications of the social changes he observed, the
growing social and moral crisis in which the following generation was involved. *The Vogelsang Documents* is an anticipation
of Thomas Mann's *Doctor Faustus*, but an innocent, naïve
anticipation, for the author has no inkling of the ' diabolical '
might of the tensions of which he writes. The loneliness of
his heroes is a naïve anticipation of one of the mightiest modern
themes.

Closely associated with this emotive and intellectual narrowness is the narrowness of social range. Raabe's favourite
setting is the bourgeoisie of the small towns, and the tensions
within the main characters arise from their double relationship, appreciative and critical, to this ' Philisterium '. To the
small-town background, therefore, there is contrasted in different books the world of the peasantry, that of the nobility,
that of the industrial modern town, and that of government and
high society. It must be said that, with one or two exceptions,
Raabe markedly fails in his presentation of these other worlds,
and this is a serious criticism, for his very intention demanded
that their moral character, their inner tensions, should be
clearly delineated.

He was most successful, in *Der Schüdderump* and elsewhere,
in his portrayal of the country nobility, the squirearchy. But
the peasantry appears continually as an undifferentiated mass

of barbarians, engrossed by material interests and vindictive
to the weak. Thus they appear in *Der Schüdderump*, in *Horacker*,
in *Restless Guests*. For the village outcasts Raabe has great
sympathy, linking their fate with that of those men and women
who are at odds with modern society ; but this sympathy is
based on the assumption of the spiritual superiority of the
bourgeoisie, and Schönow's concern for a workman, or Eckerbusch's protection of Horacker, is expressed in bullying tones
which border on arrogance.

Court-circles are portrayed in *Abu Telfan* with a petty-
bourgeois horror as homes of sophisticated heartlessness and
vice. On the whole, Raabe fortunately refrains from the
attempt to describe courts and the upper classes, for his
sketches of social gatherings do not rise above rather trite
satire of conventional elegance (*Old Iron*), and compare most
unfavourably with, say, Fontane's. His criticism of high
society is most solid when he restricts himself to the delineation
of the character of the high official, worn out and morally
distressed by social convention and the arid preoccupations
of his duties (*Der Hungerpastor*, *The Vogelsang Documents*). On
no occasion does he deal with great political and social issues
as they are fought out within ruling circles or political parties.

The industrialist plays a much bigger part in his works
as the main agent of social change, and while at first he forms
a sinister background to his stories, later he comes right into
the foreground as a characteristic and problematical figure of
the times. But, while Raabe gives great attention to the
relation of the industrialist to the old society he is shattering,
it is very noticeable that he scarcely raises the problems arising
from his relations with the modern industrial proletariat. And
this is most surprising in an age in which Social Democracy
became a great social and political force. The only communist that appears in Raabe's pages is a village carpenter in
Restless Guests, and his ' communism ' appears only as sympathy
for the village outcasts and for the charitable sister of the
parson. None of Raabe's industrialists or officials finds any
moral or practical problem arising out of his relationships with
his workmen or subordinates. We pay a visit to Asche's

factory and Schönow's quarry, but are not made aware that there are workers there.

Raabe knew of course of the existence of social conflict; there is a passing and vague reference in the early novel, *Der Hungerpastor*, to the distress and unrest in a factory. But the theme does not recur in later novels. In the first version of *A Springtide* (1857) there is a prophecy of a coming proletarian revolution, but this was deleted from the second edition of 1870. Raabe, like Dickens, has great sympathy for the poor, for social misfits, for workers in isolated occupations like shepherds, foresters, carters, millers, but he never attempts to describe factory-workers. The modern industrial masses seem to have inspired him with repugnance—in a letter he talks of the modern masses as ' pulp ' (' Bevölkerungsbrei ').[22] In his novels he often shows a horror of the great cities, the vast streets and anonymous apartment-houses, though with delightful humour he recognises, in *Pfister's Mill*, that the Berliner may be deeply attached to his flat and suburb, to his ' country ' walks through the modern cemetery.

Raabe's imaginative range is, then, very narrow. He is a bourgeois story-teller, and bourgeois too in a limited way. His best work is confined to the ' burghers ' of the small town, and the great problem of his times, the transformation of Germany into an industrial power, is grasped only in its relation to this class. The men who grow out of this class and become industrialists, bankers, or high officials, are measured not against new problems but against the old values. And within this class Raabe concentrates with preference on the professional people, those with an academic, usually classical education, the schoolmasters, parsons, officials, who are rooted in the class and yet often at odds with it. They sympathise with more humane personal relationships, they seek to guide, but they do not struggle directly against the world; ironically and humorously they admit that they can at best only modify people's attitudes within a general process which cannot be withstood. Sometimes indeed they are only onlookers, only seeking a modest refuge for themselves and their ideals. Raabe's work in general lacks the sweep and

energy of the more impassioned social novelists, like Balzac
and Tolstoy ; he was utterly at a loss with writers like Zola,
Ibsen, and the German naturalists.

While the world narrows in Raabe's imagination to this
small burgher setting, there is criticism as well as appreciation
of the ' Spiesser '. On the one hand his novels are impregnated with the philistinism of the small town, and his best
and most beloved characters are those who love the ' Stammtisch ', the familiar streets and faces, the old grooves, the
gossip. But on the other hand, the limitations of this philistinism are always firmly grasped, its moral rigidity, its lack
of enterprise, the heartlessness within its easy-going good nature.
Raabe's own character contained the two elements. He was
for nearly three decades the leading spirit of the ' Kleider-
seller ', a club of Brunswick burghers, mostly professional men
with an academic education, who met weekly to drink and
talk, to celebrate personal and national festivals with recita-
tions and speeches, at their ease in the typical ' Stammtisch '
manner. Yet they felt that they were here upholding themselves against the ' philistines ', nourishing a civic patriotism
and a moral and aesthetic culture that the practical world
around them disregarded. Raabe wrote in 1875 to Paul
Heyse : ' I have taken the old romantic battle-cry, " War
on the philistines " very seriously ', and later he said : ' We
are the people who pass freely through the ranks of the philistines.' [23] His friend Hänselmann extravagantly claimed that
they were ' a club of inquiring lovers of the naked Adam '.[24]
As Lukács has well said, Raabe lays bare the dilemma of
the petty-bourgeoisie, but within the framework of the petty-
bourgeoisie, not from outside.[25] Raabe himself was aware of
his limitations. He attributed his insight to his ' Dummheit ',
his thick-headedness, which Heess amends to ' mother-wit '.[26]
His range and insight were limited, but his works show a
remarkable harmony between capacity and intention, and a
modesty and humour which set the seal on their integrity.

CHAPTER VII

Theodor Fontane
1819–98

THE BERLINER

'THE task of the modern novel seems to me to be the description of a life, a society, a group of people, as the undistorted reflection of the life we lead ' [1]—Fontane's definition is direct and simple. He is the most clear in purpose of the German novelists, the least embarrassed by psychological troubles and social pressures. His novels are the product of his old age—the first was finished when he was fifty-nine, the greatest, *Effi Briest*, appeared in 1895 when he was seventy-six —and they express the attitude of a shrewd experienced citizen of a metropolitan city. In his novels Fontane freed himself of the provincialism which, for good and ill, marked German literature of the nineteenth century. He was the first German writer since Goethe to stand in easy contact with the public issues of the European world. And, unlike the authors of the ' Bildungsroman ', he was not concerned with inward problems of his own ; his eagerly inquisitive eyes gazed sharply and humorously outwards. He is the most adult of the German novelists.

Fontane was a Prussian and spent most of his life in Berlin, which changed during his lifetime from the staid residence of a Prussian king to the vast, agitated capital of Imperial Germany. As a young man, a dispenser in a chemist's shop, he shared the radical and patriotic enthusiasm of the middle class. He joined the Berlin literary society, the *Tunnel*, to which all the leading artistic lights belonged, and was for two decades a moving spirit in its meetings, reading and discussing poems in its convivial atmosphere, and thoroughly enjoying its free and easy provincialism. Religious and political argument was barred here, and he began to write uncontroversial patriotic poems on the great figures of Prussian history.

His discovery of the Scottish border ballads led him to take up the ballad-genre with enthusiasm, and it was as a modern ballad-writer that he was best known throughout his lifetime. His admiration for Prussia's Junker heroes, and his literary friendship with many Prussian officials and officers, placed him in an awkward dilemma at the time of the 1848 Revolution, and he has left a sincere and ironical account of his half-hearted enthusiasm during the revolutionary days.[2] After the Revolution he tried to live by his writing. A twinge of patriotic conscience sent him to enlist in the volunteer troops engaged in war with Denmark after the defeat of the Prussian troops in 1850, but he was saved in the nick of time by an invitation to join the Press section of the reactionary Manteuffel government ; and if he soon left this job, he was not much more at his ease as correspondent of two Ministerial newspapers, eking out his meagre salary with all sorts of odd jobs. Fontane was acutely aware that he was betraying his political principles ; ' egoism was stronger than patriotism ', he wrote. But he was already discouraged, and he hoped, as he wrote to his closest friend, to rescue himself ' in the past and in the circle of friends and family '.[3] It was to be his lot for two decades to work with men of the extreme Right. But his superiors did not make too stringent demands on him and though he was influenced by this conservative milieu, he always managed to preserve the inner core of his personal independence.

The next years were very difficult for Fontane, for the income from his poems and occasional journalism was pitiful. He tried teaching German in London, and spent a few years in England as a foreign correspondent, making books out of his travels. When the Manteuffel Ministry fell, he lost his connections with the official newspapers. He returned to Berlin in 1859, and from 1860 to 1870 occupied a minor editorial post on the arch-conservative newspaper, the *Kreuzzeitung*. It is characteristic of him that while he was unwilling to transfer his allegiance from one Ministry to the other, largely on grounds of personal decency, he accepted the post on the Junker paper, whose religious orthodoxy was even more distasteful to him than its politics.   Actually he got to like the editors personally, and he always admired the independence of the old-fashioned Junkers in relation to the king.   Never a party-man, he was as much a conservative at this time as a liberal—he describes his political attitude as equally opposed to absolutism and democracy.[4]

His book on Scotland had already given him the idea of writing a descriptive account of the Prussian countryside, and the first volume of his *Journeys through Mark Brandenburg* appeared in 1861.   It, like the subsequent volumes, which he was extending and re-editing to the end of his life, was the only substantial literary success he had.   Based on his journeys in the Mark and his rummaging in old books and papers, these books tell in an easy anecdotal style of the Brandenburg landscape and the homes and lives of famous Prussian families, and bear witness to his profound love of his homeland and his pride in its past.   Fontane was quite aware of their political bearing : ' The content is decidedly conservative ', he wrote.[5] But he was indignant when political opponents suggested he had written the book for the *Kreuzzeitung* party.   The Junkers themselves, in fact, were not always too pleased about what he wrote, for he refused to idealise and sentimentalise them.

It was at this time that he began to plan his first novel, on the theme of the Prussian rising against Napoleon in 1813. But the great political and military events of the 1860s threw all his plans awry.   He wrote histories of the military operations against Denmark, Austria and France, including a little book recounting his misadventures as a military correspondent when he was taken prisoner by the French in 1870.   Only when all this work was over could be settle to his novel. Meanwhile, however, things had drastically changed in Germany.   The Reich had been established, Berlin was being transformed.   And he himself had at last a congenial post. From 1870 to 1890 he was on the staff of the liberal *Vossische Zeitung*, writing regular theatre reviews.

But even now, there was no standing still for Fontane. With a lively interest in public affairs and in people (even to the point of gossip), and a most unprejudiced, forthright character, his mind and his work now really began to unfold. He was proud of Prussian and German achievements, but he began to detest the militarism, anti-semitism and vulgar megalomania of many of his compatriots. He loathed the growing ' byzantinism ', as he called it, of the court of Wilhelm II, the snobbery of all classes, and the shameless ' get rich quick ' spirit of the bourgeoisie. For all his admiration for Bismarck he saw only too clearly the latter's egoism and lack of principle.[6] His warm affection for the rural Junkers remained, but they had no longer, in his opinion, a useful function in modern society.[7] The money-making bourgeoisie of this period of capitalistic expansion he dismissed as ' frightful '. And in his old age he became ' more and more democratic ', as he says ; he turned more and more to the ' fourth estate ', the working class, for hope and comfort. Inquiring of an English friend for more information about Keir Hardie, he wrote : ' The new, better world begins with the fourth estate. What the workers are thinking, saying, writing, has made the thinking, saying, and writing of the old governing classes out of date.'[8] At this time he was actually planning a novel on a fifteenth-century community of communists, the ' Likedeeler '. None of his novels deals, however, with the modern working class ; he kept wisely within the sphere of his own direct experience. The development of his political and social opinions is more subtly revealed in the changing manner of his treatment of material long familiar to him.

In strong contrast to contemporaries and friends like Storm and Heyse, he kept pace too with the new literary tastes of the Europe of the late nineteenth century. While his romantic ballads betray the close stuffy atmosphere of mid-nineteenth-century Prussia, his novels move in a wider world ; in them he responded to the new realism of the younger generation. There was always something of Thackeray and Turgenev in his writing—the broad expansive manner, the tolerance, the prudent half-veiled realism—but he also appreciated the more stark and implacable realism of Flaubert, Zola and Tolstoy. And he was one of the most outspoken supporters of Ibsen and Gerhart Hauptmann and the ' consequent naturalists ',

though he considered their pessimism to be false and sentimental—for above all he detested romantic sentimentalism
and phrase-making.[9]   He found himself, at the end of his life,
amongst the *avant-garde*, and ironically commented on the
absence of the aristocracy and the good German bourgeoisie
from the public celebration of his seventieth birthday.   As he
often wryly remarked, only the cultured Jewish bourgeoisie
showed any real understanding and enthusiasm for his art.[10]
He remained to the end of his life remarkably free from
moral and social convention, always likely to shock even his
friends and family with the brusque outspokenness of his
views.

THE HISTORICAL NOVELS

The material of Fontane's best novels is taken from times
and places he himself knew.   He wrote, in criticism of the
ponderous reconstruction of the German past in Gustav
Freytag's *Die Ahnen* : ' The novel should be a picture of the
times to which we belong, or at least the reflection of the times
adjacent to ours, about which our parents have told us.'   He
was ready, in his usual undogmatic way, to make some allowances for other types of novel, the romantic or historical, but
the statement interprets his own work and his capacity.[11]   He
wrote only one conventional historical novel, *Grete Minde*, and
it is one of his weakest tales, sentimental and vague, without
any vigour of historical imagination.   It is noticeable, too,
that whenever Fontane sends his characters to foreign countries,
they and their circumstances become shadowy and artificial ;
Quitt, which partly takes place in America, is extremely weak.
His imagination became plastic and fertile only in the familiar
circumstances of Berlin and the Mark.

It is, however, quite a different matter with two of his
novels, *Before the Storm* (*Vor dem Sturm*, 1878) and *Schach von
Wuthenow* (1883), which both deal with the early years of the
nineteenth century, years ' about which his parents had told
him '.   His studies of the Mark and the Junkers, his Prussian
patriotism, and his concern with contemporary affairs combine

to give these historical novels the immediacy and plasticity that distinguishes his stories of contemporary life.

Before the Storm, his first novel, betrays in more than one way the influence of the novelist Wilibald Alexis, the German imitator of Walter Scott. Alexis, like Fontane, combined an admiration for the Prussian Junkers with liberal ideals of social freedom and German unity. In addition to somewhat trashy tales in the style of *Kenilworth* or *Ivanhoe*, he planned a trilogy of novels covering the years of the Napoleonic occupation of Prussia. Two of these were completed, the second, *Isegrimm* (1852), being considered by Fontane to be his best work. It describes the sporadic resistance put up by the country nobility, the peasantry, and the small-town burghers in the evil years following the defeat at Jena, and in the last chapters the story of the main characters is briefly taken up to 1848. Psychologically superficial, sensationalistic and sentimental, the novel has some good qualities which Fontane absorbed. Alexis was the first writer to make the bleak landscape of the Mark come to life ; and above all he created in his chief character, the Freiherr von Quarbitz, a significant type that appears frequently in Fontane's work—an autocratic, patriarchal Junker (' Krautjunker '), wavering between his feudal pride and his loyalty to his king, between his class-feeling and his patriotism, devoted with warm affection to his serfs and his pastor and always likely to treat them like slaves.

The milieu of *Before the Storm* is essentially the same, and it might be called the third part of Alexis' trilogy, for it depicts the response of Junkers and villagers to the defeat of Napoleon in Russia. Fontane's aim was to show, as he put it, ' how the great feeling, that was born at that time, found the most diverse people, and how it affected them '. He has chosen a simple circle of characters, he continues, in order to show how ' a great idea ' transforms ordinary people, and he has deliberately avoided grandiose events : ' I do not intend to thrill, hardly even to grip my readers.'[12]

The novel has many faults. The sensationalism of Alexis is absent, it is true, and the climax is a soberly described abortive attack by the rural irregulars on the French garrison

N

at Frankfurt on the Oder.   But there are a number of romantic elements, and a sentimental misalliance at the end that does not ring true.   The psychology is naïvely black and white, and personal love affairs tend to obscure the great issue which is the theme of the book.   It is much more broadly based than Alexis's novel, and we are given glimpses of many milieux besides the mansion and village of Hohen-Vietz—the middle class of Frankfurt, the petty bourgeoisie of Berlin, elegant aristocratic circles in the capital—but much of this remains episodic, and our interest is not only not ' gripped ', it flags. Fontane has made his task too simple, for there is little conflict within or between his characters, scarcely any psychological or dramatic tension.

The style too is broad, almost garrulous at times, and deliberately so.   Just at this time Spielhagen, the author of sensationalistic social novels, had published a book on the technique of the novel in which he had proclaimed that the novel should approximate in form to drama, and he held to the principle that Henry James was to maintain, that the author should be completely hidden behind his work.   Fontane disagreed.   He wrote that the best novelists had never been afraid to appear in person :

The continual popping-up of the puppet-player in person has an extraordinary charm for me, and it is just that that creates the ease and tranquillity that must assert itself in epic writing.   The ' dramatic ' treatment of things, now so fashionable, has led to sensationalism.[13]

The reference to the ' puppet-player ' may indicate that Fontane had Thackeray in mind, as the latter uses this image in the last sentence of *Vanity Fair*.

Fontane's distaste for sensationalism was to remain, but he was to change his attitude on the question of the intrusive author.   In *Vor dem Sturm*, however, he is only too intrusive. He stops his narrative with remarks like : ' This is the moment to give a biographical sketch of . . .'   He gives us ambulatory descriptions of churches or homes, as in his *Journeys through the Mark*.   As each character appears he gives us his biography, perhaps too the story of his ancestors and his ancestral seat.

Yet, diffuse and loose as the construction of the novel is, the separate scenes reveal a peculiar gift. Through the trivial conversations on ordinary occasions, a dinner-party, a Christmas gathering in a country mansion or a petty-bourgeois home, characters and attitudes are skilfully built up, taking shape as they rebound against or adapt themselves to one another. It is not surprising that Fontane himself spoke, in a review of Keller's *Die Leute von Seldwyla*, of his own ' predilection for genre-scenes and for the Stifter-type of detail description '.[14] In the best of the later novels Fontane was to be successful in shaping these ' genre ' scenes into organic elements of a developing story. This maturing of his art was not a mere improvement of technique ; it indicates too a surer grasp of his purpose—the depiction, through a group of personal relationships, of a general, typical situation of deep significance to his contemporaries.

It sounds queer to speak of the ' maturing ' of the art of a man of fifty-nine. Certainly it took place rapidly, for *Schach von Wuthenow*, which was started in 1878 and published in 1883, shows Fontane's art at its best. It is again a story of Prussia in the period of her downfall, a story of a small circle that, in its personal relationships and fate, mirrors the total situation of Prussia on the eve of its collapse before Napoleon. But it is without sentimentality, without digressions ; a sympathetic, but coolly even ironically observant analysis of a Junker in his class-environment. Fontane's attitude to the Prussian nobility had changed, and changed for good—we must remember of course that *Vor dem Sturm* was conceived as early as 1860, while by 1878 Fontane had detached himself from *Kreuzzeitung* and conservatives, was working on a Liberal paper, and was aware of vast economic and social changes in the Bismarck Reich.

The source of the novel was an anecdote told him by a friend. He defines its theme himself : ' A character, good and shrewd enough to recognise what is his duty, but weak enough to wish to avoid carrying it out for fear of being laughed at.' Fontane dated it exactly in the years 1804–6 and related it explicitly to this period as a typical illustration of the whole

situation.[15] He felt the anecdote to be so apt that he only
slightly altered the names of those involved.

Schach von Wuthenow, a man of forty, is an officer in a
crack Prussian regiment stationed in Berlin. He frequents the
salon of an elegant and charming widow, Frau von Carayon,
and it is rumoured that he intends to marry her ; but he holds
back, perhaps because of a naturally cold and reserved character, perhaps, as some say, because he shirks becoming the
stepfather of her daughter Victoire, who is badly pock-marked.
Under the influence of Prince Louis, who praises the charm
and intelligence of Victoire, he cedes to a momentary impulse
and seduces her. He abruptly drops the Carayons, and only
when Victoire tells her mother that she is to have a child
does Frau von Carayon summon Schach and demand that he
should marry her. Schach recognises his duty and agrees,
only asking that the announcement of the engagement should
be delayed a little so that he can prepare himself to face the
situation. But the rumour spreads among his brother-officers,
and some malicious cartoons are published showing Schach
wavering between mother and daughter. This public mockery
is too much for him, and he retires to his country mansion.
Frau von Carayon, receiving no answer to her letters, petitions
the king to intervene, and the latter summons Schach and tells
him that he expects him to marry Victoire. Schach now goes
through with the wedding, but immediately afterwards shoots
himself.

It is a story of a man whose whole being is conformity,
' morbidly dependent on the judgement of others, particularly
of the men of his class ', as an acquaintance puts it. A fellow-
officer believes that his fear of ridicule would even prevent him
from marrying a widow. On an excursion to the old church
at Tempelhof, he walks round with Victoire, enjoying her
intelligent conversation ; but when they leave the church he
joins her mother, so as to avoid being seen with an ugly companion. His sense of propriety has its good sides, too. His
brother-officers are in general a rough, reckless lot, and they
carry out a coarse masquerade through the Berlin streets, a
skit on Luther and his Käte, with an abundance of defrocked

nuns and so on. Schach's decency is shown in his revulsion against such frivolous escapades. This incident, so loosely connected with the story of Schach and Victoire, not only allows us to understand why Schach is unpopular, but shows too how the coarse frivolity of the normal officer forms a pendant to Schach's conventionalism, and thus suggests doubly the lack of *morale* in this Prussian army. The main theme is raised directly in Schach's clashes with a retired officer, von Bülow, who has read the signs of the times and never stops repeating that the Prussian army is rotten and that the Prussian state itself is doomed to disappear in the new Napoleonic world. Schach is not clever and mobile enough to answer Bülow with anything more substantial than anger, yet, while we see that his conventionality makes him blind, at the same time there is something good in his simple loyalty. Victoire, sometimes painfully aware of his vanity, also sees that he is ' chivalrous, honest, discreet and able '.

From the attitude of the Carayons we see that Fontane is not concerned to establish antithetical abstractions like convention and nature, propriety and morality, ' fashion or humanity ', as Schiller puts it in *Kabale und Liebe*. The Carayons do not stand for the ' rights of the heart '. Victoire tells Schach, it is true, that she really does not approve the public association of Prince Louis with his mistress, which Schach accepts simply because he is a prince of the royal blood. But at the same time Victoire says that it is absurd to make a fuss about such matters : ' Society is sovereign. What it tolerates, is valid ; what it condemns is to be condemned.' This is the wisdom of her clear-sighted, sophisticated mother, and it contributes not a little to Schach's admiration for them both. It is on this principle that Frau von Carayon insists implacably on Schach's preserving her daughter's honour. Victoire herself is ready to renounce any claim on her seducer, but Frau von Carayon takes matters into her own hands : ' I am not weak enough to give in to this generous play-acting of hers. I belong to society, whose conditions I fulfil, whose laws I accept.' Neither she nor Schach speaks of love ; both fully understand and accept social convention, and the marriage

is ' arranged ' without illusions on either side. Schach's
suicide is fully within this convention, and, however sharp the
shock is to Victoire, we are quite logically told nothing about
her feelings. A sort of epilogue gives us, in the form of a
letter written many months later, not Victoire's feelings but
her dispassionate reflections on Schach's behaviour and
character.

The political and social background to this private story is
indicated very lightly and subtly, through the conversations
in the Carayon salon, in the officers' club, at Prince Louis' At
Home. But it is brought into relief at the end in a long
letter written by von Bülow. He considers the Schach affair
to be symptomatic of the whole class to which he belongs, in
which the concept of ' honour ' has turned into cowardly conventionalism. Society is worshipping idols, he says, and he
warns his correspondent that a society which has thus lost its
soul must expect great disasters to come.

It might seem that this short novel should more properly
be called a Novelle, for we are interested in the main
characters only at the moment when their fates intertwine,
and are not concerned with them in any wider sense. None
makes any great demands on our interest or sympathy except
at this one moment. But, from the beginning, this slight story
opens up wide social perspectives, and it advances on a broad
front. We are continually conscious that these characters are
members of a society, and that, while for a moment Schach
occupies our main interest, at the next someone else will push
forward. We feel this broad sweep as clearly as in *Vor dem
Sturm*, though here the story is far more coherent and simple ;
its progress is both particular and general, like the irregular
advance of the incoming tide. The fact that our sympathies
are nowhere deeply engaged leaves us free to observe with a
curious interest the play of the whole.

The novel is fully characteristic of Fontane's art as a novelist.
There is an utter lack of sensationalism, in the theme as in
the tone. The crises—the seduction and the suicide—are
treated in a subdued tone, with even less emphasis than the
ordinary events of social life ; indeed, it has often been said

that Fontane fails to depict passion and thus fails to involve us emotionally in the fates of his characters. With slight, delicate touches he creates a number of varied characters, largely through their own conversation, showing a skill unparalleled in German literature in depicting social types with manifold nuances. Characteristic of his art, too, is what he called ' the clarification of a situation ', a deeper insight into men and their situation which enables us to make moral judgements without falling into rigid self-righteousness. The characters are never absolutely determined and labelled, they retain undefined potentialities. This is most clearly evident in the somewhat strange, and perhaps clumsy, ending of the novel, for Schach's death is followed by the two epilogues in which Bülow and Victoire reconsider Schach's character. On the one hand these letters point the moral, try to sum up the story's meaning ; on the other, they are only the views of people involved, betraying their own characters as much as interpreting Schach's ; they are not objective and conclusive statements, in fact they are somewhat contradictory. And so they leave us pondering, occupied with the story outside the framework of the novel.

THE NOVELS OF CONTEMPORARY BERLIN

Most of Fontane's later novels centre on aspects of social life in the capital ; the best of these are *Errors, Entanglements* (*Irrungen, Wirrungen*) (1887) and *Stine* (1890), which single out the relations between aristocratic officers and the lower class, and *Frau Jenny Treibel* (1892) which deals with the middle class.

The two first have as their theme a subject dear to the heart of magazine-writers : love affairs between officers and girls of the artisan class, the good old problem of heart versus material advantage, and in each case the girl is ' simplicity, truthfulness, naturalness personified '. But both these girls realise that marriage is out of the question and turn the young men back to their class-obligations. Fontane himself rudely refused to

believe in romantic misalliances. He wrote to a friend, in
reference to *Errors, Entanglements* :

> You have hit the nail on the head : ' Customary morals are
> valid and must be valid '. That they must is hard at times, one
> must admit. And because things are as they are, that is best ;
> keep away and don't touch. Anyone who disregards this bit of
> traditional practical wisdom—I don't like to use the word morals
> —gives his whole life a fatal twist. Yes, that's about it.[16]

In the novels, however, this rather uninspired ' moral ' raises
further, more involved issues.

Lene, the heroine of *Irrungen, Wirrungen,* is a vigorous, self-
reliant girl, devoted to her officer-friend, Botho, with that
rational forthrightness that distinguishes many of Fontane's
female characters. The market-gardener's where she lives,
the walks in the Berlin suburbs, the modest excursions the lovers
make, are described with simple and sober charm. From the
beginning Lene knows her liaison must be short-lived, and
when Botho is urged by his mother to marry a rich cousin and
so restore the family's fortunes, she tells him that it must be
so. She knows he is a nice boy, affectionate and honourable,
but also weak, average, and she accepts the fact that sooner
or later he will give in to the pressure of his social class—
' either it's your mother, or the gossip of people, or circumstances ', she tells him, that will prove too strong for him.

When Botho has to face the issue, he knows too how he
will decide. He goes for a long ride, and the thoughts that
pass through his head are those of Lene's. ' I am not the
man to challenge the world and openly declare war on its
prejudices ; I am absolutely opposed to such Quixotism.' He
passes a monument to an officer killed in a duel. He knows
that the cause of this man's death was absurd, ' an aristocratic
conception, a class-fad, which was more powerful than commonsense, more powerful too than the law '. But it only
proves that ' our behaviour is ruled by convention '. And
when a brother-officer who is proposing to marry a bourgeoise
comes to get his moral support, Botho harshly condemns his
intention, and tells him that such a marriage would only make
him wretched.

So Botho marries his cousin, a silly, fashionable creature, while Lene marries an honest, narrow-minded foreman. All ends well, with a wistful memory of the past which is by no means tragic. Yet there is more than the theme of common-sense realism in the novel. The characters develop into representative figures. On the one hand is the sturdy, humane, healthy artisan circle ; on the other the weak, trivial, class-proud aristocracy. If Botho solves his family problem, he only throws into sharper relief the decadence of a class which demands, for its existence, the abandonment of natural feeling, energy and intelligence.

Stine presents a variation on the same theme. The young Junker, Waldemar von Haldern, is a sick man. He has been retired from the army owing to a severe wound, and thus has already relinquished the duties of his class. He falls in love with a consumptive little sempstress, and challenges convention by asking her to marry him, proposing that they should emigrate. But Stine sees that neither of them is capable of sustaining the challenge. When she refuses, he commits suicide.

In contrast to them is Stine's sister, the widow Pittelkow, and her elderly lover, the Graf, Waldemar's uncle. Their liaison is without illusions and without shadows. Vigorous and practical, sharp-witted and sharp-tongued, the widow anxiously observes Stine's affection for Waldemar, for she knows her sister is too sensitive and gentle for such an affair. She tries to put an end to it, just as the Graf, a *bon viveur* whose liaison with Pittelkow is strictly within the rules, tells Waldemar that marriage with a ' bourgeoise ' is utterly out of the question.

When Fontane said that the main character of this novel was not Stine, but the widow Pittelkow,[17] he may have meant two things. On the one hand, she is a much fuller character, full of bustle and liveliness, and the scenes in her home, the grandiose party for the Graf and his friends, are full of verve. But Fontane also wishes to say, perhaps, that she is the main character because she takes the right attitude, the attitude of Lene in *Irrungen, Wirrungen*. And yet, in this respect, his statement is misleading. The widow is only a side issue, a

bit of genre-painting. What is central, once again, is the dead
weight of convention in the aristocracy, which Waldemar and
Stine have not the strength to bear. And the decisive scene,
in which the novel culminates, is the funeral of Waldemar.
Here his personal inadequacy is forgotten in the lustre of his
family and class. He himself, despite his consciousness of
being an outcast, unwanted and despised at home, had asked
that he might be buried in the family vault. High-ranking
generals arrive at the estate, and the scion of an ancient family
is laid in his grave with full military honours. The panoply
of glory is polished up ; the rock-like pride of the Junkers
rules once again ; the individual Waldemar is forgotten.
Unnoticed, the frail figure of Stine slinks to the church, the
only real mourner, to return home mortally sick. It is one of
Fontane's grand scenes, paying tribute to the past achievements and solidarity of a great class, yet pitilessly, without any
emphasis, communicating the poverty of its feeling, its unconscious hypocrisy, its shallowness.

Die Poggenpuhls (1896) is a light-hearted counterpart to these
novels. Here an impoverished aristocratic family, living
cooped up in a cheap Berlin flat, is utterly preoccupied with
schemes for making both ends meet. The eldest son, the man
of duty, is soberly making a career on the general staff ; the
younger, the favourite, who wants the usual good time of a
young officer, causes them all great anxiety. In this family,
the question of misalliance is predominant. The mother
herself is a bourgeoise. The elder daughter, a snob of snobs,
makes herself agreeable in aristocratic circles. The middle
daughter is a real middle-class ' Hausfrau '. The youngest
frequents the home of rich Jews and plans to marry her
brother to a Jewish heiress. Their problems are resolved by
a *deus ex machina*, a wealthy relative who leaves them sufficient
money to relieve them of the worst pressures. The story is
the only one of Fontane's where the theme of misalliance—so
common a practice at that time—is treated as a self-evident
habit ; but it has no seriousness as the whole is told in the
form of a skilful conventional farce. If one were to take it
seriously, one would be horrified at the heartless cynicism of

this Junker family, so shamelessly scheming to exploit their noble name. Not that Fontane was worried about this. He knew the rich bourgeoisie too well to think they might be the passive victims of the poverty-stricken Junkers.

These three novels are rather slight. It is as if Fontane purposely avoided their deeper social implications, for the tone is never tragic. His old sympathy for the Junkers is still in evidence, and the avowed ' moral ' supports the class-conventions of the Junkers. But they mark his almost involuntary change from an admirer to a ' disappointed lover ', as he often called himself, a critic of the class on whom Prussia's glories had been built. The Junkers themselves felt the bearing of these novels. *Irrungen, Wirrungen* was greeted by many hostile protests on their part, and it was this novel, above all else, that led the Junkers to be so conspicuously absent from the celebrations of Fontane's seventieth birthday.

It is perhaps not an accident that the writing of *Irrungen, Wirrungen* coincided with an absurd affair in which a Jewish friend of Fontane's, Friedländer, was convicted by a military ' court of honour ' of impugning the dignity of a higher officer —a Dreyfus case on a small scale—and from this time Fontane's criticism of the sabre-rattling militarists, with their mock-heroic gestures, grew sharper and sharper. He wrote to his friend in terms that we can apply to his novels :

When you leave the personal aspect on one side and look at the affair as signatura temporis, and not as being merely possible in Prussia but as being characteristic of Prussia, then everybody, you included, as a patriot and a human being, has to weep bloody tears.[18]

Fontane was just as unsentimental in his imaginative treatment of the Berlin bourgeoisie. One of the earlier novels, *L'Adultera* (1882), is built on a famous divorce case in wealthy Jewish circles of the capital. The banker, Van den Straaten, is an expansive, easy-going man with a sentimental streak, hiding his feelings under irony and talkativeness. His wife, Melanie, feels she needs something more, some greater natural-ness and simplicity of feeling ; she runs away with a business friend, Rubehn, and finds it hard to weather the storm of public disapproval.   But she builds a new home, on Rubehn's principle : ' Don't take it more tragically than necessary, and don't brood too much on the unpleasant old theme of guilt and atonement.'   Fontane's freedom from conventional views of morality is striking, as it was to remain : ' I am ready to swear on the Host that the old standpoint of so-called morality is absolutely idiotic, obsolete, and above all, a lie.' [19]   But he fails in this novel to show any passion or moral crisis in any of the characters, and the characters of Melanie and Rubehn are shadowy and trivial.

Frau Jenny Treibel (1892) succeeds precisely where *L'Adultera* fails, and largely because Fontane evades emotive complications and concentrates on the depiction of milieu.   The story is of the slightest.   Corinna, the daughter of a schoolmaster, Professor Schmidt, has made up her mind to marry Leopold Treibel, the son of a wealthy industrialist.   He is a poor-spirited young man whom she easily ensnares, and who as easily capitulates when his mother mobilises all her forces against the match.   Instead of the battle one expects, however, Corinna almost immediately sees she has made a mistake, and marries a schoolmaster.   At no moment is there any fear of a serious entanglement, for Corinna is a self-possessed practical girl who is never in any danger of taking things tragically, and who scarcely needs our sympathy even if she ever deserves it.

What distinguishes the book is the firm grasp of Berlin characters within their milieux.   In his likings and dislikings Fontane was never violent and one-sided, always humorously and ironically tolerant.   Professor Schmidt and his school-master friends, the ' men of the spirit ', have all the foibles and conceit of their class.   The Treibel circle, to which most of the book is devoted, reveals the traits that Fontane so detested in the plutocracy, but is seen with an amused irony rather than satire.

In the centre of the picture stands Frau Jenny Treibel, the purse-proud ambitious bourgeoise who rules the household and is determined that her son shall make a marriage in his own income-group.   But she also has pretensions to culture and sentiment.   The daughter of a greengrocer, she had as a girl

had an affair with Professor Schmidt, though she had thrown
him over for the better match, Treibel ; and this affair is her
treasured memory, she warms it up on any occasion, and at
all her parties the climax is a rendering of a lyrical tribute
which Schmidt had once composed for her. Hard as nails,
she tries to get the best of both worlds, the ideal and the
practical. Schmidt comments ironically on her character :
' Now the little doll has got a title (" Kommerzienrätin "),
and she can allow herself everything, even ideals, and even
" unswervingly ", as she puts it. A model of a bourgeoise.'
Her husband indulges her sentimentality too, knowing that
the family ' honour ' is absolutely safe in her hands. Like the
noblemen of the earlier novels, she is a social type, a representative ; and the wives she chooses for her sons are representative
too, rich Hamburg women, all artificiality and snobbishness,
narrow-minded and calculating, without the capacity for
happiness.

Treibel himself is a successful businessman of the Van den
Straaten type. Not bad at heart, aware of the falseness of
his wife and the inanity of his daughter-in-law, but avoiding
difficulties, easy-going. He is fond of Corinna and would be
glad to have her about the place, but he defers to the indignation of his wife. He too has his ambition, which leads him to
dabble in politics of the extreme Right and to court some
noble ladies who have, he hopes, influence at court. He is
standing for the Reichstag, and his agent is a reactionary
ex-officer who thinks and talks in slogans : this theme is,
however, only lightly sketched.

In this novel Fontane's style reaches its full stature. His
technique might be defined as dialogic, in the sense that
there is very little description, and what there is is a sort of
stage-direction, deliberately demanded of psychological statement, and confined to the externals of appearance. Altogether we are told little of what the characters are thinking.
We know about them through their actions, but above all
through what they say and what others say about them. The
essential structure of the novel is therefore a series of conversations. And even in these conversations, the characters

maintain the normal tone of social intercourse. Rarely does
any person speak his inmost thoughts ; these are reserved for
his privacy, and therefore are not spoken at all, scarcely
mentioned by the author, except when they have become
evident through hints. At a dinner-party, on an excursion,
the topics are indifferent, slight, the persons involved adopt
the tone they think fit, and with unsurpassed mastery out of
these scraps, out of the tone of remarks, the characters acquire
body and personality. The climaxes of the story are therefore
not moments of inward wrestling, which are passed over
lightly, nor dramatic conflicts, but these indifferent discussions
in which the figures range themselves almost imperceptibly
in their true posture.

Fontane has moved far from his earlier predilection for the
' intrusive ' author. He had largely abandoned this method
even in *Schach von Wuthenow*, where only once does he speak
confidentially of ' our Schach '. A second comment he made
on Spielhagen's advocacy of the ' dramatic ' form of the novel
shows that he was conscious of his change of attitude :

The intervention of the author is almost always harmful, or at
least superfluous. And what is superfluous is false. It is true
enough that it is often difficult to ascertain where intervention
begins. The writer must inevitably do and say a lot. Otherwise
it just doesn't work or artifice results. But he must refrain from
judging, preaching, from being clever and wise.[20]

Fontane's artistic instinct preserved him from the dogmatism
of Spielhagen, though this matter is so complicated that it is
not surprising that he could not formulate his position very
clearly. He knew that interventions from an author who
stands right outside his story are irritating ; but he knew too
that intrusions are not only unavoidable but also aesthetically
of fundamental significance. The intrusions in, say, *Middlemarch* (which were the occasion of Spielhagen's strictures) do
not break the artistic illusion like some of Gotthelf's polemics
and sermons. They construct the image of an imaginary
author, who gives the story its tone and unity on a level parallel
to the events themselves, lending it an additional dimension.[20a]

The method has obvious pitfalls, but Fontane was rarely to strain himself to avoid its dangers.

In any case, he recognised the absurdity of the aim of Naturalist writers like Holz and Schlaf to obliterate the author, for he was well aware that the author must be the organising principle of the work. Thus, for instance, in the account of Frau Treibel's dinner-party, he takes us unobtrusively and easily from one end of the table to the other, following the conversation here and there. The whole book is a series of scenes, evidently arranged by the author—what happens in between can be guessed, or can be ignored so far as it is irrelevant to the story. He manages to tell us more about Leopold's character from his chat with the waiter, who on his mother's instructions refuses to serve him with coffee, or from the manner of his announcement of his engagement, from his very silence, than he would from a long analysis of his thoughts. Only once or twice does Fontane's manner seem forced and border on that ' artifice ' of which he speaks. We hear of Treibel's political ambitions in the main through the newspaper reports of his agent's campaign and through his own reflections on them ; but Fontane makes Treibel himself read the reports aloud and talk his thoughts, even to saying to himself ' I will read the passage [from the newspaper] again '. Similarly, he makes Professor Schmidt actually speak a soliloquy.

But these are rare faults. The effect of his method is not an increase of dramatic tension, which he deliberately avoids, but a development in psychological depth. For each character acquires a many-sided reality, is seen in the light of the others and in relation to the others, and goes on acquiring substance as these relations develop. The story hardly grips us, but the characters acquire a potency which gives them a claim on us in their own right, outside the framework of these casual relationships, and they seem to go on existing beyond the confines of the story as in *Schach*—a condition of a good novel as Fontane defined it. The author does not put his own judgements round them, defining them once and for all, blacking out the background ; rather, he sets them going into wide and far perspectives. And this technique is the exact artistic counterpart or medium of his own moral outlook. For while he leaves us in no doubt about the moral constitution of his characters, and has written in this novel a sharp criticism of the psyche of the Berlin plutocracy, the criticism is tempered because Fontane does not write from an absolutist moral point of view. The criticism remains within the confines of the story, and judgements are made in terms of people who are all more or less imperfect. Thus Fontane's criticism is never final, it never becomes a condemnation. It lacks both the sharpness and the illusions that characterise, for instance, George Eliot's satire in *Middlemarch*, just as it lacks George Eliot's generalising observations. Fontane's humour was his way of overcoming the meretriciousness of the plutocracy; though he had no illusion that it was thus really overcome. In the very year in which *Frau Jenny Treibel* was published Fontane often felt incapable of taking things and describing them with this amused equanimity. ' To see this [worship of Baal] from the humorous side is the way to overcome it, but it needs a strength that I no longer have.'[21]

EFFI BRIEST

Among Fontane's novels, *Effi Briest* stands out because of the firm line of the story. Like several of the others it is based on an anecdote, ' a story of adultery like a hundred others ', which Fontane transposed to the circumstances he knew intimately, the Mark, Pomerania and Berlin; but contrary to his usual custom he wrote it swiftly and easily, ' as in a dream '.[22]

The home of Effi, the mansion of the Junker family von Briest, has an idyllic character like her own childhood, deep in the country, narrow, but carefree and easy. Her father is a limited, blunt, affectionate man, ready to avoid difficulties with his characteristic phrase: ' das ist ein weites Feld '— ' that takes us too far afield '; her mother good-hearted, contented, with a strong family-feeling. Effi herself is a little spoilt, a tomboy, by rank and character the leader among her friends, the rather dim daughters of the village pastor and precentor. Suddenly there comes an offer of marriage from von Innstetten, a most eligible man of thirty-eight, well launched on a distinguished career. Twenty years before he had loved Effi's mother but had not had the means to marry her. When the offer comes Effi is playing hide-and-seek with her playfellows ; as she goes to receive it the other girls call to her : ' Effi, come ', thinking she is in hiding. Fontane said later that it was this incident in the anecdote he heard that fascinated him and made him write his story.

Effi surprises her parents with her calm acceptance of the offer. Her mother, who is in much more of a flutter than her daughter, is a little alarmed at the swiftness of her decision and once or twice before the wedding tries to make sure that it is the right match for Effi. She knows, however, that love is not over-important in the first place, providing there is no dislike, and providing the man has the estimable qualities that Innstetten has—character, position, honourableness. She herself had not married for love. And Effi answers her careful inquiries by saying ' Why shouldn't I love him ? ' She likes a gay officer-cousin who is temperamentally akin to her, but for a husband she wants, she says, a man of character and principle, someone who will supply the firmness and seriousness she feels herself to lack. It is true she feels a little dashed at Innstetten's letters, which are formal and correct, and has a slight feeling of fear in his presence. But she believes all this will pass. The wedding goes off with the usual assembly of Junker relatives, the warmth of feeling being provided by the pastor in his address. Typical in every way, it seems a repetition of her mother's marriage, which had turned out so well. The anxiety of the parents, expressed in a long conversation after the wedding, is not more acute than the normal anxiety of all parents. They realise that Effi loves pleasure and distractions, and in the remote Pomeranian seaside town of Kessin where her husband is stationed she will lack these ; but on the other hand she is ambitious, and Innstetten is bound to advance in the civil service.

Life in Kessin is monotonous, but Innstetten is always

o

attentive and considerate, so far as his duties permit. Effi
takes a dislike to their house, old-fashioned, with queer curios,
and a strange noise in the attic that frightens her, and only
in this respect does Innstetten refuse to indulge her wishes,
saying that people in their position would seem ridiculous if
they left the house for such reasons.   Often he has to work
in the evenings, sometimes he has to spend a night at Bismarck's country place ; but he does his best for her, taking
her on excursions and introducing her to the local gentry and
townsfolk.   But her life is dreary.   The people of her own
class are narrow, illiberal, orthodox and puritanical, and view
her charm and liveliness with distrust ; the townsfolk are too
old-fashioned and quaint to make companions for her.   She
herself has few tasks and responsibilities even after her child
is born.

A new district commander of the Territorials, Major von
Crampas, is appointed, and he brings some life into the local
club.   Effi is drawn into amateur theatricals and makes friends
with this notorious ladies' man.   Out of idle adventurism he
begins to poison her mind against her husband, telling her
that Innstetten has a passion for training people and that his
behaviour to Effi is deliberately planned to mould her to his
liking.   Effi sees through Crampas, but almost idly, negli-
gently, she allows herself to be seduced.   They meet from
time to time in a hut among the dunes, but the affair with
its stealth and dissembling brings Effi little joy.   Then comes
the great news that Innstetten is promoted to one of the
Ministries in Berlin.   Effi seizes with joy the opportunity of
breaking away from this dull province, above all from her
wearisome entanglement with Crampas.

Their life in Berlin works out splendidly.   Effi likes the
distractions of the capital and becomes a normal society lady ;
their marriage seems utterly successful.   Then, after six years
in Berlin, Effi goes on holiday, and Innstetten discovers by
accident the old letters of Crampas that his wife had carelessly
kept.   He challenges and kills Crampas, and repudiates his
wife.   Effi becomes an outcast, for even her parents, though
they support her financially, will not have her in their home.

After some time she is allowed to see her daughter, but the girl has been so hardened against her sinful mother that the meeting is disastrous, and Effi has a serious collapse. She is taken home for the last few months of her life, and before she dies comes to recognise that her husband, though he was lacking in love, had throughout acted quite rightly.

Numerous *motifs* in this novel recall other works of Fontane. The partriarchal Junker on his estate appears frequently. Innstetten is a modern, more ambitious and competent Schach von Wuthenow. The problem of ' honour ', the duel-theme, not only is raised in *Irrungen, Wirrungen*, it recalls a situation in Alexis' *Isegrimm*. Effi's meeting with her daughter is exactly paralleled in *L'Adultera*. We are accustomed to minor characters like the servants, to celebrations like the wedding, the party at the Kessin apothecary's, about the excellence of which nothing more need be said. But all these incidents and persons are bound, in *Effi Briest*, in a tight knot ; they are by no means merely incidental or illustrative, they each tighten the noose into which Effi so innocently has placed her head. It is as if this piece of scandal had given Fontane the opportunity to sift in his imagination all the characteristic situations in the private life of the nobility of his day and to make a story both specific and typical : this tale of the break-down of a marriage ' grows into the shaped expression of the general contradictions of the whole of civil society '.[23]

It is characteristic that, in terms of the persons themselves, the rights and wrongs of their actions remain uncertain, puzzling. Effi is a charming girl and happiness seems to be her due ; yet she is light, frivolous, without ' character '. If the letters had not been discovered she would have become something not very different from Botho's wife in *Irrungen, Wirrungen*, elegant, ambitious, superficial. Her sin is the outcome not of passion, as with Anna Karenina, but of frivolity, almost nonchalance ; and unlike Madame Bovary she is not driven by some desperate craving and finds it easy to return to conventional proprieties. Lack of passion characterises most of Fontane's heroines, and sometimes his incapacity to express feeling is a serious failing ; in Effi's case, however, it is an

essential part of her character that she has no depth of passion.
It is quite consistent, therefore, that she is happy in those last
months at home. Even here, she does not feel contrition
except in so far as she has saddened her parents, and is content
to return to the pseudo-innocence of her childhood. That
she makes her peace with her husband is not the author's
verdict on the latter's behaviour, but Effi's, and it accords
with the affectionate lightness of her character. Her girlish
charm is the exact counterpart of the charm of her parents,
she shares their simplicity and affableness, like them she is
oblivious of intellectual and moral problems. But, at their
age and in their rural seclusion, they are safe, while she,
thrown into the larger world, is not able to contend with it,
not even able to maintain herself. Effi is not an exception,
not a peculiar case ; her own fate mirrors the whole class to
which she belongs, the rural Junker nobility to which Fontane
was so attached, and which he recognised to be so out of date,
so inadequate to modern tasks. At the very time at which
he was comparing the first draft of the novel he wrote words
which, harsh as they sound, interpret Effi's personal character
as much as that of the Junkers in general :

This country gentry—and I must almost say, without exception
—is not at all concerned with truth, knowledge, general human
progress, but merely with its own profit, its privileged position and
the satisfaction of its conceit.[24]

The moral crisis of the Junker comes into evidence more
explicitly in the character of Innstetten. The career of a high
official has obliterated the virtues that can flourish among the
rural squirearchy. Innstetten has suppressed all spontaneity,
he serves the powers that be who determine his success.
Hardworking, able, conscientious and honourable in the confines of the class-code, he is a conformist through and through.
Incapable of deep feeling, he is incapable of happiness ; and
under his controlled and correct exterior we perceive the
nervous instability that his conformism breeds. In one of the
few 'author's intrusions' in the book, Fontane caustically writes:

He was a Wagner enthusiast. It was unclear what had led him

to Wagner ; some said, it was his nerves, for however sober he seemed, he really was nervous, others attributed it to Wagner's attitude to the Jewish question. Probably both were right.[25]

The centre of gravity of the novel lies not in Effi's attitude to her adultery, for she is too light a character to wrestle with its implications. It lies in Innstetten's behaviour after the discovery of the letters.

We are told of the first shock as the servants in his house might have known of it. Then, after a few restless hours Innstetten goes out to ask a colleague, von Wüllersdorf, to call, and on returning re-reads a few of Crampas's letters. Von Wüllersdorf comes, and Innstetten asks him to act as his second, and tells him the cause. Wüllersdorf puts himself at his disposal, but suggests that time makes a lot of difference in such matters ; does he feel so wounded and angered, he asks, that a duel is inevitable ? Nervously and irritably Innstetten admits that he neither feels hatred nor a desire for revenge, that he still loves Effi, that he could forgive her. When, however, Wüllersdorf delicately hints that it might be better to drop the affair, Innstetten answers that it is impossible :

' I have thought it all over. A man is not just an individual, he belongs to a whole, and we have always to pay attention to the whole, we are absolutely dependent on it. If I could manage to live in isolation I could ignore the affair ; I should bear the whole burden on my back, it would be the end of my real happiness, but many people have to live without this " real happiness ", and I should have to do so—and could, too. You don't need to be happy, you don't have any sort of claim on happiness, and you don't inevitably have to put an end to the man who has robbed you of your happiness. You can let him off all right, if you want to turn your back on the world. But when men live together, something comes into being and can't be argued away, and we've got used to judging everything by its paragraphs, the others and ourselves. And you can't violate them ; society will despise you, and in the end you despise yourself and can't stand it and put a bullet in your brain. . . . I have no choice. I have to.'

And when Wüllersdorf demurs, Innstetten says it is too late to argue. Once he had mentioned the issue to his friend, the

die was cast, for Innstetten could never bear the feeling that
he might notice, or so much as imagine, Wüllersdorf's irony or
even sympathy.   And Wüllersdorf gives in :

'I find it terrible that you are right, but you are right.   I won't
torment you any longer with my " must it be so ? "   The world is
what it is, and things take their course not as we want, but as the
others want.   But still, when people bombastically talk about a
" judgement of God ", that's rubbish, no, it's the very opposite, our
cult of honour is idolatry, but we have to submit to it as long as the
idol is worshipped.'

And so, with exemplary efficiency, Innstetten kills Crampas,
in whose eyes he can read the ridicule at the empty formalism
of this code of honour.   And on the way back, the argument
with Wüllersdorf goes on in Innstetten's head in reverse order :

'Guilt, if it is anything at all, is not bound to time and place
and cannot disappear overnight.   Guilt demands atonement, that
makes sense.   The idea that it can lapse is something half-and-
half, something feeble, at the least something prosaic.'   And he
plucked up courage at this idea and repeated to himself that things
had happened as they were bound to happen.   But the very
moment that this was firmly established, he overturned it again.
'Guilt must lapse with time, that's the only sensible thing, it's
quite immaterial whether it is prosaic ; commonsense is usually
prosaic.   I am forty-five years of age.   If I had found the letters
twenty-five years later, I should have been seventy.   And Wüllersdorf would have said, " Innstetten, don't be a fool."   And if not
Wüllersdorf, then Buddenbrook would have said it, and if not he,
then I myself.   It's clear to me.   If you push things to extremes,
you exaggerate and grow ludicrous.   But where is the border-
line ? . . .   When I recall Crampas's last look, resigned and yet
in all his wretchedness a smile, it meant : " Innstetten, the stickler.
You could have saved yourself the trouble, and me too."   And
perhaps he was right.   Yes, if I had been full of mortal hate, if
I had been obsessed by a craving for revenge.   Revenge isn't
pretty, but it is something human and has a natural right over us.
But as it was, it all happened for the sake of an abstract idea, a
notion, it was an invented story, half play-acting.   And now I've
got to go on with the play, I've got to cast Effi off and ruin her, and
me too.   I ought to have burnt the letters, and the world should
never have heard anything about it.'

Reason and humanity speak in this man, but they cannot alter his behaviour ; they only deliver judgement on the principles by which he and his class live. It is not a real life, but play-acting ; and indeed we are indifferent to his later career. Fontane tells us little about his later life, except to mention the black fits to which he is prone. Grown cynical of the ideas of culture and honour, he tells Wüllersdorf he is thinking of throwing up everything and going to the colonies. But Wüllersdorf ridicules his notion and expresses the bankrupt philosophy of their class :

'Just stay here and exercise your powers of resignation. Is there anybody who does not feel oppressed ? Who does not tell himself every day, " It's a very dubious affair, life ". You know, I've got a load of my own too, not the same as yours, but not much lighter. It's folly to crawl about in the primeval forests or spend your nights on ant-heaps ; some people like that sort of thing, but it's nothing for us. The best thing is to stand in the breach and stick it out till one falls. And meanwhile get as much as we can out of the small, the smallest things, and have an eye for the violets when they come out or the Luise Memorial when it is covered in flowers or the little girls in their laced boots when they jump over their skipping-ropes. Or drive out to Potsdam now and again and go into the church where Kaiser Friedrich is buried, and where they are just starting to build him a mausoleum. And when you stand there, think his life over, and if that doesn't calm you, I must say you are beyond help.' [26]

And to these meagre consolations for a joyless existence Wüllersdorf adds the relaxations of the theatre, the club, and some light-hearted liaison. Though he can use the grandiose old phrases like ' standing in the breach ', they no longer ring true, they have lost their real meaning. And Innstetten remains sceptical.

Like *Schach von Wuthenow, Effi Briest* has a sort of epilogue. After Effi's death her parents, in a short conversation, puzzle once again over the failure of her life. Perhaps they were at fault, says Frau von Briest, in spoiling the child ? Perhaps her husband was not strict enough ? Perhaps she herself should have known Effi was too young to be married to Innstetten ? To all of which Briest answers ' O, Luise, don't

. . . that takes us too far afield '. And no more than Effi's forgiveness of her husband do these remarks settle the matter ; they are not the summing up of an all-wise author. They remain within the framework of the personal events, and because of this they complete the picture of good, harmless people who fall into misfortune without understanding why, precisely because they cannot view their situation from outside, because they cannot see that what is at issue is not the failings of individuals, but the failings of a class living by obsolete standards, withered, in which nature and convention are at loggerheads. The only persons who remain loyal to Effi in her disgrace are the physician and her Bavarian maid. The only inconsolable mourner is her dog. Fontane never believed in the romantic antithesis of heart and society, feeling and convention ; he refused to accept the thesis of Ibsen that the social proprieties are necessarily destructive of happiness.[27] But if convention meant, as in the case of the contemporary Junker nobility, the crushing of natural feeling, intelligence, commonsense, happiness, then it meant that the class that lived by this convention was moribund, even to the point of being incapable of understanding the causes of its failure.

Little is to be gained from an analysis of *Der Stechlin* (1898), Fontane's last novel. The description of the old Junker, Stechlin, in his remote mansion has all the excellence that we come to expect in Fontane, and it has an added interest in that this old Junker, and his parson too, are aware of the movement of the times and realise that the traditional social hierarchy is obsolete. It is Fontane's wistful farewell to a class of which he was the ' disappointed lover '. The novel lacks composition, however, and the characters and affairs of the younger generation are vague and tedious. Fontane called it ' a political novel—a contrast between the nobility as it should be and as it is ',[28] but, though there are numerous characters and scenes which illuminate the contemporary social situation, the story is lacking in contrast and tension, and shows indeed a marked falling off in imaginative power.

FONTANE'S REALISM

' Realism ' is the avowed principle of Fontane's art as a novelist, and it confronted him with a double problem : first, that of the theme—' the description of a life, a society, a group of people as the undistorted reflection of the life we lead '; and second, that of a technique.

As we have seen, he did not attempt to give an all-embracing picture of his times. Most of his books centre in the Prussian nobility, to which he was drawn by a predilection of his character, by the circumstances of his life and his studies of the Mark ; he frequently justified his choice on the grounds of the historical importance of this class in the shaping and management of modern Germany. Compared with the Junkers, the young bourgeoisie of modern Germany receives slight attention in his novels, and the petty bourgeoisie and simple folk appear only as appurtenances of the higher classes. The industrial working class appears not at all. Yet his pre-occupation with the Junkers did not strike his young con-temporaries, for all their concern with the problems of industrial Germany, as antiquated. Rather, they acclaimed Fontane as a ' modern '. For he describes the nobility as they were in actuality, without nostalgia or idealisation, and beneath his restricted themes and unassuming tales there lies, one feels, the massive totality of his times, implicit but operative.

There is little invention in Fontane's novels ; they are as sober as the Mark landscape and, indeed, might be called repetitive. He seems to be continually reconsidering in them the life around him, and the highest demand he could make on a novel was that we should feel, when reading it, that we are continuing our real life.[29] Nearly all his novels are built round anecdotes he heard. What attracted him to them was their representativeness, their embodiment of the essence of the contemporary situation. While his lesser contemporaries used anecdotal material because of its piquancy, he liked piquancy only because it laid bare important issues usually hidden beneath the surface. When Fontane relied on his invention, as in *Irrungen, Wirrungen* or *Frau Jenny Treibel*, his

story is so close to typical, everyday life that it is deficient in
sharp dramatic quality.

We can see Fontane's method most clearly in the composition
of *Schach von Wuthenow*.   The anecdote was presented to him.
He inquired carefully whether the incident occurred before
or after the Prussian collapse at Jena, so that he could relate
it unambiguously to a precise social situation.   Then he
remoulded the given characters, surrounded them with others
partly historical and partly invented, and invented minor
incidents, in order to build up the characteristic elements of
his theme.   All is individual, precise, but all is shaped and
ordered by his theme.   Even when he describes milieux which
have all the characteristics of directly experienced knowledge,
for instance Schach's Junker mansion or the church at Tempelhof, this generalising technique prevails, hidden under the
illusion of precise concrete detail.   Contemporary critics, who
found the story far-fetched, praised these milieux for their
accuracy and truth ; Fontane commented sarcastically that
he had never been to the church, that Schach's mansion was
a complete invention, while the story was the only true thing
about the novel.[30]

All Fontane's works show this combination of the typical
with the individual ; ' truth to life ' means for him both the
evocation of sensuous experience, of circumstances, objects and
people, and the uncovering of a typical social situation and
problem which is embodied in the particular.   In his ballads
—and he wrote odd ballads right to the end of his life—he
fell into romantic attitudes ; in his novels he scarcely ever
departs from this sober conscientious search for truth, avoiding
all idealisation.   In them he is nearer the new impressionist
school of painters—e.g. Liebermann—than the heroic historical
school of his old friend Menzel.   He discovered the charm
of the city landscape, the suburbs, for instance the charm
of the evening lights as his characters sit at an open-air
restaurant :

And it was not long before the lights came on.   Not only the
restaurant itself was all lit up, but also on the railway-embankment
on the other side of the river the various coloured signals appeared,

while in midstream, where the tugs were hauling the barges, a
sooty red glowed through the cabin windows.

(*Der Stechlin*)

He was aware of the difficulties facing the realistic writer.
He could see some of his younger contemporaries being
submerged under a mass of trivial material documentation.
Exact and crowded description was not his purpose, but
description which ' illuminates '. He was actually taken to
task for his use of a faulty dialect, especially in the language
of the simple Berlin folk in his novels ; and one can discover
other sorts of factual inaccuracies in his books. But he was
unconcerned about these ' errors '. An exact rendering of
dialect would have made the books inaccessible to the ordinary
reader, he said ; an absolutely precise accuracy of description
would have been boring and superfluous. It suffices, he
wrote, to ' suggest things '. ' I did my level best to describe
real life. It just doesn't work. You have to be content if the
reader gets the total impression, " Yes, that's life "." ' [31] And
this truthfulness is art, the art he recognised and admired in
the modern realists of the younger generation. In a review
of Ibsen's *The Wild Duck* he wrote :

It is the hardest thing in the world (and perhaps the highest
too) so to illuminate everyday life that what was just now indifferent and prosaic suddenly moves us with the most entrancing
magic of poetry.[32]

This is the formula of his own artistic endeavour.

He was extremely interested in the efforts of his young
contemporaries to present, as objectively as possible, the actual
and often forbidding reality of their times. It is well known
that he acclaimed the purpose of the ' consequent naturalists ',
Holz and Schlaf, to discard conventional literary expression
and present characters in their raw, natural state—' here is
the parting of the ways, the divide between old and new '.[33]
But in this same article he went on to insist that it was an
illusion to believe art is the greater the more the artist is
eliminated. Even in the works of Holz and Schlaf, he pointed
out, the artist has shaped the material ; and it is characteristic

that, in Ibsen and Hauptmann, Fontane admired immediately
the high artistic skill of their writing.　When we read a novel,
he wrote, we should feel that there is no difference between
real life and this invented life, ' except the difference arising
from that intensity, clarity, transparency and roundedness and,
consequently, that intensity of feeling, which is the trans-
figuring task of art '.[34]　On another occasion he speaks of the
' tone ' of the work of art, which interprets the poet's ' purity
of perception ' and ' transfigures the ugly '.[35]

　　Fontane was, then, very conscious of the craftsmanship of
writing, of the novel as an art.　He never falls into the faults
of naturalism, but firmly shapes his story according to his
intention ; in this respect he is the finest stylist among the
German novelists.　As his theme demands it, he gently but
firmly leads our attention from character to character, from
scene to scene.　For instance, at a dinner-party we first hear
the talk at one end of the table, then we move to the other,
and bit by bit the pieces fit together into a picture of the
whole company.　His chapters succeed one another like the
scenes of a play, as the setting for the decisive stages of the
story, intermediate stages being cut out.　He is a master of
suggestion.　Rarely is there any extended description of setting, and never any extended psychological analysis.　The
moral issues accumulate almost imperceptibly, without melodrama, from a host of slight factors.　So his ' scenes ' conclude
without sound and fury ; one can almost speak of a ' fade-
out ' technique which he often uses to conclude a chapter.

　　In this artistic arrangement of the story, the jumps in place
and time, the varying degree of reticence, the author is clearly
enough in evidence.　I have already spoken of Fontane's
attitude to the ' intrusive ' author.　But though he came to
agree with Spielhagen that it is better if the author does not
appear in person to make comments and give explanations,
Fontane was never over-anxious on this score.　He knew, of
course, that all description of circumstances is ' direct comment ', though in Fontane such description is nearly always
confined to what the characters themselves or what a chance
visitor would observe.　More important is explanatory com-

ment, particularly psychological explanations or moral judgements. On the whole Fontane, after the earlier novels, leaves
specific comments to his characters themselves. In *Schach von
Wuthenow* we have seen that he summarises the ' moral ' of
the story in letters of two of the characters. This is a somewhat clumsy device, and at other times, too, he is not too
happy in his choice of means. For instance, in order to build
out the younger Stechlin's character (which throughout
remains woefully vague), he gives us a few pages of his
diary, the content of which would be most unlikely to be
found in an intimate diary. We are disturbed too, in this
novel, by a sudden change of focus when the author gives a
synopsis of the earlier life of the young man's prospective
father-in-law.

In his greatest novel, *Effi Briest*, Fontane actually shows
himself less anxious about author's intrusions than in many of
the others. From time to time he sums up the characters, as
for instance when he comments on Innstetten's predilection
for Wagner. When Effi yields to Crampas he tells us, rather
unnecessarily, that it was because of her lack of firmness. One
intervention, a rather striking one, is worthy of analysis.
After Effi falls ill, her doctor says to her : ' Don't bother to
write ; just send Roswitha '—Roswitha is her old maid whom
she had left at Innstetten's and whom the reader has ceased
to think about. And the novel continues :

' Just send Roswitha ', the doctor had said. What, was Roswitha with Effi, then ? Indeed she was, and in fact had been there
for a long time. . . .

The author does a jack-in-the-box trick, suddenly letting us
know something he has been deliberately hiding. And the
effect is subtle. At the moment when the isolation of Effi was
becoming intolerable, this comforting news is broken, with
some of the sturdy cheerfulness of Roswitha herself. It is a
case where the author's intrusion is not an admission of failure,
but a successful artistic stroke.

In general, however, Fontane follows the practice of his
great European contemporaries in that the moral and

psychological situation becomes explicit through the situation, behaviour and speech of his characters. Partly because of this, his characters are never too precisely defined, never over-rigid ; they have numerous facets which new situations bring into view, and therefore have something of the mobility, ambiguity of real life. Thus we see the industrialist Treibel in jovial, expansive mood at the dinner-party, ironically indulgent to his wife's sentimentalism ; we see him conning his chances in politics ; and, in case we are tempted to sum him up as an ambitious *parvenu*, we see him immediately talking with humane tolerance with his wife's neurotic lady-companion. He is quite ready to approve the marriage of Corinna with his son but, though he argues with his wife, we can see he really is glad that she insists on the ' honour ' of the family. What is this industrialist really ? There can be no summing up, he is a bundle of qualities and trends. Above all, Fontane is a master of conversation—a famous talker himself, incidentally. The conversations in his novels, whether involving groups of people at parties or on excursions, or whether intimate *tête-à-têtes* like those between Frau von Carayon and Schach or between Effi's parents, are masterly. Fontane brilliantly catches the fine nuances of characters, in relation to important and trivial subjects, in serious or humorous response to others ; the whole character of social life, the subtle interplay of individuality and society, comes to expression in these conversations. They are decisive in establishing the tone of his novels, and usually they are the points at which, hardly noticeably, the characters range themselves round the major issues of the theme.

It is clear that Fontane's whole art, as a novelist, is moral in inspiration. His realism itself has moral roots. All his novels are expositions of moral dilemmas. They are not moral tracts, for though they contain much practical wisdom they leave us in some sense indetermined, aware of the complexity of the issues rather than persuaded of right and wrong. For all his satire, Fontane is far less self-assertive than, for instance, his contemporary George Eliot ; he himself, full of misgivings as he was about the trends of his times, was also very sceptical about religious and political schemes of reform. His social contribution was less ambitious :

If one can't get to grips with the matter through sermons and regulations, all the same I think much is gained if modern humanity comes to some insight into the situation, if it sees itself in a mirror and gets a fright.[36]

In this sense he justified the modern realists who were so decried because of their concern with ugliness and sin. He wrote concerning Ibsen's *The Wild Duck* that, if things might not be improved, it was ' better to stare ugliness in the face than distortion—better sin than hypocrisy '.[37] And it was characteristic of him that he was deeply distrustful of the mystical transfiguration in Hauptmann's *Hanneles Himmelfahrt*.

But his realism is of a different quality from that of the younger realists. He was not altogether won over by the Zola-tradition of delving into the most sordid aspects of the modern world ; even in Ibsen and Hauptmann he detected a pessimism which he thought was not justified and which, at any rate, was not his own view of things. In his letters he often expresses the harshest condemnation of contemporary trends—of Junker arrogance, of capitalistic greed and philistinism—but he refused to be downcast by such phenomena, and even found good words for the great industrialists of his time. In spite of all the drawbacks of modern society, he was convinced of the great progress that Germany had made, culturally as well as materially, since his youth, and retained a certain modicum of optimism, putting it down at various times to his sanguine temperament, to his avid interest in life, to his humanism, above all to his humour. His humour was his refuge and strength, and though occasionally he felt that he could no longer take things humorously, humour makes itself felt in all his works, right to the end, as the expression of his tolerance and trust in man. ' Humour is the best way.' [38] And thus he consistently demanded that art must present the reality of life mildly draped over. The essential fault of the modern realists was, in his opinion, that they lacked ' conciliatoriness, mildness, humour, naturalness '.[39] These are the qualities of his writing, as they also indicate his failings. A self-reliant man of ripe experience, his social satire lacks the bitterness and distortion of more sensitive writers and the sensationalism of the vulgar ; but it lacks passion, too, for he looks away from characters tortured by desperate needs, and slips evasively away from conflicts when they grow too harsh. That is why, even in his greatest novel, he fails to reach the stature of Flaubert or Tolstoy.

CHAPTER VIII

Franz Kafka
1883-1924

THE PROBLEM OF INTERPRETATION

KAFKA's novels, which were published posthumously, were written between 1913 and his death. With them we leap into the twentieth century ; Kafka's style, composition and purpose are startlingly original and unprepared for. Yet there is a connection between his work and the fundamental pre-occupations of the novelists of the nineteenth century. His imaginative world is, like that of Hoffmann or Poe, dominated by mysterious baleful forces, though he does not postulate two opposing worlds of imagination and reality. Like the heroes of the ' Bildungsroman ', his heroes fight for reality, though without reaching it. There is social criticism in his novels, though it is put in an entirely new context. One might say that these major themes are fused and hence transformed in Kafka's work.

He himself was tortured all his life by a father-complex, a guilt obsession, which is the material of some of his shorter tales. His family belonged to the assimilated Jewry, cut off from the Hebrew community and not at home among the Germans. His culture was German, but in Prague, his home, it was a minority-culture, and his political and social sympathies went to the Czechs. He worked as an Insurance official, and always fretted against his duties. He detested bureaucracy, and had a sneaking admiration for it. He had socialist sym-pathies, but admired the efficiency of the capitalist *entre-preneur*. He was a Zionist without religious faith. He was a vegetarian and inclined to fads like nudism or anthropo-sophy. He was often ill, and the last years of his life were largely spent in the isolation of sanatoria. All his life his will seemed to be lamed, and he seemed only to be able to know and suffer, never to master difficulties. Yet these personal abnormalities, instead of marking him off from his fellows, came to be symptomatic of the general dislocation and dilemma of his times, and particularly so in the period of triumphant Fascism, of war, and cold war.

The work of Raabe and Fontane is permeated with a deep concern over the moral health of society. But the apprehensions of both are allayed by their trust in the ultimate ' rightness ' of life ; both accept more or less sceptically the changing moral standards of a changing world, and neither challenges the prevailing positivistic realism of their times. They were able, too, to build a calm and happy private life from which the outer world could be safely contemplated. Kafka found no such ' garden of the soul ', as Raabe called it ; his inner instability matched the material and moral dissensions in the social world. He began writing at a time when nineteenth-century positivism was being assailed by Nietzsche's subjectivism, and being undermined by the phenomenalism of philosophers like Ernst Mach. In Kafka's works, the outer world loses its self-evident objectivity. Not only its morality is called into question ; the world loses its clear shape, it becomes shadowy, it appears as the construct of men's minds, perpetually disintegrating, wavering, bewildering like them. One of the characters of an early work says, characteristically : ' I hope to learn how things really are, for they sink away around me like a snowfall, while a gin-glass on the table stands in front of other people as firm as a monument.' [1]

Thus, Emrich has justifiably been able to define Kafka's work as an investigation of the nature of reality ; [2] but its centre is not a problem of logic, but spiritual anguish. His novels are about a human fate, a human bewilderment, human suffering ; this suffering grows deeper as his characters discover that their quest grows more and more intangible and elusive as they struggle towards their goal. It is Karl Rossmann's moral anxiety that leads him (in *America*) into bewildering mazes in the ship or the country house ; it is an accusation of guilt that suddenly hurls the Joseph K. of *The Trial* into the shadows that lie behind the familiar façade of normal existence. Because suffering and guilt are everywhere, the world of Kafka's characters has always the potency of becoming something unknown, unprecedented. He continually starts from, and recalls, the most banal reality that we all accept without question or thought ; in it lies the mystery. Kafka himself protested against a critic who said that his method is to introduce marvellous occurrences into the customary recognisable world ; no, he answered, ' the customary itself is a marvel '.[3] Without emphasis or shock normal things and routine slip out of our grasp—*Metamorphosis* begins typically : ' When Gregor Samsa awoke one morning out of restless dreams, he found himself in his bed transformed into an enormous bug.' This interpenetration of the normal and the fantastic makes the fascination of Kafka's style ; it asserts a new relation between men and the reality in which they try to embed themselves ; and deeper still, it is a symbolic representation of the values by which they live.

In his earliest works Kafka does not escape the pitfalls of wilful subjectivism. *Description of a Battle* (*c*. 1908) is a riot of capricious associations and a farcical parody of normal causality. *Contemplation* (1913) is more subtle, but in its impressionism suggests a deliberate obliteration of normal associations, a somewhat flatter Rimbaud. From the later works such mannerisms are absent. Puzzling symbols and fantastic situations are always there, but Kafka depicts them, one might rather say, investigates them, conscientiously and exactly, not in order to baffle us but to share the experience with us. ' The taste for the representation of my dreamlike inner life ', he wrote in 1914 in reference to his literary work, ' has reduced everything else to a subordinate position '.[4] His symbols now acquire a coherent, self-sufficient structure, like the curious figure, Odradek, in *A Country Doctor*, that represents the world as he saw it, ' The whole appears meaningless it is true, but in its own way complete.' It is this coherence that the critic must try to trace ; but immediately he comes up against a problem of the most elusive character.

When we have established the outline of any of Kafka's tales, we are no nearer establishing their coherence, however

much we may have felt it.   All the criteria by which coherence
may be tested are, on the surface, absent.   The environment
continually shifts from the normal to the unheard of ;   time
moves arbitrarily ;   causality is bewildering ;   the beliefs,
emotions, habits of characters have not the sort of consistency
with which we are normally acquainted.   How can we say
this complex is coherent, is a whole, if we have no standard.
In fact, every critic, every intelligent reader must look under
the surface for the meaning.

I have already used the term ' symbol ', and this must be
understood in a quite simple way.   Many of Kafka's shorter
tales have the unmistakable form of the fable or parable.   In
the longer works there are many directly allegorical pointers,
for instance personal names that indicate a function or temperament.   There has been some argument as to whether
Kafka's works should be called symbolical or allegorical, but
the term one uses is not of great moment.[5]   Kafka differs
from the symbolists (and from the school of abstract painting,
to which his ' Odradek ' seems to belong) in that his symbols
are much more explicit than theirs, just as his purposeful
control of his symbolic material distinguishes him from the
surrealists.   On the other hand, he differs from many alle-
gorists in that his images cannot be directly translated into
fixed moral qualities, like those in *Pilgrim's Progress*, and have
a vitality of their own, a potency within them, even if slight,
of growth and change.

The central and inescapable task with Kafka is then interpretation.   He himself gives very little help, for even in his
Journals he writes in images ;   so over his works every sooth-
sayer sees the hospitable ' All are welcome ' that advertises
Kafka's ' Nature-Theatre of Oklahoma '.   Brod and Muir see
the novels as allegories of man's search for divine grace.
Neider expounds them with abandon in terms of Freudian
psychoanalysis.   Bense interprets them as illustrations of
existentialism.   Everyone can see in them the reflection of the
position of the Jew in Western society, or that of the ' little
man ' among the gigantic paraphernalia of the modern bureaucratic state.[6]   Something is right about these and other inter-

pretations ; what is wrong about them is that each taken separately reduces Kafka's fluidity, multivalency, to the rigidity of one single purpose, and sometimes to an outlook which he himself repudiated.

There is no doubt that a few of his works are little more than symbols of Kafka's father-fixation : for instance, *The Verdict* and *Metamorphosis*, in which the hidden logic of events can be almost completely understood in terms of the love and hate of the ' hero '· for the father, his rival and his judge. But it is absurd to interpret *In the Penal Colony*, for instance, in the same way, for here the symbols are infused (perhaps in addition) with a social content. Kafka's symbols grow in depth and relevance, they come to be an image of the light refracted through various facets of his experience. What makes them bewildering is that they do not illustrate some experience already understood, but are a continual probing towards further relevancies. ' As long as you do not stop mounting, the steps will not stop, beneath your mounting feet they grow upwards.' [7] These mounting feet do not move farther away from solid earth ; Kafka's fantasies acquire more and more reality. The nightmare-horrors of *A Country Doctor* tell us how frail is the security of normal life, how dangerous it is once to subject it to question : ' Once follow the mis-ringing of the night-bell—the mischief can never be made good.' These apparent distortions are the apprehension of the perverted character of the modern world, and we can apply to Kafka what he himself is reported to have said of Picasso : ' I do not believe that he wilfully distorts. He simply notes down the distortions which have not as yet penetrated our consciousness.' [8]

AMERICA

The earliest of Kafka's three novels, *America*, was begun in 1913, when its first chapter was published under the title of *The Stoker*. We know otherwise very little about the progress of its composition ; he was still working on it in 1917, but it was never finished, and not published in his lifetime. Though he completed several chapters of the second novel, *The Trial*, in 1914, there is no doubt that *America* is the first and least mature of the longer works, and in fact it offers important clues to some of the difficult problems of the two later novels. Brod called them a trilogy, and this unfortunate term has often been repeated. It would be truer to look on the later ones as modifying and deepening the earlier.

Its title was originally ' Der Verschollene ', ' The Man who Disappeared ' or ' Lost without Trace ', and it is a pity that this very appropriate title was replaced by Brod with the nondescript *America*.[9] Karl Rossmann, a boy of sixteen, has been cast off by his parents for a minor moral offence, and sent to America. He takes sides with a stoker who complains about his treatment on board ship, but is jerked out of this entanglement by a rich uncle who takes him under his wing. A slight disregard of his uncle's wishes causes the latter to cast him off again, and he starts on an aimless trek across America, anxiously guarding his little possessions, his only link with family and respectability. Two unemployed proletarians try to exploit him, but he escapes for a time into the shelter of a vast hotel, where he becomes a lift-boy. Kindness to one of the hoodlums leads him to infringe the regulations and he is dismissed, and the sinister couple get hold of him again, partly bullying him and partly appealing to his good nature. They are themselves, now, living in squalid security on a rich but repellent woman, Brunelda, and Karl becomes their servant and in some sort guardian. Only fragments indicate Karl's service here, but it seems that at some point he breaks away and joins a mysterious ' Nature-Theatre of Oklahoma ' in which he finds employment corresponding to his abilities and taste.

How the novel was to end is uncertain. Brod, who constantly encourages us to draw comforting conclusions from Kafka's work, reports that Kafka told him his novel was to have ended with some hope for the hero. But at the same time he quotes the note from Kafka's *Journals* which tells us that Rossmann, though guiltless, was like the ' guilty ' hero of *The Trial* ' to suffer the penalty of death '.[10]

The novel is strikingly different from the others, and from most of Kafka's tales, in two respects. The boy Karl Rossmann claims our direct sympathy on simple moral grounds, because of his youth, his goodness, guilelessness, loyalty. And besides this, the whole world of this novel is directly and easily recognisable. It does not matter that Kafka had never been overseas and that the picture of America is inaccurate ; of course it is not meant to be true in this sense. The important thing is that we know the how and why of situations and characters, very much as we do in the traditional novel.

Compare, for instance, the reflection of the father-obsession in this novel with that in other tales.[11] In *The Verdict* a father's authority destroys the sensible plans of his adult son and causes him to commit suicide. On both sides the behaviour is irrational, obsessional. In *Metamorphosis* the son, the mainstay of the home, is transformed into a bug and, aware of the loathing of his family, dies by refusing food. The key to this macabre fantasy is again the son's feeling of guilt towards his father, whose place he has usurped. In *America*, on the contrary, the father-son relationship is not all-absorbing, all-consuming ; it is one among other important elements in Karl's experience, it is assimilated with others, it influences but does not bludgeon him. His father has sent him from their Prague home on a good pretext, to avoid scandal and a possible claim for alimony. Karl accepts this ' verdict ' without complaint. We see his sudden affection for the stoker, so ardent indeed that it must be ascribed to an unconscious desire for a father-substitute. And when his rich uncle snatches him from the stoker—his close relationship and his wealth fully justify this—there is simply a change of substitute, and Karl wonders : ' Will this man ever be able to replace the stoker ? ' The uncle's decision to cast him off arises from so slight an error on Karl's part that again we can understand its ruthless abruptness only in terms of the hidden passions of a father ; and the numbness of Karl on the day of his error, the nightmarish experiences at the country house, the frustration of his desire to make things good, all interpret the pathological inhibitions of the son. His anxiety to keep his bag, his money and the photograph of the family might all be interpreted as obsessional ; his inability to resent the harsh decisions of father and uncle might be considered to indicate his neurotic sense of guilt.

What is important, however, is that none of these actions, by Karl or his father (or father-substitutes), flout rationality. No doubt the full explanation for events can only be understood if we can apply psychoanalytical categories, but they are justified too in terms of normal reason and behaviour. Decency, respectability, obedience are very practical requisites for ' success ', and Karl respects these principles in those who ' condemn ' him. Though there are three ' trials ' in this book (the stoker's, and those of Karl by his uncle's friends and the hotel management), Karl in no way concurs in the verdict, and though condemned, remains spiritually intact. Karl's anxiety about his possessions never grows into an obsession, it remains on the level of normal sensible prudence. Karl is in any case a youngster, who needs a guide and can be expected to attach himself warmly to anyone who will help him or appeal to him. If, at the country house or at the hotel, all the adults seem to be in league against him, it seems to be the expression not so much of an obsession as of the natural difficulties a boy, an immigrant, has in a selfish and alien society. After a time, indeed, Karl realises that ' everyone was exploiting his power and abusing the underdog '.[12]

The social factors of the story are at least as important as the psychological ; in this respect *America* is unique among Kafka's writings, and the only one to reflect directly the humane social outlook of its author. Karl, the outcast with sympathies for the down-trodden, is out of place among the heartless rich, who are as effusive when he is in luck as they are cold when his uncle rejects him. On the way to the rich man's country house they have to make a détour to avoid demonstrations of workers ; he hears of strikes and learns that his uncle and the latter's friends are ruthless exploiters of labour. From a social-moral point of view he cannot live with them, nor can they tolerate him among them. But, in this society, where the workers claim his sympathy, the latter

also are out for what they can get. The unemployed workers
with whom he lodges are keener on exploiting him than on
getting work ; their weakness fetters him, but also their brutal
strength. Karl can belong to neither one side nor the other, he
is a victim of both, and can maintain himself only in a purely
private way, in personal decency and moral respectability.

The Brunelda episode anticipates a general situation that
recurs in the other novels. The two proletarians, and Karl,
are absorbed in the service of a woman. Their devotion is
worthy of a gracious Aphrodite ; but this massively fat,
frowsty, heartless and hysterical female, living in grotesque
squalor, has nothing to recommend her but her sex and
her wealth. Even the favoured lover, Delamarche, suffers
degrading humiliations, while his companion is satisfied with
absurd hopes. There is something in this whole situation of
that squalid authority and degrading devotion that runs
through *The Trial* and *The Castle*. But it is characteristic of
America that this service to Brunelda is not mere custom or
ritual ; it makes sense. She has the money, she provides
security.

Perhaps we should take Brunelda as a specific social symbol
as well. Karl is at first forced to stay in the apartment, and
intends to escape at the first opportunity. But a discussion
with a night-school student on the neighbouring balcony of
the huge tenement makes him resolve to stay. The student
tells him that no employee can choose his job according to
the morality of his employer, and that working for Brunelda
is morally no different from working in some huge enterprise
whose employers one does not know. With such a broad
hint, we should not go far wrong in interpreting the proletarians' unremitting thankless service to Brunelda not as the
escape from normal labour that it seems, but as a symbol of
normal labour under rugged, individualistic capitalism, with
its meaningless toil and dubious sweets ; while the capitalist,
utterly helpless in herself, tyrannises over the clumsy servants
who tend her. We might easily go further and find a fairly
obvious meaning in her abandonment of her correct husband
and luxurious apartment for these proletarians and the

disgusting filth of this stuffy room high up in the working-class tenement.

Thus the novel presents us with a series of situations symbolical of the modern capitalistic world. Karl finds no comradeship among the wealthy or among the workers, his loyal work in the giant hotel only provokes enmity, his faithful service to Brunelda is degrading and dishonourable. But at the end he finds the ' Nature-Theatre '. Its advertisement proclaims ' All are welcome ', and although his papers are not in order he is taken on and given a job where he can use the technical gifts he feels he has. The theatre is gigantic ; all can be employed. What it is, what it does, he does not ask ; but here he can find a place in its vast and inscrutable organisation. Never again was Kafka to suggest a Utopia of this kind.

Kafka himself noted a similarity between this novel and *David Copperfield*—' *The Stoker*, sheer imitation of Dickens, even more so the novel as planned ', he wrote in 1917.[13] Neider thinks the similarity lies in the technique, while Kafka's theme is ' original and mature '.[14] The reverse seems nearer the truth. Karl Rossmann is another David Copperfield or Oliver Twist ; he moves through hostile environments and maintains his goodness intact—and as a reward he enters a sheltered refuge. This is above all the immaturity of this novel ; it contains the old sentimentality of Dickens and his contemporaries. In the later novels Kafka was to describe a corrupt and senseless world, but at the same time heroes who themselves, being part of this world, are permeated too by its evil and corruption ; who are ' guilty ' simply by being part of this world. ' I am not guilty,' says Joseph K. to the priest in *The Trial*. ' It is a mistake. How can a man be guilty anyhow ? Aren't we all human beings, one like the other ? ' ' That is correct ', answers the priest, ' but that is how guilty people speak.' In the later novels we shall not have heroes who are the typical ' little men ', the innocent Charlie Chaplins, knocked about by the evil men of power, but maintaining their goodness to the end, and even finding in the end a haven. The later heroes will be representatives of their times, not outsiders in this sense.

What is original and fascinating in *America* is the Kafka method. We are not told that the world is hostile and bewildering ; we experience it as such with the hero. We learn only what is available to this young stranger, and from the first experience with the stoker we are involved in obscure impulsive forces and an unknown complex web of social relationships and personal interests. What happens must have its good logic and coherence, even though the boy cannot fathom it, or not all of it. At times this logic is so impenetrable that we border on, or enter, the world of nightmare. In the country house Karl knows that his uncle has not approved his visit, and he learns, while there, that he has been cast off ; the friends who have invited him change their attitude as they learn that he is now a mere stray. This confusion in the moral world leads to confusion of brain and senses. Karl is lost here, he gropes his way in the dark along endless corridors past dark doorways, he listens to arguments he cannot understand. In the same way he suddenly discovers at the hotel what seems to be a conspiracy among the adults to find him wrong and throw him out, in which his friend the head cook, and the porter and police enter, though there is no reason why any of these should think badly of him. At these times we enter the hostile obscurity of the worlds of *The Trial* and *The Castle* ; though in *America* ultimately there is a practical reason for the behaviour of his enemies, and in fact, too, in the labyrinth of corridors someone does turn up to guide him to the light. More explicit and optimistic than the later novels, *America* shows us a world which is bewildering and hostile to the hero, yet not ultimately senseless and not absolutely impervious to effort.

Kafka finds a striking symbol for Karl's misrelationship to the world when he looks, from Brunelda's balcony high up in the skyscraper, at an election meeting in the street below. He sees a procession, hears odd scraps of music from the band, watches the gestures of orators and hears and sees evidence of passionate support and passionate opposition. Nothing can be clearly heard and understood, it is all like a puppet-show, a parody. Brunelda holds him crushed against the balcony and tries to force him to look more closely through her binoculars, though he cannot see through them. Yet Karl is fascinated. This is the world as he can know it, in which men are passionately struggling and fighting, performing established rituals as a matter of course, but with purposes and a logic which he cannot understand. The heroes of the later novels are not allowed to stand on one side as observers ; but the world in which they move is as remote and unfathomable as the scene that takes place before Karl Rossmann's eyes.

THE TRIAL

Towards the end of *The Trial*, the prison chaplain tells the hero, Joseph K., a parable which stands in the Law Book of the Court by which he has been summoned :

Before the Law there stands a doorkeeper. A man from the country comes to this doorkeeper and begs for admittance to the Law. But the doorkeeper says that he cannot admit the man at the moment. The man thinks it over and then asks whether he may enter later. ' It is possible ', says the doorkeeper, ' but not now '. Since the gate to the Law is, as ever, open, and the doorkeeper steps to one side, the man bends down to peer through the gate. As the doorkeeper notices this, he laughs and says : ' If you find it so tempting, why not try to get in without my permission ? But take note : I am mighty. And I am only the lowest of the doorkeepers. From room to room there stand doorkeepers, one mightier than the other. Even I cannot bear the mere sight of the third.' The man from the country has not expected such difficulties, the Law, he thinks, ought surely to be accessible to everyone at all times, but when he looks more closely at the doorkeeper in his fur cloak, with his great pointed nose, his long, thin, black Tartar beard, he decides after all to wait until he gets permission to enter. The doorkeeper gives him a stool and lets him sit down at one side of the door. There he sits for days and years. He makes many attempts to get admittance and wearies the doorkeeper with his supplications. The doorkeeper often starts little examinations, questions him about his homeland and many other things, but they are offhand questions, like those that great gentlemen ask, and at the end he always tells him that he cannot yet admit him. The man, who has provided himself with much for his journey, applies everything, however valuable, to bribe the doorkeeper. The latter accepts everything but says : ' I am only taking it so that you don't think you have left anything undone.' During the many years the man observes the doorkeeper almost uninterruptedly. He forgets the other doorkeepers, and this first one seems to him to be the only hindrance to his admittance to the Law. In his first years he loudly curses his unlucky fate, but later, as he grows old, he only grumbles away to himself. He grows childish, and since in his yearlong study of the doorkeeper he has even got to know the fleas in his fur collar, he begs the very fleas to help him and change the doorkeeper's mind. In the end his sight grows dim and he does not know whether it is growing darker around him or whether it is his eyes that deceive him. But in the darkness he now does perceive a radiance that breaks unquench-ably through the door of the Law. Now he has not much longer to live. Before his death all the experiences of this whole time condense in his head into one question that he has not as yet asked the doorkeeper. He beckons to him, as he cannot any longer raise his stiffening body. The doorkeeper has to bend down low, for the difference between their heights has changed greatly to the disadvantage of the man. ' What do you still want to know ? ' the doorkeeper asks, ' you are insatiable.' ' All men strive after the Law,' says the man, ' how is it that in these many years no-one but me has asked for admittance ? ' The doorkeeper sees that the man is at his last gasp, and in order to reach his fading hearing he bellows at him : ' No-one else could get admittance, for this entrance was appointed for you alone. I am now going to shut it.'

This ' simple story ' is meant to warn Joseph K. against expecting help from the priest in his lawsuit. He protests against the injustice and the deceit of the doorkeeper's be-haviour. The priest answers : ' One must not take it all to be true, one must take it to be necessary.' ' A dismal opinion ', answers Joseph K., ' it makes lying into a universal principle.' He knows this is only a provisional conclusion, but he is too exhausted to master all the fable's implications. The parable has not cleared anything up, it has only entangled him still further. Yet, inhuman and repellent as its lesson seems to be, it does not sum up all the horrors of Joseph K.'s position. For in the parable, there is at least a Law with its traditional radiance. *The Trial* shows us Law Courts, but no Law ; it describes a frenzied search for a trial that always eludes the

accused ; it ends not with a judgement but an execution.   It
is the most implacable of Kafka's books.

Joseph K. is an able and successful bank official, a bachelor,
attached to the routine of his life, with no outstanding virtues
or vices.   One morning he is arrested, though no charge is
ever preferred against him :   the novel opens :   ' Someone
must have been calumniating Joseph K., for one fine morning,
without having done anything wrong, he was arrested.'   He
is summoned to court, which he finds in the attics of a slum
tenement, but no case is brought against him in the squalid
throng of disreputable judges and lawyers who all treat him
as if he were guilty.   Competence and procedure of the court
are quite unfathomable, and he protests with rhetorical indignation against the whole affair.   No further summons comes,
but he returns on his own initiative to clear the matter up.
The court is not sitting, and he discovers endless offices where
other litigants are hopelessly waiting.   Appalled, baffled, and
in a state of exhaustion that never again leaves him, he tries
to forget his case.   But it is already public, and his energetic
uncle comes to insist that he should take a lawyer.   The
latter, a sick old man, undertakes to help him, though since
no charge is known the defence is sheer guesswork, and the
lawyer's main hope in fact lies in personal influence with
unknown judges.   Joseph K. finds more comfort with the wife
of the janitor at the law-court, or in the embrace of his lawyer's
maid.

But Joseph K. grows obsessed with his case.   He questions
his lawyer about the courts, and hears him tell with equanimity
that there is no recognised procedure at these courts, the
accused have no rights, the judges are corrupt, the lawyers
powerless—even that no one knows what judges and what
court in the infinite hierarchy are competent to deliver
judgement.   Joseph K.'s only hope is an advocate, and yet
the advocate knows no more than he does.   He observes that
another accused, a businessman, has not only neglected all
his worldly concerns for the sake of his defence, but has also
become the fawning ' dog of his lawyer '—even the petitioner
of the lawyer's slatternly maid.   Horrified by such abasement,

and repelled by the absurdity of his lawyer's efforts, he drops the lawyer and starts on an even more grotesque plan. He begs for help from a painter merely because the latter paints the portraits of the judges. From this man he learns that the accused are never cleared in these courts, and that cases may at any moment be re-opened by the arbitrary decision of the judges : information which, like all the information he receives, simply makes his situation more obscure than before. So also his meeting with the priest, the prison chaplain, leaves him more perplexed than ever. The priest indeed puts forward the view that the doorkeeper in his fable cannot be judged by human standards, because as a servant of the Law he is ' beyond human judgement ' ; that is, Joseph K. should not try to understand and judge, but simply submit.[15] But Joseph K. will not be satisfied with this.

The only other completed chapter is that entitled ' End '. Joseph K. is formally dressed, awaiting unknown guests. Two men arrive, in morning coats and top-hats, not the visitors he was expecting. They march him like a criminal through the dark town, and he makes no resistance, no appeal for help, though he vaguely hopes for rescue. They take him to a quarry, lay him on a stone, and offer him a knife with which to kill himself. On his refusal, they ceremoniously pierce his heart with the knife ; ' like a dog ', he thinks with shame. As he lies awaiting the stroke he sees the window of a distant house thrown open—

Someone, faint and thin at that distance and height, leaned far forward with a jerk and stretched out both arms still further. Who was it ? A friend ? A good man ? Someone who felt for him ? Someone who wanted to help ? Was it one person only ? Was it everybody ? Was help still available ? Were there arguments in his favour that had been forgotten ? Certainly there were. Logic is no doubt unshakable, but it cannot withstand a man who insists on living. Where was the judge he had never seen ? Where was the High Court to which he had never come ?

Of the various interpretations of this novel, one sees it simply as an imaginative clinical study of the disease, tuberculosis, of which Kafka died. A disease is a ' punishment ' which strikes one undeserved ; the ineffectual doctors, on whom the patient utterly depends, may be seen as ' advocates ' who are at a loss about procedure ; after the regular doctors one has recourse to any quack.   The very title ' der Prozess ' is a medical term for consumption, as well as a legal term ; the executioners are dressed like doctors, and Joseph K., when seized by them, cries out : ' I am not ill.' The perpetual hallucination of hope is characteristic of this particular disease.   Apart from the fact, however, that the novel was largely completed long before Kafka's tubercular infection was suspected, this interpretation makes many important elements of the book superfluous or at best fanciful decorations.   The transference of a physical calamity into the moral realm, the problematic of the courts of justice, the fable of the Law, would merely inflate and confuse a simpler problem ; such a procedure would be highly uncharacteristic of Kafka, one of the least pretentious of authors.

A similar type of interpretation would see the novel as the direct elaboration of Kafka's father-obsession.   There is no doubt some substance in this view.   I have already mentioned instances of this obsession in other works, and it was so powerful that even in 1919, at the age of thirty-six, Kafka wrote his long incrimination of his father, partly in self-exculpation, partly in self-accusation.   In it he actually speaks of his ' lawsuit ' (' Prozess ') with his father, the subject of perpetual discussion with his sister :

All along you have been a main topic of our conversations as of our thoughts, not in order to think up something against you, I tell you frankly, but to talk over in all detail, with all the powers of our heads and hearts, this terrible lawsuit that is engaged between us and you, straining ourselves to the utmost, in fun and in earnest, with love, defiance, anger, repugnance, devotion, conviction of guilt—this lawsuit in which you constantly claim to be judge while you, at least in the greater part, are just as much a weak and confused party as we are.[16]

There is undoubtedly something pathological in Joseph K.'s preoccupation with his lawsuit.   His arrest is remarkably fictitious, for he is left completely free.   After the first summons to court he is completely ignored by the judiciary ; all that follows is due to his own initiative. The priest repeats what the warders tell him right at the beginning : ' The court wants nothing of you. It receives you when you come and dismisses you when you go.' When his executioners come, Joseph K. makes no attempt to get help. The obscurity of his guilt, the insubstantiality of the courts, are characteristic of a pathological consciousness of a guilt which has no objective reality. There is nothing apart from inhibitions to prevent him from breaking free out of the net. But this psychological interpretation again is insufficient. Why are these courts so squalid ? Why is the majesty of Law invoked ? Why is Joseph K. so engaged in battle ? Are not wider, moral or religious issues in question ?

It has been maintained that there is an objective personal guilt in Joseph K. He is a bachelor ; he is loveless ; he is a man of routine. Hence he fails in human responsibilities, and hence is punished. There is, however, no hint in the book that Joseph K. has incurred any particular, personal guilt ; he is much rather an ordinary, normal man than an exception. And then we have the religious interpretations of Brod and Muir, who see the courts as the symbol of divine justice, and Joseph K.'s execution as the judgement of God ; who even suggest that that last glimpse of possible aid is a glimpse of divine grace (or wrath). His punishment is that of those ' who do not hear the Word or who leave the true way '.[17] What a symbol of divine law, not to speak of grace, these courts are, without justice or mercy, hysterical and capricious, sordid and corrupt, inaccessible to the mediator as to the defendant ! If Heller could convincingly attack a similar interpretation of *The Castle*,[18] how much more forced and repugnant does it appear in *The Trial*.

Adherents of Kierkegaard and the ' theology of crisis ' carry this sort of interpretation to a repellent and absurd extreme, distorting the text in the process. Kelly can see Joseph K.'s execution as the ' offering ' of his life to God ; and he continues : ' A great change has come over Joseph K. since his interview with the priest. He has abandoned all attempts to

Q

escape from the jurisdiction of the court, and is in a mood to go forth joyfully and meet its sentence . . .', etc.[19]   Thus, after the execution of Joseph K., the book is executed.

These interpretations do, however, reflect significant aspects of the situation of Joseph K.   He does seek for ' grace ', for a declaration of his innocence ; he is fascinated by these courts, abhorrent as they are.   He suffers from a punishment which is not his fault, yet, like a physical illness or a neurosis pertains to human nature.   Though not personally deserved, his guilt is a general one and such as is often expressed by Kafka in religious terms : ' The condition in which we find ourselves is sinful, quite apart from guilt.' [20]   Kafka exposes this state of sin, the consciousness of suffering, the search for release ; but there is no hint of a particular cause, nor of the possibility of grace or rescue.   What is central is that Joseph K. is punished ; his ' guilt ' is only an inference and actually never accepted by him.   And this is a general human situation. For ' punishment ' is all around, the injustices of society, the malevolence of authority, the curse of poverty or disease or character.   We comfort ourselves with the platitude : ' guilt brings punishment ' ; but Kafka points out, in his paradoxical and disturbing way, that the unpalatable statement is much truer : ' punishment proves guilt '.[21]   Far from demonstrating that this is how things ought to be, as his religious interpreters would have it, he only reveals, with pain and loathing, that is how things are under the surface of the world of routine and law and customary belief.

These squalid and corrupt courts are not a symbol of divine justice.   They are the sanction of the actual world of society, the justification of the world as it is, acquiring reality and power only because they are believed in.   Joseph K. challenges their authority, he protests against his arrest, he retains his protesting spirit to the end.   But he is no hero in the ancient sense, no dragon-slayer ; he also is entangled in the web of normal existence and normal belief.   Though not admitting his guilt, he does succumb to the fascination of his lawsuit, seeking out every opportunity to hear about the courts. He invents absurd stratagems, seeking for instance the comfort of women as a distraction. He is like the mouse in Kafka's fable :

'Alas ', said the mouse, ' the world is growing smaller every day. At first it was so wide that I was afraid, I went on running and was glad when at last I saw in the distance walls to right and left, but these long walls hurry so quickly towards one another that I am already in the last room, and there in the corner stands the trap into which I am running.'

'You have only to change direction,' said the cat, and ate it up.[22]

Joseph K. is unable to change direction ; indeed, he is set on running into the trap. Though he protests he is innocent, the charge against him becomes his most precious possession, his real title to life which is at the same time his title to death, the metaphysical counterpart of the public and private life to which Joseph K. is committed. He clings to the charge as Kafka himself clung to his illness, to his Angst. In the letters to Milena Kafka calls this paralysing Angst his real companion ; it is his ' only protection '. He does not see it as something accidental, something to be cured ; it is his ' substance ', the ' best ' in him, what is ' lovable ' in him. Angst is for him, like disease, a ' fact of faith '—but a purely negative element of faith, without positive belief or hope.[23]

In the *Journals* Kafka writes :

Faith means : to liberate the indestructible element in oneself, or more correctly, to liberate oneself, or more correctly, to be indestructible, or more correctly, to be.[24]

The Trial takes the series one step further, and we might add a final term : ' or more correctly, not to be '. The indestructible element in Joseph K. is the accusation to whose fascination he succumbs, which gives sense to his life and commits him to death.

THE CASTLE

The situation in *The Castle* resembles that in *The Trial*. K., the hero, comes to a village in order to take up a post in the castle, the residence of the authorities to whom the village belongs. He seeks recognition, a right of existence, as

Joseph K. seeks a trial and a verdict ; and in the same way
the authority eludes him.   The castle is as bewilderingly
ramified in its structure, as exalted and squalid, as mighty and
ineffectual, as the court in *The Trial*.   Both heroes greedily
acquire information that only confuses, and consume themselves in their efforts.   But a new note is struck from the
beginning, for while Joseph K. is a protesting victim, K. is the
aggressor.

The castle authorities simply want to have nothing to do
with K., and the village folk only disapprove and hinder his
efforts.   It is his initiative that forces the castle into action,
a purely obstructive action, which is indeed not completely
successful.   Brod has some justification therefore in calling
The Castle Kafka's *Faust*, however slight and intangible K.'s
hope and achievement are.

In a note of 1920, two years before Kafka read the opening
chapter to Max Brod, he established the theme in its barest
form :

If you want to be introduced to a family you do not know, you
seek out a common acquaintance and ask him to oblige you.   If
you cannot find one, you put up with it and wait for a favourable
opportunity.

In the little place where we live a chance must occur.   If an
opportunity does not present itself today, it will tomorrow without
any doubt.   And if it does not, you will not shake the pillars of
the world on that account.   If the family can bear to do without
you, you will bear it at least no worse.

This is all self-evident, K. alone does not see it.   Of late he has
got it in his head that he must push his way into the family of the
lord of the manor, but instead of trying the normal social channels
he goes straight for it.   Perhaps the usual way seems too tedious,
and he is right there, but the way he tries to go is after all impossible.   Do not think I am exaggerating the importance of our
squire.   A sensible, hardworking, honourable man, but nothing
more.   What does K. want of him ?   Does he want a post on the
estate ?   No, he does not want that, he is himself well off and leads
a carefree life.   Is he in love with the squire's daughter ?   No,
no, he is free of any such suspicion.[25]

The ironic simplicity of this draft almost hides the sig-

nificance of the family and the unintelligible resolve of K. to
find contact with it. In the novel the symbols have become
infinitely richer, and irony is replaced by the bitter humour
of desperation.

K. arrives at the village in night and snow, and falls asleep
on the floor of the taproom of the inn. Awakened by a
junior official of the castle, who tells him he cannot stay
without an official permit, K. immediately shows he is out
for a battle. He truculently asks : ' What is this village I
have strayed into ? Is there a castle here ? ' He makes as
if to go there and then to the Count to get his permit, a suggestion the impertinence of which horrifies the official. Then
he states that he is a land-surveyor appointed by the Count,
and that his two assistants are on the way with his instruments.
The official rings up the castle, and the prompt answer comes
that no surveyor has been appointed ; but a minute or two
later comes another message which confirms K.'s status. He
is allowed to stay at the inn, his board and lodging being paid
by the castle. These are his curious reflections :

> So the castle had appointed him land-surveyor. That was
> unfavourable for him on the one hand, for it proved that the castle
> knew all that was necessary about him, had weighed up their
> relative strength, and was accepting battle with a smile. But, on
> the other hand, it was also favourable, for in his view it proved that
> they underestimated him, and that he would have more freedom
> than he could have dared to hope. Their recognition of him as
> land-surveyor certainly showed intellectual superiority, but if they
> thought they could thereby cow him permanently, they were
> mistaken ; it made him shiver a bit, that was all.

So, K. had never been invited to come ; even more, he is
an impostor. In his later conversation with the village Superintendent we hear that there was no such post as land-surveyor.
In this opening chapter K. claims that his assistants will be
there the next day with his instruments, but they never appear.
He speaks of his wife and child,[26] but is soon planning to
marry a village girl. He is no land-surveyor, except in the
allusive meaning of the word ' Landvermesser '—one who
audaciously lays claim to the land. His challenge has been

accepted by the castle authorities, who thus show that they know all about him ; the battle is on, and he has actually won a concession.

The next day the castle sends K. two ' assistants ', thus playing his game, and he accepts them with the ironical humour typical of Kafka. ' Who are you ? ' he asks, and continues : ' What, you are my old assistants, whom I told to follow me and whom I'm expecting ? ' When they confirm this, K. accepts the pretence, but probes a little further into the joke. ' By the way, you're very late, you're very slack. Where are the instruments ? '   ' We haven't any,' they reply. ' The instruments I entrusted you with ? ' They again say they have no apparatus and know nothing about land-survey-ing. ' But if you are my old assistants you surely must know that.' He tells them that, since they are so alike, he will treat them as if they were one person, and they respond by acting like circus clowns. It is an elaborate joke, each side joining in the make-believe but showing that he sees through it at the same time. It is continued later in the book, when K. is praised by a castle official for his excellent surveying work, though he has done none. But this game is also a fight, and the joke has a sinister undertone.

Throughout K. remains aggressive, truculent. He steals the mistress of Klamm, the castle official who is supervising his progress. He tries to waylay Klamm and displays utter con-tempt for the latter's secretary. He treats the assistants the castle sent him as if they were puppets. His restless scheming alienates his allies among the villagers, and he challenges public opinion by making friends with a family which has been ostracised because of insubordination to the castle. He can never reach Klamm or the castle, yet seizes on the chance of any intermediary. Only at the end he meets by mistake an official who offers to help him, but he is too exhausted to take advantage of the offer.

What is this castle ? It is the legal authority over the village, and consists of a vast hierarchy of officials none of whom has any real responsibility since there is always someone higher to whom decisions are referred. But does anyone take decisions ? We do not see any productive activity of any kind coming from the castle, it does not interfere in village affairs at all, it has no policy ; it is a gigantic hierarchy of control officials (' Kontrollbehörden ') we hear ; the perfect parody of an atrophied bureaucracy. The officials are respected by the villagers, but do not earn respect by wisdom, goodness, or even efficiency. They are all weary, overworked, fussy, busied with so many papers that they can never master them, hurrying to and fro with as much reason and result as the White Rabbit. They expect the village girls to yield to their contemptuous advances. Their servants are at best foolish and arrogant, but most are lewd and beastly, despised even by the villagers. One has only to divorce the castle inmates from the atmosphere of awe that surrounds them to find them absurd and ineffectual as well as repugnant.

Nor does the proximity of the castle make the villagers attractive. The peasants as a whole are dull-witted and graceless. They quarrel among themselves and are malevolent to the stranger. Many are labouring under sickness, like the Superintendent (a sort of chairman of the parish council) and the innkeeper's wife ; most are self-righteous and some arrogant. They venerate the castle and its officials, but this veneration brings no grace into their lives. The girls take it as the highest honour and happiness to receive the languid favours of the officials ; the memory of an ancient three-day liaison with Klamm constitutes the only happiness of the inn-keeper's wife. The sordidness of the village corresponds exactly to the sordidness of the castle ; and the villagers are as horrified at K.'s restless striving as the castle is obstructive.

Soon after his arrival, K. is taken to the Herrenhof inn which serves as the village office and residence of the castle officials. The barmaid, Frieda, is, he is told, the mistress of Klamm, whom he sees sitting in the back room. She hides him under the bar and they spend the night in love-making among the beer-puddles. When Klamm calls her in the morning, she shouts that she is leaving him for the land-surveyor, and they go with her little bundle to K.'s room in the other inn. K. is not sure what has attracted him to his

fiancée, for as such she is now known. She is not young or
beautiful, but has a serene competence and staunchness about
her that gives him courage. But perhaps too, he admits to
himself, he made love to her in order to use her as a channel
to Klamm ; and indeed her love for him springs largely out
of a desire to help him. She tells him as her own opinion :

   ' The innkeeper's wife says about you, " I can't abide him, but
also I can't forsake him ; you just can't control yourself when you
see a little child that can't walk properly and ventures out on his
own—you have to lend a hand." '

When they are thrown out by the landlady, who is incensed
at K.'s disrespect for the castle, Frieda loyally stands by him
even in the squalor of their quarters in the school of which
K. has become caretaker. She too is ultimately repelled by
his stratagems and lack of candour, and leaves him for one of
the assistants who needs her care. But, though she always
considers Klamm's love to have been her highest honour, she
never tries to make K. revere Klamm ; on the contrary, she
tries to wean him from his obsession with Klamm. ' There
is too much Klamm here,' she tells him, urging him to take
her away from the village and forget the castle.

   One villager only, the girl Amalia, has revolted against the
castle. With her whole family she is now ostracised, and this
family has an irresistible attraction for K. Her sister Olga
tells K. their story. One of the officials, Sortini, had summoned Amalia to him with a brutal threat, and she had indignantly torn up the note. Since that time they have become
pariahs. The father has worn himself out in his attempts to
beg for pardon and is now, like the mother, a helpless cripple.
The brother Barnabas spends most of his days waiting in the
outer offices of the castle, hoping to become a messenger, full
of doubt and despondency. Olga herself, in order to win
friends for her brother, spends her nights with the lewd castle
servants at the Herrenhof. Only Amalia has remained unconcerned and resolute. K. listens eagerly to the long tale of
their efforts, for from the outcasts he learns more about the
castle than from any of the pious, and from their failure he

hopes to learn something to his own advantage. That his
situation is in some way linked with theirs is evident, for the
first and only messages that Barnabas has ever carried are
those from Klamm to K.

It is from Olga he learns that Klamm looks quite different
at different times and to different people, and even—one of the
rare ' clues ' in the novel—that these changes are the result of
' the momentary mood, the degree of excitement, the innumer-
able grades of hope or despair in the viewer '. Equally significant is her explanation that their ostracism was not due
to any action by the castle authorities ; it was the villagers
who, hearing about Amalia's revolt, immediately broke off
contact with the family. She adds that even the village's
attitude was dependent on the family's own decision, and that
it was their own appalled consciousness of guilt that persuaded
the village that they were guilty :

> ' If we had come back again into public life, let bygones be
> bygones, and had shown by our behaviour that we had got over
> the affair, it doesn't matter how, so that public opinion would have
> been convinced that whatever the affair was, it was now closed,
> well, everything would have been all right ; we should have found
> friends again on all sides, and even if we could not completely
> forget the affair, they would have understood and helped us to
> forget it completely. But instead, we stayed at home.'

Of all the family only Amalia, with her ' proud and upright
look ', remains reserved and resolute, calmly and silently tending her crippled parents, indifferent to the ' gossip ' about the
castle. It is she that Frieda believes has captivated K. But
K. does not break through her calm aloofness, her determined
will to remain in isolation.

Since Brod's postscript to the first edition of *The Castle*, there
has been no end to interpretations which equate the castle
with Heaven and the village with the sinful world.[27] Piety
to the castle regulations and the caprices of the officials, however absurd or immoral, is defined as grace. If Kafka intended
it so, one can only say that his symbols are infinitely clumsy
and inadequate ; so much so that Heller can see the castle as
the residence of Evil, not of God. God's law may be believed

entreats him to give up his quest, he taunts her with : ' Surely you're not afraid for Klamm ? ' But perhaps above all he wants to assure himself of Klamm's existence and reality, that is, of the reality of the castle itself. He is harshly sceptical of other people's veneration for Klamm, he himself tries to trick him and catch him unawares ; Klamm responds in kind, for he sends K. a provocative letter praising him for the excellent surveying work he has not done. In so far as K. searches for and believes in Klamm and the castle, he is doomed to frustration and confusion ; yet it is only his search that brings him any reward at all. It is his great quality that he does not give up, and it is his great fault, as Frieda tells him, that he remains obsessed with the idea of getting to Klamm, no different in essence from Olga and Barnabas, the pitiableness of whose wiles he can see.

Towards the end (in a chapter not included in the first edition of the Muir translation) he is told the right method. He is called to the Herrenhof, misses his appointment, but blunders at midnight on a secretary, Bürgel, who gives him an inkling of how he should proceed. He can get admission to the castle, he is told, he can find an intermediary, but only by chance ; if he stumbles helplessly in the night upon an official, against all regulations, ' absolutely smashing all the official organisation ', then the fulfilment of his request cannot be refused. Unfortunately K. is too exhausted to understand that this is a direct offer of help. But he learns from the conversation that there is a direct approach to his goal, that he can reach it only by ignoring all the formalities and regulations.

This is the lesson he gives in the following chapter to Pepi, Frieda's clumsy successor as barmaid. She puts the blame for her personal incompetence on others, and tries to win him over by commiserating with the imaginary wrongs he has suffered. He corrects her :

' No, my dear Pepi, I have been as little misused and tricked as you. . . . You want to think you have been tricked, because it flatters you and makes you sad. The truth is, however, that you are not suited to this job. . . . It is a job like any other, but for

you it is the kingdom of Heaven, as a result you set about everything with excessive zeal, you tremble for your job, feel yourself
constantly persecuted, you are unduly obliging in the hope that
you will win over everyone who might support you, though you
merely annoy them thereby and repel them, for in an inn they want
peace and not the worries of a barmaid on top of their own. . . .
I am not at all clear about my own faults, but when I compare
myself with you, it dawns on me that both of us have been too
clamorous, too childish, too inexperienced in toiling to get something, crying, scratching, tugging, when it is to be gained easily
and imperceptibly, for instance with Frieda's calm and Frieda's
matter-of-factness. We have been like a child tugging away at
the tablecloth, who gains nothing but pulls all the fine things on
to the floor and makes them unobtainable for ever.' [28]

This would be the way; and the hindrance lies entirely
within K.   But it is not an obsessive hindrance.   If he merely
set about his job in the matter-of-fact way of Frieda, then also
Klamm and the castle would close over him as they do over
her.   But he does not want to sink to the level of the villager ;
he does not come here for grace : ' I don't want any favours
from the castle,' he tells the Superintendent, ' I want my rights.'
It may be that we can sum up his goal as entry into the community ; but it is not admission to the community as it exists
that he wants—that would be easy.   He finds the community,
his goal, sordid and inhuman, and its whole ' heavenly '
reflection the same.   He wants to find recognition in castle
and village, to enter into the most intimate realms of the
community, to share its beliefs and its values as well as to
make a living, but at the same time he rebels against the
wrongs and absurdities that the community commits and
sanctifies.   His relations with both village and castle are therefore contradictory : he needs both, he respects both, but at
the same time he loathes both, he attacks both.

K. is a tragic character.   His immediate goal he knows,
but he cannot approach it.   ' There is a goal, but no way ;
what we call " way " is wavering.' [29]   But even this goal is
illusory, for he does not know what he wants of Klamm and
the castle, nor does he think of them as a means.   It is his
tragedy that, in these desperate ruses to get to an illusory goal,

he cannot ' change direction ' ; he goes on hoping to be given
what he ought to take. He is more tragic, a fuller figure,
than Joseph K. of *The Trial*, because his failure is richer in
experience, because it is attended by a growth in self-knowledge ; because he himself is a richer person, capable of humour
and tenderness ; above all because he is active and ready for
battle. Again one thinks of a sentence from the *Journals* :
' I do not hope for victory and the battle as a battle gives
me no joy, it gladdens me only because it is the only thing
to be done.' [30] In a variant of the opening K. says indeed :
' My task is all I have ' and ' I am here to fight '.[31] This is a
tragic mood, not the mood of a sacrificial victim.

Those who see the castle as a symbol of Heaven and grace
make K. into the villain of the piece because he refuses to
submit like most of the villagers. It is true he makes errors,
makes nothing but errors, and indeed that his positive purpose
is unclear. Kafka said of himself that he had no share in
the positive inheritance of life, that he represented only the
negative, that he could accept neither the Christian nor the
Jewish faith.[32] But when, in the same passage, he says he
does not fight against the negative, his words do not fit K.,
nor *The Castle*. For the negative elements of life, its squalor
and cruelty, as reflected in castle and village, are not only
displayed in the novel in their repellent sordidness, but also
are attacked by K. His attack is not direct, for in some
respects he seems to woo the castle ; often it seems to arise
only incidentally. But these incidental rebellions of feeling
against Klamm or Sortini or the assistants, against the village
Superintendent or the schoolmaster or the peasants, become
the real substance and achievement of his battle. From them
we can gather that he has positive standards and a positive
purpose : a community governed by humane principles, a life
where a man's destiny may fulfil his will. But his hope of
finding this purpose realised is so faint that it appears only in
the negative form of disgust with actuality.

K.'s tragedy is that his goal is unattainable because it appears
to him only under the form of an illusion. He cannot remain
isolated, for the freedom of isolation is meaningless. But he

cannot accept a community at any price, with its false values
and fetishes. So he remains in a border region between community and isolation. Kafka himself was in such a position,
between the Czech, German and Jewish communities, between
bourgeoisie and proletariat, an isolation intensified by his illness which took him to one sanatorium after another. ' This
border region between loneliness and community I have
crossed extremely rarely, I have even settled in it more than
in loneliness itself.' [33]

Within this region, however, K. struggles persistently.
When Frieda tries to persuade him to take her away and live
in the isolation of married bliss, he refuses sadly but firmly :
' What could have enticed me into this desolate land but the
desire to stay here ? ' And in this sojourn which destroys him,
though he does not get nearer to Klamm, he wins something
of value. The castle is as obscure as ever, but he has learnt
that its apparent decisions are really the decisions of the village.
He has acquired contacts, even friends, among the inhabitants.
And in his last conversations with Frieda and Pepi, K. shows
that he has not only acquired some understanding of himself,
some patience ; there is also affectionate, sympathetic understanding of others in his words. This is the unique character
of *The Castle* among Kafka's works. It is the only work in
which the hero gets rid, to some extent, of his obsessive subjectivity. He does not gain his ostensible goal, but he does
break through his painful egocentricity to recognise the reality
of other persons. If ever so slightly, the nightmare world
within and around him is receding. Perhaps these are the
' incidental circumstances ' which, according to Brod's statement in the postscript to the first edition of the novel, Kafka
intended should in the end, as K. is dying, compel the grudging
recognition of the castle authorities.

THE STRUCTURE OF KAFKA'S IMAGINATIVE WORLD

The most striking characteristic of Kafka's style is the
intimate association of the contraries of a familiar reality and

a fantastic realm. Much too crude, however, is the formula, ' realism of detail within a framework of symbolism '.[34] The main point is that these contraries ' meet in one ', not only in the sobriety of the manner in which they are described, but also in their mutual relevance and relationship. If Kafka's works are comparable with dreams or nightmares, it is precisely because their fantastic elements are rooted in real experience and a real world. They are not the capricious expressions of a man who is estranged from reality, but they ' uncover the hidden estrangement of everyday life ', as Anders has well put it.[35] In this respect his theme is that of many of his contemporaries, in particular of the Expressionists. But he detested their clamorous violence, their arrogant and sentimental self-exaltation. He takes us, as it were familiarly and prosaically, into a realm where apparently normal things and people have the unusual emotional and moral charge they have in a dream ; in this world of his we can no longer take anything as indifferent or irrelevant, for all has a potency which assails us. Kafka humanises the world, or better, he depicts the world as the man-made reality it is, and makes us experience this world directly. It is not for nothing that he never takes us into the world of nature, and that the animals he describes, in *The Burrow, Report for an Academy, Josephine*, etc., are all the human animals of fable.

There is nothing purely objective in his world ; nothing purely subjective. Things are charged with value (emotive activity and meaning), feelings acquire concrete substantiality. He defined his purpose thus :

Along with his logical demonstration runs bewitchment. A logical demonstration can be evaded by escape into the world of magic, and bewitchment by escape into logic, but if both are present simultaneously they crush you in their grip, all the more since they are a third something, living magic or non-destructive but constructive destruction of the world.[36]

The logic of objective reality, the capriciousness of fantasy, in mutual interpenetration, dissolve the world ; not with a purely negative intention, but in order to reveal its innermost

character and structure.   Thus Emrich can rightly assert that
Kafka ' exactly portrays reality '.[37]

Kafka's style welds in a unique way these two elements
of rigour and fantasy.   His vocabulary is very sober and precise, extremely limited and ' ordinary ' indeed, not only when
he describes stuffy bedrooms, offices or bars, but also when we
pass to the magic regions of the court or the castle.   It is
impossible to define the point at which characters like the
proletarians or porter in *America*, the advocate in *The Trial*,
the landlady in *The Castle* cease being casual acquaintance and
acquire a baleful potency.   A ship or a country house, a
tenement or a suburb, a village or an inn imperceptibly change
into labyrinths in whose centre lurks the minotaur.   The same
subdued, sober style accompanies all phases, an ever-renewed
unemphatic rhythm ; there is no trace of rhetoric, not even
of emotionalism.   Translation fails to do justice to Kafka, for
this sober self-evidence of the truth of his words arises as
much from the order of words, the rhythm, as from the
vocabulary.

Peculiarly characteristic of Kafka's style are the immensely
long sentences, and the paragraphs that run on for many
pages.   In *The Burrow* or *Josephine* this technique may be seen
at its purest, though it is frequent in the novels also.   In them
a statement is developed in all directions, its truth is expounded,
the contrary emerges, an immense movement occurs though
it is largely circular and self-cancelling.   Neider has aptly
called it a ' breathless ' style.   In these short stories it interprets exactly the incessant activity of the animal and a pervasive doubt of the meaning and value of its labour.

In the novels these long sentences and paragraphs are used
only in particular circumstances.   K. himself falls into them
only when he is subject to tortuous arguments in which his
mind races through various possibilities without being able
to find certainty, emphasis, and pause.

Only as a village worker, removed as far as possible from the
gentry in the castle, was he in a position to achieve anything in the
castle itself, these village folk, who were still so suspicious of him,
would begin to speak once he was their fellow-citizen, if not actually

their friend, and when he had become indistinguishable from Gerstäcker or Lasemann—and that must happen very soon, everything depended on it—then at a stroke all roads would certainly be open to him which, if it were merely left to the gentry up there and their favour, would have remained for ever not only barred but invisible.[38]

The Muirs, very understandably breaking this sentence by interposing two semi-colons, make K.'s thoughts more deliberate and more sound ; the words ' only ', ' would ', ' at a stroke ', ' certainly ', simply hide his uncertainty, of course. When K. uses a similarly fluid sentence to Frieda, there is evident beneath it an almost conscious deceit ; on this occasion he is not only, not so much, wrestling with himself as trying to deceive her.[39]

We find this style frequently used for the conversation of other characters, whether in direct or indirect speech. In the twists and turns of the advocate's sentences in *The Trial*, interrupted only by commas, without energy or emphasis, we are admitted into the weary, incessant routine of the lawyer's occupation and the court's procedure. Not so much a character is portrayed thus, no more than in the advocate's actual appearance on his sick-bed in the ill-lit room, as a general situation, the situation which closes round Joseph K. A similar busy breathlessness links the statements of Olga in her long account of Amalia's misdeed and the family's efforts to win pardon. Even her short sentences run on without sharp differentiation of emphasis. The problem itself and the problematical efforts to solve it are described in all their puzzling complexity ; and with her, as often with the female characters in Kafka, perplexity leads not so much to the subtle dialectic of K. as to a gossipy inconsequence which is frequently deliciously humorous. The structure of these long sentences has nothing of the complex unity of the sentences of Thomas Mann ; the speaker or thinker does not grasp the totality of a sentence as a single statement. In their separate parts they are as simple as the shorter sentences, and as he proceeds the character gropes along, moving backwards and forwards, reaching half-unsuspected further thoughts—never coming to

R

conclusions, but going on to further qualifications or suggestions. Even the structure of the successive phrases changes, some having the character of parentheses. This is so even in Frieda's talk which, though possessing a suspicion of gossip, is much more energetic and determined than Olga's. She says to K., when she charges him with heartless duplicity in his treatment of her :

'You even imagine your interview with Klamm as a transaction, cash for cash. You calculate all the possibilities ; assuming you get your price you are ready to do anything, if Klamm wants me, you will give him me, if he wants you to stick to me, you will stay, if he wants you to throw me over, you will throw me over, but you are also ready to do some play-acting, if it is to your advantage you will give out that you love me, you will try to overcome his indifference by emphasising your insignificance and then shame him by the fact that you're his successor or by telling him my protestations of love for him which I really have made, and by begging him to take me back again, at your price of course ; and if nothing else answers, then you'll simply go on your knees to him in the name of K. and wife.' [40]

There is extremely little variety of style in the novels. The description of circumstance and event is dry, sober, laconic ; even in distress or anger or love the characters express themselves rather tonelessly. There are often hysterical outbreaks, for instance those of officials in the court (*The Trial*) or the Herrenhof inn (*The Castle*), but they occur like pieces of routine. Even the startled angry cry of the priest in the cathedral : ' Can you not see two steps ahead ? ' passes like a momentary ruffling of a pond. There is only one situation in the novels, in fact, and this situation, a confused groping, dominates the whole ; the slight and subtle variations in the speech of the characters, for instance, do not hide a fundamental identity. It is misleading, indeed, to speak of ' characters '. The people whom the hero meets exist only by virtue of their relation to him, they express themselves only in relation to his problem. There is a curious deadness about the background, it has no life and movement of its own, it comes into being when the hero enters it, it ceases to be when he goes elsewhere. The style of speech of other characters is merely a variation of the hero's style.

The Kafka heroes impose their own pattern on the world. The other characters pass across their line of vision, but never acquire substance and an existence in their own right. The hero is never inwardly changed by them ; he may be hindered by them, at best he tries to use them for his own purposes. Frieda tells K. that he simply tries to use her as an instrument ; he is incapable of feeling and of the liberation that feeling can bring. Kafka's heroes can feel the misery of others, but themselves are loveless ; to them can be applied what he wrote of himself :

That there is fear, sadness and desolation in the world, he understands, but only to the extent that these are vague, general feelings that only sweep over the surface. He denies all other feelings, and considers that what are called such are only a semblance, fairy-tale, reflection of experience and memory.[41]

The technical unity of the novels is provided, thus, by the hero. All is told from his standpoint. Only what he experiences is narrated, only what he knows is known. If we are told anything about what has occurred outside the range of his experience, we know it only as the hero is told about it, in the form it takes in the minds of his informants, the advocate or painter, the landlady, Olga or Frieda. We never enter a sphere from which the hero is absent. There is the severest unity in this structure, utterly at variance with the traditional story-telling technique.[42] Through this technique, as Beissner puts it, ' Kafka transforms not only himself, but also the reader into his main character ' ; and thereby he takes us to the very heart of the matter. We directly experience the confusions of the hero, his hopeless preoccupation with himself, his lack of knowledge about himself and his purpose. There are no interpretative or explanatory author's comments, that is, there is no hint of a secure vantage-point from which an objective view may be obtained. The confidence one of his heroes may express from time to time is always temporary and part of his illusion, even though Kafka may use a grammatical form which seems to insist on its truth. Among the tortured questions that Joseph K. asks as he awaits the executioner's blow occurs a positive sentence :

Were there arguments in his favour that had been forgotten? *Certainly there were.   Logic is no doubt unshakable, but it cannot withstand a man who insists on living.*   Where was the judge he had never seen ? . . .

Some readers have taken the italicised sentences as an ' author's comment '.   How strange if it were so !   The only such in the whole book, placed in the middle of frenzied and futile questionings, without a function, and contradicted by events. They can only be understood as one more of Joseph K.'s illusions, and their grammatical form, the dogmatic assertion, expresses only with greater intensity his harrowing incomprehension.   A close grammatical parallel is found in the incompleted chapter of *America* entitled ' Brunelda's Outing ': ' Karl scarcely listened to such remarks any longer, everybody was exploiting his power and abusing the underdog.'   The whole significance of this statement is not that it is true, but that Karl thought it was true.   At all moments in Kafka's novels we, the readers, are encased with the predicament of the hero ;   this structure interprets precisely and harrowingly the situation of man as Kafka experienced it.

Hence too the lack of rational causality in the novels.   Since this world has no objective reality, the normal connections of cause and effect are absent.   Characters are moved by motives which seem natural to them but inscrutable to us ; they accept as normal and rational what seems abnormal and irrational.   Court and castle are the most self-evident solid reality for ordinary men, while for the hero they are, to say the least, puzzling and questionable.   In the earliest work this distortion of normal relationship is due to a deliberate refusal on the part of the writer to do more than watch surface-relationships or describe dream-like hallucinations.   Even in *The Trial*, an odd fragment describes a visit to the court as a hallucination of Joseph K. as he lies on his sofa.[43]   Sometimes such abnormal causality is merely the expression of pathological mental processes.   Georg's acceptance of the verdict of his father (*The Verdict*), the feeling of Karl Rossmann for the stoker (*America*), though arbitrary in appearance, are of course fully understandable to anyone who knows anything about psychoanalysis. But the distortion of causality that occurs in the mature works is due neither to a deliberate refusal to try to understand, nor to a study of abnormal psychology. It expresses Kafka's deep questioning of the total rationality of human behaviour, of the conventional security about what is real and unreal. The logical absurdity of Kafka's imaginative world is the counterpart of its potency of horror ; man lives comfortably in this world, he tells us indirectly, only by constructing an illusion of rational causality. ' Once follow the misringing of the night-bell '—and conventional reality and causality collapse around one.

To his heroes, who have followed the misringing of this bell, the world seems senseless, but coherent ; men are bent purposively on some pursuit, but the purpose is inscrutable. In his *Journals* we often meet Kafka's preoccupation with circus-artistes, an interest that can be associated with Picasso's famous painting and Rilke's Fifth Elegy. He was fascinated by the absurdity of the plays acted by the Yiddish troupe in Prague, and some of his descriptions of their performances in the beer-hall read like pages out of his novels.[44] In *A Hunger Artist* he took as his theme a trapeze acrobat and a starvation expert. What fascinated him was the spectacle of a rigorous devotion to a meaningless task, and he makes of it the symbol of normal activity.

In the characters of his novels he similarly shows people who are absorbed in a typical conventional activity ; not individuals with their indeterminacy and potentialities, but realised types. We are reminded of the Expressionist reduction of dramatic characters to types like the father, the mother, etc. With Kafka men are above all their profession, and do nothing but fulfil their calling, as judges, lawyers, secretaries, etc. ; they are reduced to a mere social function. When Joseph K. protests against the flogging of the warders who had arrested him, the man flogging them answers phlegmatically : ' I am here to flog people, and flog them I shall.' The people around the heroes have no individuality, no personal history ; they are fixed types.   Even the women all fit into one category. The head cook in *America*, Leni in *The Trial*, the landlady and Frieda in *The Castle* are moved by pity for the heroes, their love is a type-love, a love out of pity.   Leni, we are told, loves all the lawyer's clients.   They all try to soften the hero's will, they beg him to confess or to give up his struggle, even Frieda, who is the sturdiest of them all.   It is perhaps one of the most horrifying aspects of Kafka's world that everyone is swallowed up by his function and behaves accordingly, without questioning the purpose this function serves.   In this way too it is an almost impenetrable world for the hero, for while he seeks a place in this world he seeks also to maintain his ' indestructible ' personality ;   it is not surprising therefore that the world appears to him as a grotesque hostile conspiracy.

With the disappearance of individuality and normal causality, time also becomes unrecognisable.   In the classical novel, time is a supreme reality, whether it is organic time or historical time, and the movement of events and development of persons in time shapes the structure of the story.   In Kafka there is no lapse of time.   His world is entirely a city-world (the village of *The Castle* might equally well be a tenement, there is no nature here) without seasonal changes ;   most scenes take place at night indoors.   We hear of days or weeks passing, but there is no development ;   time does not clarify or even intensify the confusion, though it shows that the labyrinth is more extensive than the hero earlier thought.   Anders uses the term ' paralysed time ', Mendilow speaks of ' a temporal vacuum '.[45]   Kafka's time is the timelessness of a dream.   His heroes set out again and again, but their new activity does not grow organically out of their earlier, it is not a true succession, it is a perpetual starting again.   His heroes might say, with the narrator of *Investigations of a Dog* : ' How my life has changed, and how at bottom it has not changed.'

This paralysis of time is intimately connected with the paralysis of the Kafka hero.   If no objective reality is perceived, then no purposive decision can be taken ;   all decisions are merely apparent and lead to no advance.   The activities of men are like the building of the Great Wall of China, in Kafka's parable. The belief that a decision to build it had ever been taken was the illusion of ' innocent Nordic peoples ' ; in fact, ' the decree existed from everlasting '—i.e. it has no purpose, it is activity for its own sake. The imperial envoy, in the same parable, can never find his way into the here and now.[46] Perhaps we can detect, in *The Castle*, a movement in time, for there is the suggestion that the hero becomes gentler and more patient. What we see in the main, in this novel and *The Trial*, is however only the growth of the hero's physical exhaustion, which is due to his successive failures ; this in itself does not mark the passage of time, it indicates only that the passage of time has been meaningless ; that is, from an aesthetic point of view there has been no lapse of time. Kafka's heroes are of course not passive in one sense, for they are extremely restless ; but they are fundamentally passive since they do not discover the right road, their activity is a perpetual ' wavering '.

In *A Country Doctor* Kafka wrote this fable :

My grandfather used to say : ' Life is astonishingly short. Now in my memory it is so compressed that I can scarcely understand, for instance, how a young man can decide to ride to the next village without fearing—quite apart from accidents—that the normal uneventful course of a life is by no means time enough for such a ride.' [47]

To the contemplative onlooker there seems not time enough. The young man, of course, confident in his purpose and the way, does not argue with his grandfather, but gets on his horse and rides off. Kafka's heroes are so preoccupied with the search for meaning that they can never ride off. Goethe wrote in his *Maxims* : ' The fairest fortune of a thinking man is, to have investigated the investigable, and to revere what is not investigable.' Kafka's heroes cannot believe in the meaning or value of what may be investigated, and consume themselves in investigating what eludes investigation. And from time to time he seems to commend those who cease from thinking and are content to believe themselves in the right.

Face to face with this world, familiar but astonishing, filled with purposes to which there is no key, Kafka like his heroes stands baffled, exhausted with the effort to understand. But the situation is not without its humour. Kafka's intelligent modesty kept him from striking tragic poses like so many of his German contemporaries, and there is much humour in his novels. It is above all a humour of parody, arising from the contrast between the apparent meaningfulness of behaviour and its actual absurdity. At the same time it approaches farce at times, since he spotlights and enlarges normal behaviour in order to bring out this absurdity in it.

Max Brod tells us that Kafka could not restrain his laughter as he read out the opening chapter of *The Trial*. The warders who come to apprehend Joseph K. act with all the insolent familiarity of the safe official before the guilty, threatening and wheedling, filching what they can ; one of them keeps butting him with his fat belly, with all the bonhomie of a bully. Joseph K.'s guilt appears here in a farcical form—as it does too in the absurd irrelevancies of his subsequent chat with his landlady and his flirtation with Fräulein Bürstner. There is the same sort of humour in his uncle's businesslike energy, or in the stoker in *America*, with his confused grievance. The castle officials nearly always appear in a farcical light. There is Momus with his arrogant and pedantic belief in the protocols that he knows no one will ever read ; Sordini surrounded with piles of documents which repeatedly collapse as he pulls one from beneath ; the morning distribution of documents at the Herrenhof, which is accompanied by hysterical excitement. Comparable is the scene in which the louts Delamarche and Robinson bathe the mountain of flesh, Brunelda, with such conscientious zeal. The humour of these and similar scenes is based on accurate observation of typical behaviour. It is never, of course, simple humour, there is always something sinister, even macabre, about it, for it is this behaviour which baffles or threatens the hero. Occasionally this parodistic humour takes a purely farcical form. K.'s two assistants behave like circus clowns, or better, like the early Chaplin or Harpo Marx, nodding and smiling to cheer him up, drooping in sympathy, playing all sorts of absurd antics, appearing and disappearing at the wrong time, etc. But they are not comic relief; they seem only to embody the inconsequence of the world in an extreme, undisguised form.

I have already mentioned what is perhaps the most subtle example of Kafka's humour—K.'s engagement of the assistants. He is no land-surveyor and has no assistants, though he says that he is and mentions that his assistants are on the way. The castle sends him new assistants who know nothing about land-surveying and yet say they are his old assistants. He keeps up the game and accepts them as such, even grumbling at them for not bringing the instruments. These farcical absurdities are a parody of commonsense causality. So, just before, K. has set out through the village in the morning, and after a short walk finds night has already fallen. This disturbance of normal time is ominous, and K. knows it; but he dismisses it humorously with the platitude : ' Short days, short days ! ' Kafka's humour is always grotesque and macabre, for while it brings out some element of the incongruous, it never releases the hero from the grip of the absurd and incomprehensible situation ; he succumbs to it in spite of his spasm of laughter.

The imaginative world of Kafka has, in all its parts, a strict coherence, and in this coherence we can find its meaning. In it are expressed and fused all the dominant elements of his experience. His obsession with his father, his love and fear of the family. The Jew who belongs neither to a religious nor a secular Jewish community ; who belongs to German culture but not to the German community ; who lives among and sympathises with Czechs under the old Austrian Empire, and who, still an alien when the Czechoslovak Republic is founded, is also by that time a sick man doomed to spend much of his time in sanatoria. An official with repugnance for his job and yet admiration for the gigantic machinery of bureaucracy. A middle-class intellectual at loggerheads with capitalistic entrepreneurs whose energy he admires, sympathising with the proletarians whom he fears (Joseph K. thinks, in the first version of *The Trial*, that the bewildering

lawcourt he attends is a socialist meeting). A man without
religion who yet hankers after the certainty of belief ; who
seeks ritualism but no church, a ' call ' but no God, service
but no master, commands but no ruler.⁴⁸ All these conflicts
are fused in the symbols of his novels so that they represent a
total situation of man, enmeshed in contradictions and vainly
seeking to release himself.

His heroes are doomed because they are consumed in the
effort to discover a meaning, because they are mysteriously
inhibited from action. Reflection, reflection that continually
turns on itself, takes the place of action ; Joseph K. and K.
are like Karl Rossmann on the balcony, fascinated by the
strange senseless behaviour in the remote street below. Ultimately, his heroes seek not so much to solve the problem as to
be redeemed, saved—as Anders puts it, they do not want
' Lösung ' but ' Erlösung '.⁴⁹ For Kafka, as for Rilke, happiness like disaster ' falls ' upon us, it can neither be earned nor
warded off.⁵⁰ In this sense he is a religious author, but in
no other, for he does not believe in divine powers that dispense
grace, and substitutes for them, in his two greatest novels,
powers of darkness who are merely the fetishes of the powers
of actual men. When, in an aphorism, he speaks of man's
earthly and heavenly ties, he uses the image of ' chains '. At
the end of his life, it was the Zionist community, not its
religion, that gave him a flicker of hope that he might enter
' a meaningful life in security and beauty '.⁵¹

It is a frozen, degenerate world that Kafka describes, without
fruitful vigour, in which the hero is paralysed. If we compare
it with that of the classical novel, we can see that there is
some justice in Burgum's statement that ' Kafka's novels cut
through the distracting irrelevancies of superficial realism and
afford a direct participation in the degeneration of personality
of the petty bourgeoisie '.⁵² It is wrong, however, to add that
Kafka was himself ' incapable of reasoned judgment upon his
material '. There is no illusion, no wishful thinking, no self-
inflation in Kafka's art. Its range and truth are restricted,
even distorted, by his situation and character, above all in
respect of the agonising paralysis which extends over all his

works. But within these limits his art is a precise, self-consistent, disillusioned spectral analysis of a world which seemed to him to be his sworn enemy, and against which his meagre strength seemed almost unavailing.

CHAPTER IX

Thomas Mann
1875–1955

THE GERMAN PROBLEM

THE form of Thomas Mann's novels is more traditional than that of Kafka's, but he too gives the novel a new character and direction. It is in fact extremely difficult to ' place ' him in the history of the German novel. He is most closely related to the tradition of the ' Bildungsroman ', but his debt to German philosophers, poets and musicians is much greater ; and he owes less to German novelists than to the French and Russians.

A highly conscious, sophisticated artist, Mann was well aware of the peculiarity of his position. Even that he is pre-eminently a novelist distinguishes him from other great German writers. In an article, *The Art of the Novel*, he asserts that the novel is ' the dominant art ' of the last two centuries, ' the vessel of the modern soul ', an opinion that is almost a challenge to the German literary tradition. He knows that the greatest German novels—he is thinking of the ' Bildungsroman '—have interpreted only ' the still, secret Germany ',[1] not its bustling social life, and that ' the novel of European stamp [" the great social novel "] is foreign to Germany '—the only exceptions he makes are Goethe's *Elective Affinities* and Fontane's *Effi Briest*. But with his own generation, he writes, something new occurred : ' At the turn of the nineteenth century there occurred something like a formal and spiritual break-through of the German novel into the sphere of European interest '[2] —and this is certainly true of Mann's own work.

Such a definition does not, however, mean that Mann was in any way un-German ; J. B. Priestley is not alone in finding his novels intolerably German. In the same article Mann defines the principle of the novel in a typically German way as ' the transformation of outward events into inward '

(' Verinnerlichung '), and he quotes with approval Schopenhauer's dictum : ' The novel will be of a higher and nobler
type, the more inward and the less outward life it presents.'
In his recognition of Wagner as a precursor on this European
path Mann makes it plain that it is at least as true that
' Europe ' has opened itself to German art as that Germany
has adapted itself to the European tradition. He · calls
Wagner's work ' the most sensational self-presentation and
self-criticism of the essential Germany that is imaginable '.[3]
As often in his essays, the phrase borders on the paradoxical,
for it is hard to find this ' self-criticism ' in Wagner. But it
can well stand for Mann's own work, and his ' Europeanism ',
somewhat like Nietzsche's, lies both in his profoundly German
character and in his constant critical preoccupation with
' Germanism '.

Schopenhauer, Wagner, Nietzsche—these were Mann's
masters and, as his essays show, with them he was at grips
throughout his life. His mode of thinking and of composition,
his style, betray their formulations and images. And this was
no local-German business, for in no writers of the nineteenth
century is the malaise of modern civilisation, of bourgeois
civilisation, more vehemently expressed. But Mann did not
remain, nor was ever engulfed by these writers. A most
sensitive seismograph, as Lukács once described him, he
reacted violently to the experiences of the twentieth century.
At first he saw life in terms of Schopenhauer's antithesis of
idea and will and adopted his aristocratic, artistic detachment ;
but later he was to judge this antithesis as ' the romantic
sickness of the nineteenth century ', and to condemn Schopenhauer's quietism and contempt for the common people—he
was to criticise Schopenhauer for seeking ' salvation ' instead
of ' liberation '.[4] As a young man he succumbed to Wagner's
ostentatious pessimism and exaltation of death, but his later
works are a continual struggle with Wagner. He absorbed
Nietzsche into his system, adopting his protest against the
banal and conventional, his revolt against the bourgeois, his
anti-mechanistic irrationalism and even, during the First World
War, his brutal anti-democratism. Later, in the cause of

humanism and democracy, he turned against Nietzsche's praise
of the instincts and of the will to power, but only very late in
life did he unambiguously repudiate a philosophy which claims
to restore mankind to health, but actually ' degenerates into
a mænadic rage against truth, morality, religion, humaneness
and everything that might serve to tame the savage in us '.[5]
The story of Mann's artistic development might be told in
terms of his continuing engagement with his three great
masters.

ARTIST AND BOURGEOIS

All Mann's early works centre in the problem of the relations
between artist and bourgeois, a theme characteristic of the
period of ' art for art's sake ', the *bohème*. The term ' bourgeois ' has not in this connection the precise meaning established
by socialism, and does not accurately translate the German
word ' Bürger ', which means ' townsman ' and ' citizen ' as
much as ' bourgeois '. In Mann's usage it indicates the staid,
old-fashioned middle class as opposed to the modern capitalist,
but it is above all a psychological term, meaning the man of
practical concerns, the unproblematical pedestrian citizen with
his private business, who feels at home in social life and does
not bother himself with questions of value. To him is contrasted the artist, a prey to irrational and ' dæmonic ' forces,
morbidly sensitive, ironically observing social life from the
outside. Art, his joy, is also his torture, for his delight in
expression and his consciousness of spiritual distinction are
attended by a painful recognition that he is unfit for life, even
that his art is sheer pretence.

These are the normal terms for the ' decadents ' of the turn
of the century. But Thomas Mann's attitude differed from
theirs. He described himself in 1918 as ' coming from
decadence, but with the emancipatory will to repudiate it ',[6]
and this contradictory relationship determined his artistic
character. In Novellen like *Tristan*, where the artist Spinell
is contrasted to a coarse and healthy brewer, the sharpest
irony is directed against Spinell ; not only are his feelings

spurious and his character feeble, but we suspect him of being a fraud as an artist. In many of the early stories Mann insists, like Nietzsche in *The Will to Power*, on the affinity between the artist and the charlatan and criminal.[6a] But the very essence of the finest of them, *Tonio Kröger* (1902), with its unmistakable autobiographical references, is the compromise position of the hero, who is at home neither with the *bohème* nor with the healthy bourgeois he feels drawn to—he is ' a bourgeois who has lost his way '. In *Death in Venice* (1912) the artist-hero, Aschenbach, has actually succeeded in reconciling the two worlds. His art itself is the product of the victory of formal discipline over the nihilistic artistic instinct, and the theme of his great book is Frederick the Great's devotion to duty. The purpose of his life is not essentially different from that of the Prussian soldiers and officials who were his forebears—self-discipline and service to the state. Only the manner and medium are different ; the moral effort is with the artist infinitely more tense and its relaxation disastrous.

Mann's first great novel, *Buddenbrooks* (1901), is built almost unconsciously round this ambivalence. Its ostensible theme is typical of the era of ' decadence '—' the decay of a family '. The Buddenbrook family is outwardly prosperous and secure, but a fateful artistic strain emerges, the business declines, and the last scion, Hanno, enraptured with Wagner, dies at an early age. Thomas, the last head of the family, still profits by the accumulated habits of the bourgeois, and for a time seems to prosper ; his artistic interests, his delight in appearances, his marriage with a gifted musician, seem nothing but the appropriate decoration of life. But his concern with business success is only a façade, he acts his life rather than lives it, form is more for him than substance ; and as he grows older his habitual moral resistance weakens. The moral crisis is reached when he greedily pores over Schopenhauer, and his death is as much an inward collapse as Hanno's. In this context the unlucky marriages of his sister Tony interpret both the lack of business acumen in the heads of the family and her own lack of a healthy mating instinct.

Yet this theme is, at least partly, at variance with the actual effect of the book.   Mann has told us, in fact, that the novel sprang from two opposed sources.   ' What originally lay near to my heart was the figure and experiences of the sensitive late-comer, Hanno '—a Novelle, that is, in the German tradition and like many others written at that time.   He continues : ' But an epic instinct drove me to begin *ab ovo* and to include all the earlier history [of the family] . . . and so there came into being a social novel disguised as a family-saga, and as such closer to the West-European type of novel than the German.' [7]

This double source, evident in the style too (Mann called it ' a curious combination of Low-German humour and the epic leitmotif-technique of Wagner '), confuses the thesis to the great advantage of the book as a whole.   Why it attracts many readers can be judged from Mann's recent statement that ' the musical pessimism, the Schopenhauer in the book, has been neglected in favour of the more agreeable aspects '.[8] The exuberance of the portrayal of normal bourgeois life, above all the great good humour with which it is described, reproduces almost involuntarily the dualism that is explicit in *Tonio Kröger* :   the attraction of ' exalted, ultimate truths ' that alienate man from society and even from life, and a deep love and sympathy for this life, a delight in life.

The uneasy feeling that the artist, however different temperamentally from the bourgeois, is intimately linked with him, and can make an alliance with him, comes to greater clarity in the rather slight novel, *His Royal Highness* (1909). The war of 1914, and the essays in *Reflexions of an Unpolitical Man* (the title is extremely ironical, for these articles are often enough blatant war-propaganda) fully brought home to Mann the deeper identity of interest between artist and bourgeois, artist and state.   He no longer saw ' spirit ' and ' culture ' as forms of protest against life and society ;   rather, the state (in this case Germany's authoritarian structure) is the cradle of culture, which he defines as ' power-protected inwardness '. In 1939, Mann roundly stated that this work brought him to the realisation that ' it was an error of the German bourgeoisie to believe that a man of culture could be unpolitical '.[9] The hero of his next great novel, *The Magic Mountain*, is no artist. True, Castorp claims to have genius, a genius for experience, for the risky venture into disease and death ; and like all artists, in Mann's conception, he lives on the edge of danger. But Mann now sees this adventurousness as only the intellectual and spiritual form of the adventurousness of his commercial forebears ; the risks Castorp runs are the counterpart of the dangers besetting the social world. Through this capacity in him, Castorp acquires the ability to overcome nihilism and to serve society. And, reflecting on this novel, Mann came to the generalisation :

When one becomes a thinker or an artist, one ' degenerates ' less than the environment from which one emancipates oneself, and less than one thinks ; one does not cease being what one's fathers were, but one is this over again, in a different, freer, spiritualised form that finds expression in symbols.[10]

When, in his later works, Mann uses the figure of an artist, it is thus that he conceives the relationship of artist and society. The artist is still marked off from the general run of men, unworldly, painfully and joyfully perceptive, engrossed with his visions, subject to a ' dæmon '. But in his symbolic medium he expresses the values by which his contemporaries live. Thus the decrepit illusionist in *Mario and the Magician* is the artist of the Fascist state and hence a symbol of Fascism —Mann says the work is concerned with ' the psychology of Fascism '.[11]

Some interpretations of Mann's most tragic novel, *Doctor Faustus* (1947), have been befuddled through a failure to realise that Mann's conception of the artist is no longer what it was in *Buddenbrooks*. On the face of it, the musician Leverkühn stands apart from the life around him. He lives a solitary, ascetic life, deliberately withdrawing from the normal concerns of his acquaintance, forgoing happiness and love. His fellow-students of theology feel him to be a doubter, ' the questioner who sits so sly ', and his rare contributions to the later discussions at Munich testify, like his taciturnity, to his scepticism of normal beliefs and enthusiasms. In his earliest

S

phase he protests with parody and irony against the cultured
'enjoyment' of music, and, challenging the whole idiom of
modern bourgeois music, he seeks with desperate sincerity a
music that will interpret his own isolation, a representative of
avant-garde revolutionism. So much does he repudiate the
bourgeois music of feeling that he is threatened with infertility ;
and his pact with the devil serves apparently simply to assure
him productiveness despite inner impoverishment : a personal
dæmonism which marks him off from others.

All this belongs to the essential theme of the novel. But
it is equally important that his music itself expresses what his
society is actually experiencing. Mann's novel is all the more
profound because he establishes this objective identity of
artist and society even when subjectively the artist believes
himself, and seems, to be detached from his fellows. Mann's
insight resulted not only from a long observation of cultural
life ; it also arose from his own personal experience. He has
several times drawn attention to the social relevance of *Buddenbrooks*, a work he thought, as he wrote it, to be of purely
personal and private relevance :

Only late in life does one learn through experience that works
of art of any importance are *socially* conceived, conceived in both
senses of the word, that of impregnation and that of conception.
You think you only give yourself, you speak only about yourself,
and lo and behold, you have given something superpersonal arising
from profound connections and an unconscious community with
others.[12]

Thus, Leverkühn's life has a double theme. There is the
story of the social relations of the artist who, as a condition
of his artistry, remains painfully apart from normal life—his
transient effort to get a share of normal happiness fails
miserably and is reflected in a falling off in his compositions.
But along with this goes the story of his compositions, which
are the symbolic expression of the life around him. This
novel is indeed, as Lukács has pointed out,[13] different from
most preceding works on the theme of artist and society, in
that it is not primarily the story of the artist's personal relations
with others, but the story of his works. The analyses of

Leverkühn's compositions, significantly preceded by those of Beethoven's later works, tell with astonishing power the story of his times.

This identity is suggested and explicitly stated many times during the book. Leverkühn's compositions are precisely and emphatically related both to the historical situation in which they were conceived, and to the moment during the Second World War at which the pseudo-narrator, Zeitblom, describes them. The *Apocalypse*, for instance, arises from the turmoil of defeat and civil war in 1919, and is described at the time in 1944 when Germany is being laid waste by aerial bombing and threatened by armies advancing from France and Russia. *The Lamentation of Doctor Faustus* is composed in 1930, the year of the breakdown of parliamentary government, and described in the year of Hitler's downfall. Explicit statements are reserved, but decisive. Leverkühn breaks away from the medieval city, Kaisersaschern, that was his birthplace, but Zeitblom writes that his music remained 'that of one who never escaped . . . music of Kaisersaschern'.[14] He tells us that in spite of the remoteness of Leverkühn's life he could not help drawing 'symbolic parallels' between his life and that of the nation. Hence Leverkühn's headaches and artistic barrenness towards the end of the war ; hence too Zeitblom's statement that the *Apocalypse* 'did not lack certain bold and prophetic associations' with the ferment of 1919, which 'it confirmed and realised on a higher creative plane'.[15] The point is driven home by the curious division of Chapter 34. In 'Chapter 34' Zeitblom begins the description of the *Apocalypse* ; in 'Chapter 34 (Continued)' he describes the politico-cultural discussions among Leverkühn's Munich friends ; in 'Chapter 34 (Conclusion)' he completes the analysis of the composition—thus suggesting that the oratorio and the public events belong together. Zeitblom closes his tale with words which utterly identify the artist and his people : 'A lonely man folds his hands and says : God have mercy on your poor soul, my friend, my Fatherland.'

The artist is in this book, like little Hanno in *Buddenbrooks*, a musician. Mann, a true German, is more susceptible to music than to other arts, and he often expresses with a mixture of horror and delight the fascination of an art that he has accused of drowning reality and reason.   He has gone so far as to relate the German inclination towards authoritarianism and barbarism with the German gift for music, in phrases which often overshoot the mark.[16]   Something of this sounds through *Doctor Faustus*, but Mann's imaginative works are consistently far deeper and more prudent than his essays ; and Holthusen misses the point when, in an indignantly hostile book on Mann, he writes that the theme of *Doctor Faustus* is, that ' music is of the devil '.[17]   Leverkühn's music is ' of the devil ', but not because music is necessarily so nor because Leverkühn wills it.   Leverkühn himself, revealing in a rare moment of candour a secret self we otherwise hardly suspect, expresses his belief and hope that music will one day become ' more cheerful and modest ', ' innocent and harmless ', ' the servant of a community ', ' an art without suffering, spiritually healthy . . . an art on easy terms with mankind '.[18]   His own music is devilish only because the times decide it so, because Germany is bedevilled—as Zeitblom once puts it, during the First World War : ' Germanism is a psychic condition threatened by its own habit of spinning itself in, by the poison of loneliness, provincial boorishness, neurotic entanglement, quiet satanism.' [19]   The pact Leverkühn makes with the devil does not simply affirm his peculiar destiny as an artist ; it is symbolic of Germany's way.

In contrast to the artist in the early works, the artist in *Doctor Faustus* is a mirror of his times, a seismograph (Mann once said he liked this definition).   Yet this formulation is doubly inadequate.   On the one hand, it points to one of the main faults of this work.   Leverkühn is a highly intelligent man, and in his behaviour and his comments he sees through the illusions of his associates ; yet his intelligence leads to nothing except a heightened consciousness of the general psychological situation amongst the cultured bourgeoisie.   His very taciturnity deepens the impression one receives of an almost automatic, mechanical response to reality.   Leverkühn is not only cold and reserved, but seems to be incapable of any positive response ; he seems to lack all moral personality, to lack human reality. On the other hand, in one respect he is more than a seismograph. He does not merely express the nihilism of his times, he expresses it with bitter comment, with parody, irony, jeering and with despairing bitterness. In finding expression for his times he is more than a recording instrument, he is a judge. This is what Zeitblom discovers in the terrible lament of Doctor Faustus, Leverkühn's last composition—the gift of utterance that is the artist's means of transcending his times. In this work Leverkühn finds ' utterance ' in grief and despair, and in so doing makes the ' breakthrough '. In the expression of man's utter abandonment lies ' the hope beyond hopelessness ', the beginning of liberation.

Yet even with this important qualification, the image of the seismograph does not correspond to Mann's latest opinions, nor to his own practice. He himself has never been a mere recorder, but has in his polemical and imaginative works vigorously championed certain positive principles. A moral purpose, even a moral thesis, is explicit in all his later works ; without it they could not have been written. The theme of *Lotte in Weimar* is the hard-won fusion of art, science and personality in the older Goethe. In an essay of 1952, *The Artist and Society*, Mann wrestles once again with this intricate problem.[20]   The artist, he says, is not primarily a moralist, and must be contrasted with the moralist ; but he has a ' loose ' relationship to morals (including in the term politics and social questions). Every artistic utterance is ' criticism ', ' criticism of life ', and is therefore concerned with morals— this is the position established in *Doctor Faustus*. But Mann goes further than this. True art, he continues, stems from a love of life and belief in man. Art is play, it is not a practical power ; but it is play ' in deep seriousness ', and it is ' bound up with the good '—' at its basis is goodness, related to wisdom, still more closely to love '.

These somewhat halting remarks mark the great revolution in Mann's work. In the earliest, the self-obsessed, endangered solitary, the artist, was contrasted with the serene, innocent practical community. In the later it is the community, including the artist, that is as guilt-laden and perverted as the imaginative world of Kafka.   But in Mann the artist is called to the further task of helping in the liberation, the restoration of society, through utterance and confession, and through love.   The artist is the comforter, the restorer.

MANN THE MORALIST

The moral principles for which Mann stands are defined by him as humanism : belief and trust in man, piety to the past and readiness for change, tolerance and reason.   They are not novel or startling, and might even be decried as banal, even as vague.   Yet he came to them only after a long and arduous struggle, with himself and with others ; his staunch advocacy of them made him a marked man in his country, an outlaw in the Hitler period, a man still looked on with suspicion and hostility in many quarters and in many lands.   At one time his problem seemed a specifically German one, arising from his own debt to German Romanticism, to Schopenhauer, Wagner and Nietzsche ; and the English reader might look with some astonishment at this struggle with tendencies which seemed to be the esoteric concern of German ideologists. No one could take this attitude today, when this moral nihilism (as Mann sums it up) has spread into all Western lands.   Mann's work has a peculiar interest and importance for us today, though here we are not concerned with his directly polemical writings in favour of democracy, peace, socialism, but with his symbolic utterances in the novel, in which he is a moralist in the sense in which he defined Goethe to be a moralist—the artist-moralist, whose moralising does not arise from his own confident harmony, but from his disharmony, difficulties, his ' problematic ', and which takes the form not of preaching but of ' confession of his own distress '.[21]

In *Buddenbrooks* the love of life, which is also a love of laughter, asserts itself almost unintentionally.   The formal climaxes of the book are Thomas Buddenbrook's submission to Schopenhauer's seductive exposition of the immortality of the soul, which decisively loosens his hold on life (though Thomas retains a wistful love of life) ; and Hanno Buddenbrook's submission to Wagner. There is no moral purpose or lesson here ; Mann is describing what he takes to be a natural process, the final blossoming of the bourgeoisie in an aesthetic dream of death. When he first (before the First World War) thought of *The Magic Mountain*, he tells us that he intended to make the sanatorium a symbol of the same theme, ' the fascination of death, the triumph of intoxicated disorderliness over a life dedicated to orderliness ', a ' comic ' counterpart to *Death in Venice*.[22] The establishment of the German Republic, and his own adhesion to democratic principles, radically changed the bearing of this novel.

Sickness remained for him, as he has often said, a means to and sign of deeper knowledge and insight—' health is idiocy '.[23] All the interesting characters of the book are seriously ill ; we are hardly at all concerned with the patients who recover. It is Castorp's ' genius ' that he is capable of the experience of disease and can meet death intimately, and that he does not see the sanatorium merely as a place to get well. But death is not the culmination of the novel : ' mental proneness to sickness is the beginning of the higher health that is imbued with spirit '. Castorp gains a philosophy of life, love of man and tolerance, and with it returns to the real world, the world engaged in a death-struggle ; and the novel ends with the question : ' Will it be that out of this universal festival of death love one day shall arise ? '

A slender hope ; and Mann engaged himself in an exhausting struggle for its realisation against the modern, savagely nationalistic and racialistic forms of German irrationalism—Spengler, Klages, Rosenberg and such. For some time he still defended his old loves, Novalis or Nietzsche, against what he held to be reactionary distortions of their attitude ; but he found a new champion, Goethe, particularly the aged Goethe. Goethe the poet knew all the seduction of ' inwardness ', was tried by spiritual and physical sickness, but tamed and canalised it by his artistic form ; he became a lover of life, a believer in the community of men, an educator, a personality. ' Life ' in Nietzsche's sense had meant all the irrational instinctive dæmonic forces of man, which had been exalted in opposition to reason, freedom, democracy, truth and social morality; 'life' in Goethe's sense, as Mann expounds it, means reconciliation between individual and community, instinct and reason, inward experience and outward achievement.[24] Mann called for a 'sobering up' of the world, and he began reluctantly to recognise that his attitude implied the rejection of much in Nietzsche that he had held dear. The latter's 'doctrine of health', he writes in 1947, is a doctrine of savagery, directed against 'truth, morality, religion, humaneness'; and he adds that Nietzsche was totally wrong in asserting that the mind, the reason, were in danger of destroying the instinctive powers of man; the contrary is and always has been the case.[25]

In the novel, the products of this most agitated period of political struggle and exile were the *Joseph* tetralogy and the Goethe-novel, *Lotte in Weimar*. Both are in appearance an escape from the tortured present into a remote world of harmonious achievement. Mann, who had an amiable weakness for taking his readers into his confidence, has told us that *Joseph* was 'a refuge, a consolation, a homeland, a symbol of constancy, a pledge of my own perseverance in the stormy fluctuation of things'.[26] But there is something more than escape implied here; there is also the need for self-confirmation—Mann calls the work 'a humorous song of man'.

The first two volumes, *The Stories of Jacob* and *The Young Joseph*, were completed before Mann left Germany in 1933. The third, *Joseph in Egypt*, was in the main the product of his exile in Europe; the fourth, *Joseph the Provider*, was written in America and finished in 1942. Mann's interpretation of the Biblical story links the work unmistakably to his earlier novels. Joseph the dreamer is the narcissistic artist, who comes into perilous conflict with the society into which he is born, but who ultimately is reconciled with the community by changing himself and it. His dreams bring him in his naïvety to the brink of disaster; but later, in his wisdom, they serve to profit himself and mankind. Mann summed up its theme for an American audience :

I told of the birth of individuality from the mythical collective, of the Abrahamite individuality which makes the audacious claim that man may only serve the Highest, from which follows the discovery of God. The claim of human individuality to central importance is the premise for the discovery of God. . . . Yet these men [the patriarchs] are still, in a large part of their being, encased in the mythical, the collective . . . and their individuality frees itself from the collective in much the same way as certain figures of Rodin wrest themselves and awaken out of the stone. Jacob too, so rich in stories, is a half-detached figure of this sort . . . He is still the venerable patriarchal form of human individualisation and emancipation, and it grows far more bold and daring in the complicated case of his son Joseph. Here is a man who has not discovered God, but who knows how to ' manage ' him ; a man who is not only the hero of his stories, but their stage-manager, yes, who invents them and ' decorates ' them. . . .

In short, we see how individuality, in the course of its emancipation, soon becomes an artistic ego, attractive, fastidious, and imperilled, a cause of tender concern for his venerable father, but with innate potentialities of development and maturity as never before existed. This artistic ego is in its youth unpardonably egocentric, it lives on the hazardous assumption that all must love it more than themselves. But through its sympathy and friendliness, to which it is never untrue, it finds as it matures its way to social life, it becomes the benefactor and provider of a foreign people and of its own family. In Joseph, the ego flows back from haughty absoluteness into the collective, the community ; and the contrast of the artist and the citizen, of isolation and community, individual and collective is reconciled in this fairy tale.[27]

This is the theme of *The Magic Mountain*, transposed into a mythical-historical setting, and expressed in religious as well as psychological and moral terms. Mann now, challengingly, relates the values of his humanism to the idea of God as it emerged with the Hebrew patriarchate ; he gives them as it were a religious sanction. It is a quite unorthodox conception of God, as we should expect from a man who calls himself a non-believer, and its origins are to be found in Strauss and Feuerbach and Nietzsche, in Freud and Jung, rather than in

Christian theology.[28] With ironical sympathy Mann plays
with the idea of the ' Chosen People ' who ascribe the success
of their guileful wisdom to the guidance and favour of God ;
in an affectionate parody of theology he pretends to explain
at the beginning of the final volume how it was that God
had need of man in his wickedness. Out of it all arises the
view that man's faith in himself is the foundation of his faith
in God : ' The claim of human individuality to central
importance is the premise for the discovery of God.' The
patriarchs do not discover God in the simple sense ; they
create him. ' Abraham is in a sense God's father.' Abraham
and Isaac and Jacob have thus ' evolved ' God ; and Joseph's
wisdom consists in his ability to go still further along this path,
assimilating features of the tribal God with the religion of the
civilisation he adopts. Mann summed up his view :

> If I am to define what I understand by religiousness, I would
> say : it is attentiveness and obedience ; attentiveness to the inward
> change of the world, to the change in the image of truth and right ;
> obedience which does not hesitate to adapt life and reality to these
> changes and thus to do justice to the spirit. To live in sin means,
> to live contrary to the spirit, to hold fast to what is obsolete and
> outworn and live in it, out of inattentiveness and disobedience.
> And when this book speaks of ' concern for God ', it speaks of the
> just fear of this sin and folly.[29]

It is a very humanised, dialectical conception of God.
God is outside man and to be worshipped ; but God is a
creation of man, an instrument in his humanisation, so that
the conception of God has continually to change. The history
of the truth of religion is for Mann this pious adaptation of
the idea of God to the highest needs of man, from that first
decisive step of Abraham, when a beast-offering was substituted
for a human sacrifice, onwards. The way is so arduous, so
full of pitfalls, that it needs piety and reverence. ' Religion ',
Mann wrote in the late essay on Nietzsche, ' is reverence—
reverence primarily for the mystery that man is . . . [a feeling]
for the difficulty and the nobility of being a man '.[30] Into
the theological complications of this heretical doctrine we
need not enter here. Some of Mann's ' theological ' com-

ments are as subtle and obscure as any schoolman's, and one doubts whether one is meant to take them seriously.

But the *Joseph* novels differ from *The Magic Mountain* not only in this religious underpinning of humanism. The earlier novel is a tale of inner struggle culminating in a moral decision ; the later shows actual achievement in the world. In Joseph himself the individual and the collective, the artist and the citizen, the heretic and the believer, are reconciled, but also Egyptian society is remodelled (Mann tells us he was thinking of Roosevelt and the New Deal [31]), and the Hebrew pastoralists are brought down to the fertile plains of Goshen. It is a story of serene achievement ; and as such, it is exemplary rather than actual. Through the absence of tension, the binding together of the patriarchal myths with the Joseph story, the confident march of Joseph to his predestined success, Mann recreates for a perverted or despairing world the myth by which it can recapture its destiny.

Mann's treatment of Goethe in *Lotte in Weimar* (1939) is similarly the creation of a myth—this time closer to the Germans. The Lotte Buff of Goethe's *Sturm und Drang* days, who recalls the glories and perils of Werther's surrender to his intuitions, appears in Weimar. She herself receives a cool and almost heartless reception from the old Goethe, the scientist, minister, and famous man, who seems determined to forget this endangered youthful self of his. His associates and son communicate to her the picture of a revered genius who dominates and tyrannises those around him. But in a last intimate conversation with Goethe Lotte herself realises that he has reached achievement in his life, personality, only by overcoming himself. Lesser personalities, like herself, hold tight to the high moments that come to them in youth ; but men who have more to contribute have to renounce in order to give—as she admits to him :

In the high dignities of your present state, do you not sometimes ask about what might have been possible ? I know, they are the work of renunciation, and therefore of impoverishment, for renunciation and impoverishment are near neighbours, and all reality and achievement is precisely an impoverishment of the possible.

There is something terrible about spiritual impoverishment, I tell you, and we lesser folk have to avoid it and set ourselves against it with all our strength. . . . But with you it was different, you had something more to contribute. Your reality, it looks like something—not like resignation and faithlessness, but like utter fulfilment and deepest loyalty. . . .[32]

This personal achievement, the marriage of the artist and the moralist, the individual and the collective, is not a success-story like Joseph's. The unity in Goethe's personality does not hide the dichotomy of art, for Goethe's ' absolute love ' of man, in Riemer's words, is allied with ' an absolute annihilation or indifference '. Goethe's achievement is not comfortable, for himself or others. It bewilders and repels, and yet imposes itself as exemplary.

From these two myths, whose form is scarcely novelistic at all, Mann returned to his own times with *Doctor Faustus*. Like all his works it is a story of men's attitudes rather than of their social or practical work. The great events that accompanied Leverkühn's life—two wars, bitter social conflict, the rise of Hitlerism—are referred to only in parentheses. Mann's aim is to present us with the psychology of a culture, through the spiritual preoccupations of the cultured class—the bourgeoisie—and so to bring home to us the dilemma of Germany. Leverkühn is the epitome of a disastrous period, when evil seized Germany and led her to her doom. The victory of the dæmonic forces does not mean, of course, that Mann goes back on the exemplary synthesis that he presented in *Joseph* and *Lotte in Weimar*. *Doctor Faustus* could have been written only by the man whose ideal and purpose is that of these earlier ' myths ', but who sees this ideal grievously betrayed.

The novel is subtly and elaborately built round the old legend of Faust the necromancer, who sold his soul to the devil, and in numerous ways the atmosphere of late-medieval Germany with its belief in the devil is evoked. But the crude devil-worship which only lingered on at that time on the social periphery, has in the twentieth century taken a sophisticated ' philosophical ' form. The original Faustus was first a theologian ; Leverkühn too first studies theology. But theology in this twentieth century has lost its innocence, and his theological teachers are convinced more of the reality of the devil than of God. Conviction of God's goodness has been replaced by conviction of the depravity of man. Holthusen seems to take these views as though they were Mann's own opinions or wishes. What Mann does is however to describe a religious situation as it has developed in modern times, above all under the influence of Kierkegaard, a situation he views with evident horror. The young theological students with whom Leverkühn consorts are fond of quoting Kierkegaard ; Leverkühn himself is reading Kierkegaard when the devil visits him, and the devil quotes phrases reminiscent of Kierkegaard (' the exquisite horror of oneself ').

The brilliant discussion of the students at Halle introduces the ideological principles of this ' satanism ' in its apparently harmless idealistic pre-1914 form. They believe that the Germans are the truly religious people in that they alone experience ' the natural and dæmonic ' aspect of being. The German people is young, destined to transform the world which has grown aged and rigid. Its individualism is not social or moral, like Western liberalism, but religious, and hence paradoxically enough the deepest individualism means loss of individuality ; some of the students assert that the true religious personality is realised only in the community, and therefore establish a transcendental meaning for the state or the ' Volk '. These ideas, taken together, form the basis of the reactionary ideology that was systematised after the establishment of the Republic. They take on a more sophisti-cated and forbidding reality in the Munich circle before 1914, and in the Kridwiss set after 1918 we meet them again, but now with a definite reactionary, racialist, brutal point, an amalgam of Nietzsche, Spengler, Rosenberg and such. Though Leverkühn stands sceptically apart from his friends and even jeers at them, it is their ideas he expresses in his music. This evil corrupt world is his world, and he differs from his friends only in having the gift of expressing in his art the depravity of his world. This is his only hope of emerging from its horror—as he says to the devil : ' Sinfulness that is so desperate that it makes a man utterly despair of salvation, that is the truly theological way to salvation.' [33]

In the person of Zeitblom, the narrator, Mann shows the helplessness of the normal decent man among these infernal forces. He is an old-fashioned humanist, a teacher, bewildered and horrified by what goes on about him ; deeply attached to Leverkühn as to Germany, but incapable of understanding or altering the one or the other. He is easily misled, too. He repeats the nationalistic claptrap during the First World War ; and when he finds what it has led to, Hitlerism, he is powerless, like his friends in the Church. He is by no means an obtuse man. But his intelligence cannot break through the bourgeois tradition and circle in which he lives, and within it he can discern no remedy. All he can look for is a remedy from outside—from a communist revolution, perhaps, as he says at the time of the Republic ; from the victory of the United Nations, which he awaits at the end in grief and relief. But these are solutions which fall outside his own competence, and they leave the inward moral regeneration of Germany still a question.

In *Buddenbrooks* Mann built the structure of his novel upon a general thesis which seemed to him to sum up the central spiritual problem of his times. He does the same in *The Magic Mountain*, but now with a moral purpose ; the moral development of his hero is in some sort representative even though it is halting and inconclusive. The *Joseph* novels and *Lotte in Weimar* present us with exemplary figures which exist in an atmosphere utterly remote from present-day Europe. *Doctor Faustus*, returning us to modern Germany, seems on the surface to abandon the educative tendency of the other novels of the middle period, and to return to the psychology of culture characteristic of *Buddenbrooks*. But in every way we perceive that this psychology is a criticism as well. The book has been felt to be an attack on Germany and on German music, and it is in effect a harsh condemnation of all those trends towards irrationalism and authoritarianism that proved dominant in Germany. It is above all the book of a moralist. If it lacks any moral struggle or development in its characters, if it lacks anything exemplary, this is because all its characters are utterly bounded in their experience and vision by the bourgeois culture which had gone bankrupt—within these bounds the highest moral achievement for them is ' confession ', the ' lamentation ' in which lies ' the hope beyond hopelessness, the transcendence of despair '.

MANN THE WRITER

The moral purpose of Mann's novels and other writings seems to contradict the conception of the artist that he had adopted from Schopenhauer. Yet there is something of Schopenhauer underlying all his practice as an imaginative writer. Art for Schopenhauer is a realm of freedom, where man can observe and reproduce the world of ' will ', of life, without being subject to its illusion ; and this idea of the freedom of the artist is characteristic of Mann. Art, he insists in practice and theory, is play and pretence. On the other hand, he was influenced by the Naturalists (above all the Goncourt brothers), and though he never pretends that art can reproduce nature, he is exceptionally attentive to the impressions of the exterior world and reconstructs environments and characters with meticulous care. This combination of playful superiority to his imaginative world and disciplined subjection to experience is the aesthetic counterpart to the Artist-Bourgeois dualism defined in his early works.

It has made him a most sophisticated artist. He invites the reader to participate in an ironical but friendly game. Often delighting in the exact rendering of appearances, of interiors, dress, feature and gesture, he does so like a virtuoso, almost asking us to admire his skill—as he himself admires Hans Castorp's skilful sketch of Peeperkorn, ' we could not have done better ourselves '. The little subterfuges of story-telling, like the abrupt opening of *Buddenbrooks*, are frankly enjoyed, and the author proceeds to help out with a few explanatory remarks, conversing with the reader without embarrassment : ' The fact was, the old gentleman was not on the best terms with Ida Jungmann ', etc. This familiarity of author and reader is more reserved in *Buddenbrooks* than in the later novels, but in them all the author is in a friendly conspiracy of illusion with his readers, often speaking to them directly and at length.   Only *Doctor Faustus* and the unfinished *The Confessions of Felix Krull* vary from this plan, since both have a fictitious story-teller, Zeitblom and the adventurer himself, Krull.   But they too, like Mann in the other novels, take us fully into their confidence.

If Mann is telling us, through his comments and his tone, ' don't be taken in by my realism ', he is at the same time telling us to look for something else : namely, the secrets of his artistic composition.   Consider for example, the diverse methods he uses to indicate the lapse of time.   In *Buddenbrooks* he keeps us precisely informed of the passage of the years, chronicling the deaths, births and marriages, and telling us in what year each scene takes place.   Time here is the objective social time of history.   In *The Magic Mountain* time moves quite erratically, sometimes slowly, sometimes swiftly, sometimes almost stopping ; it is the subjective time of Hans Castorp in a realm which approaches death in life.   In the *Joseph* novels there is no real lapse of time, past and present are interwoven as in myth ; all the events are spread out like a tapestry and might almost as well be read backwards.   In *Doctor Faustus* there is a double time, the time of Leverkühn's life and that in which the pseudo-narrator writes, perhaps even a treble time, for verbally the sixteenth century also is conjured up.   In all cases we are invited to recognise that the time-structure of the novel is not an absolute, but arranged by the author to correspond to the psychological situation of his characters, and beneath this to the total vision of the book.

The dress, gestures, speech of characters impose the illusion of real appearance and seem to belong to the tradition of the psychological-realistic novel.   But we soon notice that certain habits or gestures are repeatedly mentioned—Thomas Buddenbrook's nosegay, Tony's quivering upper lip and the ever-repeated phrases that she took from the student, her first love, Mme Chauchat's door-slamming, Settembrini's check trousers, Frau Kestner's tremulous head.   These acquire the significance

of Wagnerian leitmotifs, they are not only marks of a psychological type, but elements of the total structure in which event
and moral meaning are fused.[34] They are discreetly used,
and often are modified with time as the character itself develops
—only in some of the shorter tales like *Tonio Kröger*, and in
His Royal Highness, are they absolutely fixed. But they provide
a pattern of colour which gives depth to the linear pattern of
the story.

The characters of novels constructed upon a thesis tend to
lose individuality and to become representative symbols.
Mann's characters and events certainly acquire a representative and symbolic meaning, but in general they have plasticity
and individuality as well. It is in fact wrong to believe that
his novels were constructed purely abstractly. *Buddenbrooks*
and *The Magic Mountain*, we know, grew in conception as he
was writing them. He himself asserts that his intentions
became clear only in the actual process of writing : ' What I
myself was, what I wanted and did not want . . . what was
my attitude to life and death : I learnt all this as I wrote.' [35]
A study of the form of his novels informs us how far this statement is true.

Buddenbrooks is the most discursive of the novels. It started
from the figure of Hanno, but grew out of all expectation into
a family-saga as Mann dwelt on the circumstances of his
childhood and drew on the information provided by a relative.
In the result, the scenes and figures acquire such a full and
sharp-cut individuality that they not only come to exist in
their own right, but even challenge the whole original intention.
We see the members of the family less as a group ' overshadowed
by the idea of decline ' than as individuals wrestling each with
his own character and circumstances. So too, the individuals
around the family are significant for their personal character
and personal relationship with members of the family, rather
than as types. We can, if we wish, discern that the rollicking
bounder Permaneder is a representative Bavarian, and is
introduced as a contribution to that much discussed theme,
the contrast between South and North German, between
' Gemütlichkeit ' and ' Tüchtigkeit '; but such reflections are

T

really superfluous. What this episode tells us is that the elegant, snobbish Tony has a secret longing for the more natural, easy-going life, but makes a great mistake when she tries it. Of course, some of the characters have a more general significance. The rise of the plebeian, coarse-grained Hagenströms, which balances the decline of the Buddenbrooks, introduces the theme of the replacement of the cultured old burgher class by the modern bourgeois. It is characteristic of Mann's cast of mind that this theme is only lightly touched upon.

In most of Mann's early stories the practical bourgeois world is described with an irony that sometimes becomes biting, and to some extent this is true of *Buddenbrooks*. But there is here, also, good-humoured sympathy, even tenderness, and because of this the aesthetic effect of the novel contradicts the writer's original intention ; or rather, a new pattern emerges. What was meant to be the climax of the family-history, the story of Hanno, comes to appear as an episode, not a fulfilment. We return to the family scene after his death with the feeling that here is the indestructible fabric of life. The curious result is that Tony, the failure, comes to be the central and symbolic figure, never admitting defeat, obstinately tenacious and courageous. So also Thomas Buddenbrook emerges not primarily as the man infected by ' decadence ', but as the man who, in contrast to his effete brother, struggles and to some effect. This transformation of values must be attributed in the main to the sincerity of Mann's imagination. After conjuring up these figures and dwelling upon them, he remained loyal to their spirit. Perhaps it was this imaginative experience above all that led him to recognise, in *Tonio Kröger*, the dual and contrary values which were the essence of his own character and art.

The power of Mann's imagination to transcend his theoretical principles is evident even when he reaches the incidents which were intended most unambiguously to illustrate his theme. The Schopenhauer experience, the seduction of the contemplative life that destroys in Thomas Buddenbrook the old bourgeois virtues, belongs to Mann's primary intention. But in the novel this typical ' thesis ' of decadence not only loses its abstractness but even changes its character. Thomas is already, when the volume of Schopenhauer falls into his hands, an old, weary, and unsuccessful man, aware that his son will not carry on the business. He gratefully embraces Schopenhauer's doctrine that life is suffering and that it is impossible to conquer life's difficulties except by withdrawing from the struggle into contemplation. But Schopenhauer does not appear here as the philosophy of the novel ; it is only the outlook of this particular man in his particular situation. Even then, Thomas does not renounce his ' bourgeois instincts '; he takes comfort in the mystical thought that after death he will live on in every vigorous individuality. And when we read that he relapses into his old bourgeois habits, after ' his hands had reached out towards exalted and ultimate truths ', we do not take these last words as an objective assessment of Schopenhauer, but ironically as the illusion of this worn-out man. This is one example of many where Mann's artistic instinct is deeper than his avowed intention.[36]

The German novelist, Spielhagen, criticised George Eliot's *Middlemarch* because our attention is not riveted the whole time on the heroine : ' the angle of vision changes every moment '.[37] *Buddenbrooks* does not change focus in this way, for the family remains the centre of attention ; but it has a manifold variety and spaciousness that is rare in the German novel. Germans have in general been very unsuccessful with the spacious novel, most successful in the most egocentric form of novel, the ' Bildungsroman '. *Buddenbrooks* is a rare exception ; in it the centripetal and centrifugal forces of the novel are balanced with a fineness hardly ever met in other German novels.

The other early novel of Mann's, *His Royal Highness*, shows the dangers of his typifying procedure. Here all is general, all is imposed pattern, stylisation, there is no individuality and no tension. It is tolerable only because the tone is so light and unpretentious. The novel has some biographical importance as representing Mann's first attempt to sketch a possible reconciliation between inwardness and society, the culture of

the past (the Prince) and the money-making of the present
(the American millionaire), but it is not much more than an
agreeable trifle.

Mann's realism and symbolism are fully developed in *The
Magic Mountain*, but only a few summary remarks are necessary
to supplement the analysis given earlier in this book.[38]
Although a large part of the book is taken up with discussions,
Mann shows an incomparable artistry in suggesting the massive social reality implied by ideas. The battle of the hero is
none the less tangible for taking place in the spirit, and his
final choice, appropriately expressed in the form of the hallucination in the snowstorm, is persuasively real. But the
theoretical mode of conception of this book is betrayed by its
weaknesses. The subsidiary characters represent certain
dominant social attitudes, and they as symbols are static ;
they fulfil their function in providing Castorp with alternatives.
They enter the story ready-made, and we are not concerned
with their inner life nor with their fate as persons. They lack
the potentialities of movement and change that true characters
must have.

The *Joseph* novels show a consistent and appropriate development of Mann's symbolic method. Far from reducing the
myth to realistic human proportions, Mann brings out its
symbolical character ; ' it is, it ever is, even though in popular
parlance we say, " it was " '. All the characters become
archetypes. Not for a moment are we allowed to believe this
all really happened. With a subtle and sophisticated irony
Mann builds out the story with a mass of historical knowledge
which seems, perhaps, at first sight, to belong to the tradition
of the historical novel ; but what he really does is to remind
us continually that we are reading this story in the twentieth
century and musing over a well-known myth. Thus, in the
last part, when Joseph becomes ' the provider ', Mann even
goes so far as to use anglicisms, in order subtly to suggest that
he had in mind the modern provider, Roosevelt, and his New
Deal. In the same spirit he fills the story with commentary.
The first volume is prefaced with a long essay on the likeness
between the obscure origins of race and the unconscious source

of individuality, and their fusion in myth, that prepares us to approach the old Biblical story in a new way, and to perceive the meaning of Mann's style. In an essay on this novel Mann defines his purpose :

The exactness, the making real of the legend, is an illusion, a game, a pretence of art ; with all the means of language, psychology, description, and of commenting investigation, something real and present is achieved, the soul of which, with all its human seriousness, is humour. In particular, all the essay-like discussion in the book is humorous, the critical and scientific commentary : all this is, as much as the narrative, a descriptive technique, a means of achieving reality. . . . Here is an aesthetic problem with which I have often busied myself. Discursive speech, the author's intrusion, does not need to be alien to art, it can be part of it, and itself be a means of art. My book knows this and asserts it, for it even comments on the commentary. It says of itself that this story, which has been so often told and has passed through so many media, is now going through a medium in which it as it were becomes aware of itself and discusses itself as it enacts itself. The discussion here belongs to the play, it really is not the speech of the author but that of the work itself, taken up into its linguistic sphere ; it is indirect, stylised and playful, it contributes to the illusory exactness of the work, very near to persiflage or anyhow to irony : for when scientific resources are applied to something totally unscientific and legendary, the result is pure irony.[39]

It is an extremely bold purpose. All the traditional realistic techniques are used only partly to make us believe that the events are real ; they also are meant to persuade us that all is play. And, *vice versa*, the author's intrusions which traditionally break through the illusion are here meant to be part of the illusion, part of the story, provoked by the story itself. And the result is ' irony ', a curious mixture of surrender to the work and distance from it, a combination of the two which suggests why Mann loved *Don Quixote*. This ' romantic irony ', to use Friedrich Schlegel's term, is different from the affectionate paternal irony with which the story of Hans Castorp is told. The irony of *Joseph* is not directed towards the characters but to the whole form of the work of art. These characters are not actual, historical living beings, moving from one predicament to another, groping into the unknown. They are

' enacting ' their prescribed parts, and we should resent it if
they were to ' pretend ' that the play was real.   They are like
the actors in a mystery play, acting a story that is well known
to them and their hearers—Mann actually calls Joseph the
hero, stagemanager, and author of his own story, all rolled
into one.[40]   What is serious and real is what their play means
for them and for us.   The commentary, the modern turns of
expression, even the sophistication of the speech of the characters, focus the whole and make of it a new sort of reality
compounded of conscious pretence.   We are reminded of the
intrusions of Old Gower in Shakespeare's *Pericles*, which in
confirming the legendary character of the play reconcile us
with its truth.

Mann's treatment of the story of Tamar exemplifies his
whole method.[41]   This startlingly candid tale is curiously
linked, in *Genesis*, with the history of the race, in that one of
the children of the guileful and determined Tamar and the
outwitted Judah is the ancestor of David.   In retelling it,
Mann includes Tamar's consciousness of her high destiny in
the story itself.   As she eagerly listens to Jacob's stories she
imbibes the conviction of a divine destiny that is worked out
through the practical wisdom of man.   Her whole scheme is
not merely the outcome of her claim for justice, but also of
her determination to play her part in the blessed history of
the Chosen People.   The whole story is ironised, both in the
exaltation of Tamar and the nonplussed behaviour of Jacob
and Judah, for the significance of Tamar's acts is an attribution
of later interpreters, and her drastic cunning stands in the
queerest relation to its exalted outcome.   God moves here,
certainly, in a most mysterious way.   By enriching Tamar's
actions with this significance, Mann makes of them a symbol
of Jacob's religious attitude, when it is adopted by a devoted
and determined character ;   it is a simple form of Joseph's
own story, told with an amused playfulness that does not hide
its exemplary truth.

This playful seriousness characterises the whole vast reconstruction of ancient Israel and Egypt, which is impressively
real and yet avowedly a pretence.   The old phrase of ' going

down into Egypt ' recurs over and over again in humorously
serious variations. Egypt is the land of the dead, of the cult
of the dead, and through this death lies the path of renewal.
Joseph imagines his whole life as the rite of the myth of the
slaughtered and resurrected God ; the pit and the prison into
which he is thrown are forms of his ritual death. His dreams
are the pit of his unconscious ; his attention to them almost
destroys him in his youth, but is a source of strength when he
learns how to manage them. All these related themes are
subtly interwoven as the novel majestically constructs the myth
of earthly life.

Mann has therefore not tried to rival or improve on the
Genesis story ; what he has done is to express what it means
for modern times in the modern consciousness. He does not,
like many novelists who have used Biblical subjects, try to say
how it ' really ' happened ; his intention is even less like that
of the historian or archæologist—though he amuses himself and
us by seeming to come close to their purposes. What he
shows is that it was a myth, and that it remains a myth. He
knew that people would say he had spoilt a simple and lovely
story by elaboration, but his answer, and a complete one,
would be that it was necessary to pull this antique story out
of its shrine, where it is reverently preserved, and set it to
work in the modern world.

It is questionable whether Mann has been fully successful in
this impressive work. The very size of the four-volumed
novel is a risk, for it calls for a high degree of concentration
in the reader. The constant accretion of historical detail
puts a heavy strain on the attention, particularly as it is to
some extent playful ; Mann had a typically German taste for
games of scholarship. The style is intricate and subtle. Mann
always writes for the highly cultured ; perhaps this is not a
true drawback, but certainly he demands an imaginative and
intellectual effort from his readers that few other novelists dare
ask for. In this and all his other novels, however, there is no
dead, flat learning or discussion. Like the exposition of
Schopenhauer in *Buddenbrooks*, or the arguments of Settembrini
and Naphta in *The Magic Mountain*, which plastically build

up character and situation, the descriptions in *Joseph* are rigorously subject to the dynamism of the story and the theme. Like his stylistic master Nietzsche, Mann has an uncanny gift (for which the German language is a peculiarly apt medium) for giving abstractions gesture, colour, and movement. He is an artist in words, a virtuoso on the instrument of language, which means not only that he has a remarkable power of creating the illusion of a real scene or character, but that he can extract out of words their manifold meanings, their concrete energies, the human purpose behind them.

In the later novels of Mann the novel has largely broken with its traditional form ; he must be associated with the two other initiators, Joyce and Proust. There is nothing experimental about his form, of course, for it arose out of the nature of his experience and intention. He himself observes that the *Joseph* novels were ' forced ' to become something different from what is normally understood to be a novel. There can be no objection to this on principle ; but the third volume, *Joseph in Egypt*, which Mann calls ' the most novelistic part of the work ',[42] raises certain doubts precisely where it is nearest to the traditional form of the novel. Here Mann has elaborated the story of Potiphar's wife into an ' interesting ' plot, full of psychological refinement and tension. Yet this is the sort of improvement on the original that we can dispense with. The dramatic tension is out of place, and much of it is tediously irrelevant ; both method and emphasis contradict the formal intention and principle of the novel as a whole.

In the *Joseph* novels, apart from this episode, action is divested of its dramatic quality ; in *Lotte in Weimar* there is almost no action, certainly no plot. Bit by bit the problematical character of the Goethe of 1816 is unfolded in a series of conversations between Frau Kestner and members of Goethe's circle, in Goethe's morning thoughts, at a *soirée* at Goethe's house, and in a final conversation between Lotte and Goethe. The arrival of Frau Kestner at Weimar sets the theme : in what relation does the great poet stand to his early life, when his ' glorious feelings ' threatened to destroy him ? What she hears about, however, as her visitors loquaciously unburden their hearts, is how Goethe now stands to the people around him. They are normal, humdrum people like Lotte herself. With an abundance of sympathetic humour they tell how they are used and abused by the great man, how they resent his tyranny, and yet are ready to sacrifice their careers and themselves to him because he gives them an indefinable worth. And it slowly emerges that this is the theme, the problem Lotte has come to investigate. It is the theme of Goethe's own life, an unrelaxing struggle with himself, renunciation and self-sacrifice for the sake of fulfilment. Goethe is the formal centre of this book, not merely because he is the subject of all conversations and the object of Lotte's visit, but also because all the characters involuntarily repeat his phrases and use his language. The formal, reserved elegance of expression which characterises the whole novel is a deliberate assimilation of the mature style and character of Goethe.

The tension of the book grows round the simplest issue : will Goethe actually meet Lotte, will he actually face his past ? And when he does so, the cold reserve and formal politeness of his behaviour, so vexatious for the old lady, interpret his refusal to turn backwards and glorify his Sturm und Drang, tell us too that his present balance is precarious and always menaced. We are not sure that that final meeting in the coach is real or only imagined by Lotte ; its meaning is not unclear, however, for she detects his affectionateness and realises that his indifference was due not to coldness of heart but to the need to master himself and mature.

Doctor Faustus is the most subtly constructed of all Mann's works, and only an exhaustive analysis would do it justice. There are, in fact, many references which are of a rather esoteric interest. The whole novel is modelled on the sixteenth-century tale, and practically all the incidents of the folk-book are recalled : Faust's parentage, his prowess in theology and mathematics, his ' famulus ', his pact with the devil, his scientific investigations, his lapses of remorse, his love for Helen, their mysterious child, the final lamentation, and so on. But even for those readers who ignore these parallels, the frequent use of a sixteenth-century jargon, by Leverkühn and others, recalls the atmosphere of a period that believed in a very tangible devil.

One sort of environment that is conjured up, therefore, is the German sixteenth century. But with these motifs others are interwoven which recall a nearer epoch—well-known incidents from the life of Nietzsche and other moderns. These are embodied in Leverkühn himself and form the second environment of the book, the first thirty years of this century, of which Nietzsche and Kierkegaard are as it were heralds. But there is a third environment, that in which the pseudo-narrator is writing the work, the period of war and disaster 1940–5. All three periods are intertwined with the most refined skill in a triple time-scheme. Individual facts, persons, and scenes of the two modern environments are described in concrete and precise realistic detail, but the manner in which the present and recent past are mingled and linked, and related to a remoter legendary past, continually makes us conscious that we are here concerned with something more than a biography. Mann himself speaks of his ' montage technique ' in this novel, and compares it with the panoramas one used to see at fairs, where the tangible objects of the foreground merge into a painted illusionistic perspective.[43]

A musician is chosen to be the representative of a Germany which has sold its soul. Mann set himself the stupendous task of laying bare the psychical structure of his times through the analysis of musical compositions, largely therefore in symbolic terms. He had as his master Nietzsche, who, particularly in Section 8 of *Beyond Good and Evil*, had done something similar. The astounding thing is that Mann succeeds ; the analyses of Beethoven early on, and those of Leverkühn's imaginary works, are astonishingly plastic descriptions of a state of mind, a state of civilisation. Compared with them, the accounts of actual social behaviour and opinion are shallow and summary, and hardly equal to the great issues they are meant to illuminate. Altogether, Mann tends to fixate the characters of this book over-rigidly. Leverkühn himself seems to respond almost mechanically to life, and all the others are puppet-like—except the narrator Zeitblom who tells us of his anxieties and thoughts. Most of the characters are in fact defined by their name—Dragfoot (Schleppfuss), the devil-obsessed theologian, Daniel from the Height (Daniel von der Höhe), the aesthete, Squire (Schildknapp) Leverkühn's loyal friend, etc., etc. (the names sound rather absurd when translated into English). They are often characterised by a particular gesture or turn of speech, comparable with the leitmotifs of Mann's earlier phase. But these gestures and phrases do not develop, they mark the man for ever, and there is something stony and inhuman about this trick ; it is nearer caricature than characterisation.

Yet though this impression remains, it is considerably modified by the actual form of the book. Events and characters are often artistically inadequate to the great issues of the times. But they are related by Zeitblom at moments of national disaster, and his comments on the tragic fate of the whole nation give depth and meaning to apparently trivial and personal incidents, which thus appear as representative and ominous. The function of the narrator in this book cannot be over-valued. It is Zeitblom who, of course, describes Leverkühn's works and deeds, and it is an essential part of the pathos of this book that the devil-harrowed musician and nation are described by a man who loves them, is ingrown with them, abhors them, and sees the justice of their horrible fate. Zeitblom is an ineffectual character, his values have no strength in them and seem to have no future ; yet he is the principle of ' confession ', he is ' utterance ' as Leverkühn seeks it ; in his mourning lies ' the hope beyond hopelessness '. It is his existence and his attitude which prevents the book from becoming a diatribe against Germany, which infuses love and grief and hope into this sombre work.

The most bewildering of Mann's novels is *Der Erwählte* (1949). It is built on the medieval legend of Pope Gregory, a story of repeated incest, repentance and finally exaltation to the papacy. Mann tells us that in spite of the playfulness, travesty and laughter in his treatment of this old legend, ' it preserves in pure seriousness its religious core, its Christian faith, the idea of sin and grace '.[44] But the novel fails to make us feel anything of the reality of sin and grace, and Mann's treatment only accentuates the contrast between the pious intention of the legend and its absurd incoherence. Mann's linguistic and stylistic virtuosity is always a danger ; here it luxuriates without the discipline of a worthy theme. The elaborate evocation of a medieval atmosphere, through an assumed chronicle style which includes scraps of medieval French, Low-German, and a number of strange anglicisms, the sophisticated comments on incest, the absurdities of the hero's hermit-existence, make the whole seem an overdone joke.

Mann's novelistic work, taken as a whole, shows a pronounced movement in the direction of myth and pseudo-myth. Keen psychological insight and precise factual observation are never absent, but they are used more and more to create, not individual and unique personalities, but symbolic. In this respect his novels are a criticism of the European novel-tradition, and a very German criticism. Wolfgang Kayser has drawn attention to what he considers to be the essential limitation of the novel-form, in that the world of the novel presents man only in his mundane relationships, and characters, society and nature in their specific, historical reality. The figures of the novel lack the mysterious multiplicity of significance of poetry—Kayser contrasts Goethe's Euphorion (in *Faust*) with Mignon ; the former's significance remains boundless, while Mignon, as we learn of her history, becomes an individual and loses in symbolic value.[45] This real limitation of the novel-form has always been felt most acutely by the Germans ; they have been happiest in the symbolic world of music, and Wagner, rather than any novelist, represents their highest achievement in the epic form. Mann, a devotee of Wagner, remains true to the German tradition. All his novels have a symbolic structure. At the same time he rebels against Romantic metaphysics, for his world remains mundane and natural, without transcendental relationships—his gods and devils are only symbols of human characteristics. But always his characters and situations take on a representative, symbolic character, they incorporate a general human predicament, they are heavy with meaning. Mann has thus enriched and deepened the novel, but he has at times overstrained its capacity, freezing its warm Protean life into the fixed gestures of symbolic forms.

MANN'S REPRESENTATIVE POSITION

Mann once wryly observed that he felt his character to be that of a representative German, though in fact he had been constantly engaged in partisan struggles. We may say that, precisely because he has been so deeply committed in struggle, he is the most representative German of this century. The conviction that he belongs to a precise cultural epoch, that his task is to express it, runs through all his works, from *Buddenbrooks* to *Doctor Faustus*, and the definition that he gives of it hardly varies. He calls it a ' late ' culture, more precisely the last epoch of bourgeois culture.

Bourgeois existence appears in his imaginative works essentially in its ideological form, in its cultural tastes, its philosophy, its attitude to life and death. *Buddenbrooks* is the only work in which he writes in any detail of the practical bourgeois world, of business and money ; but even here this side of bourgeois activities is only slenderly developed. He hardly ever treats of political or social conflicts, not even of the predominant social question of his times, the relations between bourgeoisie and proletariat. The *Joseph* novels, in which the form of life of the ancient Hebrews and Egyptians is reconstructed, characteristically dwell above all on the spiritual constitution of these peoples ; the method reminds us most, in spite of the gigantic research appropriated by the author, of Herder's imaginative reconstructions of the ' spirit of a people '. It is characteristic, too, that the reform of Egyptian life is carried through from above, not through social struggle.

This preoccupation with spiritual situations is most strikingly exemplified in Mann's continual concern for the character and fate of the artist. In this respect, his work is German through and through, for it is a curious feature of the German novel, from *Wilhelm Meister* and the Romantics onwards, that over

and over again the central theme is built round art and the
artist. For Mann's great masters, Schopenhauer, Nietzsche
and Wagner, art is a function of supreme importance. In this
German tradition, the artist is the symbol of spirit, of inner
values, and the work is the battle-ground between these and
outer, social values. The aestheticism of the generation to
which Mann belonged meant a devotion to art to the exclusion
of other concerns, and many of Mann's early short stories
show an almost wearisome preoccupation with the personal
fate of the artistically gifted. But already in *Buddenbrooks* the
theme is widened and given greater substance, for the real
centre of this novel is not the artist, but social man, more
precisely the bourgeoisie and its welfare—one might compare
with this the wider scope and deeper implications of Joyce's
Ulysses as contrasted with *A Portrait of the Artist*. The artist
continues to play a leading part in all Mann's novels, for not
only Goethe and Leverkühn are artists, but also Castorp and
Joseph are artistic temperaments. But Mann is not primarily
concerned with their success or failure as artists; they are
central because, exceptionally sensitive and reflective, exceptionally capable of experience, they focus in themselves a
general situation, the situation of man.

In his first novel Mann was concerned only to portray the
late culture of the German burgher class, where refinement of
the spirit goes hand in hand with decadence, an unconscious
longing for death. By the time he wrote *The Magic Mountain*,
however, he established too the possibility of overcoming this
death-wish. The Soviet and German Revolutions had brought
him to a clearer conviction that the social pre-eminence of
the bourgeoisie was doomed and that a new social form was
emerging through the rise to power of the working class; but
he was equally convinced, and has remained so, that the
decline of the bourgeois class did not necessarily mean the
disappearance of its values.[46] These values are not those of
its decline, but the values it established in its heyday: love,
reason, tolerance, ' humaneness, humanism, human culture '
as he defines them. Humanism means for him piety to the
perpetual change in human activity, organisation and relation-

ships ; but also piety to the past, to the great moral tradition
of the bourgeoisie, which men must struggle to preserve in
the future society. In this spirit he creates his exemplary
figures and stories, and in this spirit he shows how the modern
forms of Romantic irrationalism were perverting and destroying
the German people. His work is an exposition and criticism
of his times from within the bourgeoisie, not from any point
outside.[47] It is all the more deeply embedded in the German
bourgeois tradition, and the more profoundly representative,
in that he himself received such a powerful impetus from the
very forces he criticises, from the Romantic Novalis, from
Schopenhauer, Nietzsche and Wagner, and that he fully
experienced and appreciated the liberation and deepening of
the spirit that remained in his view their positive achievement.

The three middle novels are all ' Bildungsromane ' ; the
heroes overcome or have overcome the Romantic fever and
have reached the moral position of the best bourgeois culture.
But this position never appears to be a natural and simple
norm, as it does so often in the English novel of the nineteenth
century. The natural, instinctive trend of men seems, in
Thomas Mann's novels, to be towards nihilism, refined egoism,
even barbarism ; and the achievement of Castorp, Joseph,
Goethe is set against a dark background. The dangers of the
world, particularly of the contemporary world, cannot be
withstood by the simple and naïve soul ; they demand
strenuous intellectual effort and spiritual audacity. Intellectual superficiality sweeps Leverkühn's associates into the
stream of barbarism. Easy-going ' Gemütlichkeit ' always
has something sinister about it in Mann's works, barbarous
with Permaneder and diabolical with Kumpf—he calls
it ' murderous easy-goingness '.[48] Underneath the German
' soul ', with its naïve love of nature, its vague Romantic
yearning, Mann discovers an implicit hostility to life and social
co-operation that has been exploited by the philosophers of
Hitlerism. In the loveliness of Schubert's *Winterreise* Castorp
and Leverkühn feel above all the seduction of solitariness and
death.

So Mann is the reverse of a naïve writer, and the simple

unreflecting joys of life scarcely appear in his works—or if they
do, they suggest something subtle and evil beneath the surface.
There is no loveliness of landscape in his works. The sea and
the high mountains appear not in romantic charm but as
inhuman and ' stupid ', something that seems to try to crush
man. His heroes are incapable of simple love. The only
passions he describes are the passion for art or the infatuation
with ideas, particularly the infatuation with the destructive
forces of the unconscious ; abstract passions that are almost
obsessions and that impede human contacts. Love never
grips his characters, they never find simple expression for it,
it is always tainted. Thomas Buddenbrook and Tony give
up their first, socially unsuitable, loves without a struggle, and
contract marriages which are at least problematical ; the
affairs of Castorp and Leverkühn are involved and infertile.
Even the friendships of these men are reserved and perverse.
Thus Ermatinger can speak of the ' terrifying soullessness ' of
Mann's works.[49] The lack of passion means that there are
regions of his characters that remain unilluminated, veiled,
mysterious, there is something dead in their soul. But one
cannot let the charge of soullessness remain at that. There
is a great tenderness in Mann's writing, just as there is
bitterness. And the soullessness of his world is part of his
theme that soulfulness has become ' putrefied and stuffy ';
emotive impotence, eroticism, perversion, are a mark of his
times.

The structure and style of Mann's novels are similarly the
reverse of naïve. He comes nearest to telling a simple story
in *Buddenbrooks*, but the later books are immensely complex in
construction, full of subtle suggestion and hidden relations.
At every stage in the story one is aware of an underlying meaning, and the novels are so cunningly constructed that this
meaning, the principle of the construction, demands the
attention and learning of the connoisseur. Technical virtuosity
is for Thomas Mann a necessary characteristic of the artist.
His style is extraordinarily complex ; language is an instrument on which he plays. He has unwittingly defined his own
style in an article purporting to define that of the Romantic

author, Chamisso—as in many of his literary essays, his remarks are truer of himself than of his subject :

. . . this profound intimacy with the last refinements and secrets of language, this sublime and cunning awareness of tone and movement, of the reflex action of words upon one another, of their sensuous flavour, their dynamic, stylistic, curious, ironic, emotive value.

Mann's long and complex sentences are not dynamic, successive in character ; they have nothing of the simple movement of a story, nothing of the fits and starts, the sudden alterations of direction, of Kafka's. They are ' composed ' like his novels, rounded off, full of subtle modifications, rich with epithets, essentially static and reflective. His superb mimic gift, evident in his descriptions of external appearances, is brilliantly displayed in his language, where all the subtleties of character appear in the choice of vocabulary, the phraseology, the grammar itself. His evocation of the style of past periods, of Goethe or the Middle Ages, is incomparably skilful. But there is a lack of simple, lapidary statement, as Holthusen has complained. Except for a few minor characters like servants, all his characters are burdened with oversubtlety, not because the characters are necessarily subtle in themselves, but because the times invest even simple characters with ambiguity. Zeitblom is an essentially simple character caught in a diabolical network. Frau Kestner is a simple woman ; but in the problematical environment of *Lotte in Weimar* even her thoughts and conversation become subtle and involved.

The truth is that Mann's characters (and Mann himself), even if they come at the end to simple conclusions, have had to fight their way through subtle entanglements ; and the conclusions they reach are marked with the arduousness of the way. Hans Castorp finds his way back to the simple life with the words : ' Man must, for the sake of goodness and love, cede to death no dominance over his thoughts.'[50] It is an involved and cautious thought, a clumsy sentence ; but in its clumsiness there lies the groping of the man who makes it,

U

who is not yet liberated. Mann can never be simple. For that is his achievement, that he has passed through modern times, not by-passed them. The moral health he advocates lies not in naïvety, which is not strong enough to resist evil, but in intellectual and spiritual audacity. As Leverkühn once said, it would need a new society if art is again to become ' innocent and harmless '.

CHAPTER X

General Characteristics of the German Novel

THESE *Studies* do not amount to a history of the German novel. But the novels discussed illuminate successive phases of German cultural history of the last 150 years. Even more, they have a coherence which is not, I believe, the result of a selective bias on my part, for I have tried to discuss those works which are widely held, or may reasonably be held, to be the best German novels. In them, the struggle between personal and social values, which forms the theme of so many European novels, tends to take the form of a struggle between the claims of inner, transcendental values and outer social reality. The German novel may in fact, I believe, best be understood and appreciated in relation to the metaphysical aspiration, the longing for night and death, which was formulated most comprehensively by German Romanticism. The Romantic movement, in Germany as elsewhere, is too complex a phenomenon to be summed up under any single heading. It contained progressive and reactionary elements in its social philosophy, it promoted a new communal consciousness and was aristocratically individualistic, it was over-sentimental and over-intellectual, it was often sharply realistic and often soaringly fantastic. But it is no accident that its transcendental and socially reactionary trends were much more prominent in Germany than elsewhere, and that its legacy in Germany has fortified above all the ideology of irrationalism and authoritarianism.

The battle over irrationalism, which rumbles in all German thinking of modern times, takes its own special shape in the novel. The novel was felt from the beginning to be the peculiar literary form of the middle class. Hegel calls it ' a bourgeois epic ' ; all epic, he writes, has as its field ' the broad background of a total world ', but for the novelist this total world is the ' prosaic reality ' of modern bourgeois society.[1] As an artistic form, the novel, in contrast with the lyric, is involved directly with the world of social experience and practical reality ; as Henry James said : ' It is on manners, customs, usages, habits, forms . . . that a novelist lives—they are the very stuff his work is made of.' Or, in Hazlitt's words, the scope of the novel is ' the very web and texture of society as it really exists '.[2] Whatever the philosophical intention of the novelist, his art demands that he portrays the lineaments of ' prosaic reality '.

The efforts of the German Romantics to disregard the artistic scope of the novel only vindicate the latter. Novalis, lacking respect for external reality, fails utterly to create character and situation. Carlyle rightly doubts whether Novalis' unfinished novel could ever have been completed, since the hero was to have passed into ' a mythical, fairy and quite fantastic world '—it would be even truer to say he never emerges from it. Jean-Paul Richter is more successful in his shorter, satirical pieces, but the longer novels are inchoate, again because of his Romantic disregard for the exigences of the novel-form. His admirer Carlyle can again be quoted : ' There is solid metal enough in them [the best of his novels] to fit out whole circulating libraries, were it beaten into the usual filigree.' The grotesque fancies of E. T. A. Hoffman, on the other hand, are much more successful, because beneath them is acute psychological observation and social satire. However, the great German novels of the nineteenth century have been those in which the rights of the external world have been recognised and, in most, respected and loved ; those in which the claims of the novel-form have chimed in with the philosophical attitude of the writer. The realism of technique has a symbolical significance : ' the realism of the symbol becomes the artistic vindication of a lovable world '.[3] The great German novel is the outcome of a perpetually renewed struggle with Romanticism.

In other European literatures the novel seems to have established itself as a major artistic medium without desperate difficulties. Even the Romantic English and French novelists do not seem to force themselves in ' conjuring up the spatial dimensions of a life and recounting a happening ' ; [4] Pushkin or Lermontov adopt the form of the prose-narrative with extraordinary ease. The world that is thus 'artistically vindicated' is not 'lovable' in the simple sense, for it is frequently depicted as harsh and abominable ; but its reality is acknowledged, and respected as morally binding. The novelist has, in Leavis's words, 'a kind of reverent openness before life'.[5] The Germans, however, come to this philosophical position only with the greatest difficulty. The 'Bildungsroman' is the representation of an arduous journey out of inwardness into social activity, out of subjectivity into objectivity, and for this reason it is 'the German species of the modern novel'.[6] The theme is not absent from the literature of other peoples, but it is central and predominant only in the German novel. The 'Bildungsroman' is peculiarly German, too, in that it deals essentially only with the weaning of the heroes from their inwardness, with their spiritual preparation for social life, and stops or falters when they actually enter upon it. The structure and style of the four books analysed indicate, as I have tried to show, how difficult was the way and how precarious the attainment.

The metaphysical question is absent from the novels of Gotthelf, Raabe and Fontane, for these authors confine themselves to the theme of moral adaptation within the practical social sphere. But this limitation does not go without some spiritual impoverishment. From Gotthelf's world the great issues of modern life, its potentialities and subtle seductions, are shut out. Raabe's intellectual vision is limited, and his conception of man's powers is modest and subdued. Fontane, with his robust commonsense, sidles away from tragic involvements. Neither of these two grapples with the fierce energies at work in modern society, and their tolerant humanism stops at accommodations which lack penetration and spiritual adventurousness.

With Kafka and Thomas Mann we enter the modern period of acute social and international crisis, when a forbidding reality made the moral accommodations of an earlier period seem shallow or false. In one sense Kafka seems to reverse the whole process of the German novel, for he not only ignores

the possibility of a moral order but also implacably undermines any comforting trust men may have in the solid reality
of the external world. Not, however, like a Romantic to
contrast to it the compensating reality of an inner or transcendental world ; his heroes are as uncertain and tortured in
spirit as the world which torments them. He has no lesson
to give ; all he can do is to express the savage incoherence
of this world. Hence the precision of his writing, his novelistic
quality. There is a close relationship between his imaginative
vision and that of Thomas Mann. But Mann critically and
constructively relates the moral incoherence of the outer and
inner world, as expressions of one single situation ; and he
does not confine himself to utterance, but seeks to shape and
change. His strong moral sense has led him continually to
fight again the battle of the ' Bildungsroman ', to confront his
times with his humanism—not as confidently as the earlier
writers, for his writings are permeated with irony and parody,
but even more determinedly. Thus he exhibits an extraordinary skill in depicting both the dæmonic seduction of
inwardness and the delight of the concrete real social world,
so that each aspect ironically modulates the other ; out of
their interplay the structure of his novels arises. Even his
earlier works bear witness to his subsequent identification of
Romantic inwardness with social authoritarianism, and his
resistance to Romanticism is expressed in his combined
realism and moralism.

The good novel, as Leavis puts it, must be adult and
intelligent ; it must centre in a serious moral issue, and the
characters must learn and develop. Such definitions are
particularly appropriate to most of the novels considered in
this book, particularly if we understand adultness in Grillparzer's sense (see above, p. 19) as man's emergence from
infantile subjectivism. The growth of personality through the
renunciation of dreams and the sober recognition of the
lovability of reality is the predominant theme ; or, with Kafka
and Mann's *Doctor Faustus*, the tragic powerlessness to find and
love a real world that has become evil and senseless. Social
novels like Freytag's *Soll und Haben*, so famous in its day, do

not stand up to this test, for its crude pragmatism allows of no questionings and no spiritual development. And on the other hand, some of the most estimable modern German novelists, like Hermann Hesse, Hermann Broch and Robert Musil, still remain befogged among vague intimations and ' inner monologues ' which obstruct the development of character and the shaping of events.

Leavis further defines the great English novelists as ' distinguished by a vital capacity for experience '. This term is so vague as to be almost useless, but it may serve to introduce what I consider to be the greatest weakness of the German novel. To take it at its most banal level, it reminds us that the private lives of most of the novelists I have discussed were extraordinarily subdued. Except for Goethe, none of them was subject to the intricate passions, the hatreds and obsessions, that characterise the life of Dickens, for example, or of so many of the French or Russian novelists. Even Thomas Mann, who has been thrown about by violent events and has played a distinguished part in them, would not be a grateful subject for a biographer as far as his private life is concerned. Of course, the characters of most of them were complex and intricate ; Keller and Stifter, even Gotthelf, were highly problematical personalities, and Kafka is a goldmine for the psychologist. But their difficulties never took an energetic, passionate form, and scarcely ever involved them in significant activity. The critic will say, all this is quite irrelevant to the quality of the novels ; the ' capacity for vital experience ' is often allied, in the greatest writers, with a reserved life and an apparently equable temperament. But I believe it is worth considering because this almost ' philistine ' monotony in the lives of the German novelists at least points to something that is lacking in their works.

Goethe, as I have said, was an exception, and was subject, right up to his old age, to acute rapture and distress ; *Werther* and *The Elective Affinities* bear witness to them. *Wilhelm Meister*, too, in the earlier parts, recaptures the sharp joys and pains of experience. But in most of even the best German novels there is a sad lack of the energy and bite of passion. It is certainly lacking in the later parts of *Wilhelm Meister*. Perhaps there is more effective feeling, feeling that drives to action, in Gotthelf's works than in the others, though it has with him a very uncomplicated character as befits the peasantry of whom he writes.   In the novels of Raabe and Fontane feeling is never violent, always ready to renounce ; it hardly belongs to Kafka's world.   Mann's characters sometimes have passion, but it is an abstract or introverted passion, a love of art, an obsession with themselves.   As Clavdia Chauchat tells Hans Castorp, the Germans are incapable of passion—' passion, that is, to live for the sake of life, self-forgetfulness '.   Certainly Mann's characters can never achieve this self-forgetfulness.

To point out this blind spot in the German novel is not simply equivalent to saying that there is no German *Madame Bovary*, *Red and Black*, or *Anna Karenina*.   It is only in passion that man shows what he really is or what his potentialities may be ;   in this sense, even his obsessions and perversions reveal the truth.   The ' self-forgetfulness ' of which Clavdia Chauchat speaks is the means to self-discovery.   But the thrill of this kind of discovery is rarely experienced in the German novel ;   the outstanding exception is the first part of Keller's *Green Heinrich* which is full of sharp penetration.   The German novelists seem to shelter anxiously behind the defences that men have to erect round themselves for the purposes of a settled daily life.   There is something provincial, philistine, about their novels, something ' bourgeois ' as Mann uses the term.

They have other faults that result from this lack of adventurousness.   There is too little freshness of perception in their writing, and a lack of liveliness in incident and plot.   There is sharp delineation of character in *Wilhelm Meister*, and luminous evocation of situation in *Green Heinrich* ; Gotthelf's novels are full of the delight of sensuous perception ;   Stifter is a master in landscapes, Fontane in the conversation-piece. But the reader rarely gets that thrill that he feels when Jane Eyre, behind the curtains, looks at the misty country and the rain beating on the window-pane.   *Buddenbrooks* often gives us this delight, but elsewhere in Thomas Mann it is damped by the ironical undertone. It seems as if the characters of the German novel will not allow the outer world to make a direct sharp inpact on them ; they seem capable only of limited or muted responses. Altogether the characters of the German novels seem less alive, less avid of life, less capable of overflowing exuberance, than those of the great European novels.

The action of the novels suffers likewise from a lack of vividness. Traditional English criticism used to distinguish between the ' plot ' and the ' characters ' of novels ; but it would hardly occur to the critic of German novels to invent such categories, for there is rarely any plot at all, and what there is has no meaning except as the interaction of the characters. There is an extraordinary paucity of incident in the ' Bildungsroman ', except in the sense of the inward change in the chief character ; but there is very little also in the other novels I have discussed. All these writers seem to believe, with Schopenhauer, that the less external incident, the better the novel. There are, of course, many lesser German novels that have plenty of incident and plot, for instance those of Spielhagen and Feuchtwanger, and it is no accident that in their time these authors have been far more popular abroad than most of the writers I have chosen. But in these novels, the action becomes melodramatic and sensational, and is not a function of a moral development ; it is for this reason that I do not consider them worth consideration in this book.

The modern trend in English literary criticism is to pay little attention to liveliness of plot ; but in relation to the German novel one cannot help recognising that liveliness of action, skilfulness and clarity of plot, is as much an artistic desideratum in the novel as in the drama. Without this shaping of the outer world of action, the inner world lacks clarity and the moral development of character lacks plasticity. It is not only that nearly all foreign critics find the German novels ponderous ; the Germans find this too. Our ' classic ' novels are read by English children with passion ; bothered parents have to forbid too much of it and tell them to get on with their ' work '. Later on, they get seized by the French

and Russians in the same way. But even for Germans, to
read the great German novels is mostly a ' cultural task '—
infinitely rewarding, I believe, but never likely to become a
dangerous passion in the reader !

A counterpart of this lack of immediate appeal in the German
novel is the prominent, often heavy, symbolism that characterises it. With Goethe I would take a symbolical ' object '
to be one that both ' exists for itself' and expresses something
general ; a symbol is ' an image concentrated in the mirror
of the mind, yet identical with the object '.[7] The English
novel is rich in symbolical situations which fully belong to the
actual world of the story and have a natural function in the
narrative, and at the same time sum up the inward, moral
situation. All the elements of a story are in fact in this sense
symbolical, but certain of them stand out startlingly, revealing
the very heart of the matter. One thinks of Robinson Crusoe
discovering the footprint, Maggie Tulliver drifting with
Stephen down the Floss, the excursion to the Marabar caves
in *A Passage to India* ; in these typical examples the occurrence
seems to ' exist for itself' at the same time as it brings into
evidence a whole moral crisis. In the German tradition the
symbol is more forced, it often seems to come from another
world. Mignon has this unworldly character, and it is
significant that, in order to complete *Wilhelm Meister*, Goethe
did his best to reduce her to normal stature. In *The Elective
Affinities* he deliberately allowed himself mysterious associations
which give this novel something of the character of a legend.
Wolfgang Kayser has said that there is something ' artificial '
about the structure of the ' Bildungsroman ',[8] and I believe
this artificiality is due to the fact that characters and incidents
exist less in their own right than as bearers of a meaning. In
this century more and more use has been made of abstract
symbols, that is, of allegorical constructs, such as one finds in
Hesse, Jünger, and many lesser writers like Kasack or Lang-
gässer. Where they are aesthetically justifiable, as in Kafka
and Thomas Mann, these symbolical figures are recognisably
individual at the same time as they represent a world, the
modern world, in which all that the individual is and does is

bound up with, and to some extent a function of, entities larger than himself.

I have put these criticisms very sharply, too sharply, of course ; it is only when German novels are compared with the best foreign novels that their failings loom up so large. Their good qualities have, I hope, been made clear enough. But I have tried to see them in the light of what the European novel has achieved, and not to make for them claims which would seem extravagant to any reader who takes them up for the first time. They offer abundant ' profit and delight ', and it is only to be regretted that they are so little known outside specialist circles. English and French studies on the novel almost without exception show no trace of acquaintance with the German novel. It is typical of this situation that an informed French critic such as Thibaudet can write that there are no novels showing the growth of intelligence in the adolescent ; [9] for this is the repeated theme of the ' Bildungs-roman ', and no novelists have shaped this process, and the world in which it takes place, so subtly and tenderly as the Germans.

The German novel is not lacking in artistry. The art of the German novelists is their manner of seeing and imaginatively shaping the world, and this manner is distinctive because of the peculiar character of their world and its spiritual problems. I do not wish, however, simply to commend the German novel to those with a sympathetic interest for Germany's problems. There is, of course, no need to commend Kafka and Thomas Mann, who are widely and often wildly popular. But Kafka and Mann are not simply better writers than other German novelists, nor does their eminence mean that they have somehow ceased to be German—though no one could deny that there are cosmopolitan features in their work. It is important to recognise how they are linked, in sympathy and hostility, with the German cultural tradition, and especially with the metaphysical issue which so often appears in the German novel. Their popularity indicates, I believe, a greater understanding today for this issue abroad, a confluence of German and non-German culture. It no longer is specifically

German to wrestle in novel-form with the claims of socially
experienced reality and social morality ; only too frequently,
in fact, it is the subjectivist elements in Kafka and Mann that
constitute their appeal to many readers abroad. But these
are times when these issues, which declared themselves earlier
in Germany than elsewhere, are taken seriously in other lands ;
and it is now above all that an understanding of the older
German novel is desirable, and an appreciation of it possible.

Notes

CHAPTER I.—GOETHE—*WILHELM MEISTER*

[1] To Schiller, 27 August 1794. Goethe, *Gedenkausgabe*, Zürich 1948–54, xx, 18. Roman numerals in text and notes refer to this edition of Goethe.

[2] The 'Dichter' makes similar statements in *Faust*, 'Vorspiel auf dem Theater'.

[3] K. Viëtor, *Goethe*, Berne 1949, 134–5. Wilhelm is right, says Viëtor, in choosing the theatre as his profession, if he wants to influence the moral culture of his contemporaries; he is following in the steps of Lessing. For the rôle of the theatre in eighteenth-century Germany, see W. H. Bruford, *Theatre, Drama and Audience in Germany*, 1950.

[4] Tag- und Jahreshefte. xi, 620–1.

[5] To Goethe, 8 July 1796, xx, 205.

[6] F. Grillparzer, *Tagebücher*, ii, 76. *S. Werke* ed. Sauer, Wien 1916–24.

[7] H. A. Korff, *Geist der Goethezeit*, Leipzig 1930, ii, 343.

[8] G. Lukács has given a masterly exposition of this essential theme of the novel in *Goethe und seine Zeit*, Berne 1947, 31–47. Korff's analysis is misleading precisely because he fails to appreciate the concrete content of all these principles, *Geist der Goethezeit*, ii, 341–62.

[9] Schiller points out how the confrontation of Wilhelm and Werner at the end shows how ' ennobled ' is the reality to which Wilhelm returns, ' equally distant from freakish fancy and philistinism '. To Goethe, 3 July 1796, xx, 193.

[10] Also in the *Wanderjahre*, where Montan (Jarno) says : ' What a man is to achieve must detach itself from him as a second self ' (viii, 43). The same view emerges in Tasso's discussion with the Princess, *Torquato Tasso*, Act 2, Sc. I. Lukács can properly call the moral of *Wilhelm Meister* ' a great polemic against the moral theory of Kant ' (op. cit., 38).

[11] Goethe used the term ' metamorphosis ' to indicate this double source of growth, and Günther Müller has interpreted *Wilhelm Meister* in terms of this concept—*Gestaltung-Umgestaltung in W. Ms. Lehrjahre*, Halle 1948. In my view, Professor Müller does not prove his case except in regard to the central figures of Wilhelm and Mignon.

[12] Goethe, reported by F. von Müller, 22 January 1821, xxiii, 119. Schiller to Goethe, 28 November 1796, xx, 280.

[13] *Dichtung und Wahrheit*, Book 13, x, 636.

[14] See G. Müller, op. cit., 27–9.

[15] The account is broken up in the novel. The main incidents are found vii, 551–4, 561–4, 583–4.

[16] To Goethe, 2 July 1796, xx, 185–6.

[17] Grillparzer, *Werke* ed. Sauer. *Tagebücher*, ii, 327.

[18] To Goethe, 3 July 1796, xx, 190. The insight with which Schiller

understood Goethe's intention may be judged from Goethe's remark on ' the beautiful soul '—' the whole rests on the noblest self-delusions and the most delicate confusion of the subjective and the objective '. To Schiller, 18 March 1795, xx, 69.

[19] See C. F. Harrold, *Carlyle and German Thought*, 1934, 202–30.

[20] *Geist der Goethezeit*, ii, see particularly 345–8.

[21] The word ' Gesinnung ' means partly ' opinion ', or ' moral sentiment ', but also the ' disposition ' which unites and expresses the ' opinions '. Carlyle uses the somewhat ambiguous ' sentiment '.

[22] It is of some significance that one of the earliest representatives of the modern ' stream of consciousness ' type of novel finds confirmation of her conception of the novel in this passage from *Wilhelm Meister* —Dorothy M. Richardson, *Pilgrimage*, Foreword to the 1938 edition.

[23] Goethe on *Wilhelm Meister*, to Eckermann, 18 January 1825, xxiv, 141–2.

[24] Viëtor, *Goethe*, 131.

[25] One thinks of Virginia Woolf, but as distinct from Wilhelm Meister her characters do not seek to understand or direct their inward movement.

[26] Schiller to Goethe, 5 July 1796, xx, 195.

[27] These stylistic qualities are excellently analysed in R. Riemann, *Goethe's Romantechnik*, Leipzig 1902.

[28] Schiller to Goethe, 28 November 1796, xx, 280.

[29] Particularly in the letter of 8 July 1796, xx, 202–7.   Goethe acknowledged the help he had received from these criticisms, pp. 207–10.

[30] *Notiz*, quoted Viëtor, *Goethe*, 144.

[31] Viëtor, *Goethe*, 133.   Albert Thibaudet, forgetting the German ' Bildungsroman ', could write in 1912 : ' Pourquoi le roman de la jeune intelligence n'a-t-il pas été écrit ? ' *Réflexions sur le Roman*, Paris 1938, 13.

[32] Reported by F. von Müller, xxiii, 295.

CHAPTER II.—GOTTFRIED KELLER—*GREEN HEINRICH*

[1] It may seem that I dismiss the Romantic novel too harshly.   No doubt my criticism is too summary, but very few specialists would find serious fault with it.   Richard Samuel, who has written sympathetically on German Romanticism, is just as harsh on the Romantic novel in his article ' Theodor Fontane ', *Journal of the Australasian Universities Modern Language Association*, No. 12, August 1954.

[2] See Keller's important letters to his publisher Vieweg, 3 May 1850, and to his friend Hettner, 4 March 1851, *Briefe und Tagebücher*, Zürich 1943, i, 328–32 and 371–9.

[3] *Der grüne Heinrich*, Part i, Chapter 17.

[4] ibid., Part ii, Chapter 7.

[5] Keller himself met Feuerbach in 1849 in Heidelberg, where the philosopher gave a course of lectures published as *The Essence of Religion*. His comments at the time sum up an influence that was to be per-

NOTES

309

manent : ' Only now am I beginning really to seize hold of and feel
nature and man. . . . I am glad that at last I have a definite and
energetic philosophical outlook ' ; ' Since reading Feuerbach the
world seems to be infinitely more lovely and deep, life is more valuable
and intense, death more serious, more challenging, urgently calling
me to fulfil my task.' Letters of 8 February 1849 and 27 March 1851.
Briefe i, 286–7, 380.

[6] See Keller's observations in his letters of 25 June 1878 and 21 April
1881. *Briefe* ii, 279–80, 370.

[7] 4 March 1851. *Briefe* i, 377–8.

[8] *Der grüne Heinrich*, Part iii, Chapter 9. This incident is admirably
discussed in H. Boeschenstein, *Gottfried Keller*, Berne 1948, 88–91.

[9] 21 April 1881. *Briefe* ii, 370. The episode occurs Part iv, Chapters
5 and 8.

[10] *Der grüne Heinrich*, Part i, Chapters 4 and 5.

[11] 11 April 1880. *Briefe* ii, 366. The tale occurs Part iii, Chapter 10.

[12] *Der grüne Heinrich*, Part i, Chapter 12.

[13] ibid., Part ii, Chapters 11 and 12.

[14] ibid., Part iii, Chapter 6.

[15] 21 April 1881. *Briefe* ii, 370.

[16] *Der grüne Heinrich*, Part ii, Chapters 13–18 ; Part iii, Chapters 13 and 14.

[17] In the first version of the novel Lys dies of his wound in the duel, and
remorse for the deed contributes to Heinrich's death. It was a great
improvement to make the duel as absurd as the Carnival.

[18] See H. Boeschenstein, op. cit., 103 ; Lukács, *Deutsche Realisten des* 19
Jahrhunderts, p. 203. Those of Keller's works that deal with the
problems of capitalistic society are his weakest : *Das verlorne Lachen* ;
Martin Salander.

[19] See Keller's letters of 3 April and 10 September 1871, 4 June 1876,
25 June and 13 August 1878.

[20] 4 June 1876. *Briefe* ii, 236.

[21] Boeschenstein (op. cit., 86) has well defined the ironical tone of the
first form, and the salutary effect of the change. ' Instead of being
an insertion, the " youth " is now genuine, experienced time, the
sustaining source of the life that is to come.'

[22] *Der grüne Heinrich*, Part i, Chapter 8.

[23] See for instance Keller's letters of 31 January and 25 February 1860.
Briefe ii, 75, 76–7. J. Fränkel, *Keller's politische Sendung*, Zürich 1939,
45–50.

CHAPTER III.—ADALBERT STIFTER—*INDIAN SUMMER*

[1] 11 February 1858. *Briefwechsel* iii, 93 (A. Stifter, *Sämmtliche Werke*,
vol. xix, *Bibliothek deutscher Schriftsteller aus Böhmen, etc.*, Prag and
Reichenberg, 1901–39—all references to Stifter's works and letters
apply to this edition).

[2] Apart from the articles he wrote in 1848 and 1849, see the numerous
statements in his letters of these years, particularly of 6 March,

4 September, and 13 October 1849, 22 February 1850.   *Briefwechsel*
i, 322 ; ii, 9–15, 29.

[3] *Der Nachsommer,* vol. 1.   *SW* vi, 233.

[4] ibid., vol. 2.   *SW* vii, 126–7.

[5] The story of Risach and Mathilde is similar to that of the most perfect
of Stifter's shorter tales, *Brigitta,* which tells how a middle-aged pair
make good the error and estrangement caused by uncontrolled passion.
In 1852 Stifter advised a young relative, as a supreme condition of
a good and happy life, to rid himself of all passion.   *Briefwechsel* ii,
126–7.

[6] 17 July 1858.   *Briefwechsel* iii, 122.

[7] *Der Nachsommer,* vol. 2.   *SW* vii, 206–7.

[8] July 1847.   *Briefwechsel* i, 240.

[9] *Der Nachsommer,* vol. 1.   *SW* vi, 23.

[10] ibid., vol. 2.   *SW* vii, 22, 27.

[11] ibid., vol. 2.   *SW* vii, 157.

[12] ibid., vol. 1.   *SW* vi, 135–6, 235 ; vol. 2.   *SW* vii, 41.

[13] Stifter himself hardly crossed the borders of Austria.   He saw the sea,
the Adriatic, for the first time when he was just finishing the proofs
of *Der Nachsommer,* and was so moved by it, and by the fragment of
Italy he caught sight of, that he said his novel would have been quite
different if he had written it after this journey.   20 July 1857.   *Briefwechsel* iii, 39.

[14] *Der Nachsommer,* vol. 3.   *SW* viii (i), 217.

[15] For instance the letters of 22 April 1850 and 29 February 1856.   *Briefwechsel* ii, 38 and 299.

[16] *Der Nachsommer,* vol. 3.   *SW* vii, 350–4.   Risach says, most people are
fitted to carry out the subordinate, commonplace tasks of life.   Considerable talents will find their rightful place ; and even if they do
not, the struggle is sufficient in itself, it ensures them the essential
' freedom of soul ', which would be lacking if everyone found without
difficulty the sphere for which he is best suited.

[17] See his letter of 22 March 1857.   *Briefwechsel* iii, 14.   The French July
Revolution of 1830 is the watershed, and the liberal battle may be
said to have been opened with Anastasius Grün's *Spaziergänge eines
Wiener Poeten* of 1831.

[18] *Der Nachsommer,* vol. 1.   *SW* vi, 12.

[19] ibid., vol. 1.   *SW* vi, 130.

[20] He protested against the proposed illustrations to the first edition
because they indicated that the Drendorf family belonged to the less
affluent middle class.   *Briefwechsel* ii, 284 passim.

[21] *Der Nachsommer,* vol. 3.   *SW* viii (i), 236.

[22] ibid., vol. 2.   *SW* vii, 247.

[23] Cf. the letters of 6 March, 4 September, and 13 October 1849.   *Briefwechsel* i, 322 ; ii, 9–15.

[24] Stifter himself, as opposed to Heinrich, always longed to get back to
Vienna, at least for part of the year, to enjoy the company of intelligent
and artistic friends.   One cannot help thinking that the rural life of

Risach and Heinrich would have seemed to Stifter in actuality an ' exile ', a ' real martyrdom ', as he called his life in Linz. See the letter of 1 June 1851 and others. *Briefwechsel* ii, 65 passim.

[25] In a letter of 13 February 1847, Stifter wrote the characteristic words : ' He who has the greatest cleanliness and simplicity in his body, will mostly have them also in his soul : and he who rightfully keeps his property intact, will also keep his morals intact.' *Briefwechsel* i, 205.

[26] *Der Nachsommer*, vol. 2. *SW* vii, 28.

[27] ibid., vol. 1. *SW* vi, 235.

[28] W. Rehm, *Nachsommer. Zur Deutung von Stifters Dichtung*, Berne 1951, 109. See too Erik Lunding's very interesting ' existentialist ' interpretation of the work in his *Adalbert Stifter*, Copenhagen 1946.

[29] In a letter of 16 February 1847, referring to *Die Mappe meines Urgrossvaters*. *Briefwechsel* i, 208-9.

[30] The point is well made by F. Beissner, *Der Erzähler Franz Kafka*, Stuttgart 1952, 33-4.

[31] Schmidt's review, from *Der Grenzbote* of 1858, is partly summarised, partly reproduced, in the introduction to *Der Nachsommer*, *SW* vi, lxxxii-xc.

[32] Compare also the excursion to the medieval altar at ' Kerberg ', which takes Risach and his companions into Bohemia. Nothing hangs on this excursion except its explicit purpose—the examination of this masterpiece from the school of Riemenschneider, which Stifter himself so admired.

[33] *Der Nachsommer*, vol. 2. *SW* vii. 72-6. As the tutor of Mathilde's brother Gustav, his method must give rise to serious misgivings, for the boy is left alone a great deal, and subjected to a rigid routine.

[34] ibid., vol. 2. *SW* vii, 283. See also vii, 8, 19, 183, 195, 223, etc.

[35] E. A. Blackall, *Adalbert Stifter*, 1908, 15. An excellent, I think the best, study of the writer.

[36] *Der Nachsommer*, vol. 2. *SW* vi, 305.

[37] ibid., vol. 2. *SW* vi, 191, 194.

[38] ibid., vol. 1. *SW* vi, 135-6. Stifter's language is at times a trifle quaint, even awkward, and I have tried to preserve this quality.

[39] ibid., vol. 1. *SW* vi, 273.

[40] ibid., vol. 2. *SW* vii, 216-22.

[41] ibid., vol. 3. *SW* vii, 306-7.

[42] ibid., vol. 3. *SW* vii, 312.

[43] ibid., vol. 2. *SW* vii, 243.

CHAPTER IV.—THOMAS MANN—*THE MAGIC MOUNTAIN*

[1] *Lübeck als geistige Lebensform*, Lübeck 1924, 27-8.

[2] *Rede und Antwort*, Berlin 1922, 281. ' Release in death ' (' Erlösung ') might be rendered ' redemption ', ' salvation ', but without a religious implication.

[3] *Bemühungen*, Berlin 1925, 272.

[4] *Der Zauberberg*, Berlin 1924, ii, 76–8.

[5] *Lübeck als geistige Lebensform*, 44.

[6] *Der Zauberberg*, i, 163–6, 333–8.

[7] ibid., i, 437–49.

[8] ibid., ii, 570–3. Compare Mann's essay, *Okkulte Erlebnisse* (1923), in *Altes und Neues*, Frankfurt 1953.

[9] *Der Zauberberg*, i, 559–78.

[10] ibid., ii, 425.

[11] ibid., ii, 375, 431, 439–40, 477.

[12] *Lübeck als geistige Lebensform*, 48.

[13] *Der Zauberberg*, ii, 224–62.

[14] ibid., ii, 348–9.

[15] ibid., ii, 165–77.

[16] ibid., ii, 63 and 78 ; i, 576 and ii, 117.

[17] ibid., ii, 361.

[18] H. J. Weigand, *Thomas Mann's Novel, Der Zauberberg*, New York 1933, 80–1. There are many admirable observations in this study.

[19] *Der Zauberberg*, ii, 521.

[20] ibid., i, 57–8.

[21] H. E. Holthusen, *Die Welt ohne Transzendenz*, Hamburg 1949, 6.

[22] Bruno Walter, *Recollections of Thomas Mann*, in *The Stature of Thomas Mann*, ed. Charles Neider, New York 1947, 105.

CHAPTER V.—JEREMIAS GOTTHELF

[1] G. Muret, *Jérémie Gotthelf*, Paris 1913. W. Muschg, *Gotthelf. Die Geheimnisse des Erzählers*, München 1931. Jeremias Gotthelf, *Sämtliche Werke*, 24 vols., ed. Hunziker and Bloesch, Erlenbach-Zürich 1911–54—this edition is referred to below as *SW*. A useful introduction to Gotthelf is H. M. Waidson, *Gotthelf*, Blackwell, 1953.

[2] That is, in the novels. Many of his shorter tales were inspired by the aesthetic taste of popular romanticism, particularly those with a legendary or historical theme, and their literary quality is poor.

[3] 1845. *Briefe*, *SW* Ergänzungsband 6, 149–50. ' It always seems to me as if my literary work were not writing but fighting '—to the Princess of Prussia, April 1850. *Briefe 8*, 49.

[4] 26 December 1838. *Briefe 4*, 288.

[5] For his conception of the popular writer, see the long letter of 28 September 1843. *Briefe 5*, 331–5.

[6] Even in his most ferocious attack on the Berne townsfolk, *Der Herr Esau*, which on the advice of friends he left unpublished, he by no means idealises the peasantry.

[7] 29 December 1840. *Briefe 5*, 107–8.

[8] 16 December 1838. *Briefe 4*, 279–83.

[9] 30 October 1842. *Briefe 5*, 243. There are many similar comments in his letters about this ' spirit ' that ' possessed ' him, cf. *Briefe 5*, 35, 85, 164, 335 ; *6*, 90.

[10] He jokingly commented on the fact. Of *Uli der Knecht*, which was given

the sub-title ' A present for servants and masters ', he wrote that people were puzzled as to whom it was written for—' it is not for the gentry, not for peasants, not for masters, not for farmhands '. 15 November 1841. *Briefe 5*, 169.

11 The Berlin publisher could offer him larger editions and royalties than any of the Swiss, and Gotthelf was interested both in driving a hard bargain and in being widely known. Muschg makes much of his love of money, to which he even attributes a pathological character. But there seems as little evidence of an obsession with money as there are grounds for attributing Gotthelf's co-operation with Springer to purely material calculations. It is not insignificant that the Berliner showed so much more tact and understanding in his handling of Gotthelf, and had a keener eye for his quality, than the Swiss.

12 15 November 1841. *Briefe 5*, 167.

13 23 March 1839. *Briefe 5*, 38.

14 29 June 1846. *Briefe 6*, 300.

15 *Die schwarze Spinne.* 8 December 1842. *Briefe 5*, 257–8.

16 *Die Armennot. SW* xv, 159.

17 *Uli der Knecht. SW* iv, 195.

18 *Erlebnisse eines Schuldenbauers. SW* xiv, 126.

19 It is certain that Gotthelf would have approved the aesthetic of Ruskin and the later Tolstoy. Ruskin was a great admirer of his novels— see H. M. Waidson, ' Gotthelf's Reception in Britain and America ', *Modern Language Review*, xliii, No. 2, April 1948.

20 G. Büchner, *Lenz. Werke* (Inselverlag), 92.

21 See the comments of his friends Pupikofer and Fröhlich, *Briefe 6*, 73 and 7, 182 ; and of Burkhalter, *6*, 57.

22 Keller. Review of *Uli*, 1849.

23 W. Günther, *Der ewige Gotthelf*, Zürich 1934.

24 27 October 1840. *Briefe 5*, 89–90.

25 27 October 1840. *Briefe 5*, 92.

26 7 December 1843. *Briefe 5*, 361.

27 *Leiden und Freuden eines Schulmeisters*, ii. *SW* iii, 281–301, 381.

28 *Anne Bäbi Jowäger*, ii. *SW* vi, 63–6.

29 16 July 1842. *Briefe 5*, 227.

30 For instance, the reasonable protests of Fueter, 18 May 1842. *Briefe 5*, 223.

31 Keller, review of *Uli*, 1849, of *Die Käserei in der Vehfreude*, 1951, and of *Der Schuldenbauer*, 1855. With some justice Keller called *Die Käserei* ' an excellent field-study to Feuerbach's *Essence of Religion* '.

32 Xaver Herzog, 1 May 1846. *Briefe 6*, 287.

33 10 December 1840. *Briefe 5*, 101.

34 *Uli der Pächter. SW* xi, 39.

35 F. Grob, in his excellent study, *Gotthelfs Geld und Geist*, Olten 1948, 30.

36 Gotthelf's conscious attitude in this work is critical, even harsh, to Hans Joggeli and Anne Marei, and he seems not to realise how in fact he wins us for them—for instance, it is quite unnecessary that he should assure us that though the mother seems narrow-minded and faulty

to the reader, she is loved and needed by her family, *Der Schuldenbauer*. *SW* xiv, 315.

[37] *SW* xix and xx.

[38] *Uli der Knecht*. *SW* iv, 195.

[39] Keller, review of *Die Käserei*, 1851. Keller's remarks are particularly true of sketches like *Michels Brautschau* or *Wie Christen eine Frau gewinnt*.

[40] Lukács repeats this charge. *Deutsche Realisten des 19 Jahrh.*, Berlin 1951, 222.

[41] Gotthelf expounds this point in *Zeitgeist und Bernergeist* where he states that Gretli's love for Benz is more than personal, since it sums up her whole longing to become a 'Bäuerin'. *Zeitgeist und Bernergeist*. *SW* xiii, 82.

[42] Hence the strangest misapprehensions have been held on Meyeli's character, as is pointed out by T. Salfinger, *Gotthelf und die Romantik*, Basel, 1945, 58–60.

[43] See the letters of Pupikofer, 21 July 1844, and Burkhalter, 28 May 1844 : 'You are setting up ideals'. *Briefe 6*, 73 and 57.

[44] To Burkhalter, 22 January 1837. *Briefe 4*, 223. *Der Herr Esau*, Einleitung. *SW* Ergänzungsband i.

[45] Muschg has pointed out that the sexual perversions and crimes that Gotthelf met in the course of his parochial duties are scarcely mentioned in the novels. *Gotthelf*, 404. The reality of the ' Kiltgang ' itself is glossed over in the later novels.

[46] *Die Wassernot*, Vorwort. *SW* xv.

[47] Muschg, *Gotthelf* 260.

[48] Muschg, *Gotthelf* 237.

[49] *Geld und Geist*. *SW* vii, 86.

[50] *Zeitgeist und Bernergeist*. *SW* xiii, 244–5.

[51] *Der Geldstag*. *SW* viii, 57. This negative procedure lends itself rather too readily to direct moralising.

[52] In the obituary article, 1855, attached to his review of *Der Schuldenbauer*.

[53] *Wie Christen eine Frau gewinnt*. *SW* xviii, 419–20. Similarly *Die Käserei*. *SW* xii, 395.

[54] *Anne Bäbi*, ii. *SW* vi, 386.

[55] *Uli der Pächter*. *SW* xi, 304–5 ; *Uli der Knecht*. *SW* iv, 190–5.

[56] *Geld und Geist*. *SW* vii, 88–90. *Zeitgeist und Bernergeist*. *SW* xiii, 205–9.

[57] *Uli der Knecht*. *SW* iv, 310.

[58] Carl Bitzius to Gotthelf, 30 January 1848. *Briefe 7*, 108–9. Carl Bitzius urged Gotthelf to model himself closer on the old chapbooks with their crude morality and sensational and romantic characters and incidents. The romantic and mysterious Hagelhans of *Uli der Pächter* was much to his taste, ibid., 230–1.

[59] *Leiden und Freuden eines Schulmeisters*, i. *SW* ii, 320–2.

[60] See for instance the descriptions in *Uli der Knecht*. *SW* iv, 369–71. *Zeitgeist und Bernergeist*. *SW* xiii, 205–10.

[61] T. Salfinger gives a useful analysis of the Romantic elements in Gotthelf's style, *Gotthelf und die Romantik*, Basel 1945, 89–106. Muschg's analysis of style and language is very helpful, *Gotthelf*, 435–99.

[62] *Zeitgeist und Bernergeist.* *SW* xiii, 96.
[63] *Anne Bäbi*, ii. *SW* vi, 224-5.
[64] ibid., ii. *SW* vi, 27-9.
[65] 28 September 1843 and 25 February 1839. *Briefe 5*, 335 and 23.

CHAPTER VI.—WILHELM RAABE

[1] W. Raabe, *In alls gedultig (Briefe)*, Berlin 1940, 356 (1901).
[2] F. Martini, *Der Realismus in 19 Jahrhundert und Raabe. Dichtung und Volkstum*, 1935, xxxvi, 281.
[3] At the end of *Der Schüdderump* Raabe links the three novels, and it has become customary to refer to them as a ' trilogy '. This term is quite misleading. The novels were in no sense conceived together, and the development in theme and style is such as to put a great distance between them. Raabe's friend, Wilhelm Brandes, was surely right in insisting that the three novels form a unity only in the sense that they mark ' die Stationen seines Weges der Erkenntnis '—*Wilhelm Raabe*, Wolfenbüttel 1901, 8-9. The first sketch-plan of *Der Hungerpastor* avoids the happy end and leaves the hero still hungering at the end, so that its original conception was nearer to that of *Der Schüdderump*. See W. Brandes, *Aus Raabes Werkstatt* in *Raabestudien*, ed. Bauer, Wolfenbüttel 1925.
[4] *Abu Telfan.* W. Raabe, *Sämtliche Werke*, Berlin n.d., Serie 2, Bd. i, 29-33.
[5] *Der Schüdderump.* *Werke*, Serie 2, Bd. ii, 378-80.
[6] e.g. H. Spiero, *Geschichte des deutschen Romans*, Berlin 1950, 309.
[7] *Gutmanns Reisen.* *Werke*, Serie 3, Bd. iv, 242.
[8] *Christoph Pechlin.* *Werke*, Serie 2, Bd. ii.
[9] *Die Leute aus dem Walde.* *Werke*, Serie 1, Bd. v, 58.
[10] *Pfisters Mühle.* *Werke*, Serie 3, Bd. ii, 335.
[11] *Alte Nester.* *Werke*, Serie 2, Bd. vi, 239.
[12] ibid., 295.
[13] *Pfisters Mühle.* *Werke*, Serie 3, Bd. ii, 313.
[14] Raabe, *In alls gedultig*, 253 (1890).
[15] *Die Akten des Vogelsangs.* *Werke*, Serie 3, Bd. v, 374. Krumhardt is quoting the reason given by Lessing for his publication of *Die Fragmente des Ungenannten*. H. J. Meinert's *Die Akten des Vogelsangs*, Berlin 1940, gives a valuable analysis of the form and style of this novel, and contains a useful Raabe bibliography.
[16] *Abu Telfan.* *Werke*, Serie 2, Bd. i, 113-19.
[17] See my ' The Reminiscence-Technique in Raabe ', *Modern Language Review*, xlix, No. 3, 1954.
[18] B. Fairley, *The Modernity of Wilhelm Raabe* in *German Studies presented to Willoughby*, 1952.
[19] H. Meyer, *Raum und Zeit in Raabes Erzählkunst*, Dt. Vierteljahrsschrift für Lit.wissenschaft, 1953, xxvii.
[20] *Stopfkuchen.* *Werke*, Serie 3, Bd. v, 59-60.

[21] Raabe, *In alls gedultig*, 375 (1905).

[22] 1887. Quoted in W. Heess, *Wilhelm Raabe*, Berlin 1926, 164.

[23] Raabe, *In alls gedultig*, 141 ; and *Werke*, Serie 3, Bd. vi, 545-7.

[24] Quoted by Heess, op. cit., 183. See W. Brandes, *Raabe und die Kleider-seller*, 1912.

[25] G. Lukács, *W. Raabe* in *Deutsche Realisten des 19 Jahrhunderts*, Berlin 1951, 254-5.

[26] W. Heess, op. cit., 14, 76.

CHAPTER VII.—THEODOR FONTANE

[1] T. Fontane, *Gesammelte Werke*, Berlin 1905-10, 2nd Series, ix, 269. All references are to this edition, the first series of which contains his poems and novels, the second some of his critical and historical works and his letters. Most of the novels were published in shortened form in periodicals before they appeared as books, and I give the dates of the first book editions.

[2] In his autobiography, *Von Zwanzig bis Dreissig*. *Werke*, 2nd Series, iii.

[3] To B. von Lepel, 7 January 1851. *Theodor Fontane und Lepel*, ed. Petersen, München 1940, i. 293.

[4] See letters of 20 November 1858 and February 1859. *Werke*, 2nd Series, x, 198, 201.

[5] 31 October 1860. *Werke*, 2nd Series, x, 211.

[6] For instance, letter of 5 August 1893. *Werke*, 2nd Series, xi, 303-5.

[7] See in particular the letters to Friedländer—*Briefe an Friedländer*, ed. Schreinert, Heidelberg 1954.

[8] To James Morris, 22 February 1896. *Werke*, 2nd Series, xi, 380. Also *Von Zwanzig bis Dreissig*, *Werke*, 2nd Series, iii, 157 passim, and similar statements in his letters to his wife and daughter, *Werke*, 2nd Series, vi and vii.

[9] See for instance his essays on Alexis, Goethe and Keller in *Aus dem Nachlass*, *Werke*, 2nd Series, ix ; and his review of H. von Kleist in viii, 92-5.

[10] Letters of 23 and 25 January 1890. *Werke*, 2nd Series, xi, 242-3, 245.

[11] *Werke*, 2nd Series, ix, 242-4.

[12] To Hertz, 17 June 1866. *Werke*, 2nd Series, x, 247.

[13] To Hertz, 14 January 1879. *Werke*, 2nd Series, x, 405-6.

[14] *Aus dem Nachlass*. *Werke*, 2nd Series, ix, 253.

[15] See letters of 11 August 1878, 3 June 1879, 14 March 1880, and 5 November 1882. *Werke*, 2nd Series, x, 390-1, 414, and xi, 3, 78-9.

[16] To Stephany, 16 July 1887. *Werke*, 2nd Series, xi, 132.

[17] To Dominik, 3 January 1888. *Werke*, 2nd Series, xi, 144.

[18] The case is referred to in numerous letters to Friedländer in the course of 1887 and 1888. See e.g. 7 December 1887 and 12 April 1888. *Briefe an Georg Friedländer*, ed. Schreinert.

[19] To Schlenther, 22 June 1888. *Werke*, 2nd Series, xi, 155-6.

[20] To Spielhagen, 15 February 1896. *Werke*, 2nd Series, xi, 373.

20a See the illuminating remarks on the function of the story-teller in
R. Koskimies, *Theorie des Romans*, Helsinki 1936, and W. Kayser,
Das sprachliche Kunstwerk, Berne 1954.

21 29 September 1892. *Briefe an Friedländer*, 189.

22 To Hans Hertz and to Spielhagen, 2 March 1895 and 21 February
1896. *Werke*, 2nd Series, xi, 341-2 and 377-8.

23 G. Lukács, *Der alte Fontane. Deutsche Realisten des 19 Jahrhunderts*,
Berlin 1951, 300-1.

24 28 February 1892. *Briefe an Friedländer*, 173.

25 The higher Prussian officialdom was deeply involved in the anti-
semitism of the 1890s.

26 Kaiser Friedrich, the son of Wilhelm I and the father of Wilhelm II,
was the great hope of German liberals. He was ill with cancer
before he came to the throne and reigned only a few months, bearing
his illness with great dignity.

27 See for instance *Kritische Causerien über Theater. Werke*, 2nd Series,
viii, 180-4.

28 To Lessing, 8 June 1896. *Werke*, 2nd Series, xi, 388.

29 *Aus dem Nachlass. Werke*, 2nd Series, ix, 269.

30 To Friedrich, 19 January 1883. *Werke*, 2nd Series, xi, 83-4.

31 To Schiff, 15 February 1888. *Werke*, 2nd Series, xi, 147-8.

32 *Kritische Causerien über Theater. Werke*, 2nd Series, viii, 190-1.

33 *Kritische Causerien. Werke*, 2nd Series, viii, 313.

34 *Aus dem Nachlass. Werke*, 2nd Series, ix, 269.

35 On Hauptmann's *Vor Sonnenaufgang*, in *Kritische Causerien. Werke*, 2nd
Series, viii, 303-4.

36 27 May 1891. *Briefe an Friedländer*, 147.

37 *Kritische Causerien. Werke*, 2nd Series, viii, 189-92.

38 To Stephany, 10 October 1889. *Werke*, 2nd Series, xi, 219.

39 *Aus dem Nachlass. Werke*, 2nd Series, ix, 270.

CHAPTER VIII.—FRANZ KAFKA

1 *Beschreibung eines Kampfes. Gesam. Schriften*, New York 1946, 44.

2 W. Emrich, *Franz Kafka* in *Deutsche Literatur im 20ten Jahrhundert*, Heidelberg 1954.

3 G. Janouch, *Gespräche mit Kafka*, Frankfurt 1951, 38.

4 *Tagebücher. Gesam. Werke*, New York 1951, 420. As the new edition
of Kafka's writings, entitled *Gesammelte Werke*, is not yet complete,
I have had to refer on some occasions to the older edition, called
Gesammelte Schriften. In every case I give the title of the volume
rather than its number.

5 For instance in Edwin Muir's Introduction to his and Willa Muir's
translation of *The Castle* ; in A. Camus, *Le Mythe de Sisyphe*, Paris
1942 ; and E. Heller's essay on Kafka in *The Disinherited Mind*,
Cambridge 1952.

6 From the numerous studies of Kafka mention may be made of the

following : Max Brod, *Franz Kafka*, Prague 1935, the invaluable biography ; and also his *Franz Kafkas Glauben und Lehre*, Winterthur 1948, together with Brod's postscripts to his editions of Kafka's works. C. Neider, *Kafka, his Mind and Art*, London 1949. G. Anders, *Kafka, Pro und Contra*, Munich 1951 (a provocative but very helpful work). M. Bense, *Die Theorie Kafkas*, Berlin 1952. A compendium of views is given in *The Kafka Problem*, ed. A. Flores, New York 1946, which contains a valuable bibliography of works by and on Kafka.

7 *Beschreibung eines Kampfes*, 139.

8 G. Janouch, *Gespräche mit Kafka*, 88. I must confess that I cannot repress suspicions of this book. So many of Kafka's statements here answer so neatly the questions one would like to ask him. Can the memories of a boy, even when prompted by a notebook, carry so far ?

9 Kafka's titles have not received very respectful treatment from many of his translators either. *The Trial* is far more correctly *The Lawsuit* ; *The Judgment*, occasionally called *The Sentence*, is better *The Verdict*. To avoid confusion I have used the more familiar titles. Translations of the texts are my own, though the Muir translations are in general accurate as well as skilful.

10 M. Brod, *Kafka*, 168–9, and Postscript to *Amerika*, Berlin 1935, 311. F. Kafka, *Tagebücher*, New York 1951, 481. The entry in the journal belongs to 1915.

11 There is no point in recapitulating the facts of Kafka's obsessional neurosis in relation to his father. The main direct statement, his letter to his father of 1919, is now available in full in the volume *Hochzeitsvorbereitungen auf dem Lande*, New York 1953, 162–223.

12 *Amerika*, 308.

13 Kafka, *Tagebücher*, New York 1951, 535–6.

14 C. Neider, *Kafka, his Mind and Art*, 93–4.

15 This is the theme of several of Kafka's shorter sketches, e.g. *The Great Wall of China*, *The Problem of our Laws*, *The Refusal*. The two sides of the problem are put : ' There is something tormenting in being ruled by laws that one does not know ' and ' Seek to understand the orders of your leaders, but only to a certain limit, then stop thinking '.

16 *Brief an den Vater*. *Hochzeitsvorbereitungen auf dem Lande*, 193. I have already remarked that the title of *The Trial* should correctly be *The Lawsuit (Der Prozess)*.

17 See particularly Brod, *Kafkas Glauben und Lehre*, 8, 32, 48 passim.

18 E. Heller, *The World of Kafka* in *The Disinherited Mind*.

19 J. Kelly, *The Trial* in *The Kafka Problem*, 151–71. Similarly, the inhuman governor of *In The Penal Colony*, and his lieutenant who worships the monstrous death-machine, are said to be God and his servant. The death of the officer and the destruction of the machine are taken to be the (regrettable) results of rational humanism, which Kafka is supposed to hope will not prevail for long. One wavers between astonishment at the arbitrary interpretation and abhorrence over the barbaric obscurantism of these critics, who outdo Kierke-

gaard in regretting, apparently, that the God who asked Abraham to sacrifice his son was ' rationally liberal ' enough to substitute a ram.   See the contributions of Austin Warren and J. F. Warren in *The Kafka Problem*, 140–2 and 242–3.

[20] Kafka, *Hochzeitsvorbereitungen*, 84.

[21] G. Anders, *Kafka Pro und Contra*, 37–8.

[22] Kafka, *Kleine Fabel. Beschreibung eines Kampfes*, 121.

[23] See Kafka, *Briefe an Milena*, ed. Haas, New York 1952, pp. 68, 70, 105, 148, 246.

[24] *Hochzeitsvorbereitungen*, 89.

[25] ibid., 298.

[26] In the Muir translation, ' wife and child ' is replaced by ' home ' (*The Castle*, ed. 1947, 16).   K. is, however, not using ' wife and child ' as a mere synonym for ' home '.

[27] One of the most elaborate is Herbert Tauber, *Franz Kafka*, Zürich 1941 (translated into English in 1948).

[28] *Das Schloss*, ed. 1935, 351–5.   The chapter is not included in the first edition of the Muir translation.

[29] *Hochzeitsvorbereitungen*, 303.

[30] *Tagebücher* (ed. 1937), 157.

[31] *Das Schloss* (ed. 1935), 366.

[32] *Tagebücher* (ed. 1937), 158.

[33] ibid. (ed. 1937), 109–10.

[34] Max Lerner in *The Kafka Problem*, 45.

[35] G. Anders, *Kafka Pro und Contra*, 11.

[36] *Hochzeitsvorbereitungen*, 125.

[37] W. Emrich, *Franz Kafka*, in *Deutsche Literatur im zwanzigsten Jahrhundert*, ed. H. Friedmann and O. Mann, Heidelberg 1954.   I cannot, however, agree with Emrich that Kafka prepares in any explicit form ' the way for the break-through of truth and freedom '.

[38] *Das Schloss*, 36–7.   The Muir translation (ed. 1947), 38.   Unfortunately an accurate examination of this and related problems is not yet possible, as Brod admits that he has altered Kafka's text in some respects—see the postscripts to his editions of the novels.

[39] ibid., 289–90.   J. Pfeiffer has given a subtle analysis of this style in his essay on Kafka's *Eine Kleine Frau* in *Wege zur Erzählkunst*, Hamburg 1953.

[40] *Das Schloss*, 183–4.   I have kept to the punctuation of the original. The Muirs give Frieda undue deliberateness and clarity by adding two semi-colon pauses.

[41] *Hochzeitsvorbereitungen*, 281.

[42] See the skilful analysis of this technique in F. Beissner, *Der Erzähler Franz Kafka*, Stuttgart 1952.   Kafka does not always carry it off perfectly—e.g. the end of *Metamorphosis*, after the death of Gregor.

[43] *Der Prozess* (ed. 1935), 256–9.   The passage is not given in the first edition of the Muir translation.

[44] See *Tagebücher* (ed. 1937), 11, 13, 15, 18, 56 ff., 82–5.

[45] A. A. Mendilow, *Time and the Novel*, 1952, 139.

[46] *Beim Bau der Chinesischen Mauer.* In *Beschreibung eines Kampfes* (ed. 1946), 75 and 77–8.

[47] *Erzählungen* (ed. 1935), 153.

[48] G. Anders, *Kafka Pro und Contra*, 75–7.

[49] ibid., 29.

[50] Rilke, *Duineser Elegien* X.

[51] G. Janouch, *Gespräche mit Kafka*, 17.

[52] E. B. Burgum, in *The Kafka Problem*, 299.

CHAPTER IX.—THOMAS MANN

[1] *Leiden und Grösse Richard Wagners*, 1933. *Adel des Geistes*, Stockholm 1945, 465.

[2] *Die Kunst des Romans*, 1939. *Altes und Neues*, Frankfurt 1953.

[3] *Leiden und Grösse Wagners. Adel des Geistes*, 467.

[4] *Schopenhauer*, 1938. *Adel des Geistes*, 337–97.

[5] *Nietzsches Philosophie im Lichte unserer Erfahrung*, 1947. *Neue Studien*, Frankfurt 1948, 137.

[6] *Betrachtungen eines Unpolitischen* (1918), Berlin 1922, 171.

[6a] In his last (unfinished) novel, *Die Bekenntnisse des Hochstaplers Felix Krull* (1955), which was begun in this early period, Mann has developed this theme. In this gayest, most humorous of his works, the hero is an artist in his instinct for disguise, and his gift for swindling is delightfully balanced by the earnest conscientiousness with which he devotes himself to pleasing others.

[7] *Zu einem Kapitel aus Buddenbrooks*, 1947. *Altes und Neues*, 567–8.

[8] In an interview reported in *Süddeutsche Zeitung*, Sonderdruck, January 1953.

[9] *Kultur und Politik*, 1939. *Altes und Neues*, 648.

[10] *Lübeck als geistige Lebensform*, 1926. *Altes und Neues*, 309, 300.

[11] *Sechzehn Jahre*, 1948. *Altes und Neues*, 679.

[12] *Tischrede bei der Feier des 50ten Geburtstages*, 1925. *Altes und Neues*, 288.

[13] G. Lukács, *Thomas Mann*, Berlin 1949, 73.

[14] *Doktor Faustus*, Stockholm 1947, 133.

[15] ibid., 541.

[16] See for instance *Deutschland und die Deutschen*, 1945. *Neue Studien*, 14–16, 25–9.

[17] H. E. Holthusen, *Die Welt ohne Transzendenz*, Hamburg 1949, 11.

[18] *Doktor Faustus*, 494–5.

[19] ibid., 475.

[20] *Der Künstler und die Gesellschaft. Altes und Neues*, 433–42.

[21] *Goethes Laufbahn als Schriftsteller*, 1932. *Adel des Geistes*, 154.

[22] Mann's Introduction to the Stockholm edition of *Der Zauberberg*, 1946, xiv–xv.

[23] *Zur Begrüssung Gerhart Hauptmanns*, 1929. *Adel des Geistes*, 354–5. See e.g. *Dostojewski, Neue Studien*, 102.

24 See the big essays, *Goethe als Repräsentant des bürgerlichen Zeitalters* and *Goethes Laufbahn als Schriftsteller*, both of 1932. *Adel des Geistes*, 104–45, 146–79.
25 *Nietzsches Philosophie im Lichte unserer Erfahrung. Neue Studien*, 137–8.
26 *Sechzehn Jahre*, 1948. *Altes und Neues*, 677.
27 *Joseph und seine Brüder*, 1942. *Neue Studien*, 173–4. The English text, *The Theme of the Joseph Novels*, Washington 1942, bears clumsy marks of the translator ; though it should be said that Mann is extremely difficult to translate.
28 See *Freud und die Zukunft*, 1936. *Adel des Geistes*, 587–91.
29 *Joseph und seine Brüder*, 1942. *Neue Studien*, 175.
30 *Nietzsches Philosophie im Lichte unserer Erfahrung. Neue Studien*, 156.
31 *Sechzehn Jahre. Altes und Neues*, 687–8.
32 *Lotte in Weimar*, Stockholm 1946, 447.
33 *Doktor Faustus*, 382.
34 See R. Peacock, *Das Leitmotiv bei Thomas Mann*, Berne 1934.
35 *Lübeck als geistige Lebensform. Altes und Neues*, 295.
36 Lukács has repeatedly drawn attention to the workings of this process in Mann and other writers. I am indebted to him for this particular example, *Thomas Mann*, 13–15.
37 F. Spielhagen, *Der Held im Roman*, 1874. *Beiträge zur Theorie und Technik des Romans*, Leipzig 1883, 78–84.
38 See above, pp. 76–98.
39 *Joseph und seine Brüder. Neue Studien*, 160–1.
40 ibid., 173.
41 *Joseph der Ernährer*, Stockholm 1943, 311–57.
42 *Joseph und seine Brüder. Neue Studien*, 167.
43 T. Mann, *Die Entstehung des Doktor Faustus*, 1949, 33.
44 *Bemerkungen zum Roman ' Der Erwählte '*, 1951. *Altes und Neues*, 262–3.
45 W. Kayser, *Entstehung und Krise des modernen Romans*, 1954.
46 See *Lübeck als geistige Lebensform. Altes und Neues*, 312.
47 This is the central thesis of Lukács, op. cit.
48 *Goethe als Repräsentant des bürgerlichen Zeitalters. Adel des Geistes*, 144.
49 Quoted by L. Erlacher, *Untersuchungen zur Romantechnik Manns*, Liestal, 1932, 24.
50 *Der Zauberberg*, ii. 260 : ' Der Mensch soll um der Güte und Liebe willen dem Tode keine Herrschaft einräumen über seine Gedanken.'

CHAPTER X.—GENERAL CHARACTERISTICS

1 Hegel, *Vorlesungen über die Aesthetik. Werke*, Berlin 1835–8, xii, 395–6.
2 Quoted by F. V. Matthiessen, *The James Family*, New York 1947, 502, and by W. D. Allen, *The English Novel*, 1954.
3 E. Heller, *The Disinherited Mind*, 1952, 86.
4 J. Pfeiffer's definition of the novel. *Wege zur Erzählkunst*, Hamburg 1953, 11.
5 F. R. Leavis, *The Great Tradition*, 1948, 9.

[6] K. Viëtor, *Goethe*, Berne 1949, 133.

[7] Goethe, *Werke*, Gedenkausgabe, Zürich 1954, xiii, 124, 868.

[8] Wolfgang Kayser, *Entstehung und Krise des modernen Romans*. *Deutsche Vierteljahrsschrift für Literaturwissenschaft und Geistesgeschichte*, 1954, No. 28.

[9] A. Thibaudet, *Réflexions sur le roman*, Paris 1938, 13.

Appendix

To page 8.

' Wenn der Edelmann im gemeinen Leben gar keine Grenzen kennt, wenn man aus ihm Könige oder königähnliche Figuren erschaffen kann ; so darf er überall mit einem stillen Bewusstsein vor seinesgleichen treten ; er darf überall vorwärts dringen, anstatt dass dem Bürger nichts besser ansteht, als das reine stille Gefühl der Grenzlinie, die ihm gezogen ist. Er darf nicht fragen : was bist du ? sondern nur : was hast du ? welche Einsicht, welche Kenntnis, welche Fähigkeit, wie viel Vermögen ? Wenn der Edelmann durch die Darstellung seiner Person alles gibt, so gibt der Bürger durch seine Persönlichkeit nichts und soll nichts geben. Jener darf und soll scheinen ; dieser soll nur sein, und was er scheinen will, ist lächerlich und abgeschmackt. Jener soll tun und wirken, dieser soll leisten und schaffen ; er soll einzelne Fähigkeiten ausbilden, um brauchbar zu werden, und es wird schon vorausgesetzt, dass in seinem Wesen keine Harmonie sei, noch sein dürfe, weil er, um sich auf eine Weise brauchbar zu machen, alles übrige vernachlässigen muss.

An diesem Unterschiede ist nicht etwa die Anmassung der Edelleute und die Nachgiebigkeit der Bürger, sondern die Verfassung der Gesellschaft selbst schuld ; ob sich daran einmal etwas ändern wird und was sich ändern wird, bekümmert mich wenig ; genug, ich habe, wie die Sachen jetzt stehen, an mich selbst zu denken, und wie ich mich selbst und das, was mir ein unerlässliches Bedürfnis ist, rette und erreiche.

Ich habe nun einmal gerade zu jener harmonischen Ausbildung meiner Natur, die mir meine Geburt versagt, eine unwiderstehliche Neigung.'

GOETHE : *Wilhelm Meisters Lehrjahre*, Buch V, Kapitel 3.

To page 22.

Im Roman wie im Drama sehen wir menschliche Natur und Handlung. Der Unterschied beider Dichtungsarten liegt nicht bloss in der äussern Form, nicht darin, dass die Personen in dem einen sprechen, und dass in dem andern gewöhnlich von ihnen erzählt wird. Leider viele Dramen sind nur dialogierte Romane, und es wäre nicht unmöglich, ein Drama in Briefen zu schreiben.

Im Roman sollen vorzüglich Gesinnungen und Begebenheiten vorgestellt werden ; im Drama Charaktere und Taten. Der

Roman muss langsam gehen, und die Gesinnungen der Hauptfigur
müssen, es sei auf welche Weise es wolle, das Vordringen des
Ganzen zur Entwickelung aufhalten. Das Drama soll eilen, und
der Charakter der Hauptfigur muss sich nach dem Ende drängen,
und nur aufgehalten werden. Der Romanheld muss leidend,
wenigstens nicht im hohen Grade wirkend sein ; von dem drama-
tischen verlangt man Wirkung und Tat. Grandison, Clarisse,
Pamela, der Landpriester von Wakefield, Tom Jones selbst sind,
wo nicht leidende, doch retardierende Personen, und alle Begebenheiten werden gewissermassen nach ihren Gesinnungen gemodelt.
Im Drama modelt der Held nichts nach sich, alles widersteht ihm,
und er räumt und rückt die Hindernisse aus dem Wege, oder
unterliegt ihnen.

So vereinigte man sich auch darüber, dass man dem Zufall im
Roman gar wohl sein Spiel erlauben könne ; dass er aber immer
durch die Gesinnungen der Personen gelenkt und geleitet werden
müsse ; dass hingegen das Schicksal, das die Menschen, ohne ihr
Zutun, durch unzusammenhängende äussere Umstände zu einer
unvorhergesehenen Katastrophe hindrängt, nur im Drama statt
habe ; dass der Zufall wohl pathetische, niemals aber tragische
Situationen hervorbringen dürfe ; das Schicksal hingegen müsse
immer fürchterlich sein, und werde im höchsten Sinne tragisch,
wenn es schuldige und unschuldige, voneinander unabhängige
Taten in eine unglückliche Verknüpfung bringt.

GOETHE : ibid., Buch V, Kapitel 7.

To page 30.

Die Eltern lagen schon und schliefen, die Wanduhr schlug ihren
einförmigen Takt, vor den klappernden Fenstern sauste der Wind ;
abwechselnd wurde die Stube hell von dem Schimmer des Mondes.
Der Jüngling lag unruhig auf seinem Lager, und gedachte des
Fremden und seiner Erzählungen. Nicht die Schätze sind es, die
ein so unaussprechliches Verlangen in mir geweckt haben, sagte er
zu sich selbst ; fern ab liegt mir alle Habsucht : aber die blaue
Blume sehn' ich mich zu erblicken. Sie liegt mir unaufhörlich im
Sinn, und ich kann nichts anders dichten und denken. So ist mir
noch nie zumute gewesen : es ist, als hätt' ich vorhin geträumt,
oder ich wäre in eine andere Welt hinübergeschlummert ; denn
in der Welt, in der ich sonst lebte, wer hätte da sich um Blumen
bekümmert, und gar von einer so seltsamen Leidenschaft für eine
Blume hab' ich damals nie gehört. Wo eigentlich nur der Fremde
herkam ? Keiner von uns hat je einen ähnlichen Menschen
gesehn ; doch weiss ich nicht, warum nur ich von seinen Reden

so ergriffen worden bin ; die andern haben ja das nämliche
gehört, und keinem ist so etwas begegnet. Dass ich auch nicht
einmal von meinem wunderlichen Zustande reden kann ! Es ist
mir oft so entzückend wohl, und nur dann, wenn ich die Blume
nicht recht gegenwärtig habe, befällt mich so ein tiefes, inniges
Treiben : das kann und wird keiner verstehn.

NOVALIS : *Heinrich von Ofterdingen*, Kapitel 1.

To page 47.

Einige Tage darauf behielt mich der Lehrer zu meiner Ver-
wunderung nach der Schule zurück, sowie jene vier angegebenen
Knaben, welche mir wie halbe Männer vorkamen, da sie an Alter
und Grösse mir weit vorgeschritten waren. Ein geistlicher Herr
erschien, welcher gewöhnlich den Religionsunterricht gab und
sonst der Schule vorstand, setzte sich mit dem Lehrer an einen
Tisch und hiess mich neben ihn sitzen. Die Knaben hingegen
mussten sich vor dem Tische in eine Reihe stellen und harrten der
Dinge, die da kommen sollten. Sie wurden nun mit feierlicher
Stimme gefragt, ob sie gewisse Worte in meiner Gegenwart aus-
gesprochen hätten ; sie wussten nichts zu antworten und waren
ganz erstaunt. Hierauf sagte der Geistliche zu mir : ' Wo hast
du die bewussten Dinge gehört von diesen Buben ? ' Ich war
sogleich wieder im Zuge und antwortete unverweilt mit trockener
Bestimmtheit : ' Im Brüderleinsholze ! ' Dieses ist ein Gehölz,
eine Stunde von der Stadt entfernt, wo ich in meinem Leben nie
gewesen war, das ich aber oft nennen hörte. ' Wie ist es dabei
zugegangen, wie seid ihr dahin gekommen ? ' fragte man weiter.
Ich erzählte, wie mich die Knaben eines Tages zu einem Spazier-
gange überredet und in den Wald hinaus mitgenommen hätten,
und ich beschrieb einlässlich die Art, wie etwa grössere Knaben
einen kleineren zu einem mutwilligen Streifzuge mitnehmen. Die
Angeklagten gerieten ausser sich und beteuerten mit Tränen, dass
sie teils seit langer Zeit, teils gar nie in jenem Gehölze gewesen
seien, am wenigsten mit mir ! Dabei sahen sie mit erschrecktem
Hasse auf mich, wie auf eine böse Schlange, und wollten mich mit
Vorwürfen und Fragen bestürmen, wurden aber zur Ruhe gewiesen
und ich aufgefordert, den Weg anzugeben, welchen wir gegangen.
Sogleich lag derselbe deutlich vor meinen Augen, und angefeuert
durch den Widerspruch und das Leugnen eines Märchens, an
welches ich nun selbst glaubte, da ich mir sonst auf keine Weise den
wirklichen Bestand der gegenwärtigen Szene erklären konnte, gab
ich nun Weg und Steg an, die an den Ort führen. Ich kannte
dieselben nur vom flüchtigen Hörensagen, und obgleich ich kaum

darauf gemerkt hatte, stellte sich nun jedes Wort zur rechten Zeit
ein. Ferner erzählte ich, wie wir unterwegs Nüsse herunter-
geschlagen, Feuer gemacht und gestohlene Kartoffeln gebraten,
auch einen Bauernjungen jämmerlich durchgebleut hätten, welcher
uns hindern wollte. Im Walde angekommen, kletterten meine
Gefährten auf hohe Tannen und jauchzten in der Höhe, den
Geistlichen und den Lehrer mit Spitznamen benennend. Diese
Spitznamen hatte ich, über das Äussere der beiden Männer nach-
sinnend, längst im eigenen Herzen ausgeheckt, aber nie verlautbart ;
bei dieser Gelegenheit brachte ich sie zugleich an den Mann und
der Zorn der Herren war ebenso gross, als das Erstaunen der
vorgeschobenen Knaben. Nachdem sie wieder von den Bäumen
heruntergekommen, schnitten sie grosse Ruten und forderten mich
auf, auch auf ein Bäumchen zu klettern und oben die Spottnamen
auszurufen. Als ich mich weigerte, banden sie mich an einen
Baum fest und schlugen mich so lange mit den Ruten, bis ich alles
aussprach, was sie verlangten, auch jene unanständigen Worte.
Indessen ich rief, schlichen sie sich hinter meinem Rücken davon,
ein Bauer kam in demselben Augenblicke heran, hörte meine
unsittlichen Reden und packte mich bei den Ohren. ' Wart ihr
bösen Buben ! ' rief er, ' diesen hab' ich ! ' und hieb mir einige
Streiche. Dann ging er ebenfalls weg und liess mich stehen,
während es schon dunkelte. Mit vieler Mühe riss ich mich los und
suchte den Heimweg in dem dunklen Wald. Allein ich verirrte
mich, fiel in einen tiefen Bach, in welchem ich bis zum Ausgange
des Waldes teils schwamm, teils watete, und so, nach Bestehung
mancher Gefährde, den rechten Weg fand. Doch wurde ich noch
von einem grossen Ziegenbocke angegriffen, bekämpfte denselben
mit einem rasch ausgerissenen Zaunpfahl und schlug ihn in die
Flucht.

Noch nie hatte man in der Schule eine solche Beredsamkeit an
mir bemerkt, wie bei dieser Erzählung. Es kam niemand in den
Sinn, etwa bei meiner Mutter anfragen zu lassen, ob ich eines Tages
durchnässt und nächtlich nach Hause gekommen sei ? Dagegen
brachte man mit meinem Abenteuer in Zusammenhang, dass der
eine und andere der Knaben nachgewiesenermassen die Schule
geschwänzt hatte, gerade um die Zeit, welche ich angab. Man
glaubte meiner grossen Jugend sowohl, wie meiner Erzählung ;
diese fiel ganz unerwartet und unbefangen aus dem blauen Himmel
meines sonstigen Schweigens. Die Angeklagten wurden unschuldig
verurteilt als verwilderte bösartige junge Leute, da ihr hart-
näckiges und einstimmiges Leugnen und ihre gerechte Entrüstung
und Verzweiflung die Sache noch verschlimmerten ; sie erhielten

die härtesten Schulstrafen, wurden auf die Schandbank gesetzt und überdies noch von ihren Eltern geprügelt und eingesperrt.

Soviel ich mich dunkel erinnere, war mir das angerichtete Unheil nicht nur gleichgültig, sondern ich fühlte eher noch eine Befriedigung in mir, dass die poetische Gerechtigkeit meine Erfindung so schön und sichtbarlich abrundete, dass etwas Auffallendes geschah, gehandelt und gelitten wurde, und das infolge meines schöpferischen Wortes. Ich begriff gar nicht, wie die misshandelten Jungen so lamentieren und erbost sein konnten gegen mich, da der treffliche Verlauf der Geschichte sich von selbst verstand und ich hieran so wenig etwas ändern konnte, als die alten Götter am Fatum.

GOTTFRIED KELLER : *Der grüne Heinrich*, Teil I, Kapitel 8.

To pages 54–5.

In diesem Augenblicke ertönte durch das geöffnete Fenster klar und deutlich Mathildens Stimme, die sagte : ' Wie diese Rosen abgeblüht sind, so ist unser Glück abgeblüht.'

Ihr antwortete die Stimme meines Gastfreundes, welche sagte : ' Es ist nicht abgeblüht, es hat nur eine andere Gestalt.'

ADALBERT STIFTER : *Der Nachsommer*, ii. Kapitel 4.

' Gegen den Herbst kömmt wieder eine freiere Zeit. Da haben sie gleichsam einen Nachsommer und spielen eine Weile, ehe sie fort gehen.'

STIFTER : ibid., i. Kapitel 6.

To page 72.

' Ihr habt da einen reizenden Sitz,' bemerkte ich.

' Nicht der Sitz allein, das ganze Land ist reizend,' erwiederte er, ' und es ist gut da wohnen, wenn man von den Menschen kömmt, wo sie ein wenig zu dicht an einander sind, und wenn man für die Kräfte seines Wesens Thätigkeit mit bringt. Zuweilen muss man auch einen Blick in sich selbst thun. Doch soll man nicht stetig mit sich allein auch in dem schönsten Lande sein ; man muss zu Zeiten wieder zu seiner Gesellschaft zurück kehren, wäre es auch nur, um sich an mancher glänzenden Menschentrümmer, die aus unsrer Jugend noch übrig ist, zu erquicken oder an manchem festen Thurm von einem Menschen empor zu schauen, der sich gerettet hat. Nach solchen Zeiten geht das Landleben wieder, wie lindes Oel, in das geöffnete Gemüth. Man muss aber weit von der Stadt weg und von ihr unberührt sein. In der Stadt kommen die Veränderungen, welche die Künste und die Gewerbe bewirkt haben, zur Erscheinung : auf dem Lande die, welche nahe

Y

liegendes Bedürfniss oder Einwirken der Naturgegenstände auf einander hervor gebracht haben. Beide vertragen sich nicht, und hat man das Erste hinter sich, so erscheint das Zweite, fast wie ein Bleibendes, und dann ruht vor dem Sinne ein schönes Bestehendes, und zeigt sich dem Nachdenken ein schönes Vergangenes, das sich in menschlichen Wandlungen und in Wandlungen von Naturdingen in eine Unendlichkeit zurück zieht.'

Ich antwortete nichts auf diese Rede, und wir schwiegen eine Weile.

STIFTER : ibid., i, Kapitel 4.

To page 73.

' Ich weiss nicht, wie lange ich gegangen bin,' antwortete sie, ' ich ging zwischen den Feldern hin, auf denen die ungeheure Menge des Getreides steht, ich ging an manchem Strauche hin, den der Rain enthält, ich ging an manchem Baume vorbei, der in dem Getreide steht, und kam zu dem rothen Kreuze, das aus den Saaten empor ragt.' . . .

' Und jetzt führt Euch Eure Neigung öfter in das Freie ? ' fragte ich.

' Ich gehe gerne herum, wo ich nicht beengt bin,' antwortete sie, ' ich gehe zwischen den Feldern und den wallenden Saaten, ich steige auf die sanften Hügel empor, ich wandere an den blätterreichen Bäumen vorüber und gehe so fort, bis mich eine fremde Gegend ansieht, der Himmel über derselben gleichsam ein anderer ist und andere Wolken hegt. Im Gehen sinne und denke ich dann. Der Himmel, die Wolken darin, das Getreide, die Bäume, das Gras, die Blumen stören mich nicht. Wenn ich recht ermüdet bin und auf einem Bänklein, wie hier, oder auf einem Sessel in unserem Garten oder selbst auf einem Sitze in unserem Zimmer ausruhen kann, so denke ich, ich werde nun nicht wieder so weit gehen.'

STIFTER : ibid., ii, Kapitel 3.

To page 74.

' Ich habe sehr wenig Schlaf gefunden ; aber ich habe es nicht unangenehm empfunden,' entgegnete ich, ' die Fenster meiner Wohnung, welche mir Eure Mutter so freundlich hatte einrichten lassen, gehen in das Freie, ein grosser Theil des Sternenhimmels sah zu mir herein. Ich habe sehr lange die Sterne betrachtet. Am Morgen stand ich frühe auf, und da ich glaubte, dass ich Niemand in dem Schlosse mehr stören würde, ging ich in das Freie, um die milde Luft zu geniessen.'

'Es ist ein eigenes, erquickendes Labsal, die reine Luft des heiteren Sommers zu athmen,' erwiederte sie.

'Es ist die erhebendste Nahrung, die uns der Himmel gegeben hat,' antwortete ich. 'Das weiss ich, wenn ich auf einem hohen Berge stehe und die Luft in ihrer Weite, wie ein unausmessbares Meer, um mich herum ist. Aber nicht bloss die Luft des Sommers ist erquickend, auch die des Winters ist es, jede ist es, welche rein ist, und in welcher sich nicht Theile finden, die unserm Wesen widerstreben ' . . .

'Die Kunstgebilde leiten die Augen auf sich, und mit Recht,' antwortete ich, 'sie erfüllen mit Bewunderung und Liebe. Die natürlichen Dinge sind das Werk einer anderen Hand, und wenn sie auf dem rechten Wege betrachtet werden, regen sie auch das höchste Erstaunen an.'

'So habe ich wohl immer gefühlt,' sagte sie.

'Ich habe auf meinem Lebenswege durch viele Jahre Werke der Schöpfung betrachtet,' erwiederte ich, 'und dann auch, so weit es mir möglich war, Werke der Kunst kennen gelernt, und Beide entzückten meine Seele.'

STIFTER : ibid., iii, Kapitel 1

To page 88.

Lebewohl, Hans Castorp, des Lebens treuherziges Sorgenkind! Deine Geschichte ist aus. Zu Ende haben wir sie erzählt; sie war weder kurzweilig noch langweilig, es war eine hermetische Geschichte. Wir haben sie erzählt um ihretwillen, nicht deinethalben, denn du warst simpel. Aber zuletzt war es deine Geschichte; da sie dir zustiess, musstest du's irgend wohl hinter den Ohren haben, und wir verleugnen nicht die pädagogische Neigung, die wir in ihrem Verlaufe für dich gefasst, und die uns bestimmen könnte, zart mit der Fingerspitze den Augenwinkel zu tupfen bei dem Gedanken, dass wir dich weder sehen noch hören werden in Zukunft.

Fahr wohl—du lebest nun oder bleibest! Deine Aussichten sind schlecht; das arge Tanzvergnügen, worein du gerissen bist, dauert noch manches Sündenjährchen, und wir möchten nicht hoch wetten, dass du davonkommst. Ehrlich gestanden, lassen wir ziemlich unbekümmert die Frage offen. Abenteuer im Fleische und Geist, die deine Einfachheit steigerten, liessen dich im Geist überleben, was du im Fleische wohl kaum überleben sollst. Augenblicke kamen, wo dir aus Tod und Körperunzucht ahnungsvoll und regierungsweise ein Traum von Liebe erwuchs. Wird auch aus diesem Weltfest des Todes, auch aus der schlimmen Fieberbrunst,

die rings den regnerischen Abendhimmel entzündet, einmal die
Liebe steigen ?

THOMAS MANN : *Der Zauberberg*, Letztes Kapitel.

To page 130.

Hansli Jowäger war ein braver Mann, und Anne Bäbi, sein
Weib, meinte es auch gut, aber uf sy Gattig. Hansli Jowäger
hatte noch Speckseitenkutten, Gilet, wo die Säcke Deckel hatten,
und wenn er nicht Spitzhosen trug, so waren seine Hosen doch
aufgeschlitzt bis zum Knie, und selten war der lange Schlitz
zugeknöpft. Sein Hut hatte keinen hohen Gupf ; desto breiter
war der Schirm, und wenn er an einem Stock zMärit ging, so stellte
er gerne das Kinn auf selbigen ab, während er um eine Kuh
märtete. Sein Weib Anne Bäbi plagte ihn nicht mit der Hoffart.
Ihrer Grossmutter Hochzeitkittel trug sie an den heiligen Sonn-
tagen, und ihren eigenen Hochzeitkittel sparte sie der Nach-
kommenschaft auf. Sie hatte noch Schuhe mit währschaften
Böden, aber weit ausgeschnitten, dass sie mit den Zehen kaum
anhängen konnte, und für Ärgäuer Fürtücher hatte sie noch keinen
Kreuzer ausgegeben. Sie schämte sich, sagte sie, ein solches
Hüdeli umzuhängen, in welches man nicht einmal herzhaft
schneuzen könne, wenn man nicht wolle, dass die Nase am andern
Ort zum Vorschein komme. Halbrystigs, das sei das Fundament
in einer Haushaltung, sagte sie. Hansli Jowäger hatte seine Anne
Bäbi erst geheiratet, als seine Mutter gestorben und beide weit
über die Dreissig hinaus waren. Er wolle seinem Muetti keinen
Verdruss mit einem Söhniswyb machen, sagte er ; man wisse wohl,
wie es öppe gehe, wenn zwei an einer Feuerplatte zusammenkämen.
Die Frucht dieser Ehe war ein Söhnlein, welches man Jakobli
nannte, gar wert hielt als das einzige, späte Sprösslein, und das
ein Ausbund von Tugend und Frömmigkeit werden sollte vor
Gott und Menschen.

JEREMIAS GOTTHELF : *Anne Bäbi Jowäger*, i, Kapitel 1.

To page 133.

In aller Farbenpracht hing das welke Laub an den Bäumen, im
Schimmer seiner eigenen Abendröte ; unter ihm streckte sich grün
und munter die junge Saat aus, spielte lustig mit den blinkenden
Tautropfen, die an ihrer Spitze hingen ; geheimnisvoll und düftig
dehnte sich über alles der Himmel aus, der geheimnisvolle Schoss
der Wunder Gottes. Schwarze Krähen flogen über die Äcker,
grüne Spechte hingen an den Bäumen, schnelle Eichhörnchen

liefen über die Strasse und beguckten von einem rasch erreichten Ast neugierig die Vorüberfahrenden, und hoch in den Lüften segelten in ihrem wohlgeordneten Dreieck die Schneegänse einem wärmeren Lande zu, und seltsam klang aus weiter Höhe ihr seltsam Wanderlied.

GOTTHELF : *Uli der Knecht*, Kapitel 24.

To page 134.

Ich lief hinauf nach Gytiwyl und sah dort am frühen Morgen bei einem der ersten Häuser den Gerichtsäss mit einem Pferd an der Hand am Brunnen stehen und tränken.   So in der Hast und ohne es böse zu meinen, frug ich ihn, ob sie den Brief nicht erhalten, und warum niemand darauf gekommen sei.   Der Gerichtsäss antwortete : sie liessen sich nicht so mit einem Briefe befehlen ; das wäre eine kommode Sache, wenn da ein jeder nur zu befehlen brauche.   Wenn ich etwas von ihnen wolle, so tue es mirs sauft, sie dafür z'ha und selbsten zu kommen, das sei anständig.   Ein Schulmeister müsse nicht meinen, dass er Meister sein wolle im Dorfe, sie seien auch noch da daheim.   Damit führte er sein Pferd, das die nasse Nase schon lange an seinem Ärmel abgerieben hatte, in den Stall und liess mich draussen stehen.

Ganz bedächtlich füllte er seinen Futterkübel aus dem Futterkasten, netzte das Futter und schüttete es dann wohlgerührt in die Krippe, legte den Mist zurecht und trat aus der Türe.   Dort redete ich ihn wieder ganz demütiglich an : ich sei eben jetzt dafür da, um für ein Fuhrwerk zu bitten, und wegen des Briefes sollte er nicht zürnen, ich hätte schier nicht Zeit gehabt und gedacht, ein Brief versäume nichts, hingegen ich einen oder fast zwei Tage.   Er lüpfte die Hosen und sagte, er wolle ein Ross geben, ich solle nun zu denen und denen gehen, deren Häuser er mir zeigte ; wenn die auch fahren wollten, so sei es ihm recht.   Damit ging er ins Haus hinein, ohne mich mitgehen zu heissen.   Im zweiten Hause ging es mir ähnlich.   Als ich doppelte an der Haustüre, sah jemand aus dem Läufterli, zog aber den Kopf schnell zurück.   Wahrscheinlich kannte mich der Kopf, und drinnen hob eine Beratung an, was ich wohl wolle, und ob man mich solle hineinkommen heissen oder nicht.   Da wird die Frau gesagt haben : ' Gang du use, Hans, dStube isch ṇo nüt gwüscht, u mr hei nume gwärmts Krut u bösi Milch, u mi weiss no gar nit, was er für eine isch, u drum bigehri ih nüt, dass er dNase i alles icheheig.' Und dr Ma wird gesagt haben : ' Er wird wohl warte, ih will emel zerst näh, bis ih gnue ha.' Und da tat die Frau das Läufterli wieder auf, um erstlich mich auch zu sehen und zweitens mir zu

sagen : ' Es chunnt grad neuer.' Und während Hans langsam
mit der Gabel das Kraut und mit dem Löffel die Milch nahm und
zuletzt noch ein Stücklein Brot als Dessert, musste er der neugierigen
Frau Bescheid geben, was das wohl sei, dass ich da zu ihnen komme.
    Endlich kam er heraus, gab mir den gleichen Bescheid wie der
Frühere und wies mich zu einem dritten.   Dort kam eine grosse,
mächtige Frau eben mit zwei Säumelchtern von den Ställen
zurück, wo sie ihre Morgensfreude genossen hatte an den lustigen
Fasel- und den gschlachten Mastschweinen, die, wie die weisse
Melchter bezeugte, ebensoviel Nidle erhielten als Milch, auf alle
Fälle bessere Milch, als die Leute selbst auf dem Tische hatten.
Ich will wetten, die reichen Basler Herren haben nicht so gutes
Weisses in ihrem Kaffee, als zirka viertausend Bernerschweine von
Martistag bis Fastnacht in ihrem Troge haben.   Die Frau war
aufgeweckt ; wahrscheinlich hatte sie mit ihren zusammen-
geknüpften Strumpfbändern ihre Lieblinge gemessen und gefunden,
dass sie im letzten Monat wieder fast um ein Viertel zugenommen.
    Sie fragte resolut : ' Was hesch welle ? '
        GOTTHELF : *Leiden und Freuden eines Schulmeisters*, i, Kapitel 30.

To page 157.

    ' Das sage ich Ihnen, Dichter, Denker und Doktor,' brummte
er, ' auf den Tisch steigen wir heute morgen nicht.   Und du,
Junge, bilde dir ja nicht ein, dass ich nach Pfisters Mühle heraus-
gekommen sei, um mir Weltuntergangsgefühle aus deines Vaters
verstänkerter Kneipidylle herauszudestillieren.   Idylle hin, Idylle
her ; trotz Weihnachten, Ostern und Pfingsten in einer Wehmuts-
träne habe ich jetzt die Absicht, ruhig unter den Philistern auf
gegebenem, bitter realem Erdboden so gemütlich als möglich mit
zu schmatzen, zu schlucken, zu prosperieren und möglicherweise
auch zu propagieren.'
        WILHELM RAABE : *Pfisters Mühle*, Blatt 14.

To page 172.

    ' Woher stammen im Grunde des Menschen Schicksale,
Eduard ? ' fragte er zuerst, und ehe ich antworten konnte (was hätte
ich antworten können ?), meinte er : ' Gewöhnlich, wenn nicht
immer aus Einem Punkte.   Von meinem Kinderwagen her—du
weisst, Eduard, ich war seit frühester Jugend etwas schwach auf den
Beinen—erinnere ich mich noch ganz gut jener Sonntagsnachmit-
tagsspazierfahrtstunde, wo mein Dämon mich zum erstenmal
hierauf anwies, in welcher mein Vater sagte : ' Hinter der roten

Schanze, Frau, kommen wir gottlob bald in den Schatten. Der
Bengel da könnte übrigens auch bald zu Fusse laufen ! Meinst
du nicht ? '—' Er ist so schwach auf den Füssen,' seufzte meine
selige Mutter, und dieses Wort vergesse ich ihr nimmer. Ja,
Eduard, ich bin immer etwas schwach, nicht nur von Begriffen,
sondern auch auf den Füssen gewesen, und das ist der besagte
Punkt ! Ich habe mich wahrhaftig nicht weiter in der Welt
bringen können, als bis in den Schatten der roten Schanze. Ich
kann wirklich nichts dafür. Hier war mein schwacher oder, wenn
du willst, starker Punkt. Hier fasste mich das Schicksal. Ich habe
mich gewehrt, aber ich habe mich fügen müssen, und ich habe
mich seufzend gefügt. Dich, lieber Eduard, haben Störzer und
Mr. Le Vaillant nach dem heissen Afrika gebracht, und mich haben
meine schwachen Verstandeskräfte und noch schwächern Füsse im
kühlen Schatten von Quakatzenhof festgehalten. Eduard, das
Schicksal benutzt meistens doch unsere schwachen Punkte, um
uns auf das uns Dienliche aufmerksam zu machen.'

Dieser Mensch war so frech-undankbar, hier wahrhaftig einen
Seufzer aus der Tiefe seines Wanstes hervorzuholen. Natürlich
nur um mir sein Behagen noch beneidenswerter vorzurücken.
Ich ging aber nicht darauf ein. Den Gefallen, meinerseits jetzt
noch tiefer und mit besserer Berechtigung zu seufzen, tat ich ihm
nicht.

RAABE : *Stopfkuchen.*

To pages 203–4.

' Ich habe mir's hin und her überlegt. Man ist nicht bloss ein
einzelner Mensch, man gehört einem Ganzen an, und auf das
Ganze haben wir beständig Rücksicht zu nehmen, wir sind durchaus
abhängig von ihm. Ging es, in Einsamkeit zu leben, so könnt
ich es gehen lassen ; ich trüge dann die mir aufgepackte Last, das
rechte Glück wäre hin, aber es müssen so viele leben ohne dies
"rechte Glück", und ich würde es auch müssen und—auch
können. Man braucht nicht glücklich zu sein, am allerwenigsten
hat man einen Anspruch darauf, und den, der einem das Glück
genommen, den braucht man nicht notwendig aus der Welt zu
schaffen. Man kann ihn, wenn man weltabgewandt weiter
existieren will, auch laufen lassen. Aber im Zusammenleben mit
den Menschen hat sich ein Etwas ausgebildet, das nun mal da ist
und nach dessen Paragraphen wir uns gewöhnt haben, alles zu
beurteilen, die andern und uns selbst. Und dagegen zu verstossen
geht nicht ; die Gesellschaft verachtet uns, und zuletzt tun wir
es selbst und können es nicht aushalten und jagen uns die Kugel

durch den Kopf. Verzeihen Sie, dass ich Ihnen solche Vorlesung
halte, die schliesslich doch nur sagt, was sich jeder hundertmal
gesagt hat. Aber freilich, wer kann was Neues sagen ! Also noch
einmal, nichts von Hass oder dergleichen, und um eines Glückes
willen, das mir genommen wurde, mag ich nicht Blut an den
Händen haben, aber jenes, wenn Sie wollen, uns tyrannisierende
Gesellschafts-Etwas, das fragt nicht nach Liebe und nicht nach
Verjährung. Ich habe keine Wahl. Ich muss.' . . .
      Wüllersdorf war aufgestanden. 'Ich finde es furchtbar, dass
Sie recht haben, aber Sie haben recht. Ich quäle Sie nicht länger
mit meinem "muss es sein". Die Welt ist einmal wie sie ist, und
die Dinge verlaufen nicht, wie wir wollen, sondern wie die andern
wollen. Das mit dem "Gottesgericht", wie manche hochtrabend
versichern, ist freilich ein Unsinn, nichts davon, umgekehrt, unser
Ehrenkultus ist ein Götzendienst, aber wir müssen uns ihm
unterwerfen, solange der Götze gilt' . . .
      'Schuld, wenn sie überkaupt was ist, ist nicht an Ort und Stunde
gebunden und kann nicht hinfällig werden von heute auf morgen.
Schuld verlangt Sühne, das hat einen Sinn. Aber Verjährung
ist etwas Halbes, etwas Schwächliches, zum mindesten was Pro-
saisches.' Und er richtete sich an dieser Vorstellung auf und
wiederholte sich's, dass es gekommen sei, wie's habe kommen
müssen. Aber im selben Augenblicke, wo dies für ihn feststand,
warf er's auch wieder um. 'Es muss eine Verjährung geben,
Verjährung ist das einzig Vernünftige, ob es nebenher auch noch
prosaisch ist, ist gleichgültig ; das Vernünftige ist meist prosaisch.
Ich bin jetzt fünfundvierzig. Wenn ich die Briefe fünfundzwanzig
Jahre später gefunden hätte, so war ich siebzig. Dann hätte
Wüllersdorf gesagt : "Innstetten, seien Sie kein Narr." Und
wenn es Wüllersdorf nicht gesagt hätte, so hätt es Buddenbrook
gesagt, und wenn auch der nicht, so ich selbst. Dies ist mir klar.
Treibt man etwas auf die Spitze, so übertreibt man und hat die
Lächerlichkeit. Kein Zweifel. Aber wo fängt es an ? Wo liegt
die Grenze ? Zehn Jahre verlangen noch ein Duell, und da heisst
es Ehre, und nach elf Jahren oder vielleicht schon bei zehneinhalb
heisst es Unsinn. Die Grenze, die Grenze. Wo ist sie ? War sie
da ? War sie schon überschritten ? Wenn ich mir seinen letzten
Blick vergegenwärtige, resigniert und in seinem Elend doch noch
ein Lächeln, so hiess der Blick : "Innstetten, Prinzipienreiterei.
. . . Sie konnten es mir ersparen und sich selber auch." Und
er hatte vielleicht recht. Mir klingt so was in der Seele. Ja, wenn
ich voll tödlichem Hass gewesen wäre, wenn mir hier ein tiefes
Rachegefühl gesessen hätte. . . . Rache ist nichts Schönes, aber

was Menschliches und hat ein natürlich menschliches Recht. So
aber war alles einer Vorstellung, einem Begriff zuliebe, war eine
gemachte Geschichte, halbe Komödie. Und diese Komödie muss
ich nun fortsetzen und muss Effi wegschicken und sie ruinieren und
mich mit. . . . Ich musste die Briefe verbrennen, und die Welt
durfte nie davon erfahren.'

THEODOR FONTANE : *Effi Briest*, Kapitel 27–9.

To page 208.

Und nicht lange mehr, so waren diese Lichter auch wirklich da.
Nicht nur das ganze Lokal erhellte sich, sondern auch auf dem
drüben am andern Ufer sich hinziehenden Eisenbahndamme
zeigten sich allmählich die verschiedenfarbigen Signale, während
mitten auf der Spree, wo Schleppdampfer die Kähne zogen, ein
verblaktes Rot aus den Kajütenfenstern hervorglühte.

FONTANE : *Der Stechlin*, 'Nach dem Eierhäuschen '.

To page 226.

'Vor dem Gesetz steht ein Türhüter. Zu diesem Türhüter
kommt ein Mann vom Lande und bittet um Eintritt in das Gesetz.
Aber der Türhüter sagt, dass er ihm jetzt den Eintritt nicht
gewähren könne. Der Mann überlegt und fragt dann, ob er
also später werde eintreten dürfen. "Es ist möglich," sagt der
Türhüter, "jetzt aber nicht." Da das Tor zum Gesetz offensteht
wie immer und der Türhüter beiseite tritt, bückt sich der Mann,
um durch das Tor in das Innere zu sehen. Als der Türhüter das
merkt, lacht er und sagt : "Wenn es dich so lockt, versuche es
doch, trotz meinem Verbot hineinzugehen. Merke aber : Ich bin
mächtig. Und ich bin nur der unterste Türhüter. Von Saal zu
Saal stehen aber Türhüter, einer mächtiger als der andere. Schon
den Anblick des dritten kann nicht einmal ich mehr vertragen."
Solche Schwierigkeiten hat der Mann vom Lande nicht erwartet,
das Gesetz soll doch jedem und immer zugänglich sein, denkt er,
aber als er jetzt den Türhüter in seinem Pelzmantel genauer
ansieht, seine grosse Spitznase, den langen, dünnen, schwarzen,
tartarischen Bart, entschliesst er sich doch, lieber zu warten, bis er
die Erlaubnis zum Eintritt bekommt. Der Türhüter gibt ihm
einen Schemel und lässt ihn seitwärts von der Tür sich nieder-
setzen. Dort sitzt er Tage und Jahre. Er macht viele Versuche
eingelassen zu werden und ermüdet den Türhüter durch seine
Bitten. Der Türhüter stellt öfters kleine Verhöre mit ihm an, fragt
ihn nach seiner Heimat aus und nach vielem anderen, es sind aber

Y*

teilnahmslose Fragen, wie sie grosse Herren stellen, und zum
Schlusse sagt er ihm immer wieder, dass er ihn noch nicht einlassen
könne. Der Mann, der sich für seine Reise mit vielem ausgerüstet
hat, verwendet alles, und sei es noch so wertvoll, um den Türhüter
zu bestechen. Dieser nimmt zwar alles an, aber sagt dabei :
"Ich nehme es nur an, damit du nicht glaubst, etwas versäumt
zu haben." Während der vielen Jahre beobachtet der Mann
den Türhüter fast ununterbrochen. Er vergisst die anderen Türhüter, und dieser erste scheint ihm das einzige Hindernis für den
Eintritt in das Gesetz. Er verflucht den unglücklichen Zufall in
den ersten Jahren laut, später, als er alt wird, brummt er nur noch
vor sich hin. Er wird kindisch, und da er in dem jahrelangen
Studium des Türhüters auch die Flöhe in seinem Pelzkragen
erkannt hat, bittet er auch die Flöhe, ihm zu helfen und den Türhüter umzustimmen. Schliesslich wird sein Augenlicht schwach,
und er weiss nicht, ob es um ihn wirklich dunkler wird oder ob ihn
nur die Augen täuschen. Wohl aber erkennt er jetzt im Dunkel
einen Glanz, der unverlöschlich aus der Türe des Gesetzes bricht.
Nun lebt er nicht mehr lange. Vor seinem Tode sammeln sich in
seinem Kopfe alle Erfahrungen der ganzen Zeit zu einer Frage,
die er bisher an den Türhüter noch nicht gestellt hat. Er winkt
ihm zu, da er seinen erstarrenden Körper nicht mehr aufrichten
kann. Der Türhüter muss sich tief zu ihm hinunterneigen, denn
die Grössenunterschiede haben sich sehr zuungunsten des Mannes
verändert. "Was willst du denn jetzt noch wissen ? " fragt der
Türhüter, "du bist unersättlich." "Alle streben doch nach dem
Gesetz," sagt der Mann, " wie kommt es, dass in den vielen Jahren
niemand ausser mir Einlass verlangt hat ? " Der Türhüter
erkennt, dass der Mann schon am Ende ist, und um sein verge-
hendes Gehör noch zu erreichen, brüllt er ihn an : " Hier konnte
niemand sonst Einlass erhalten, denn dieser Eingang war nur für
dich bestimmt. Ich gehe jetzt und schliesse ihn.""

FRANZ KAFKA : *Der Prozess*, Kapitel 9.

To page 241.

' Nein, liebe Pepi, ich bin so wenig missbraucht und betrogen
worden wie du. . . . Du willst immerfort betrogen worden sein,
weil dir das schmeichelt und weil es dich rührt. Die Wahrheit
aber ist, dass du für diese Stelle nicht geeignet bist. . . . Es ist
eine Stelle wie eine andere, für dich aber ist sie das Himmelreich,
infolgedessen fasst du alles mit übertriebenem Eifer an, schmückst
dich, wie deiner Meinung nach die Engel geschmückt sind—sie
sind aber in Wirklichkeit anders—, zitterst für die Stelle, fühlst

dich immerfort verfolgt, suchst alle, die deiner Meinung nach dich
stützen könnten, durch übergrosse Freundlichkeiten zu gewinnen,
störst sie aber dadurch und stösst sie ab, denn sie wollen im Wirts-
haus Frieden und nicht zu ihren Sorgen noch die Sorgen der
Ausschankmädchen. . . . Ich weiss nicht, ob es so ist, auch ist
mir meine Schuld gar nicht klar, nur wenn ich mich mit dir
vergleiche, taucht mir etwas Derartiges auf, so als ob wir uns beide
zu sehr, zu lärmend, zu kindisch, zu unerfahren bemüht hätten,
um etwas, das zum Beispiel mit Friedas Ruhe, mit Friedas Sach-
lichkeit leicht und unmerklich zu gewinnen ist, durch Weinen,
durch Kratzen, durch Zerren zu bekommen—so wie ein Kind am
Tischtuch zerrt, aber nichts gewinnt, sondern nur die ganze Pracht
hinunterwirft und sie sich für immer unerreichbar macht— ; ich
weiss nicht, ob es so ist, aber dass es eher so ist, als wie du es erzählst,
das weiss ich gewiss.'

KAFKA : *Das Schloss*, Kapitel 20.

To page 246.

Nur als Dorfarbeiter, möglichst weit den Herren vom Schloss
entrückt, war er imstande, etwas im Schloss zu erreichen, diese
Leute im Dorfe, die noch so misstrauisch gegen ihn waren, würden
zu sprechen anfangen, wenn er, wo nicht ihr Freund, so doch ihr
Mitbürger geworden war, und war er einmal ununterschiedbar von
Gerstäcker oder Lasemann—und sehr schnell musste das geschehen,
davon hing alles ab—, dann erschlossen sich ihm gewiss mit einem
Schlage alle Wege, die ihm, wenn es nur auf die Herren oben und
ihre Gnade angekommen wäre, für immer nicht nur versperrt,
sondern unsichtbar geblieben wären.

KAFKA : ibid., Kapitel 2.

To page 248.

' Die Unterredung mit Klamm stellst du dir als ein Geschäft vor,
bar gegen bar. Du rechnest mit allen Möglichkeiten ; vorausgesetzt, dass du den Preis erreichst, bist du bereit, alles zu tun, will
mich Klamm, wirst du mich ihm geben, will er, dass du bei mir
bleibst, wirst du bleiben, will er, dass du mich verstösst, wirst du
mich verstossen, aber du bist auch bereit, Komödie zu spielen,
wird es vorteilhaft sein, so wirst du vorgeben, mich zu lieben, seine
Gleichgültigkeit wirst du dadurch zu bekämpfen suchen, dass du
deine Nichtigkeit hervorhebst und ihn durch die Tatsache deiner
Nachfolgerschaft beschämst oder dadurch, dass du meine Liebes-
geständnisse hinsichtlich seiner Person, die ich ja wirklich gemacht

habe, ihm übermittelst und ihn bittest, er möge mich wieder
aufnehmen, unter Zahlung des Preises allerdings ; und hilft nichts
anderes, dann wirst du im Namen des Ehepaares K. einfach
betteln.'

KAFKA : ibid., Kapitel 13.

To page 273.

'Findest du nicht, alter Freund, und fragst du nicht auch
mitunter dem Möglichen nach in den Würden deiner Wirklichkeit ? Sie ist das Werk der Entsagung, ich weiss es wohl, und also
doch wohl der Verkümmerung, denn Entsagung und Verkümmerung, die wohnen nahe beisammen, und all Wirklichkeit und
Werk ist eben nur das verkümmerte Mögliche. Es ist etwas
Fürchterliches um die Verkümmerung, das sag' ich dir, und wir
Geringen müssen sie meiden und uns ihr entgegenstemmen aus
allen Kräften, wenn auch der Kopf zittert vor Anstrengung, denn
sonst ist bald nichts von uns übrig, als wie ein Hügel im Badischen.
Bei dir, da war's etwas anderes, Du hattest was zuzusetzen. Dein
Wirkliches, das sieht nach was aus—nicht nach Verzicht und
Untreue, sondern nach lauter Erfüllung und höchster Treue und
hat eine Imposanz, dass niemand sich untersteht, dem Möglichen
davor auch nur nachzufragen. Meinen Respect ! '

THOMAS MANN : Lotte in Weimar, Kapitel 9.

Index

344   INDEX

Spengler, O., 269, 275.
Spielhagen, F., vii, 76, 143, 152, 184, 196, 210, 281, 303, 321.
Spiero, H., 315.
Spiessbürger, see *Philistinism*.
Springer, J., 105, 313.
Stendhal (Beyle, H.), 141.
Le rouge et le noir, 302.
Sterne, L., 167.
Stifter, A., 28, 32, 52–75, 185, 301, 302.
Briefwechsel, 309, 310, 311.
Brigitta, 310.
Bunte Steine, 56.
Die Mappe meines Urgrossvaters, 66, 311.
Der Nachsommer, 52–75, 96, 97–8, 327–9.
Witiko, 60.
Storm, T., 45, 152, 181.
Strauss, D. F., 109, 271.
Sue, E., 140.
Symbol, symbolism, 17–19, 35–44, 89–96, 133–4, 148, 163, 217–19, 279–91, 298, 304–5.

Tauber, H., 319.
Thackeray, W. M., 167, 181.
Vanity Fair, 26, 184.
Thibaudet, A., 305, 308, 322.
Tieck, L., 30, 101.
Time in the novel, 24–5, 71, 89, 126–7, 144, 145, 252–3, 255, 278.
Tolstoy, L., 177, 181, 214, 313.
Anna Karenina, 141, 201, 302.
Turgenev, I. S., 181.

Viëtor, K., 4–5, 29, 307, 308, 321.

Wagner, R., 76, 77, 259, 261, 268, 269, 290, 292, 293.
Waidson, H. M., 312, 313.
Walter, Bruno, 97, 312.
Warren, A., 319.
Warren, J. F., 319.
Wassermann, J., vii.
Weigand, H. J., 92, 312.
Werfel, F., vii.
Woolf, Virginia, 308.

Zola, E., 177, 181, 213.